CHICAGO AS IT WAS IN 1820.

ILLINOIS AS IT IS;

ITS

HISTORY, GEOGRAPHY, STATISTICS, CONSTITUTION, LAWS, GOVERNMENT, FINANCES, CLIMATE, SOIL, PLANTS, ANIMALS, STATE OF HEALTH, PRAIRIES, AGRICULTURE, CATTLE-BREEDING, ORCHARDING, CULTIVATION OF THE GRAPE, TIMBER-GROWING, MARKET-PRICES, LANDS AND LAND-PRICES, GEOLOGY, MINING, COMMERCE, BANKS, RAILROADS, PUBLIC INSTITUTIONS, NEWSPAPERS, ETC., ETC.

BY

FRED. GERHARD.

WITH

A PRAIRIE AND WOOD MAP, A GEOLOGICAL MAP, A POPULATION MAP, AND OTHER ILLUSTRATIONS.

CHICAGO, ILL.:
KEEN AND LEE.
PHILADELPHIA:
CHARLES DESILVER,
1857.

STEREOTYPED BY J. FAGAN, PHILADELPHIA.

Dedicated

TO

THE BRAVE AND INDUSTRIOUS CITIZENS OF

ILLINOIS,

AND

TO ALL THOSE WHO INTEND TO BUILD A HOME THERE,

MAY THE FLOURISHING AND FERTILE

PRAIRIE-STATE

UNFOLD, FROM YEAR TO YEAR, MORE AND MORE GLORIOUSLY;

AND

MAY VIRTUE, WEALTH, AND HAPPINESS,

FOR EVER

HAVE THEIR ABODE WITHIN

HER BORDERS.

CONTENTS.

PREFACE.

In presenting this book to the Public, it seems proper to me, to make a brief, but candid and respectful, mention of the motives which have induced me to write it, as well as the means I adopted to collect and secure, in a reliable form, the large amount of material and truthful information that will be found to make up its contents.

Having for a long while past endeavored. in seeking to aid and direct the great mass of the emigration from Europe, to find and to point out what seemed the best way to the advancement of their welfare, my attention was early given to the remarkable developments which have been, and are still, made in the Western States. While thus employed, I made myself fully acquainted with the prevalent literature of the West, and became a close observer of "the progress of events" in the new States. Through this employment, and by such observations, my judgment, I trust, has been rightly matured, so that I may freely utter my own convictions, as entitled to some weight, that Illinois is, if really not the most attractive, at least one of those States which offer the amplest guarantees for the rapid thriving and ultimate success and welfare of those who may seek to establish for themselves a "Home in the West."

After having thus sedulously made myself acquainted with the character of the West in general, and especially still more carefully studied everything relating to Illinois, I resolved upon the preparation of this work; and, for the purpose of facilitating my labors, I made a personal visit through the State, in the fall of the year 1855, and examined things with my own eyes. It has not, however, been my object to write a merely pleasing and saleable book, without the strictest regard to the authenticity and truthfulness of its statements. Well knowing the aptitude of even the most honest observer and candid writer, while travelling through a State in order to gain a more intimate knowledge of it, to be filled with false first-impressions, misapprehensions, and monotonous judgments, I have not, therefore, solely relied upon my own personal observations and experience; but sought, in all that I have written, to base it substantially upon the testimony of many other persons, such as farmers, merchants, physicians, clergymen, &c., who have been long residents of the State, and whose personal experience is of much weight. In the course of my journey through the State, I accordingly made it one of my principal aims to cultivate the acquaintance of such persons, and to procure their impartial statements and opinions as to the existing state of things in Illinois. Among numerous others, who have very much favored me in this respect, I feel myself under particular obligations to Governor J. A. MATTESON, Lieutenant-Governor G. KŒRNER, and FRANCIS A. HOFFMANN, Esq. In making my further acknowledgments, it is but an act of justice to mention the following-named gentlemen, through whose kind letters and valuable written communications I have been enabled to make up a great part of the matter of this book, viz.: —

F. J. Arenz, Esq., Arenzville, Cass co.
I. A. Arenz, Esq., Beardstown, Cass co.
S. A. Armstrong, Esq., Morris, Grundy co.
I. Atkinson, Esq., Pekin.
Edgar Babcock, Esq., Metamora, Woodford co.
R. G. Bailey, Esq., Mt. Carroll, Carroll co.
Wm. M. Bean, Esq., Metropolis, Massac co.
Edw. Bebb, Esq., Fountaindale, Winnebago co.
L. M. Beels, Esq., Belvidere, Boone co.
A. Berlin, Esq., Granville, Putnam co.
Jas. Biddlecom, Esq., Waukegan, Lake co.
Chs. Biel, Esq., Somonauk, De Kalb co.
Dr. Fred. Bock, Waterloo, Monroe co.
D. Bonar, Esq., Cambridge, Henry co.
A. K. Bosworth, Esq., Greenup, Cumberland co.
G. W. Bowyer, Esq., Pontiac, Livingston co.
Rev. C. A. Brauer, Addison, Du Page co.
Fred. Brendel, M. D., Peoria.
A. B. Briscoe, Esq., Marshall, Clark co.
James N. Brown, Esq., late President of the State Agricultural Society Island Grove, Sangamon co.
F. Bumann, Esq., Bunkerhill, Macoupin co.
Geo. Bunsen, Esq., Belleville.
Ph. Burk, Esq., Hardin, Calhoun co.
Z. Cadley, Esq., Knoxville, Knox co.
Thos. H. Campbell, Esq., Auditor of the State, Springfield.
J. J. Cole, Esq., Oswego, Kendall co.
A. Collins, Esq., Hadley, Will co,
Dan. Converse, Esq., Waterloo, Monroe co.
T. R. Courtney, Esq., Ottawa, La Salle co.
F. E. Cummings, Esq., Lincoln, Logan co.
C. Dairly, Esq., Caledonia, Pulaski co.
F. S. Day, Esq., Peru.
Rosw. Dow, Esq., Sycamore, De Kalb co.
M. M. Dudley Esq., Naperville, Du Page co.
Wm. Eddy, Esq., Hennepin, Putnam co.
W. D. Edwards, Esq., Lacon, Marshall co.
John McElvain, Esq., McLeansboro, Hamilton co.
N. D. Elwood, Esq., Joliet.
Theo. Engelmann, Esq., Belleville.
Steph. Feussner, Esq., St. Clair co.
Edw. Forcht, Esq., Concord.
Henry Funk, Esq., Stout's Grove, McLean co.
H. W. Good, Esq., Vandalia, Fayette co.
R. S. Graham, Esq., Carmi, White co.
John McGraw, Esq., Clinton, De Witt co.
J. G. Hall, Esq., Shawneetown, Gallatin co.
Edson Harkness, Esq., Southport, Peoria co.
Wm. H. Haskell, Esq., Canton, Fulton co.
Jul. Heinrich, Esq., Peru.
John Hertel, Esq., Rock Island.
G. F. Hilgard, jr., Esq., Belleville.
John Hinton, Esq., Taylorville, Christian co.
C. Hofmann, M. D., Pekin.
F. A. Hoffmann, M. D., Beardstown.
Mich. Hogle, Esq., Middleport, Iroquois co.
Rev. F. W. Holls, Centreville, St. Clair co.
Rev. Hoppe, Belleville.
Jos. C. Howell, Esq., Carlinville, Macoupin co.
James S. Johnston, Esq., Mt. Carmel, Wabash co.
I. S. Irwin, Esq., Mt. Sterling, Brown co.
M. Kleinhenz, Esq., Henry, Marshall co.
E. M. Lamb, Esq., Woodstock, McHenry co.
J. A. M. Laurie, Esq., Urbana, Champaign co.
Wm. Leighton, Esq., Winchester, Scott co.
L. B. Leisenbee, Esq., Thebes, Alexander co.
Geo. W. Lowder, Esq., Jerseyville, Jersey co.
Jas. G. Madden, Esq., Monmouth, Warren co.
Jas. S. Martin, Esq., Salem, Marion co.
N. W. Matheny, Esq., Springfield.

W. L. Mayr, Esq., Albion, Edwards co.
Henry Menke, Esq., Beardstown.
Chas. Molitor, Esq., Springbay, Woodford co.
Henry T. Mudd, Esq., Pittsfield, Pike co.
Chrs. W. Murtfeldt, Esq., Oregon, Ogle co.
Messrs. Casp. & Hy. Oertley, Princeville, Peoria co.
W. W. Oglesby, Esq., Decatur, Macon co.
J. N. Onstot, Esq., Havana, Macon co.
James F. Oulton, Esq., Monticello, Pratt co.
S. G. Paddock, Esq., Princeton, Bureau co.
J. N. Pearce, Esq., Vienna, Johnson co.
James M. Perry, Esq., Kankakee.
John W. Pyatt, Esq., Pinkneyville, Perry co.
John Ranney, Esq., Keithsburgh, Mercer co.
S. W. Raymond, Esq., Ottawa.
Jos. Reinhard, Esq., Granville, Putnam co.
C. Reuske, Esq., Petersburg, Menard co.
Const. Rilliet, Esq., Highland, Madison co.
B. Roberts, Esq., Shelbyville, Shelby co.
Wm. Ross, Esq., Pittsfield, Pike co.
Benj. Sammons, Esq., Hillsboro, Montgomery co.
T. Sears, Esq., Oregon, Ogle co.
Rev. A. Selle, Crete, Will co.
A. Shaw, Esq., Lawrenceville, Lawrence co.
J. C. Short, Esq., Danville, Vermillion co.
James G. Soulard, Esq., Maple Lawn, Jo Daviess co.
Thos. McSoy, Esq., Ewington, Effingham co
Rev. S. Spies, Mascoutah, St. Clair co.
Dan. Stahl, M. D., Quincy.
I. Trautham, Esq., Macomb, McDonough co.
John Trousdale, Esq., Fairfield, Wayne co.
J. B. Turner, Esq., Elizabethtown, Hardin co.
Isaac Underhill, Esq., Peoria.
Pet. Unzicker, Esq., Groveland, Tazewell co.
A. Vetterhœffer, Esq., Washington, Tazewell co.
P. H. Walker, Esq., Rushville, Schuyler co.
R. A. Warfield, Esq., Raleigh, Saline co.
Dr. Welsch, Mascoutah.
Alb. Weinberger, Esq., Whitefield township, Marshall co.
F. Wenzel, M. D., Belleville.
John H. White, Esq., Marion, Williamson co.
Jas. Wightman, Esq., Carlyle, Clinton co.
J. Winn, Esq. Toulon, Stark co.
Dr. J. G. Zeller, Springbay, Woodford co.

I am, also, under particular obligations to Dr. Fred. Brendel, of Peoria, for the drawings and delineations, which he had the kindness to furnish me, and which will be found appended to this book. They consist of three maps, viz.: —

1. A Prairie and Wood Map.
2. A Geological Map.
3. A Population Map.

These maps, I am confident, the reader will find to form a very excellent and valuable supplement to the work.

The literary resources of which I made use, are —

Brown's *History of Illinois.*
Ford's *History of Illinois.*
Reynold's *My own Times.*
Reynold's *Pioneer History of Illinois.*
Reynold's *Sketches.*
Peck's *Gazetteer of Illinois.*
Illinois in 1837.
Curtiss' *Western Portraiture.*
Hall, *The West.*
Drown's *Records of Peoria.*
Campbell's *Glance at Illinois.*
Transactions of the Illinois State Agricultural Society.
Revised Statutes of Illinois.
F. A. Hoffmann's *Commercial Reports,* &c. &c.

—together with many *newspapers*, printed in the State, which the publishers had the kindness to send regularly to me.*

It was a part of my original intention to append to this work a complete *Gazetteer* of the whole State; but, for the want of room, I am compelled, very much to my regret, to desist from doing so. The very valuable material which I had collected for this purpose, and which I have now in my possession, I will, however, reserve, and prepare for the publication of a Gazetteer at some future period.

May this book meet a kind approbation, and benevolent criticism, and prove as welcome and useful to the citizens of Illinois as to new settlers.

THE AUTHOR.

NEW YORK, December the 25th, 1856.

---

* It being my intention to follow up, in future editions of this work, the progressive history and development of Illinois, and as I consider its newspapers as furnishing the best resources for this purpose, the publishers of newspapers in Illinois will greatly oblige me by sending me their papers regularly. If directed, "Gerhard's German Reporter, New York," they will certainly come to my hands.

IN THE PLACE OF AN

INTRODUCTION.

"THE brilliant destiny of Illinois is now fairly beginning to unfold, and to be read in the speed with which she is bounding forward upon the highway to prosperity and greatness. Earth holds not, upon all its broad surface, a more fertile and favored land than this, our own beautiful Prairie State. What a mighty aggregation of natural advantages do we behold within her borders! In the very centre of the great Mississippi Valley, and in the heart of the Confederacy, she is embraced by magnificent lakes and rivers. With a soil of unsurpassed richness, resting upon a bed of coal sufficient to "keep the hearthstone of the world bright for a thousand centuries"; with a climate genial and healthful; with a level contour of surface, inviting the construction of great works of internal improvement; abounding in mineral resources; destined to be the crossing for the grand lines of oceanic intercommunication, connecting the extreme sections of the Union — those lines which must become the highways of nations, over which will pass the products of every clime, and a great moving human tide, in one unceasing flow; — blessed with all these advantages, nothing is wanting further to constitute the elements of physical greatness. We have an ample guarantee, in the character of her population, that her unbounded natural resources will receive a speedy development. The heavy debt, from the contemplation of which so many shrank back appalled, now presses no more heavily upon her energies, than the curtain of morning mist that rests upon the bosom of her prairies. Her whole population are excited to unwonted activity by the brilliancy of the future; and, from every quarter, emigrants throng to her fertile plains. Inhabited by an honorable people, who kept her escutcheon free from the deep stain of repudiation, in the terrible ordeal of temptation through which she passed — inhabited by a generous people, who, although weighed down with onerous burdens, cheerfully submitted to additional taxation, to provide asylums for the stricken and unfortunate — inhabited by a brave people, whose valor upon the field has illuminated some of the brightest pages of the Republic's history, and heard of wherever the "birds of fame have flown."

(*From an Oration, delivered by* ROBERT BELL, ESQ., *at Fairfield, Illinois.*)

ILLINOIS AS IT IS.

HISTORY.

CHAPTER I.

The State of Illinois was, originally, a part of Florida, and belonged to Spain, and was so laid down upon the old Spanish map of North America. The Spaniards, led on by the daring Fernando de Soto, were the first Europeans who had discovered the Mississippi; they had erected the standard of Spain on its shores in the year 1541, and, according to the views at that time prevailing, had thus established the title of their country to the whole of that vast region watered by its tributary streams, so that thenceforth the State of Illinois became a Spanish colony, and its native inhabitants vassals of the Spanish crown. But, although the Spaniards claimed the State by right of possession, its settlement was never entered upon by them, but was first carried into effect by the French.

At the very time that the Spaniards under Fernando de Soto were exploring Florida and the valley of the Mississippi, several attempts were made on the part of the French by two enterprising adventurers, Cartier and Roberval, to plant settlements on the banks of the St. Lawrence; but these enterprises proving abortive, nothing effectual was done by the French to colonize North America, until the year 1603, when certain merchants at Rouen having formed themselves into a company for this purpose, Champlain, a man of untiring energy and great intrepidity, who had been charged with the direction of their enterprise, succeeded in establishing the first permanent French settlement upon the North American Continent. As early as 1608, he laid the foundation of Quebec, and, in the following year, explored the region occupied by the Indian Nations of Northern New York.

By a charter from Louis XIII, granted to him in the year 1627, he obtained a patent of New France, embracing the whole basin of the St. Lawrence and Canada, and entered upon its government in the year 1632. Perceiving that the climate of New France would offer but little encouragement to immigration, he thought, that the settlement of the new country could not be more effectually promoted than by establishing missions, to call upon religion to aid him in the execution of his designs, and to enter into a close alliance with the native Indians. No sooner, indeed, had the French established their authority in Canada, than numbers of Jesuit missionaries resorted thither, and commenced preaching the gospel to the untutored savages, and forming alliances, in the name of their king, with the numerous savage tribes that inhabited the "Far West." In August, 1665, Father Claude Allouez set out to travel among the Indians, visited the Chippeways, entered their councils, displaying before the wondering savages pictures of hell and of the last judgment, and lighted the Catholic torch at the council fires of more than twenty nations, whom he claimed for his country and his king. In his endeavors to extend the influence of France he was assisted by various missionaries employed for that purpose; among others by James Marquette, who labored incessantly for the cause of his Redeemer and his country, travelling far and wide, exposed to the inclemencies of the season, often subsisting on no other food than the unwholesome moss which he gathered from the rocks, and sleeping beneath the skies on the open ground, without the comfort of a fire. Whilst he was preparing to leave St. Mary's, the outlet of Lake Superior, where he then was, in order to explore the Mississippi, Louis XIV. and his minister Colbert having formed a plan for the extension of the dominion of France in North America, Nicholas Perot appeared at St. Mary's as their agent, and convoked a universal congress of the Indian nations at that place. The remotest Indian nations, from the St. Lawrence, the Mississippi, and the Red River being assembled in council, in the presence of brilliantly-clad officers from the veteran French armies, it was announced to the amazed savages by Allouez, who acted as interpreter, that they had been placed under the protection of Louis XIV., king of France; and thereupon "a cross of cedar was raised, and the whole company, bowing before this emblem of Christianity, chanted to its glory a hymn of the seventh century;" after which a cedar column, with the arms of the Bourbons engraved on it, being planted by the side of the cross, the faith and the rule of France were supposed to be permanently established upon the Continent.

In 1673 James Marquette, with five Frenchmen as companions and two Indians for guides, reached the great "father of waters," on which they embarked "with a joy that could not be expressed," and hoisting the sails of their bark canoes, floated down the majestic river, "over broad clear sandbars," and glided past islets swelling from its bosom with tufts of massive thickness, between the "broad plains of Illinois and Iowa, all garlanded with majestic forests and chequered with illimitable prairies and island groves." After descending the Mississippi for about sixty leagues, they discovered an Indian trail, and unhesitatingly left their canoes to follow it. After walking for some six miles, they came to an Indian village, whence four men immediately advanced to meet them, offering the pipe of peace, their calumets "brilliant with many colored plumes," and speaking to them in language which Marquette understood: "We are Illinois;" that is, "we are men." "How beautiful is the sun, O Frenchman, when thou comest to us! our whole village awaits thee, thou shalt enter in peace all our dwellings." After staying with that hospitable people for a while, James Marquette and his companions further descended the Mississippi River until they were satisfied of its flowing into the Gulf of Mexico, when they returned, and having reached the 39th degree of North Latitude, entered the Illinois River and followed it to its source. The tribe of Illinois Indians, which occupied its banks, invited Marquette to remain and reside among them. But expressing a desire to continue his travels, he was conducted by one of the chiefs and several warriors to Chicago, in the vicinity of which place he remained to preach the gospel to the Miamis, whilst his companions returned to Quebec to announce their discoveries. Two years afterwards Marquette entered the little river in the State of Michigan, called by his name, and erecting on its bank a rude altar, said mass after the rites of the Catholic Church; and being left alone at his own request, "he kneeled down by its side, and offering to the Mightiest solemn thanks and supplications, fell asleep to wake no more. The light breeze from the lake sighed his requiem, and the Algonquin nation became his mourners."

The fame of Marquette induced others to follow in his wake; and among these was Robert Cavalier de la Salle. In 1667, when the attention of Europe was directed to New France, he resorted thither, and first established himself as a fur-trader at La Chine, being in habits of daily intercourse with the warriors of the Iroquois, the Five Nations of Northern New York. Hearing from them the most glowing accounts of the Far West, he resolved to annex the same to France, and to establish a close connection between the valley of the Mississippi and New France by a line of military posts, and for that purpose repaired to France, where he sought and obtained an interview with Colbert, then the prime minister of Louis XIV. Colbert listened with delight to the gigantic schemes of La Salle, and a paper having been obtained from the king commissioning La Salle to explore the valley of the Mississippi, he arrived with a number of mechanics, and military stores and merchandise for the Indian trade, at Fort Frontenac, in the year 1678. In the fall of that year a boat of ten tons, the first that ever entered the Niagara River, conveyed part of his company to the Niagara Cataract. He immediately established a trading-house in its vicinity, and laid the keel of a vessel of sixty tons, called the Griffin, which in the summer of 1679 was launched on the Upper Niagara, being the first vessel that ever rode on the waters of Lake Erie. The roar of its artillery reverberated from shore to shore, arousing the savages in their forests and making them come forward in their swift canoes and look with astonished curiosity upon it. He sailed across the lake and cast anchor on the 27th of August in Green Bay, where he exchanged his goods at an immense profit for a rich cargo of furs, which he shipped in the Griffin to Niagara River to be disposed of, in order that he might make a remittance to his creditors. He next entered the river St. Joseph, on the banks of which he erected a small fort, known as the fort of the Miamies; and after waiting for a long time to hear tidings of the Griffin, being weary of delay, he resolved to explore the interior of Illinois. He left ten men as the garrison of his little fortress, and descended the Illinois as far as Lake Peoria, where he met large parties of Illinois Indians, who, desirous of obtaining axes and firearms, offered him the calumet and assented to an alliance. They received him and his companions with great joy, and when they learned, that colonies were to be established in their neighborhood, the happiness of these simple-minded savages was complete. They offered to conduct him to the Mississippi. But after building a fort a little above where Peoria now stands, which fort he named Crève Cœur, La Salle, destitute of almost every means required to prosecute his voyage, and ruined in fortune by the loss of the Griffin, set out on foot for Canada to procure aid, taking but three men to accompany him and leaving the rest to guard the fort, the command of which he entrusted to Tonti, with directions to fortify Rock Fort, a cliff on the Illinois River, rising to a great height above its banks. During the absence of La Salle, a large body of warriors of the Iroquois or the five Indian Nations of Northern New York, excited to hostilities by the enemies of La Salle, forced Tonti to abandon the construction of the fort and to seek refuge in the country of the Miamies. When La Salle afterwards returned, with a supply of men and stores, he found the fort entirely deserted, and thereupon visited Green Bay, recommenced trade and established friendly intercourse with the natives, found Tonti and his companions, left Chicago on the 4th of January, 1682, and having built a spacious barge on the Illinois River, descended the Mississippi to the sea. La Salle saw at once the unparalleled resources of this vast valley, and his exultation knew no bounds, when he planted the arms of France on the shores of the Gulf of Mexico. Claiming the country for France, in honor of Louis XIV., under whose patronage its discovery was achieved, he called it Louisiana. Having descended the Mississippi to the sea and informed himself about everything he wanted, he returned. On ascending the river a part of the company left behind settled at Kaskaskia and Cahokia, and their vicinity, being afterwards joined by other emigrants from Canada. La Salle himself returned to France by way of Canada, and having given a most glowing description of his discoveries to the king, was entrusted with the command of another expedition, fitted out by the king himself for the purpose of effecting the settlement of Louisiana; but having inadvertently passed the mouth of the Mississippi, was obliged by his companions, who were unwilling to return, to land in Texas, where he founded the first settlement, and after suffering innumerable privations with his party, every one of his ships being wrecked, and his colony diminished from 250 to 50 persons, he resolved to leave 20 men at the fort, and to go with the residue to Canada in search of supplies. Whilst on his way thither, he was treacherously murdered on the 17th of March, 1687, by two of his own men, who, stung to madness by disappointment in their expectations of boundless wealth, resorted to assassination as the means, by which to avenge themselves upon the person of their generous commander. Thus perished miserably La Salle, no doubt the founder of the French dominion in the Mississippi valley, who by his courage, his vast comprehension, his restless energy, and untiring efforts to promote the interests of his country, has secured to his name an immortality of renown.

Two years after his death war was declared between France and England; but though the French and English colonists devastated and plundered each other's *frontiers*, the military occupation of Illinois was continued without interruption. Public documents of the year 1696 mention a fort named St. Louis, and the wish of Louis XIV. to preserve it in good condition. The actual settlement of Illinois, however, advanced but slowly. Gravier succeeded Allouez at the Jesuit mission of Kaskaskia, "the village of the Immaculate Conception." Sebastian Rasles joined him in the year 1693 as fellow-laborer. He investigated the principles of the Illinois language and established its principal rules, and preached the gospel, though surrounded by perils and opposed by Indian sorcerers. After the recall of Gravier and the decease of several of the missionaries, Gabriel Marest joined the mission, and for some time administered its affairs. "Our life," said Marest, "is passed in wading through marshes, where we plunge sometimes to the girdle, over boundless prairies, and in rambling through thick woods and forests, in climbing over hills, in paddling the canoe across lakes and rivers to catch a poor savage, who flies from us, and whom we can neither tame by teachings nor caresses."

At the request of the Peorias, Marest established a mission among them. He was aided by Marmet, whose fervid eloquence, according to the testimony of Marest himself, made him the soul of the mission. His pupils at early dawn attended church neatly dressed in large deer skins, or in robes made of several. After receiving lessons they chanted canticles. Mass was then said in presence of the French and the converts, the women on one side and the men on the other. After prayer the missionaries visited the sick and administered medicine. In the afternoon they instructed in the catechism both young and old, every one of whom had to answer their questions. In the evening all assembled at church for instruction, to offer prayers to the Most High, and to chant the hymns of the Church. On Sundays and festivals, as also after vespers, the people were edified with an eloquent sermon. After sunset, parties would meet in each other's cabins to spend the night in reciting the chaplet in alternate choirs, and in singing psalms, which were frequently homilies, with the words set to familiar tunes. Saturday and Sunday were the days appointed for confession and communion, every convert confessing once in a fortnight. Many of the Indians were converted, and their daughters married to the French emigrants, according to the rites of the Catholic Church.

In 1699 Lemoine de Ibberville was appointed Governor of Louisiana, and arriving with a French colony at the mouth of the Mississippi, built a fort twelve miles west of Pensacola River. From that time the Territory of Illinois was included in and became part of Louisiana. A line of fortified posts now existed between the Gulf of St. Lawrence and the Gulf of Mexico. Jealous of the growth of French power in America, the English planned an expedition for the reduction of Canada, and fitted out a fleet of fifteen ships of war and forty transports, with seven veteran regiments from Marlborough's army on board, under the command of Sir Hoveden Walker. The news of the intended expedition soon reached Quebec, the fortifications of which were immediately strengthened, and the Indian nations of the Far West, including the Illinois, summoned for its defence. Whilst the Indian warriors were assembling at Quebec and Montreal, the fleet, which, on the 25th of June, 1711, had arrived in Boston, took in supplies of stores, and the colonial forces which were to participate in the expedition, and sailed for the St. Lawrence. As it ascended the river, the fleet became enveloped in a dense fog, the Admiral proceeding too incautiously, eight of the vessels suffered shipwreck, and nearly a thousand men were drowned. At a council of war it was resolved to return; and thus this expedition, undertaken at great expense, ended in ignominious failure.

Peace being at length concluded between France and England, Louisiana and Canada were confirmed to the former. Obliged by the sanguinary and expensive wars in which he was involved, to withhold from Louisiana the usual supplies of money and men, and notwithstanding determined to prevent his enemies from taking possession of the same, the King of France, on the 14th of September, 1712, granted Louisiana, including also the State of Illinois and its territory of Wisconsin, to Anthony Crozat, whose character and abilities were sure pledges, that he would make the colony prosper under his direction, and put an end to the dissensions between the provincial authorities. Admitted into partnership with Crozat, De La Motte Catilla was appointed Governor of Louisiana under the royal grant, and entered accordingly upon its government. Agriculture being neglected by the settlers, large sums were expended for provisions by Crozat, who, at the end of five years, finding his disbursements to exceed his receipts by about 125,000 livres, and being unwilling to incur further loss, surrendered his grant to the Crown, two years after the death of Louis XIV. A trading company, known as the Western Company, divided into 200,000 shares of 500 livres each, was formed, and the grant surrendered by Crozat conferred upon it. The capital of the Company was composed of State Securities, then selling at a discount of 78 per cent. John Law, a Scotchman by birth, a gambler and banker by trade, a daring speculator throughout, and at that time a favorite of the French Regent, because, by establishing a bank which flooded the country with paper money to the amount of 1,000,000,000 livres, and enabled its unscrupulous founder to pay the interest on the public debt with its worthless issues, he had for a moment succeeded in arresting the national bankruptcy, paid also the whole of the interest due on this part of the public debt; in consequence whereof a sudden rise in its value took place to par, and John Law was entrusted by the Duke of Orleans, who governed the State in the name of Louis XV, then a minor, with the direction of the affairs of the said Western, now called the Company of the Indies, the number of whose shares were immediately increased by him to a very large amount. Carrying on his system of colonization and trading with the utmost prodigality, John Law in 1720, when at the height of his fortune, built at a cost of several millions of livres, Fort Chartres, in the vicinity of Kaskaskia, and near the centre of the French settlements in Illinois. At length, however, his downfall, which cool reflecting men from the beginning had seen to be inevitable, took place. No sooner had more notes been issued, than the natural state of the business of the country could call for, and the specie been driven out of circulation by a superabundance of paper money, for the redemption of which nothing whatever of value had been pledged, than the bank exploded with a great crash. John Law, but a short time before the most influential person in the State, escaped with difficulty being torn to pieces by the excited populace, and died at Venice in the most wretched poverty in 1729.

The failure of the master spirit, who through his bank had so liberally supplied the India Company with the funds required to carry on their business, resulted of course in the dissolution of the said company. Louisiana being retroceded to the Crown in the year 1730, its interests were again the care of government; Louis XV. and his minister, Cardinal Fleury, being very anxious to promote its prosperity. Louisiana at that time included the entire valley of the Mississippi and its tributary streams; all the countries west of the Alleghany mountains, with the head-springs of the Alleghany, the Monongahela, the Kanawha, the Tennessee, the Cumberland, and the Ohio, were claimed by Frenchmen as forming part of it. The French incessantly labored to extend their power and authority through the valley of the Ohio, and built forts intended to control the Indians. Having induced the Shawnee nation to place themselves under the protection of Louis XV., they erected a fort on the north bank of the Ohio, in the State of Illinois, in the vicinity of the Shawnees. Displeased with the threatening aspect of this stronghold, the savages devised the following ingenious stratagem for its capture. A number of Indians, each of whom was covered with a bear skin and walked on all fours, appeared at daybreak on the opposite side of the river. Supposing them to be bears, the greater part of the garrison crossed the river and went in pursuit of them, whilst the remainder went to the bank of the river to witness the sport. Meanwhile the Indian warriors rushed forth from their hiding places in the woods near by, entered it without opposition, and having thus possessed themselves of the fort, surprised and massacred the French on their return.

The French afterwards built another fort near that fatal spot, which, in commemoration of this disaster, they called Fort Massacre. It was occupied by the French until about 1750, when it was abandoned, and is now, like most of the ancient forts in America, but a heap of ruins.

On the 18th of May, 1756, another war broke out between France and England, of which war, since it resulted in the cession of Canada and the countries east of the Mississippi, Illinois included, to the English Crown, we shall state the general facts.

A British trading company having, previous to the declaration of war, encroached upon French territory, the French took the alarm, built the Fort Du Quesne on the site of the present city of Pittsburgh, and dispersed a party of British workmen engaged in building a fort on the Ohio. Having received information of these open acts of hostility, the Legislature of Virginia despatched, in the year 1754, a military force under the command of Col. Washington, afterwards the illustrious President of the United States, to the scene of action. A party was sent from Fort Du Quesne to surprise him, but was itself surprised by Col. Washington, and every man taken prisoner. After this action Col. Washington was assailed in a fort previously erected by him, by a much superior force of French and Indians, and, after a gallant resistance, obliged to surrender the fort and to retreat to Virginia.

In the summer of the following year Gen. Braddock, at the head of 2500 British veterans, and a body of Virginia militia, marched against Fort Du Quesne. Whilst proceeding through the woods in careless security, the troops were suddenly saluted with a tremendous fire of musketry from all sides, by an invisible foe. The panic at once became general. The American militia fought and died like soldiers, but the British veterans fled in the utmost confusion, notwithstanding the efforts of their officers, and especially of Col. Washington, who, during the whole action, displayed the most heroic bravery and admirable presence of mind, and was the only mounted officer who escaped unhurt; though four balls pierced his coat, and two horses were shot under him, he remained unwounded, his life being evidently preserved by Providence, which destined him to play, at a later period, so noble and prominent a part in the history of the country which hails him as her founder. Such was the terror which struck the army, that they left all the artillery, ammunition and baggage to the enemy, and never stopped in their flight until they reached Fort Cumberland. In this action the British loss amounted to 700 killed, while the French force opposed to them was but 400, all told. Two subsequent expeditions undertaken against the French proving equally abortive, the campaign of 1755 ended in the disgrace of the British arms.

In the year 1756 war was again declared between France and Great Britain. Whilst the British army was lying idle at Albany, the French, under the command of the vigilant and brave Marquis De Montcalm, captured Fort Oswego and conducted the whole garrison, 1400 men, as prisoners of war to Canada.

Lord Loudon opened the campaign of 1757 by proceeding with 12,000 men to attack Louisburg, but finding the fortress in a formidable state of defence, concluded it to be the better part of valor to postpone the attack to some more convenient opportunity. His departure leaving the State of New York exposed to an attack, the vigilant Montcalm invaded the State, laid siege to Fort William Henry, and compelled its garrison, numbering 3000 men, to surrender at discretion. "Thus," as the English historian Smollet very justly observes, "ended the third campaign, where, with an evident superiority of numbers and resources, we abandoned our allies, exposed our people, and relinquished a large tract of country, to the shame and disgrace of the British name."

The English opened the campaign of 1758 with the prodigious force of 50,000 men, one half of whom were regular troops, under the command of Gen. Abercrombie. Their fleets cruised at the same time along the American coast, and prevented any reinforcements whatsoever from reaching the hands of the French in America. Gen. Abercrombie, at the head of 17,000 troops, attacked Ticonderoga, but was repulsed. The expedition against Fort Du Quesne was more successful. All reinforcements, either from France or from Canada, having been intercepted, the garrison, entirely destitute of provisions as well as materials of war, found themselves obliged to abandon the fort without a struggle, at the approach of Col. Washington: and after setting it on fire, proceeded in boats down the river. The forts of

Niagara, Ticonderoga and Crown Point, attacked by superior numbers, were also abandoned by the French. About this time another powerful army, under the command of the young and gallant Wolfe, arrived from England in America, to aid Gen. Abercrombie in the reduction of Canada. The cause of the French had now become hopeless; their numbers were too small, and their communication with France being cut off, all their valor and bravery could afford them no chance of success in a struggle against such fearful odds, but would only contribute to their destruction. Louisburg was taken, and although the victorious career of Gen. Wolfe was momentarily checked by his defeat at the Falls of Montmorency, where, in an attack upon the French, he lost 500 men, the subsequent battle fought by him upon the plains of Abraham, on the 13th day of September, 1759, against the French and Indian forces under the command of the Marquis De Montcalm, in which both the contending Generals were killed, the one in the moment of his victory, the other in the moment of his defeat, broke forever the French power in North America. Quebec surrendered, and with Quebec all Canada.

When the news of this eventful battle reached England, so much were the people of that country astonished at their own success, that a day of most solemn thanksgiving was appointed by royal proclamation throughout the British empire, and the General, whose defeat at Montmorency had made all Great Britain grumble, and who on the fields of Abraham had only done his duty, was now extolled to the skies as the greatest hero the world had ever seen, &c. &c.

In the conquest of the country the English had not conquered the hearts of the native Indians. Pontiac, the great Indian chief, apprehended danger from the English, from whose arrogant and insolent behaviour he had reason to infer, that they were much inclined to expel him and his people from the country of their fathers altogether. "When the French came hither," said a Chippeway chief, "they came and kissed us: they called us children, and we found them fathers: we lived like children in the same lodge." The French, in fact, had lived with the Indians, had assisted in their councils, smoked the calumet with them, had made them presents, and evinced much anxiety on their behalf. "On the other hand," said Pontiac, "the English neglected all those circumstances, which made the neighborhood of the French agreeable, and which might have made their own at least tolerable. The conduct of the French never gave rise to suspicion, the conduct of the English never gave rest to it."

Pontiac, who clearly discerned that the British usurpations would terminate in the total extinction of his race, began to excite the Indians with the story of their wrongs, and to dream dreams, in which he pretended to have interviews with the Great Spirit, during one of which the Great Spirit had asked him: "Why do you suffer these dogs in red clothing to enter your country and take the land I give you? Drive them from it, and when you are in distress I will help you." Having thus roused the savage multitude to bloody vengeance, he concerted a plan to secure the co-operation of the savage tribes along the English frontier for more than a thousand miles, and having completed his arrangements, made in the month of May, 1763, a simultaneous attack upon each of the twelve British forts between Green Bay and Pittsburgh. Nine of them were immediately captured, without the slightest previous suspicion on the part of the British that the Indians had any hostile intentions. Ingenious artifices were used by the savages to effect the capture of the forts. Thus the Ottowas, before committing their assault upon Fort Mackinaw, arranged a great game of ball, to which the British officers were invited. While engaged in play, the Indians managed to throw the ball once or twice over the pickets, and were suffered to procure it from within the fortress. Suddenly the ball was again thrown into the fort, and all the Indians rushed after it. The troops were butchered and scalped, and the fort destroyed.

Peace was at length concluded between France and England, and a treaty to that effect signed at Paris on the 10th of February, 1763, in virtue of which France ceded to England Nova Scotia, the whole of Canada and its dependencies, and all that portion of Louisiana east of the Mississippi, together with the French posts and settlements on the Ohio. The State of Illinois was included in the above cession, and therefore, after the 10th of February, 1763, became part of the British empire. News having been received in America of peace being restored, Pontiac soon relaxed in his efforts, the tomahawk was buried, and the war-whoop no longer resounded through the thickets of the forests. Unable to bear the sight of the red-coats, Pontiac

left the country and repaired to Illinois, where he was assassinated by a Peoria Indian. His nation, the Ottowas, and the Pottawatomies and Chippeways, determined to avenge the death of their revered leader, commenced a war upon the Peorias and their confederates, the Kaskaskias and Cahokias, in which these tribes were nearly exterminated.

At the time this State was ceded to England, the French portion of the population amounted to about 3000 souls. They resided along the Mississippi and Illinois Rivers, and their largest towns were Kaskaskia and Cahokia, of which the former contained about 100, and the latter about 50 families. Other small villages were in their vicinity, and one at Peoria, on the Illinois River. Prairie Du Rocher contained 14 families, and Prairie Du Pont, a short distance from Cahokia, about as many. Another considerable settlement was in and about Fort Chartres; but the whole did not exceed 3000 individuals. The French settlements were laid out by common consent on the same plan or system. The blocks were about three hundred feet square, and each block contained four lots. The streets were rather narrow, but always at right angles. Lots in the old times were enclosed by cedar posts or pickets, planted about two feet in the ground and extending five feet above. These pickets were placed touching each other, the whole forming a light and safe paling around each proprietor's lot. The upper ends of the pickets were sharpened, so that it was rather difficult to get over the fence. A neat gate was generally made in the fence opposite to the door of the house, and the whole concern was kept clean and neat.

Each village had a tract of land for common fields, containing several thousand acres, which was surrounded by a common fence, each family possessing a separate and well-defined portion of the land exclusively for itself. Besides this, a common, which contained frequently several thousand acres, and in which each villager had a joint, instead of a separate interest, was appended to every village for wood and pasturage. Each proprietor of land was bound to make and keep in repair the fences on his land.

The French in those days mostly sowed spring wheat. Sometimes wheat was sowed late in the fall. Indian corn was not so much cultivated as wheat, or used as much by the inhabitants. A species of

Indian or hominy corn was raised for the voyagers, which was an article of commerce. The French did not use Indian corn meal for bread to any great extent, but raised it for stock and to fatten hogs.

Their farming implements were neither well made nor of the proper kind. Their ploughs had not much iron about them. A small piece of iron was on the front part, covering the wood. They had no coulter, and had a large wooden mould-board. The handles were short and almost perpendicular, the beam was nearly straight, resting on an axle supported by two small wheels, the wheels low, and the beam so fixed on the axle with a chain or rope of raw hide, that the plough could be placed deep or shallow in the ground. Horses were seldom used for ploughing, oxen being preferred. The carts of the French, like the ploughs, were constructed without iron. When the Americans under Gen. Clarke came to the country, they called these carts "barefooted carts," because they had no iron on the wheels.

The French houses were generally one story high, and made of wood. A few of them were of stone. There was not a single brick house in the country for one hundred or more years from its first settlement. These houses were formed of large posts or timbers, the posts being three or four feet apart in many of them. In others the posts were closer together, and the intervals filled up with a mortar made of common clay and cut straw. The mortar filled up the cracks, so that the wall was even and regular. The whole wall, outside and inside, was usually whitewashed with fine lime, so that these houses presented a clean, neat appearance. The other class of houses having the posts further apart, the spaces were filled up with puncheons. The posts were grooved for the puncheons to fit in. These houses were used for stables, barns, &c. &c. The covering of the houses, stables, &c., was generally of straw, or long grass cut in the prairie. All the houses had porticoes around them, the posts of which were generally of cedar or mulberry. A garden was assigned to each house. The doors were plain batton work, of walnut usually. The windows were generally glazed, and the sash opened and shut on hinges. Close by the houses were neat clean wells, nicely walled with stone, having a windlass fixed in them, so that water was convenient and clean.

Hats in those times were very little used. The *capot,* made of white blanket, was the universal dress for the laboring class of people.

The capot was a kind of cap, attached at the cape, and raised in cold weather over the head. Coarse blue stuff was used by the working-men for pantaloons in summer, and buckskin or cloth in the winter. Moccasins made from the skins of cattle were used instead of boots. The females generally wore the deer skin moccasins. Both sexes kept always on hand something tasty and neat for the church and ball-room.

The French in those days turned their attention to the Indian trade and to hunting, in a great measure, for support. Game was then plenty; buffalo, and other wild animals, were found in the prairies between Kaskaskia and Vincennes, sufficient to supply the inhabitants with animal food. The Indians called the Kaskaskia, Raccoon River, from the number of those animals living about it. A great many of the inhabitants were expert voyagers and hunters, and a hardy and energetic race of men, who could not be terrified by hardships or perils, and who often performed their laborious service without anything to eat, for days together. The women spun, wove, and made the garments, and carefully attended to their household affairs. Both sexes spent their leisure time in lively conversation, in dancing, or other amusements, according to the customs of their nation; which, as true Frenchmen, even at so great a distance from their native country, they had not been able to renounce.

The State of Illinois, although ceded in 1763, continued in the possession of France until 1765, when Captain Stirling, sent by Gen. Gage, then commander-in-chief of the British forces in America, to take possession of the territory, arrived, and assumed its government in the name of His Britannic Majesty. He established his head-quarters at Fort Chartres, and issued a royal proclamation, granting to the Roman Catholic subjects of His Majesty the free and undisturbed exercise of their religion, according to the rites of the Roman Catholic Church, as it had already been granted to the Canadians.

Captain Stirling was succeeded by Major Farmer, and the latter superseded by Col. Reed, in 1766. Col. Reed remained also but a short time, and was succeeded by Lieutenant-Colonel Wilkins, who arrived at Kaskaskia, on the 5th of September, 1768. Ever since the occupation of the territory by the British, the administration of justice had been in the hands of the military commandant, which caused no little annoyance to the public, and occasioned frequent complaints. A Civil Court, consisting of seven judges, was afterwards established, but trial by jury being refused, it did not become popular. Many of the French inhabitants, finding the British rule insupportable, emigrated to Louisiana.

The war of 1756 had increased the public debt of Great Britain to an alarming magnitude, and various expedients were proposed for the payment of its interest and the liquidation of its principal. To raise part of the money necessary for this purpose, the British Parliament claimed the right and power of taxing the American Colonies, although they were entirely without representation in the Parliament, and Great Britain had not even the slightest claim upon their gratitude, since nothing whatever had been demanded by the proud and independent American Colonists, or granted and provided by the niggardly hand of the British Government, to promote the settlement and welfare of the Colonies. The American people, too intelligent not to understand their rights, denied, repeatedly, the existence of any legal power on the part of Parliament to tax the Colonies; but Parliament not only established it as a fundamental principle, "that Great Britain had a right to tax America," authorizing the imposition of duties upon tea, glass, paper, &c., but also passed a bill for quartering troops upon the Colonists, another for depriving them of trial by jury, and another for transporting persons charged with offences, beyond the high seas, for trial, and various others of a similar despotic nature. Such acts of tyranny and oppression would not be endured by a generous people, and met, therefore, with the most decided resistance on the part of the American people, which led to the outbreak of hostilities in 1775, inaugurating the glorious American Revolution, and causing the last ligaments that bound the descendants of England to the land of their fathers, to be severed for ever.

About the time of the commencement of the Revolutionary War, or rather, before, the American Colonists had extended their settlements west of the Alleghanies, and occupied Kentucky. Of the first settlers, who repaired thither to seek a new home, the most conspicuous were Daniel Boone, who arrived there in 1769, and George Rogers Clarke, who came thither from Virginia, in 1775. The population of Illinois was then about the same as at the time of its cession to England, a majority of it consisting of French and Catholics. Kaskaskia, Cahokia, Saint Vincennes, in Indiana, Detroit and Mackinaw, were garrisoned by English troops.

Preparing themselves for the approaching struggle, in which they were to be so ignominiously defeated, the British, by promises and gifts, had pacified the savages, and made them their allies, by representing to them the Americans as bent upon their extermination, supplied them with arms and ammunition, and paid them liberally in advance for the scalps they were to bring in. Immediately upon the commencement of hostilities, the savages attacked the frontier settlements and burnt them to the ground, causing the forests to resound with the heart-rending shrieks of helpless women and children, who fell beneath the murderous tomahawk and scalping-knife of an enemy that knew no quarter.

Clarke, tracing the incitement of the Indian ravages to the British settlements at Kaskaskia, Detroit, and Vincennes, his heart dilating with joy at the idea of annexing to his country a territory, the splendid resources of which he had found, on examination, to be unrivalled any where, conceived the plan of carrying the war into Illinois. He hastened to Williamsburgh, then the capital of Virginia, sought and obtained an interview with the Governor, was promised a bounty of 300 acres for every person who should enlist, furnished with £1200 by the Governor, and authorized to raise seven companies of militia; and, in order that the enterprise might be kept secret, was publicly instructed to proceed to Kentucky for its defence; being thus "clothed with all the authority he could wish," he set off on the 4th of February, 1778, to make haughty Britain feel the power of the American arms. After reviewing his little band of four companies, equipped in the simplest manner, he commenced his march across the country, passed over the Ohio some distance above Fort Massacre, and continued to advance by the nearest route against the ancient French village of Kaskaskia. Whilst on his march, he fell in with a party of hunters, who communicated to him, that the town had no regular garrison; that the inhabitants, who entertained most horrid apprehensions of the Virginians, had not even the slightest suspicion of an attack being contemplated; so that, if they could reach the town without being discovered, they could not fail to render themselves masters of it Resolved to profit by this intelligence, Clarke, after an arduous march of several days, when his provisions were now quite exhausted, arrived with his party near Kaskaskia. They entered a farm-house about a mile's distance from the village, where they learned, that though the militia had been called out the day before, they had been since dismissed, as no cause of alarm existed, and everything was apparently tranquil and quiet. Clarke immediately divided his detachment into several small parties, assigning to each a place of attack, and causing notice to be given to the inhabitants that whosoever of them should dare to appear in the streets, would be instantly shot down. Everything turned out as well as could be wished; both the town and the fort were taken, and the British Governor, together with his British troops, were made prisoners of war. Resolving to make good use of the dread, in which the Virginians were regarded, Col. Clarke at once posted guards at every avenue of the town, so as to prevent all transmission of intelligence from without, disarmed the inhabitants in the short space of two hours, and ordered his troops to patrol the town in every direction during the night, making the most horrible uproar, and whooping after the most approved Indian fashion. On the next day the troops were withdrawn and placed in different positions about the town, and the inhabitants were strictly forbidden to have any intercourse, either between themselves, or with the soldiers. Several Kaskaskians, who had congregated and conversed with each other, were arrested and put in irons, without being allowed to utter a single word in their defence. The whole town was at once overspread with terror, and neither mercy nor compassion any longer expected. At last, the priest, and several of the most influential citizens of the village, were granted an audience by Col. Clarke. Addressing Col. Clarke in a low and submissive voice, the priest, in the name of the inhabitants, begged permission for them all "to assemble once more in the church to take final leave of each other, as they expected to be separated never to meet again on earth." This being granted, the priest, feeling his drooping spirits revive, made an attempt at some further conversation, but was rudely interrupted by Col. Clarke, who told him that he had no time to listen any further to him. The whole town then went to church, remaining there for a long time, after which the same deputation waited again upon Col.

Clarke to express their thanks for the indulgence they had received; also to solicit him not to separate their families, and to allow them some clothes and provisions for their further support; and also to assure him that they would have long ago declared themselves in favor of the Americans, had they dared so to do in the presence of their British rulers. Regarding it as useless to terrify the people any more, Clarke, throwing aside all disguise, told the people, who stood in utter amazement, not knowing whether to trust their ears, that he had none, save the most friendly intentions towards them, that the king of France, having united his arms with those of America, he, Clarke, expected the war shortly to cease, and that he was glad to be convinced of their being friendly to the American cause, notwithstanding the prejudices excited against the latter by British officers "And now," continued he, "to prove my sincerity, you will please inform your fellow-citizens that they are at liberty to go wherever they please, and that their friends in confinement shall immediately be released." The joy of the village seniors on hearing, and of the inhabitants, at the communication of the speech of Col. Clarke, was immense, so as to baffle all attempts at description. Suffice it to say, that the church was instantly filled, and devout thanks were offered to the Most High for the miraculous manner, in which he had subdued the minds of their savage conquerors. Nor did the gratitude of the people to Col. Clarke display itself in mere words; for, when Col. Clarke resolved to capture, if possible, in the same way, Cahokia, which yet remained in the hands of the enemy, several Kaskaskians offered to aid him in the enterprise, assuring him that the Cahokians were their relations and friends, and would, at their request, be ready to join his cause. Accepting their services, Col. Clarke despatched them in company with a party of his own troops, to Cahokia, which they reached before the surrender of Kaskaskia was even known there. The garrison of the British Fort at Cahokia was at once compelled to surrender at discretion; the Indian force near Cahokia was dispersed, and the inhabitants, easily persuaded by their Kaskaskian friends, a few days afterwards took the oath of allegiance to the American Republic. Thus, the State of Illinois, in territory larger than the whole of Great Britain, was annexed to the Republic by the energy of a single man, at the head of but four companies of militia, who, for this purpose, had marched and transported their provisions and ammunition for one thousand three hundred miles, by land and water, through a wild and inhospitable region, inhabited by the allies and mercenaries of England.

Having with a handful of trusty followers penetrated into the heart of a hostile country, Col. Clarke, considering his situation rather delicate, since he had no prospect of being speedily relieved or reinforced in case of need, and being aware that the position he now occupied would be unsafe as long as Fort Vincennes, which impeded his communication with Virginia, was in the hands of the British, determined to reduce this fort. As a preliminary step, wishing to conciliate to himself the favors of the Illinoisians, he organized courts, held by French judges elected by the people, with a right of appeal to himself—which courts became very popular and aided essentially in increasing his influence; and further, besides instructing his soldiers to speak of the troops at Kaskaskia as a detachment only from the main body, stationed somewhere at the Ohio, he caused the rumor to be circulated, that reinforcements were hourly expected to arrive. The warm attachment of the Kaskaskians to him rendered these measures of precaution superfluous, for when Col. Clarke prepared in earnest for an expedition against Fort Vincennes, Mr. Gibault, the Roman Catholic priest at Kaskaskia, offered, if it met with his approbation, to take the whole business on himself, assuring him "that he had no doubt of being able to bring that place over to the American interest without the trouble of sending a military force against it." The offer being accepted, the priest set off for Vincennes. On his arrival he explained the object of his mission to the inhabitants, who, two days afterwards, threw off their allegiance to the British king, and in a solemn assembly at their church, proclaimed their political union with the Commonwealth of Virginia, The American flag being hoisted, and a Provisory Commandant elected, the priest returned to Kaskaskia with the agreeable intelligence, that Vincennes had gone over to the Americans. On hearing this, Col. Clarke appointed Leonard Helm commandant at Vincennes, and agent for Indian affairs in the department of the Wabash. He also sent a detailed report of his campaign to the Legislature of Virginia, urging the same to appoint a civil commandant to take charge of the political affairs of the region which had now submitted to his arms: whereupon in October, 1778, the said Legislature passed an act to establish "as the county of Illinois," all that part of Virginia west of Ohio, surpassing in its dimensions the whole of Great Britain, and appointed Col. John Todd Civil Commandant and Lieutenant Colonel of the said county.

Having established a garrison at Kaskaskia and another at Cahokia, as also a military post at the Falls of the Ohio, on the site of Louisville, the present great commercial emporium of Kentucky, Col. Clarke exerted himself to the utmost to bring about a good understanding between the Indians and Americans, and being perfectly well acquainted with the Indian character, with the most consummate skill (indicating also a deep knowledge of human nature) induced them to abandon the British cause, and to conclude treaties of peace and of alliance with him.

On the 29th of January, much to the dissatisfaction of Col. Clarke, intelligence was received at Kaskaskia, that Gov. Hamilton, of Detroit, had subjected Fort Vincennes once more to British sway, and that, but for the lateness of the season, he would have marched against Kaskaskia; that he contemplated, however, at any rate, opening early in the spring a grand campaign against Kaskaskia.

At the time Gov. Hamilton had arrived with a considerable force before Vincennes, Capt. Helm and one soldier, by the name of Henry, constituted the whole of its garrison. No sooner had Gov. Hamilton approached within speaking distance of the fort, than Capt. Helm, standing with a lighted match by the side of a well-charged cannon, then placed in the open gateway, halloed out at the top of his voice, "Halt!" Gov. Hamilton immediately halted, and on seeing the cannon in the gateway, peremptorily demanded the surrender of the place. Uttering a frightful oath, Capt. Helm exclaimed, "No man enters here until I know the terms." Hamilton at once replied, "You shall have the honors of war," whereupon Helm surrendered the fort, and the whole garrison, to the unspeakable mortification of the warlike British, consisting of one officer and one private, marched out with the honors of war.

On hearing this, and on being further informed, that Gov. Hamilton had then only eighty men at Vincennes, and was impatiently awaiting the arrival of about 700 Indian auxiliaries, Col. Clarke, who on this occasion remarks in his journal, "I knew, that if I did not take him, he would take me," at once resolved to carry the war into Africa. Having fitted out a large Mississippi boat as a galley, he put six pieces and forty-six men, under the command of Capt. John Rogers, on board of it, and ordered the men to ascend the Ohio and enter the Wabash as far as the White River, where they were to await further instructions. He then raised, with the utmost dispatch, two companies of militia in Kaskaskia and Cahokia, which, his own force included, amounted to about 170 men, and before eight days had elapsed, was on his way to Vincennes. After a most toilsome march through woods, and over marshy, swampy prairies, he and his men came in sight of Fort Vincennes, and advanced within fifty yards of it. Col. Clarke, notwithstanding his galley, laden with ammunition and military stores, had not yet arrived, ordered his men to open a fire of musketry upon the British soldiers at their guns, which was done with such effect, that Gov. Hamilton found it impossible to keep them at their cannon, which, moreover, from their elevated position, had done no damage to the Americans. The rest of the tale is soon told. Gov. Hamilton, who knew what kind of an enemy he had to fight, finding all further resistance useless, surrendered the fort on the 24th of February, and the whole garrison, consisting of 79 men, and thirteen pieces of cannon, and half a million of dollars' worth of military goods and stores, fell into the hands of the victors, who for the second time, on the ramparts of the fort, destined to remain American, unfurled the star-spangled banner, the ensign of freedom, to the breeze. Col. Clarke appointed Capt. Helm once more commandant of the fort, and embarking on his galley, which had now come up, returned to Kaskaskia.

Such was the renown Col. Clarke had acquired by this successful expedition, and the rapid conquest of the territories between the Mississippi and Ohio, that Buckongahelas, the head warrior of the Delawares, on a day in which he happened to meet Col. Clarke in council, "thanked the Great Spirit for having brought together two such great warriors as Buckongahelas and Col. Clarke!"

The surrender of Cornwallis with his whole army on the 19th of October, 1781, to the Americans, spreading terror and consternation throughout Great Britain, a treaty of peace was signed between England and the United Colonies, in virtue of which the independence of the latter was fully recognised, and all the land east of the Mississippi, and south of Lakes Ontario, Erie, Huron, Superior, and the Lake of the Woods, including therefore Illinois, was ceded to the Americans. That portion of the western lands which constituted what was then called the "Northwestern Territory," including the present States of Ohio, Indiana, Illinois, Michigan and Wisconsin, was claimed wholly by the State of Virginia, and in part by New York, Massachusetts and Connecticut; but in consideration of the all-important object, to secure harmony among the States of the Confederacy, which were then without any special bond of union, the people of the States, which claimed to have a title to the said "Northwestern Territory," moved by a noble spirit of patriotism, ceded all their right and title to the Federal Government. Soon after these cessions had been made, Congress, in the summer of 1787, passed an ordinance "for the government of the territory of the United States north-west of the River Ohio." A governor was appointed by Congress for three years, and a secretary for four. A Court, consisting of three judges, was organized, and the governor and judges authorized to adopt and publish such laws of the original States as were necessary and best suited to the circumstances of the territory. As soon as there should be 5000 free male inhabitants of full age in any district, they were authorized to elect representatives for two years to a General Assembly. The Governor, Legislative Council, consisting of five members appointed by Congress, and a House of Representatives, could make any laws, provided they were not contrary to the ordinance of Congress. The Legislature were also authorized to elect by joint ballot a delegate to Congress.

Arthur St. Clair, an officer of the Revolutionary army, who had served with some distinction, was appointed the first Governor and Commander-in-chief of the Territory.

The white population of the Territory was but small: that of Illinois had remained stationary. Struck with the fertility of the soil of Illinois, several of the soldiers of Col. Clarke settled in that country. They were the earliest American settlers in Illinois. They lived mostly in stations, or block-house forts, which they had been compelled to erect for their protection, since the Indians committed great depredations on the habitations of the new settlers. The general construction of these block-house forts was about this: The lowest order of these forts was a single house, strongly built, a story and a half or two stories high. The lower story was provided with port-holes to shoot through, and also with substantial puncheon doors, three or four inches thick, with strong bars, to prevent the Indians from entering. The second story projected over the first three or four feet, and had holes in the floor, outside the lower story, to shoot down at the Indians attempting to enter.

Another higher grade of pioneer fortifications was made thus: Four large, strong block-houses, fashioned as above, were erected at the four corners of a square lot of ground, as large as the necessities of the people required. The intervals between these block-houses were filled up with large timbers, placed deep in the ground, and extending twelve or fifteen feet above the surface. Within these stockades were cabins built for the families to reside in. A well of water, or a spring, was generally found to be necessary in these forts. In perilous times the horses were admitted into the forts for safe keeping. Generally there were two strong gates to these garrisons, with bars in proportion, to secure the doors against the savages. Port-holes were cut in the stockade at about seven feet high, and platforms raised to stand on when shooting.

The timber in the vicinity of these forts was carefully cleared off, so as to afford no hiding-places to the Indians. In the mornings it was often dangerous to open the gates and walk out. The Indians frequently attacked the milking parties and others first going out of the fort. Sentinels were kept up all night in dangerous times.

Emigrants from the remotest parts of the Union and of Europe would come together in these forts. Many were the quarrels, which such a mixed state of society would naturally lead to. The property of one man was often so contiguous to that of another as to excite strong temptations in the mind of the latter to annex it to his own; nor does it appear, that the women were an exception to this rule. Whenever a violation of the sixth commandment took place, in which case, owing to the extremely limited space, detection was sure to follow, the grave old ladies would put on their spectacles and hypocritically exclaim: "Oh the sins of the world! It is no wonder we have an Indian war upon us!"

The customs of these early American settlers were much on the French model, extremely gay, polite, and merry.

In personal appearance these pioneers were rough and unrefined, yet were they kind, social, and generous. They were brave, energetic, and hospitable, and ready to share with their neighbors or newly-arrived strangers their last loaf.

Their habits and manners were plain, simple, and unostentatious. Their dwellings were log cabins of the simplest structure, their furniture, utensils and dress were also as simple and economical as possible.

For clothing, dressed deer-skins were extensively used, for hunting-shirts, pants, leggins and moccasins; the red skin of the prairie wolf or fox was converted into the hat or cap. Dressed skins of the buffalo, bear and elk furnished the covering of their beds. Wooden vessels were used instead of bowls. A gourd formed the drinking-cup.

Every man carried his knife in his girdle, while the whole family had often to use the solitary remaining one. If a family chanced to have a few pewter dishes, knives and forks, it was in advance of the neighbors.

The American settlers were hunters and stock-growers, raising, be sides a small amount of wheat, chiefly corn, which was beaten for bread in the mortar, and ground on a grater, or in a hand mill.

Many of these settlers observed the Sabbath with an austerity that would have become a Puritan.

To the French, on the other hand, the Sabbath always had been and still was a day of hilarity and pleasure. They would strictly attend mass in the morning and practise their devotions in the church; and in the afternoon would assemble in parties at private houses for gay social intercourse, when cards, dances, and various sports, made the time pass. Intemperance, either in eating or drinking, was never witnessed among them.

CHAPTER II.

THE Indians had not been included in the treaty of peace signed between Great Britain and America. Several tribes, therefore, wrought upon by British gold, continued their hostilities as before, and between 1783 and 1790 nearly 2000 men, women and children in Kentucky alone had been killed or carried away into captivity. All peaceable remonstrances on the part of the United States government having been in vain, it became incumbent upon the latter to pacify the Indians by force of arms. Gen. Harmar was accordingly despatched with a body of militia, amounting to 1433 men, into the country of the Miamies, but imprudently dividing his forces, he was attacked and defeated in detail by Little Turtle, the renowned warrior-chief of the Miamies, and obliged to return with a loss of 200 men.

In the subsequent year, 1791, a new force of 2000 soldiers and a large body of militia were raised, and the previous Governor, Arthur St. Clair, though from physical debility altogether disqualified for service, appointed commander of it. Gen. St. Clair commenced his march, and having reached with part of his troops a tributary stream of the Wabash, encamped, intending to entrench himself and to await the arrival of the remainder of his troops. Penetrating his design, Little Turtle, at the head of about 1500 warriors, assailed the camp about midnight. The militia gave way, and the Indians rushed after them, spreading terror everywhere. The greatest confusion at once ensued throughout the whole camp. Gen. St. Clair being unable to walk, was borne upon a litter into the hottest of the engagement, and exerted himself to the utmost to restore order, but seeing all his efforts to be in vain, he ordered a retreat, which immediately degenerated into a precipitate flight. Such was the panic, which had seized the army, that they abandoned their entire artillery train and baggage to the Indians, threw away their arms, and could not be brought to a stand before they reached Fort Jefferson. The Americans lost nearly one half of their whole force engaged, or about 600 men, the Indians only 58.

This disastrous defeat rendered it necessary, that the American Government should prosecute the war with the utmost vigor, in order to retrieve the credit of its arms. Negotiations were at first attempted, but failed, the savages being too much elated with their victory to think of peace. A new and still larger force was therefore raised, and its command entrusted to Gen. Wayne, famed for the gallant manner, in which he stormed Stony Point during the Revolutionary war, "where, after wading through a deep morass and surmounting a double row of abattis, and forcing his way up to the strong works on the summit of the hill amid a shower of shells and shot of every kind, being struck on the head by a musket-ball, he fell, and immediately rising on one knee, he exclaimed: 'March on and carry me into the fort; if the wound be mortal, I will die at the head of the column!'" With such a leader the event of the expedition could hardly be doubtful. His offers of peace being rejected, Gen. Wayne advanced on the 15th of August, 1794, to Roche Debout, where he erected a small fort, which he called Fort Deposit. Five days afterwards he marched against the enemy and discovered them, about 2000 strong, in a position difficult of attack, their front protected by trees overthrown by a tornado, their right flank covered by thickets, and their left resting on the river Miami. As he was forming his army in order of battle, a brisk fire was opened upon his advance-guard from a thicket of underwood. He immediately ordered the "front line of legionary infantry to rouse the Indians out of their thickets with the bayonet, and when up to deliver a tremendous fire on their backs, followed by a brisk charge, so as not to give them time to load again." So furious was the onset of the troops, and so irresistible their bayonet charge, that the Indians were completely routed before any of the other corps could have come up. The American loss was 107, while that of the Indians was far greater. Gen. Wayne was not remiss in following up this victory, laying waste whole villages and cornfields, for a distance of fifty miles around. The destruction of their cabins and cornfields at last broke down the savage obstinacy of the Indians, and they sued for peace, which was promptly granted, and mutually concluded on the 7th of August, 1795. With the termination of this bloody war the lives and property of the settlers were secured to them, and a new impulse was given to immigration, which began to pour slowly in.

In 1803, a new territory, known as the territory of Indiana, which embraced the whole of the North-western Territory, with the exception of the present State of Ohio, was formed, and William H. Harrison, since President of the United States, appointed its first Governor. Illinois remained a part of the new territory until 1809, when it was erected into an independent territory, and Ninian Edwards appointed its first Governor.

Peace had been made, and the white man had permanently established himself in the region, once a favorite hunting-ground of the Indian. No effort of the latter to recover the heritage of his fathers could have prevailed against the superior will and discipline of the former. Despair filled the minds even of the boldest of the Indian race, and the indefatigable and enterprising Little Turtle himself, who had beaten the foreign intruder in many a bloody engagement, becoming satisfied of the impossibility of making the Ohio the boundary-line between the red and white man, relaxed in his efforts, and at last acquiesced in the rule of the white man. But when he ceased to battle for the rights of his people, a hero arose among the Indians, no doubt the most gifted and exalted of his race, who, collecting the nearly exhausted strength of his people for a last and desperate struggle, placed himself at their head, and fought foremost in their ranks, until his untimely death on the field of battle forever sealed the doom of his unhappy race.

The name of this extraordinary man, with whom we will next occupy ourselves, is Tecumseh. He was a patriot, and the love of his country rendered him an irreconcilable enemy of the white man, upon whom, he was heard to declare, he could never look without feeling the flesh crawl upon his bones. His penetrating mind foresaw the total extinction of his race, the cause of which he traced, with unerring certainty, to the white immigration. He studied the subject as a statesman, and having satisfied himself that justice was on the side of his countrymen, with his heart oppressed by grief and inflamed with implacable vengeance, he tasked his mighty brain to find means to avert from his people the tide which threatened to engulf them.

Upon the great work contemplated by him, Tecumseh entered in the year 1805 or 1806, when he had attained his 38th year. As a preliminary step, he sought to improve the morals of his people, whom the intercourse with the whites had only debased, and with this view caused their original manners and customs to be re-established, and the use of ardent spirits, and the intercourse with the whites to be strictly forbidden. Being aware of the superstitious character of his race, he communicated his plan to his brother, the prophet, who immediately entered into his designs. At first, he began by dreaming dreams and seeing visions; afterwards he became an inspired prophet, commissioned by the Great Spirit to decide over life and death, and to restore to the Indians their lands and original happy condition. The fame of the prophet soon penetrated to the frozen shores of the Lakes, and far away beyond the Mississippi, and pilgrims from the remotest tribes hastened to see him. Tecumseh himself, seemed to believe, and mingling with the pilgrims, won their hearts by his address, and through them diffused a knowledge of his plan among the most distant Indian nations. He himself travelled far and wide, and by his brilliant eloquence, soon persuaded his countrymen to join his cause. It is related, that whilst among the Creeks in Alabama, he visited a chief called the Big Warrior, explained to him the object of his call, and perceiving that the Big Warrior wanted to keep aloof from fighting, told him that he knew the reason of his so declining to fight was his disbelief in the Great Spirit's having sent him, but that he would conclusively prove his divine mission, by shaking down to the ground every house in his village by stamping with his foot on the earth, the moment he should have arrived at Detroit. He thereupon left him. The Big Warrior and his people anxiously watched the arrival of the day, on which they supposed, Tecumseh would reach Detroit. The anxiously looked-for day came, and with it a mighty earthquake, which levelled with the ground every house in Tuckhabatchee, the village of the chief. It was afterwards ascertained, that this earthquake had happened on the very day, on which Tecumseh arrived at Detroit, as he threatened it would. It was the famous earthquake of New Madrid, on the Mississippi.

In the meantime, whilst laboring day and night in his great work, he had three different interviews with Gen. Harrison, during which he proposed to become even an ally of the Americans, provided they would deliver up the lands lately purchased, and never make another treaty without the consent of all the tribes. Gen. Harrison promised to refer the matter to the President, although, said he, he will not be very likely to listen to the proposition made; whereupon Tecumseh declared, that the Great Spirit would determine the matter, and he and Harrison would be obliged to fight it out. The Governor then proposed to him, that, in the event of a war, he should do his best to put an end to the cruel mode of warfare as carried on by his countrymen, to which Tecumseh at once assented, being perhaps, the only Indian, who scrupulously kept his word in this respect.

On the 27th of July, 1811, he again visited Gen. Harrison, at the head of about 400 warriors, probably with a view of impressing the whites with an idea of his strength. Several murders had previously been committed in Illinois by the Indians, and Gen. Harrison, notified of these occurrences, was rather in a bad humor, when he met Tecumseh at their fourth conference. Tecumseh, whose manner and behaviour were always very respectful, and on this occasion most remarkably polite and dignified, openly declared to Gen. Harrison, "that, after much trouble, he had united all the western tribes under his lead and placed them under his direction; that, in so doing, he had merely imitated the example set by the United States themselves, and claimed to have the same right to do this; that the murders spoken of ought to be forgiven, since the Indians had suffered similar injuries at the hands of the whites; and lastly, that the Indians were going to reoccupy, in autumn, their ancient hunting-ground, at Tippecanoe, which the Americans were then about surveying." The Governor replied, "that the President would put his warriors in petticoats sooner than give up the country he had fairly acquired, or to suffer his people to be murdered with impunity."

Whereupon, Tecumseh left him, and shortly afterwards resumed his travels among his countrymen.

In the meantime, his brother, the prophet, collected around himself in Tippecanoe, the restless and daring spirits of every tribe, haranguing them daily, and protecting them, by a hundred charms, from the weapons of the white man, encouraging, rather than controlling, their lawless desires. Several murders were committed, and one of Gov. Harrison's own soldiers fired upon by the Indians. The

Indians apparently intending hostilities, Gov. Harrison, with a force of nearly 1,000 men, proceeded to their village to restore peace, if necessary, by force of arms. He found their town, Tippecanoe, fortified with great care, and on the 6th of September, 1811, encamped at the distance of a mile from it. The prophet had taught his followers to believe, that the village was wholly impregnable, and that in the coming contest the Great Spirit would strike the eyes of the Americans with blindness, and would make their bullets fall harmless at the Indian's feet. Encouraged by these assurances of their holy prophet, the savages, early on the morning of the 7th of September, sallied forth from their town, and attacked the camp of Gov. Harrison, with an apparent determination to conquer or to die.

They encountered a desperate resistance, but believing themselves fated to conquer, continued the battle until daylight, when they were in their turn charged by the troops with the bayonet, and after a bloody conflict, driven into a swamp. The Indians lost 38 killed, besides a great many wounded; the Americans 60 killed and 120 wounded. The town of the prophet was burnt, the corn in its vicinity destroyed, and the savages compelled to sue for peace. The exasperated Indians abused and nearly killed the prophet, whose claims to magic power were forever destroyed.

When Tecumseh returned and heard of this disastrous battle, which had been fought against his most positive orders, and saw his people dispersed, overpowered by indignation, and losing for a moment his wonted self-control, he reproached his brother in the most bitter terms, seized him by the hair, and came very near taking his life. His anger and disappointment we may readily understand, since, by striking the western Indians with terror, the battle of Tippecanoe resulted in postponing, if not wholly frustrating, the execution of the vast undertaking — to which he had devoted the best years of his noble manhood — of uniting all the Indian nations in a powerful confederacy, which he was to direct and govern. After an interview with the Indian agent, during which he blamed Gen. Harrison for having made war upon his people during his absence, he departed to Canada to fight under the banners of the British, — not because he either loved or respected them, for this was impossible to him, who hated every white man without distinction, and only too well understood the policy pursued by Great Britain towards his people, — but because, after the battle of Tippecanoe, he could expect no success in his undertaking against the Americans, unless by making the British interested in them.

The opportunity, which Tecumseh had so anxiously awaited, of avenging the injuries of his people upon the Americans, at last presented itself. Ever since the close of the revolutionary war, the most illiberal policy was pursued towards the United States by Great Britain; desirous of repressing the growth of the republic, which already at that time threatened to become her great commercial rival, she violated every commercial and maritime right of the nation, and filled the measure of her arrogance by searching the American vessels on the high seas, impressing such as were unable to prove on the spot, that they were Americans, into her public service. Ignominious outrages and atrocious injuries were thus inflicted by Great Britain upon the American people, until the latter, unless indeed willing to be considered as her subjects, if not her slaves, found themselves compelled to declare war against her. A force of several regiments of regulars and militia was immediately raised, and placed at the disposal of Gen. Hull, who, on the 12th of July, 1812, crossed the Canadian frontier, and issued a proclamation to the inhabitants, exhorting them to join his standard; but either from want of courage or lack of judgment, after "an inglorious occupation of less than a month," withdrew his forces from the Canadian territory.

Sir Isaac Brock was then Governor of Upper Canada, and commander of the British forces, which were then but small. They were afterwards considerably increased. Apprised at an early day of the declaration of war by Congress, he transmitted the intelligence at once to his outposts, and "ere the tardy and blundering movements of the American secretary had begun, his legions were in the field." Having collected a force of 300 English troops and 600 Indians, he arrived at Fort Mackinaw before the declaration of war was even known there, and compelled its small garrison of 58 men to surrender.

About that time Capt. Brush, at the head of a company of volunteers, reached the river Raisin with supplies for the army of Gen. Hull. As he did not dare to proceed any further, the country around being infested with savages, Major Van Horn with 150 men was sent to escort him to head-quarters. He was attacked near Brownstown, by a large body of British regulars and Indians, and defeated, with a loss of 19 killed; whereupon Lieut. Col. Miller, with 300 regulars and 200 militia, was despatched to the relief of Capt. Brush. Though Col. Miller advanced with great caution, he fell into an ambuscade, being unexpectedly attacked by a party of British regulars, and Indians, commanded by Tecumseh in person. The battle raged with great fury; a bayonet charge, however, executed with great spirit by the Americans, drove back the British, whilst the Indians under Tecumseh maintained their ground, fighting with the most desperate valor. Unwilling, that their Indian allies should excel them in bravery, the British returned to the charge, continuing the combat for two hours, after which they beat a hasty retreat. The loss in killed and wounded amounted to about 100 men on either side. Lieut. Col. Miller, while in Brownstown, making preparations to pursue his march, received orders to return immediately to head-quarters. Gen. Hull, in order to secure himself a regular supply of provisions, and at the same time to keep open his communication with the Ohio, had fixed his camp at Detroit. The vigilant Sir Isaac Brock, perceiving the isolated and perilous position of Gen. Hull, appeared on the 15th of August, 1812, before Detroit, with about 1000 men, both regulars and Indians, and summoned Gen. Hull to surrender. To the astonishment and indignation of the whole garrison, who, equal as they were in numerical force to the British, confidently expected to repel the latter with great slaughter, in case they should dare an attack, Gen. Hull, whom no doubt old age had rendered imbecile, ordered his troops to stack their arms, and surrendered, not only his own precious person, but also the place, the Territory of Michigan, and all of the northwestern army under his command, to the British under Sir Isaac Brock, on the 16th of August, 1812. A provisional government having been established in Detroit under Col. Proctor, Sir Isaac Brock returned to Niagara, and in the second invasion of Canada by the Americans, was slain at the battle of Queenstown.

The fall of Detroit was not the only reverse the American arms were destined to sustain, before they should vindicate the cause of their country by splendid victories. Other forts, more remote, and, owing to the utter incompetence of Gen. Hull, but miserably provided for.

had to be abandoned to the British, and at the very time of the fall of Detroit, Chicago was the theatre of barbarous cruelties and a savage massacre, in which its garrison was nearly exterminated. Chicago was then but a small fort, which the United States government had erected in 1804, in order "to supply the Indians' wants and to control the Indians' policy." Sixty men, under the command of Capt. Heald, constituted the whole of its garrison. Gen. Hull, who, as commander of the Northwestern army, was also entrusted with the defence of the forts of the Northwestern Territory, despatched a friendly Indian to Chicago with such orders as could only emanate from such a man, directing Capt. Heald to evacuate the fort, and to distribute all of the United States property, arms and ammunition included, among the neighboring Indians, and repair to Fort Wayne. This Indian arrived on the 7th of August, and urged Capt. Heald to evacuate the fort without a moment's delay, before the Pottawatomies, a numerous and warlike tribe, through whose country they had to pass, could receive intelligence, and collect a force sufficient to harass him on his march. Capt. Heald neglected to follow this prudent advice, so that at the time he read the order of evacuation to his troops, the Indians were already apprised of his intentions. Several of the officers of Capt. Heald, considering his project as little short of madness, remonstrated against it, urging Capt. Heald to remain in the fort, and to strengthen it as well as possible; but in obedience to the order of Gen. Hull, Capt. Heald insisted upon marching out. Although the Indians of the adjacent villages had already become troublesome, and manifested symptoms of hostility, so infatuated was Capt. Heald, as to hold, on the 12th of August, a council with them, in which he requested them to escort him to Fort Wayne, promising large rewards on their arrival thither, in addition to the goods, ammunition and provisions they were to receive, in pursuance of the absurd order of Gen. Hull. On the next day Capt. Heald distributed the goods in the factory store among the Indians, but being struck with the folly of delivering to them arms and ammunition, which they might use against the Americans, or liquor, which might arouse their savage temper, emptied the liquor into the stream flowing near by, and destroyed of arms and ammunition whatever was not required for immediate use. Notwithstanding all the precautions which had been taken, the Indians perceived what had been going on, and on the following day, when again meeting Capt. Heald in council, reproached him in the severest terms for having violated his promises. After the council had adjourned, Black Partridge, one of their chiefs, repaired to Capt. Heald, and delivered to him a medal, given him by the Americans as a token of friendship, assigning as the reason for so doing, that he could no longer restrain his warriors, and would not wear a token of peace when compelled to act as an enemy. Information was also received from another Indian chief, that the Pottawatomies, who had promised to protect the troops, could not be trusted.

Notwithstanding these repeated warnings, Capt. Heald, at the head of his garrison, marched out of the fort on the morning of the 15th, with the families and baggage of the soldiers, and the invalids, being followed in the rear by about 500 Pottawatomies, who were to escort the troops to Fort Wayne. Whilst the soldiers pursued their march, the Pottawatomies suddenly left the road, and turning the flank of the troops, poured in a volley of musketry upon them. The treacherous plot of the Indians could no longer be mistaken. The battle at once became general; the Americans fought with the greatest gallantry, till two-thirds of their number were slain; the remainder, 27 in all, surrendered, after stipulating for the safety of their families and themselves. In the hurry of the moment, the wounded prisoners were not thought of; therefore the Indians, considering them as excluded from the stipulation, tomahawked and butchered them with the most savage ferocity, during the following night, when they had returned with their captives to their camp, near the fort. A soldier, mortally wounded, and writhing in agony on the ground, was attacked with a pitchfork by an old squaw, and literally stabbed to death. Another of the savages, in direct violation of the treaty, assailed a baggage-wagon, and massacred and scalped in cold blood the children who were within, twelve in number. Whilst many other atrocities of a like nature were committed by the blood-thirsty savages, it is but just to observe, that a few of them, amongst whom Black Partridge, the magnanimous chief, was the most conspicuous, did the utmost in their power to save the lives or soothe the sufferings of their prisoners. Capt. Heald and his wife, the former twice, the latter seven times wounded, were nobly released by the Indian, who had taken them prisoners, and afterwards conveyed to Detroit. The soldiers, with their families, were dispersed among the Pottawatomies, and eventually ransomed; the fort was plundered and burnt to ashes.

These repeated disasters, and the actual occupation of Michigan, Northern Illinois and Mackinaw, by the British, aroused the nation to extraordinary efforts. Whole regiments and large bodies of volunteers were raised and equipped in a surprisingly short time. Gen. Hopkins and Gen. Edwards, of Illinois, undertook expeditions against the Indians of the Illinois and Wabash rivers, many of whom had participated in the massacre at Chicago. They destroyed several of their villages, and laid waste their fields, thus punishing them for the cruelties they had perpetrated at Chicago.

Appointed by Congress in the latter part of the year 1812, commander of the Northwestern army, Gen. Harrison undertook to drive the British from the Northwestern Territory; nothing was achieved, however, except the reduction of Fort Defiance, by Gen. Winchester, the next in command.

Thus terminated the land campaign of 1812.

On the sea, contrary to expectation, the Americans had been signally successful, and in three decisive engagements had humbled the flag of the proud mistress of the seas.

Early in the year 1813, the inhabitants of Frenchtown notified Gen. Winchester, that a large body of British and Indians were hovering about their town, and requested him to relieve them. Yielding to the entreaties of his volunteers, Gen. Winchester moved to the town, but before he arrived thither with the main body of his army, his vanguard, under Cols. Allen and Lewis, had attacked the British and Indians, and after a severe conflict, expelled them from the town. Two days after having joined his troops, on the 22d of January, he was assailed by nearly double the number of British and Indians. He was taken prisoner, and his troops, after a desperate defence, in which nearly one half of them, about 300, were killed, finding further resistance useless, surrendered, under promise of protection from Col. Proctor, the commander of the British force. The unfortunate troops paid dearly for their reliance on British faith; being delivered up to the Indians to be brought in the rear of the army to Malden, in Upper

Canada, they were, with scarce an exception, massacred and tomahawked by the blood-thirsty savages, without the interference of the British officers, who witnessed the scene. Their bleeding bodies were mutilated and scalped, and left to putrefy on the ground. But a very small remnant reached Fort Malden alive.

Gen. Harrison about that time had built a fort at the Rapids, which, in honor of the Governor of Ohio, he called Fort Meigs. He returned afterwards to Ohio for reinforcements. Receiving intelligence that the British threatened to attack Fort Meigs, he repaired thither, and was besieged by a powerful force under the former Col. Proctor, whom the British government, by way of approving his barbarous, fiend-like cruelty, had then promoted to the rank of Brigadier General. Gen. Clay, from Kentucky, marched to the relief of Gen. Harrison with 1200 men. Before reaching the fort, part of his troops, under Col. Dudley, were attacked and defeated by Tecumseh and Proctor, with a loss of 250 men; Col. Dudley himself being killed. Having driven the prisoners into a ruined fort, the Indians commenced a frightful slaughter among them, in presence of Gen. Proctor himself, and several of his officers, who seemed to delight at the inhuman spectacle. "While this carnage was raging," relates Drake, in his life of Tecumseh, "a thundering voice was heard in the rear, and in the Indian tongue; and on turning round, Tecumseh was seen advancing on horseback with the utmost speed to where two Indians had an American down, and were in the act of killing him. He sprang from his horse, caught one by the throat, the other by the breast, and threw them to the ground; and drawing his tomahawk and scalping knife, he ran in between the Americans and Indians, daring any one of the hundreds that surrounded him to attempt the murder of another American. They were all confounded, and immediately departed. He then demanded where Proctor was, and eyeing him at a distance, sternly inquired why he had not put a stop to the inhuman massacre. 'Sir,' said Proctor, 'your Indians cannot be commanded.' 'Begone,' thundered Tecumseh: 'You are unfit to command; go and put on petticoats!' "

On the 9th of May the siege of Fort Meigs was raised. Proctor departed with all his forces, but soon returned with reinforcements, this time selecting Fort Stephenson as the theatre of savage massacre.

He summoned the garrison to surrender; but they, determined to be cut to pieces sooner than to entrust their persons to his tender mercies, returned for answer: "When the fort shall be taken, there will be none left to massacre, as it will not be given up while a man is still alive." He then made an assault upon the fort, and was repulsed once, with a loss of 150 men, by a force scarcely a tenth of his own, not daring another assault.

On the 10th of September, a splendid naval victory was gained on Lake Erie, by the gallant Commodore Perry, in which the whole British squadron, consisting of six vessels, were captured, and more prisoners taken, than there were men in Perry's whole fleet. By this decisive victory the road to Canada was effectually opened, and Gen. Harrison, reinforced by a body of 4000 volunteers, under the command of Col. Johnson, was enabled to invade Canada without further delay. He advanced against Fort Malden, but on his arrival thither, found that it had been destroyed by Gen. Proctor, and that the latter, together with the gallant Tecumseh and his warriors, had retreated to the Moravian towns. After delivering the Northwestern Territory from the odious presence of the British, and hoisting again the American flag on the ramparts of Detroit, Gen. Harrison set out in pursuit of Gen. Proctor, reaching him on the banks of the river Thames. Determined to make his last stand here, Gen. Proctor, on the 7th of October, 1813, drew up in battle array his entire force of 800 of the line, and 2000 Indians; the greater part of the former, with the chief part of the artillery, occupied the left wing, resting on the river bank, and the Indians under Tecumseh the right wing, between two swamps. The position was skilfully chosen; Gen. Proctor, however, who knew, that the Americans had a numerous and well-appointed cavalry force, committed a grave error in forming his troops in open order, with intervals of three or four feet between the files, since he might have foreseen, that his troops, thus drawn up, would be unable to resist a cavalry charge.

Gen. Harrison, who had a force of 3500 men, inclusive of cavalry, with him, no sooner perceived the tactical error of the enemy, than he ordered two of his battalions of mounted men, of which one was under the immediate command of Col. Johnson, to the charge. So spirited and vigorous was the charge made by these troops, that at their first onset the rank and file of the British were scattered like leaves before the blast, and all the efforts of the British officers to form the broken ranks again, proved utterly unavailing. Seventy of the British regulars were killed and wounded, and more than 600 taken prisoners. Gen. Proctor's escape was merely due to the fleetness of his horse.

A far more serious trial awaited the Americans, who had to attack the Indians, commanded by the brave and noble Tecumseh. For although Col. Johnson succeeded in breaking their lines at the second charge, the Indians, unlike the British, disdaining to yield, continued the fight with desperate valor, and had nearly forced their way through the American lines, when they were repulsed with great slaughter by a regiment of Kentucky volunteers, led on by the intrepid Shelby. Still the Indians, to the number of 1200, stimulated to extraordinary efforts by their beloved commander, whose voice could be distinctly heard in every part of the battle, continued the combat, with heroic self-devotion, gathering round their illustrious chief, with an apparent determination to conquer or die by his side. But after Proctor's defeat, the event of the battle could no longer be doubtful. Unwilling to survive the slaughter of his countrymen, the generous Tecumseh fell, nobly battling at their head. About the same time Col. Johnson, conspicuous by the white horse he rode, was pierced by several balls, and fell. The Indians, whom the voice and example of Tecumseh could no longer animate, at last gave way on every side. Where Tecumseh had fallen, 36 men, both whites and Indians, were found literally cut and stabbed to pieces.

Thus fell Tecumseh, no doubt the greatest and most exalted of his race, and respected by all his enemies as a great and magnanimous chief. To a powerful intellect uniting the soul of a hero, he was in war the bravest of the brave, most eloquent in council, and generous and humane in every one of his acts. He died the greatest champion of his people; his death deprived them of their last protector, and sealed their doom forever.

Long afterwards his grave was to be seen beside a large fallen oak. He was there left alone in his glory. The British government having previously appointed him a brigadier-general, afterwards granted a pension to his mourning family.

The victory at the Thames, the fall of Tecumseh, and the inglorious defeat of Proctor, terminated the war in the Northwestern Territory, which was once more united to the republic, never again to be separated from it. The middle and northern part of Illinois for some time continued to be afflicted with the depredations of the Sacs, Foxes, Shawnees, Kickapoos, and other Indian nations, but peace being at length concluded between Great Britain and the Republic, on the 24th of December, 1814, the savages, abandoned by Great Britain, were soon brought to terms.

On the 20th of May, 1812, Illinois, for the first time, sent a delegate to Congress. The right of suffrage was extended to all its inhabitants, and the property qualification required by the ordinance of 1787 in the voter, was abolished. By this ordinance the President appointed a Governor, who held his office for three years, resided in the district, and had a freehold estate of 1000 acres of land; a Secretary for four years, who resided in the district, and had a freehold estate of 500 acres of land; and a Court of three judges, to reside in the district, and have, each of them, a freehold estate of 500 acres of land. The governor and the judges had power to adopt and publish such laws of the original States as were necessary and best adapted to the circumstances of the territory, and the governor was to have also the power of appointing all magistrates, civil officers, and all military officers under the rank of brigadier-general, and of dividing the district into counties and townships.

This was the form of government under which Illinois was ruled from 1809–1812.

In 1812 the governor was appointed and commissioned as before, but a Legislative Council of five members, and a House of Representatives, elected by the people, were now authorized to make laws "for the government of the district, not repugnant to the principles and articles established and declared in the ordinance above alluded to." The Legislative Council was appointed by the President and Senate, and commissioned by the former, from a list of 10 persons to be furnished by the House of Representatives in the district. A delegate to Congress was also elected by the people. In this manner the Territory was governed from 1812–1818, Ninian Edwards continuing as governor during that time.

The population of the Territory in the year 1812 did not exceed

12,000 souls. After the termination of the war in the year 1814, people began to arrive from the old States. They brought money with them,—quite a novelty to the people of Illinois,—for till then the skins of the deer had answered, with that primitive people, the purpose of a circulating medium; and introduced some changes into the habits and customs of the people. Education and learning, however, were still much neglected. There were few schools; in these few nothing but reading, writing, and the four cardinal rules of arithmetic, were taught. Scientific and professional men came from abroad. Of preachers, it is true, they had many that were born and brought up in the country, but their chief excellence consisted not in the profundity of their learning, which was wholly made up by a superficial knowledge of the gospel, but rather in the power of their lungs, the rapidity of their gesticulations, and the skill, with which they were wont to spin out a few barren ideas into a sermon of astonishing length, overladen with florid bombast. Their enthusiasm knew no bounds; by reason whereof many of them turned fanatics. Unlike our modern divines, they would, in times of scarcity, preach gratuitously, and be satisfied with the coarsest food; often they would accost and warn strangers, whose souls these poor fanatics imagined they saw rushing into the fire of eternal damnation. Of the fine arts, even the art of singing was unknown. The attempt of a New England singing master to introduce better music among the Illinoisians, resulted in a disastrous failure; for at the very first lesson he gave, his pupils, in spite of all his remonstrances, cried at the top of their voices, producing a deafening noise, which proving too much for his feeble constitution, forced him to desist from the enterprise.

The occupations of the people were still those of farming or hunting. They raised their own provisions, and often supplied their wants in a manner that shows them not deficient in originality and fertility of genius. To illustrate this, the example may be quoted of a farmer of the name of Lemon, who on a certain day turned out to plough, and, missing his horse-collar, which his waggish son had hidden, being perplexed for but a moment, in the twinkling of an eye pulled off his leathern breeches, stuffed them, and straddled them across the horse's neck, ploughing lustily all day, without any covering to hide his natural inferiorities from the prying eye of an insolent criticising curiosity.

CHAPTER III.

Up to the year 1818 the population of the Territory of Illinois had increased to about 50,000 inhabitants. At the commencement of that year, the people of the Territory unanimously resolved to have Illinois admitted into the Union as an independent State, and ordered Nathaniel Pope, their delegate to Congress, to take measures to that effect. Nathaniel Pope brought the subject at once before Congress, and reported a bill thereon. About that time the danger, already vaguely apprehended before, of the dissolution of the confederate States of the Republic, had assumed a very threatening aspect. Nathaniel Pope justly observed, that if Illinois, which, by reason of the great extent of its territory, its fertile soil, and the facilities it offered for the support of a crowded population, was destined to become a chief instrument either in the preservation or in the dissolution of the Union, — was given a large boundary on the Northern Lakes, the increase of the commerce on which was very confidently expected, then, united as Illinois already was by the bonds of interest to the States west of the Mississippi, it would also become connected by the closest ties of business and commerce with the Eastern States, and thus be bound to sustain the Federal Union forever; whilst, on the other hand, if no such extensive territory should be given to her, the interests of the State would compel her to enrol herself among the States of a new Southwestern confederacy, whenever the Union should be dissolved. Nathaniel Pope's views met the full approbation of Congress, and the bill, in virtue of which the Territory of Illinois was to be raised to the rank of an independent State, was passed as a law, in the month of April, 1818; it granted to Illinois the extension of her northern boundary to the parallel of 42° 30′ north latitude, and the privilege of applying the money arising from the sale of the public lands, to the encouragement of learning within the borders of the State.

Congress having passed this act, a Convention, of which Elias K. Kane, a lawyer, was the leading member, was convoked during the summer of 1818 in Illinois, to form its Constitution. By this Constitution the Governor and Lieutenant-Governor were required to have been citizens of the United States for 30 years previous to their election. The qualifications for the office of Lieutenant-Governor were afterwards in so far modified, that any citizen of the United States who had resided in the State for two years, could be elected to that office. Power was vested in the Governor to nominate, and in the Senate to confirm all officers, except those, whose appointments had already been provided for by the Constitution, including also the Judges of the Supreme and Inferior Courts, State Treasurer, and Public Printer. The Convention, however, in order to please a favorite of theirs, inserted a schedule in the Constitution, declaring "that an Auditor, Attorney-General, and other officers of the State, may be appointed by the General Assembly." This schedule was productive of innumerable intrigues and quarrels between the Governors and the Legislature, which ended in the Legislature, who had at first contented themselves with electing an Auditor and Attorney-General, depriving the Governor, as was the case with Gov. Duncan, of the power of appointing any public officers, save notaries public and public administrators.

Shadrach Bond, a farmer by occupation, and a man of plain common sense, without pretensions to a refined education, who had already been several times elected to the Territorial Legislature, and once as a delegate of the Territory to Congress, was elected the first Governor, and entered upon the discharge of his duties in October, 1818. At the same time, the Legislature assembled in Kaskaskia. In his first message to the Legislature, he earnestly recommends the construction of the canal, which was to run through Illinois, and to connect the Mississippi with Lake Michigan. He died in the year 1834.

The Legislature convened in Kaskaskia elected Joseph Philips, a lawyer by profession, who had been a captain in the United States Army, and afterwards Secretary of State to the Territory, as Chief Justice; and John Reynolds, Thomas C. Brown, and William P. Foster, a great rascal, who soon resigned his office, as Associate Justices of the Supreme Court. Ninian Edwards, and Jesse B. Thomas, who had been chosen President of the Convention, were elected first Senators. Daniel P. Cook was appointed first Attorney-General, Elias K. Kane, Secretary of State, John Thomas, State Treasurer, and Elijah C. Berry, Auditor of public accounts.

Having thus organized the State Government, the Legislature adjourned to meet again in winter, at which adjourned session they elaborated and adopted a *Code of Statute Law,* mostly collected and made up from the Statutes of Kentucky and Virginia. This first Code was altered and amended several times, till in 1827 a revised copy was published. It contained a most important act concerning negroes and mulattoes. The early Legislatures of Indiana and Illinois had not been hostile to the introduction of slavery, but had allowed emigrants to bring their slaves with them; these, if they voluntarily consented to serve their master for a term of years, were then held to perform their contract, but if they refused to consent, might be removed by their masters out of the territories in sixty days. Children of such slaves were registered, and bound to serve their masters, until they were 32 years old. This first Legislature of the State of Illinois, enacted laws as severe and stringent as could be found in a Slave State, where the number of negroes is equal to, or greater than that of the whites; though, in fact, the negroes constituted but a very small portion of the population of Illinois. These laws, which were passed by men from the Slave States, and were intended to preserve the purity of the white race, by discouraging free negroes from settling in Illinois (which they effectually did), have now become a dead letter, having never been carried into effect within the memory of the present generation.

The Legislature and Government removed to another place on the Kaskaskia River, which was afterwards called Vandalia, owing to the information imparted by some wag to the Commissioners who were surveying the ground for the new seat of government, that the name of Vandalia would not only sound very agreeably, but at the same time perpetuate the memory of the Vandals, once a powerful and warlike, but now extinct Indian nation; on the strength of which information the Commissioners, believing the same to be correct, and not troubling themselves much about matters of history, adopted the name proposed to them, which has ever since inflicted some slight stigma upon the character of the people inhabiting the place.

As already mentioned, upon the conclusion of the war of 1812, emigrants began to arrive from the Eastern States, and settle in Illinois; they brought money with them, which soon superseded the skins of the deer and of the raccoon as a circulating medium, and brought about a radical change in the material condition of the people, by creating new desires, and especially a mad desire for speculating in lots and lands. At that time the United States sold land at two dollars per acre, eighty dollars on the quarter section, to be paid cash down on the purchase, and the residue payable in five years. Everybody was eager to buy at that price, confidently expecting to be able to sell the lands, with the houses and other improvements thereon, at a large profit, to the immigrants who were sure to arrive. This proceeding was proudly styled "developing the infant resources of a new country." Several banks were incorporated, and speculation ran high, being favored by the circumstance, that money was then very abundant, and in consequence, every man's credit very good. Lots were purchased on credit, and towns laid out, all over the country; if money could not be had, notes were taken in place of, and considered as good as cash, until, two years afterwards, in the year 1820, the entire population had become indebted to a vast amount. The immigrants, whose arrival had been so anxiously looked for, did not come, the lots and houses could not be sold, and the price of the lands purchased of the United States remained unpaid. Bank notes, and paper of every kind and description, had long since driven the specie out of circulation, since it could be far more easily supplied to any amount wanted by notes, and nobody was willing to pay in cash, what he could pay for in paper. Commerce being then utterly insignificant, nothing was exported; and the people, being left to settle their debts among themselves, began to sue one another, though without any prospect of recovering their amounts, since, in consequence of the total absence of money, even the richest man would have found it impossible to satisfy his creditors.

To put an end to these crying evils, a State Bank, with several branches, was created by the Legislature of 1821; which bank, being wholly supported by the credit of the State, was to issue one, two, three, five, ten and twenty dollar notes, bearing two per cent. per annum, and payable by the State in ten years. It was the duty of the bank to advance, upon personal property, money to the amount of $100, and a larger amount upon real estate mortgages, to anybody, who should require such a loan. All taxes and public salaries could be paid in such bills, and if a creditor refused to take them, he had to wait three years longer before he could collect his debt. The people imagined, that simply because government had issued the notes, they would remain at par, and although this could evidently not be the case, were yet so infatuated with their project as actually to request the United States Government to receive them in payment for the public lands. Although there were not wanting men who, like John McLean, the Speaker of the House of Representatives, foresaw the danger and evils likely to arise from the creation of such a bank, by far the greater part of the people were in favor of it; the new bank was therefore started, and began to transact business in the summer of 1821. The new issues of bills by the bank, of course, only aggravated the evil, heretofore so grievously felt, of the absence of specie, so that the people were soon compelled to cut their bills in halves and quarters, in order to make small change in the trade. And further, most persons tried to borrow as much money from the bank as they could, considering whatever they got as clear gain, never pretending to pay it afterwards. And finally, the paper currency so rapidly depreciated, that three dollars in these bills were only considered worth one dollar in specie, so that the State not only did not increase its revenues, but lost full two-thirds of them, and expended three times the amount required to pay the expenses of the State Government.

In the year 1822, the term of office of the first governor, Shadrach Bond, expired. The question, which then agitated the whole Union, whether Missouri was to be admitted into the Union as a Slave State or not, had resulted in starting two parties in Illinois, one favorable, the other hostile to the introduction of slavery, each proposing a candidate of their own for governor. Although the slave party did everything in their power to secure the election of their candidate, and could boast of many of the most influential men in the State as belonging to their party, the people at large being decided, as they ever since have been, in favor of a Free State, Edward Coles, an anti-slavery man, was elected.

The Legislature, at their next session (1824–1825), ordered that the Supreme Court, consisting of four judges, should be held twice a year at the seat of government, and created five judges to hold all the Circuit Courts in the State, each of whom was maintained at a yearly salary of $600, while each of the Supreme Court Judges received $800 per annum. Considering this to be an extravagant outlay of the public money, the people were so clamorous for a reduction of it, that the Legislature of 1826–7 annulled and repealed the act passed by their predecessors, discharged the Circuit Judges, and ordered the Judges of the Supreme Court to hold the Circuit Courts instead of them.

The same Legislature of 1824–1825 appointed, by another law, the Judges of the Supreme Court to revise the laws, and to present the new revision to the Legislature at their next session.

Senator Duncan, afterwards governor, presented to the Legislature a bill for the support of schools by a public tax; and William S. Hamilton presented another bill, requiring a tax in proportion to property, to be used for the purpose of constructing and repairing the roads; both of which bills passed the Legislature and became laws. But although these laws conferred an incalculable benefit upon the public, by highly improving both the condition of the schools and the roads, the very name of a tax was so odious to the people, that rather than pay a tax of even the smallest possible amount, they preferred working as they formerly did, five days during the year on the roads, and would allow their children to grow up without any instruction at all. Consequently both laws were abolished, and the former system restored, by the Legislature, at their session of 1826–1827.

In the year 1826 the office of Governor became again vacant. Ninian Edwards and Adolphus Frederick Hubbard, were the principal candidates for it. Ninian Edwards, a lawyer by profession, and Governor of Illinois Territory for the nine years previous to its admission into the Union as a sovereign State, had made himself many enemies by urging strict inquiries to be made into the corruption of the State Bank, so that, had it not been for his talents and noble personal appearance, he would most probably not have been elected. In a contest for office with a man of the talents of Ninian Edwards, Adolphus Frederick Hubbard, if judged merely by his personal merits, had but little chance of coming off victor, although he himself claimed to be able to govern his fellow-citizens as well as anybody else; which, moreover, in his opinion, did not require a "very extraordinary smart man." Of this same man, tradition has preserved, among other curious sayings, a speech on a bill granting a bounty on wolf-scalps, which we cannot withhold from the knowledge of our readers; we communicate the same just as it has been preserved. This speech, which Mr. Hubbard delivered before the Legislature, is as follows: "Mr. Speaker, I rise before the question is put on this bill, to say a word for my constituents. Mr. Speaker, I have never seen a wolf. I cannot say, that I am very well acquainted with the nature and habits of wolves. Mr. Speaker, I have said, that I had never seen a wolf. But now I remember, that once on a time, as Judge Brown and I were riding across the Bonpas prairie, we looked over the prairie about three miles, and Judge Brown said, 'Hubbard, look, there goes a wolf.' And I looked, and I looked, and I looked, and I said, 'Judge, where?' And he said, 'There;' and I looked again, and this time, in the edge of a hazel thicket, about three miles across the prairie, I think I saw the wolf's tail. Mr. Speaker, if I did not see a wolf that time, I think I never saw one. But I have heard much, and read more, about this animal. I have studied his natural history. By-the-bye, history is divided into two parts; there is first the history of the fabulous, and secondly, of the non-fabulous, or unknown ages. Mr. Speaker, from all this sources of information, I learn that the wolf is a very noxious animal: that he goes prowling about, seeking something to devour; that he raises up in the dead and secret hours of the night, when all nature reposes in silent oblivion, and then commits the most terrible devastation upon the rising generation of hogs and sheep. Mr. Speaker, I have done, and return my thanks to the house for their kind attention to my remarks." The primitive naïveté, and wonderful ingenuity, as displayed in this remarkably choice speech, show better than anything else could have done, the state of civilization then existing in Illinois, especially when we bear in mind, that the speech was delivered by no less a personage than the Lieutenant-Governor himself.

6

Governor Edwards commenced his term in 1826. Remaining still as hostile to the old bank as ever, in his messages, he charged the officers of the bank with corruption and fraud. The friends and employees of the bank immediately took the alarm, and were certainly not remiss in retorting an equally disgracing charge upon the Governor, by accusing him of base motives in having instituted an inquiry into the management of the bank. Their influence was so great, that the accusations of the Governor were at once dismissed as wholly devoid of proof of mismanagement on the part of the officers of the bank.

Judges Lockwood and Smith, who had been appointed by the Legislature to revise the laws, presented to them, during their session of 1826–1827, a newly-revised code of laws, which was adopted, and of which the principal laws have ever since remained in full force, although the code was revised several times subsequently.

The Indians, who had remained quiet since the termination of the war of 1812, became again troublesome in the summer of the year 1827. The Winnebagoes, Sacs and Foxes, and other Indian tribes, had been at war for more than a hundred years, and although the United States had tried to settle the feuds existing between them, these tribes nevertheless remained at bitter enmity with each other, being always ready to inflict, one upon the other, a maximum of injury. In the summer of 1827, a war-party of the Winnebagoes surprised a party of 24 Chippeways, and killed 8 of them. Four of the murderers were arrested, and delivered by the commander of the United States troops at St. Peter's, to the Chippeways, by whom they were immediately shot. This was the first irritation of the Winnebagoes. They were further grieved at seeing the whites taking possession of their country; for many of them had penetrated into it as far as the Wisconsin river, in search of lead mines. Red Bird, a chief of the Winnebagoes, in order to avenge the execution of the four men of his own people, attacked the Chippeways, but was defeated, and being determined to satisfy his thirst for revenge by some means, surprised and killed several white men. Upon receiving intelligence of these Indian murders, the Illinoisians who were working the lead mines in the vicinity of Galena, assembled in Galena, formed a body of volunteers, and, reinforced by a company of regular United

States troops, marched into the country of the Winnebagoes. To save their nation from the miseries of war, Red Bird, and six others of the most influential men of his nation, voluntarily surrendered themselves prisoners of war; part of them were executed, part of them imprisoned, and destined, like Red Bird himself, ingloriously to pine away within the narrow confines of a jail, whereas formerly even the vast forests of their native country had proved too limited for their daring and adventurous disposition.

Resenting the defeat he had sustained at the hands of his enemies, when pressing an investigation of the affairs of the old State Bank, Gov. Ninian Edwards devised another scheme to embarrass and annoy them. Hitherto the United States had enjoyed undisturbed possession of various public lands within the State of Illinois. But now, for the first time, Gov. Edwards, in a message delivered to the Legislature, claimed the whole of the public lands of the United States lying within Illinois, as belonging to the latter; making good his claim by arguing, that inasmuch as Illinois had been admitted into the Union as an independent and sovereign State, all the lands within her own limits must necessarily belong to her. The measure was far from being unpopular, since the Legislature unanimously approved of it, although the people did not eventually enforce it. Gov. Edwards was mistaken, however, in imagining, that his enemies would oppose the bill, for on seeing the bill favorably received by the Legislature, and part of the public, being fearful to sacrifice their own popularity, they prudently abstained from throwing any obstacle into the way of the bill, and having learned from experience, that Gov. Edwards was too subtle an enemy for them to grapple with, never afterwards resisted any one of his measures. Gov. Ninian Edwards died in 1833.

Of the public lands owned by the United States Government within Illinois, Congress had already granted 300,000 acres to the State, for the construction of the Illinois and Michigan Canal, being prevailed upon to make this grant by Daniel P. Cook, the first Attorney General, and then Senator to Congress, to whose active and unceasing exertions in behalf of the measure, the credit of the donation must be mainly attributed. Although Daniel P. Cook had thus acquired some claim upon the gratitude of his fellow-citizens, which might have caused him to be re-elected Senator in the year 1826, having rendered himself unpopular, on the other hand, by giving, in the year 1824, when John Quincy Adams, Gen. Jackson, William H. Crawford, and Henry Clay, being candidates for the Presidency, and none of them receiving a majority, it became the business of the House of Representatives to elect one of them, the vote of Illinois to John Quincy Adams, instead of to Gen. Jackson, then the general favorite of the people, he was defeated, and Mr. Joseph Duncan elected in his stead.

At first Mr. Duncan manifested the greatest sympathy and attachment to Gen. Jackson, whose ardent admirer he was; but after Gen. Jackson had annulled the charter of the United States Bank, and denied the appropriation of money for the improvement of the Wabash river, Mr. Duncan began visibly to grow cold towards him, and, at last, became altogether estranged from him, ceasing to support his administration. Although Duncan was generally esteemed a man of honesty and upright principles, and could not be reproved for adhering to a particular opinion of his own in regard to a public matter, he was, nevertheless, severely blamed for his conduct by the friends and followers of Gen. Jackson, who were of opinion, that since they had put him in an office, by which he had grown rich, he should have remained faithful to the cause of Gen. Jackson, and that by abandoning the same, he had acted in a manner becoming only a man of a treacherous and ungrateful character.

Since the repeal of the law introduced by Mr. Duncan, then a Senator, for supporting the schools by a public tax, the Legislature sold the school lands, and applied the money arising from the sales to the payment of the school expenses. Still, the means provided by government for education and instruction, would have been very insufficient, had not Congress generously donated to the State one township of six miles square, and the thirty-sixth part of all the residue of the United States Government lands within the State, besides three per cent. of the net proceeds of the sales of the remainder. The Legislature ordered at first, that lands of the school section of each township should be leased out, on payment of a certain rent, but the lessees and newly-arrived immigrants, who had settled on these lands and were entitled to vote, wishing to establish themselves permanently, by their joint influence prevailed upon the Legislature, the majority of whom needed their votes for the coming election, to discontinue collecting the taxes, to sell the lands, to borrow the proceeds of the sale and the three per cent. school fund from the counties, and to use them for the public service; paying an annual interest, for the benefit of the schools, to the respective counties, on the moneys so borrowed. To meet the wants of the lessees, the lands were sold at low prices, in consequence of which the State incurred another debt, amounting to nearly half a million of dollars; and the schools lost part of their revenues, all which might have been easily avoided, if the State had adopted a system of taxation, in order to defray all the expenses of the public instruction and education.

Here it may not be improper to state the principal facts regarding the improvements, which, from the year 1820 to 1830, had been taking place in the manners and habits of the Illinoisians, their modes of thought, and the character of their institutions.

Until the year 1820, the early preachers of Illinois enjoyed undisputed sway over the minds of the people. In that year, several educated and well-instructed ministers arrived from the Eastern States, whence they had been sent as missionaries, by several religious societies. Relying, at first, mainly upon the support afforded to them, in case of need, by these societies, they founded Bible Societies and Sunday Schools, and started a number of religious prints or tracts in the State, patiently waiting until the people should gradually become accustomed to the new state of things. Their arrival caused no little uneasiness to the old preachers. Knowing, that from the moment their new rivals should have ingratiated themseles into the favor of the people, their own services would no longer be needed, they affected to deride the nice and fashionable dress of their young colleagues, whom they believed destitute of all religion, and whom they represented, not without some good show of reason, to be utterly unfit to travel through the wilderness, sleep in the open air, suffer hunger and thirst, in short, to suffer the same privations which they themselves had suffered, while engaged in providing for the spiritual wants of the people. They openly and boldly accused the new ministers of being less concerned about the salvation of the souls of their flocks, than about the size of their purses, and of selling their bibles and tracts with a view of securing to themselves a handsome profit thereby. The new ministers, paying no regard to their declamations, settled themselves wherever a more refined style of preaching had become acceptable, and being satisfied with the salary offered to them, commenced building churches and organizing congregations. Success attended their enterprises, and their less erudite brethren were soon exiled from the towns into districts, where the people still believed the chief merits of an orator to consist in the power of his lungs, and the theatrical display of his gesticulations. A large part of the people, however, continued to be prejudiced against the new ministers, whom they forbade to establish theological departments in any college or seminary, which had been built by them, and incorporated by an act of the Legislature.

During the years from 1820 to 1830, a great change took place in the appearance and modes of dressing of the people. The coon-skin cap, the hunting-shirt, and leather breeches, the moccasins, and the belt around the waist, to which the butcher-knife and tomahawk were appended, had entirely disappeared before the modern clothing apparel. The women had exchanged their cotton and woollen frocks, manufactured, and striped with blue dye, by themselves, for modern dresses of silk and calico; they had laid aside the cotton handkerchiefs, which formerly covered their heads, and adopted bonnets instead; they would not, as formerly, walk barefooted to church, but would often be seen riding on fine horses to the house of worship. They would go to church flattering themselves with a secret hope, that they would make the best figure in the whole assembly, and outshine their neighbors by the brilliancy of their dress. To be able to gratify their ambition for fine dresses, they were obliged to become industrious and enterprising in business. The desire for fine dress soon also superinduced a similar desire for polite society and knowledge, so that the old folks, who would have much preferred remaining undisturbed in their sluggish tranquillity and repose, thoroughly taken by surprise, everywhere uttered loud complaints, that the prodigalities, luxuries and innovations of the young, would speedily cause the ruin of the country.

At the time, that such a rapid improvement was taking place in the manners and customs of the people, commerce comparatively made but little progress. Of steamboats, which had been introduced in the western country about the year 1816, the Illinoisians possessed but two small ones in 1830, which were running up the Illinois river as far as Peoria. A majority of the merchants of the country were retailers of dry-goods and groceries, who, with but a small amount of money and goods in their hands, sold only for cash, or notes payable on sight in cash, which they remitted to their Eastern creditors, so that they would have soon been drained of their last specie, had not the money of the newly-arrived immigrants supplied them again with the sinews of trade. Nothing was exported, save a few skins, hides, furs, with tallow and beeswax. The merchants of Illinois used to go to St. Louis to purchase Eastern exchange, but upon the suppression of the United States Bank in that city, these facilities of commerce no longer existed, and the traders of Illinois, when the high rates of premium had rendered it impossible for them to remit either money or bills of exchange to their Eastern creditors, were compelled to purchase the productions of the country, and to remit them to their creditors in place of cash. Most of the exports were shipped to New Orleans, at that time a place of inconsiderable importance. Since there were no merchants or express companies to forward the goods to market, the Illinoisian farmer would build his own boats, load them with his goods, and, with the assistance of a few men, sail down the river to New Orleans. After a long and troublesome voyage, he would arrive in New Orleans, only to fall an easy victim to the runners and sharpers, who abounded in that city, and to go home penniless. On his return home he would find his farm neglected, and yet, notwithstanding this wholesome lesson, undertake, perhaps, another expedition to New Orleans at the earliest possible period. Even after, in consequence of the great improvements in steamboat navigation, excellent opportunities had been afforded to the people, not only to expand their commerce, but also their ideas about it, they still persevered in pursuing a narrow-minded, selfish commercial policy. They would, for instance, raise no surplus of produce, except when prices were high, and even then, perhaps, demand a higher price for their produce, than they could have sold it for in the market. They would never be in a hurry to sell, when prices were below their expectations, but rather wait, even for the space of a whole year, until they should be able to sell at the prices they had fixed upon; or they would even cease producing altogether, when prices continued low. The necessary consequence of such a proceeding was, that by allowing their produce to waste away and rot, they would lose more money than they could have gained, even if they had sold it at the highest market price, and would incur still another loss by being obliged to borrow money at high rates of interest, in order to pay for many necessities of life, or to carry on their enterprises, since, having sold nothing, they were often entirely destitute of money. However evident the folly of their course might be to others, they could not be prevailed upon to abandon it, having, it appears, an unshaken confidence in the infallibility of their own judgment.

In regard to the state of politics, of the government, and the administration of justice, the following appears worthy of notice. The majority of the Illinoisians were new immigrants, who had come with the avowed purpose of bettering their own condition. Bearing this fact in our mind, we shall not be surprised to hear, that they evinced an utter indifference for all matters connected with government, confiding these entirely to the hands of cunning politicians, in whose rule they seemed to acquiesce, provided the latter would leave them undisturbed, and in possession of the largest personal freedom. The original pioneers, though now but a small minority of the people, easily to be distinguished by their linsey shirts, leather breeches, moccasins, and the large butcher-knives in their belts, which knives were an indispensable part of their dress, were apt to take a more active interest in politics, as appears from the predominating influence they exercised upon the elections, at which, by a mere parade of superior physical force and reckless spirit, they would frequently decide the contest in favor of the candidate identified with their own party and interests. Politicians were very careful not to offend this class of men, known as the Butcher-Knife Boys; but, for the rest, taking advantage of the want of regard paid to politics by the people at large, secured to themselves nearly all the offices and emoluments of the government; created others, the salaries of which they diligently pocketed; passed laws for their own benefit, and whilst hypocritically pretending to watch over the welfare of the people, in whose name they governed, were always ready to deceive them in the most shameful and barefaced manner. Nor were honest politicians and office-holders safe from their intrigues, for they knew how to gain the confidence of such honorable folks, by the most cunning devices and most artful manœuvres, using them for their own purposes without their being aware of it. Thus it was, that Samuel Crozier, a man of most irreproachable honor, and a member of the Senate, whom the politicians had used, with great success, as an instrument for the accomplishment of their own ends, without the slightest suspicion on his part, after having been in the Senate for two sessions, was heard to say, at the close of the second, that he "really did believe, that some intrigue had been going on." Such politicians, as by their polished and winning manners had gained the favors of credulous people, whom they afterwards imposed upon, in a slang phrase, were said to have "greased and swallowed their victims."

The elections in Illinois during that time were at first by ballot, but as nobody was willing to make known, whom he had voted for at the elections, since, to vote against a candidate was then considered as a personal insult, and as balloting, by opening a vast field for intrigue, fraud, and corruption, brought the system of voting thus into disgrace, the Legislature, at their session in the year 1828–9, made it unlawful to elect by ballot.

The judiciary system of those times appears to have been a very simple one. People then did not require judges to be possessed of profound learning and erudition, but would be satisfied with one reputed a man of sagacity and good common sense. The state of civilization then enjoyed by the country, and the small amount of business then transacted by the judges, not having yet rendered necessary the erection of large and splendid halls of justice, the judges would hold their courts in log-houses, or in the bar-rooms of inns, fitted up with temporary seats for the judges, lawyers, and jurors. It is related, that on the opening of the first Circuit Court held by Judge John Reynolds, the sheriff went into the court-yard and said to the people: "Boys, come in; our John is going to hold Court." Judges seem to have been considered as very amiable, harmless men. In fact, the judges, whenever they could do so, would leave the decision of a case to the juries, lest they might give offence to any of the parties concerned, or expose their incompetence. They would tell the jury: "If the jury believe from the evidence, that such a matter is proved, then the law is so and so." One of these judges used to say to the lawyers asking him for instructions: "Why, gentlemen, the jury understand the case; they want no instructions; no doubt they will do justice between the parties." The same judge once had to pronounce sentence of death upon a man by the name of Green. He said to him: "Mr. Green, the jury in their verdict say you are guilty of murder, and the law says you are to be hung. Now, I want you and all your friends down on Indian Creek to know that it is not I, who condemns you, but it is the jury and the law." He then asked him, what time he would like to be hung. The prisoner replied, he was ready to die at any time the Court would appoint. The judge then told the prisoner, that the Court would give him four weeks' time to prepare himself for death. The Attorney General of the State, who prosecuted the case, interposed here, and required the Court to state to the prisoner, the particular reasons of the judgment pronounced upon him, and solemnly to exhort him to repent and prepare for death. To this the Judge replied: "O, Mr. Green understands the whole matter as well as if I had preached to him a month. He knows he's got to be hung this day four weeks. You understand that, Mr. Green, don't you?" "Yes," said the prisoner, whereupon he was taken back to prison to await the day on which he was to be hung.

Except during the period of the universal bankruptcy, the lawsuits were mostly small cases, actions for trespass, slander, indictments for assault and battery, riots, and unlicensed rum-selling; the latter occurring most frequently. Jurors were disposed to forgive minor offences, and would even discharge a murderer, when it could be shown, that an altercation and an ungovernable fury had driven him to murder; but would always convict the murderer, who had assassinated his victim in cold blood, and in a cowardly, clandestine manner. The character of the Illinoisians was in many respects violent and impetuous, which will account for the willingness on the part of jurors to dismiss indictments for assault and batteries, or even murder. This spirit of the Illinoisians is best shown in the following instance. In the year 1827, there was a very excited election for State Treasurer, in which the former occupant of the office was defeated. After the election the Legislature adjourned, but before they had left the hall, the defeated candidate walked in and gave a valiant thrashing to four of the strongest of his opponents, who had voted against him. Before him the members dispersed and scattered like sheep before the intruding wolf. He not only escaped unpunished for this offence, but during the same session was appointed Clerk of the Circuit Court, and Recorder of a county; which will go far to show the respect in which physical force was at that day held by the Illinoisians.

Whilst displays of physical force, bribes, and intrigues of all kinds, were thought by aspiring politicians to be very serviceable instruments for securing their election, the power of liquor was not overlooked by them. A candidate would frequently hire the taverns and liquor-stores for several weeks previous to the election, and furnish the people with liquor at his own expense. The people, of course, quite unwilling to miss so precious an opportunity of gratifying their taste for liquor, were sure to visit these taverns regularly every Saturday.

The candidates would at first harangue the people from stumps of trees, whence the name of stump speeches; and after the addresses of the candidates had been delivered, all present would freely partake of liquor, until, a majority of them having become drunk, they would march about, raising loud shouts for their candidates, and making preparations to fight them into office, if necessary. Having satisfied their desire for free fights and pugilistic encounters, they would, at a late hour in the night, mount their ponies and gallop home.

In the year 1830, the office of Governor becoming again vacant, William Kinney, who belonged to the "whole hogs," a party devoted body and soul to Gen. Jackson, and Judge Reynolds, were the candidates for it; the former, who electioneered for himself, with the Bible in one hand, and a bottle of whiskey in the other, notwithstanding he was thus armed with "the sword of the Lord and of the Spirit," was defeated; and the latter, a man of fine talents, elected.

At the same time a new Legislature was elected, a majority of whom were Jackson men. Upon this Legislature devolved the odious duty, the fulfilling of which had been so long prorogued and delayed by their predecessors, of making some provision for the redemption of the old "State Bank" notes, then nearly due. Whilst some members were fearful to be branded with infamy for neglecting, and others afraid of losing a hardly-acquired popularity, by fulfilling their duty, a majority of the Legislature, in both houses, convinced of the necessity of saving the honor of the State, authorized the famous Wiggins loan of $100,000, which being taken, the notes of the bank were redeemed, and their popularity ruined, at the same time. 'Twas altogether in vain for them to apologize for their conduct; the people, paying no regard to their representations, ducked every one of these unfortunate politicians in the tempest-ridden sea of popular indignation, and down they went, never to rise again.

About this time serious Indian disturbances broke out, occasioning the celebrated Black Hawk war, which, as it marks quite an important epoch in the history of Illinois, will be described at length in the following chapter.

CHAPTER IV.

In the year 1804, a treaty was concluded between the United States and the chiefs of the Sac and Fox nations, in virtue of which the Americans acquired, together with other territory, all the lands of these Indians on Rock river. One old chief of the Sacs, however, called "Black Hawk," who had fought with great bravery in the service of Great Britain during the war of 1812, had always taken exception to this treaty, and pronouncing it to be void, established himself, with a chosen band of warriors, upon the disputed territory, ordering the white settlers to leave the country at once. The settlers complaining, Gov. Reynolds despatched Gen. Gaines, with a company of regulars and 1500 volunteers, to the scene of action; taking the Indians by surprise, these troops burnt their villages, and forced them to conclude a treaty, by which they ceded all right and title to the lands east of the Mississippi, and agreed to remain on the western side of the river. Necessity had compelled the proud spirit of Black Hawk into submission, which made him more than ever determined to be avenged upon his enemies at the earliest possible moment. Having rallied around him the warlike braves of the Sac and Fox nations, he crossed the Mississippi river, in the spring of 1832, and directed his march into the countries of the Winnebagoes and Pottawatomies, intending to make them his allies. Upon hearing of the invasion, Gov. Reynolds hastily collected a body of 1800 volunteers, divided into four regiments, and a spy battalion, of which Col. Dewitt commanded the 1st, Col. Fry the 2d, Col. Thomas the 3d, Col. Thompson the 4th regiment, and Col. James D. Henry the spy battalion, while the command of the whole brigade was entrusted to Brig. Gen. Samuel Whiteside, of the State militia.

The army marched to the Mississippi, and having reduced to ashes the Indian village known as "Prophet's Town," proceeded for several miles up the river to Dixon, to join the regular forces under Gen.

Atkinson, and to await the arrival of provisions. They found at Dixon two companies of volunteers, amounting to 275 men, who, sighing for glory, were despatched by Gen. Whiteside to reconnoitre the enemy. They advanced, under the command of Major Stillman, to a river afterwards called "Stillman's run," and whilst encamping there, espied a party of mounted Indians at the distance of a mile. Several of Stillman's party mounted their horses, and charged the Indians, killing three of them; but, attacked by the main body of the Indians under Black Hawk, they were routed in their turn, and by their precipitate flight spread such a panic through the camp, that the whole company ran off to Dixon as fast as their legs could carry them. On their arrival thither, eleven were missed, who had been killed by the Indians. At a council of war, immediately convoked by Gen. Whiteside, it was agreed to march back the next day to the battle-ground. Upon reaching the battle-field, Gen. Whiteside could discover no Indians; being short of provisions, he buried the dead, put up a rude board to their memory, and returned to Dixon, where Gen. Atkinson joined him with the regular forces. The whole brigade was now 2400 strong, so that the war would have been speedily brought to a close, had not a majority of the militia, whose term of service had expired, left the army, to attend to their affairs at home.

The Indians in the meantime committing depredations everywhere, and massacring the inhabitants of some small frontier settlements, the Governor called out several new regiments of militia, one of which was sent in advance, to spy out the country between Galena and Rock river. This regiment, surprised by a party of 70 Indians, was on the point of being thrown into disorder, when Gen. Whiteside, then serving as a private in the regiment, shouted out that he would shoot the first man, who should turn his back to the enemy. Order being at once restored, the battle began; at its very outset Gen. Whiteside shot the leader of the Indians, who thereupon commenced a hasty retreat.

Up to the 15th of June, 1832, nearly 4000 volunteers had been organized; this force was fully sufficient, not only to prosecute the war, but, at the same time, keep in check various Indian tribes who seemed to evince much friendship to the cause of Black Hawk.

About this time Black Hawk, with a band of 150 warriors, attacked the Apple River Fort, situated 12 miles from Galena, and defended by 25 men. This fort, a mere palisade of logs, in the form of a square, the corners of which were flanked by block-houses, was erected to afford protection to the miners living in its vicinity, in case of an Indian war. For fifteen consecutive hours the garrison had to sustain the assaults of the savage enemy, but knowing very well, that no quarter would be given them, they fought with such fury and desperation, that the Indians, after losing a great many of their best warriors, were compelled to retreat. Galena itself had been threatened with an assault, but on learning the formidable state of its defences, the Indians did not dare to attack it.

Another party of 11 Indians murdered two men near Fort Hamilton; they were afterwards overtaken by a company of 20 men, under Gen. Dodge, and every man of them killed.

About this time an engagement took place between Capt. Stephenson, of Galena, and a party of Indians, who had taken up their position in a dense thicket of the prairie. A desperate charge was made upon the Indians by the whites, and a number of volleys fired by both parties, those of the whites taking no effect, whilst those which the ambushed Indians delivered, killed several of the whites, causing Capt. Stephenson, himself severely wounded, to order a retreat.

Whilst the Indians were scattering their war-parties over the northern part of Illinois, cutting off the communication between the isolated frontier towns, the regular soldiers and newly-organized volunteer regiments, under the command of Gen. Atkinson, assembled on the banks of the Illinois, in the latter part of June. Sent in advance to explore the country, Major Dement fortified a camp at Kellogg's Grove, in the midst of the Indian country; having sallied out with a small party to reconnoitre the movements of a large body of Indians, known to be somewhere in the vicinity of his camp, he suddenly found himself confronted by some 300 Indians, whose endeavors to surround him made it advisable for him to retire to his camp. This the Indians attempted to storm, but after suffering severe losses in consequence of their exposure to the deadly fire of the men within, retreated, carrying their dead with them. Upon hearing of this engagement, Gen. Atkinson sent a detachment to intercept the flying Indians, whilst he himself, with the main body of his army, moved into the territory of the Winnebagoes, to meet the Indian forces under Black Hawk, then said to have occupied a strongly fortified position near the four lakes, with a determination to decide the fate of war by a general battle. The troops, all of whom were totally unacquainted with the nature of the country they were to enter, and unable to gather information with regard to it, since it was not deemed advisable to trust to the statements of the Winnebagoes, known to be much disposed to join Black Hawk, proceeded slowly and very cautiously through the country: and having passed through Turtle village, marched up along the Rock river to Burnt village, a considerable town of the Winnebagoes. On their arrival thither, news was brought of the discovery of the main trail of the Indians. Preparations were made to examine and follow it the next day. At an early hour of the morning, two soldiers, who had gone to the river, flowing at the distance of 150 yards from the camp, were shot by two Indians from the opposite bank, on being notified of which, Gen. Atkinson questioned some of the Winnebagoes, who followed the camp: being informed by them, that the opposite bank was a large island, on which Black Hawk's entire war-party was fortified, he resolved first to send a detachment on the main trail, and afterwards to cross over to the island, where Black Hawk was reported to have entrenched himself. Part of the volunteers went, accordingly, in search of the trail, and after a most toilsome and arduous march over the so-called "trembling lands," which are large tracts of turf, about a foot in thickness, resting upon water and beds of quicksand, having exerted themselves in vain to discover the trail, were obliged to return to Burnt village. Neither had the companies, who had crossed over to the island, and overrun it in every direction, been able to discover any vestige of Indians, save of the two, who had shot the two soldiers.

Dissatisfaction soon became general among the volunteers, few of whom, before enlisting, had duly reflected upon the fatigue, drudgery, and great hardships of an Indian war, in an entirely unknown country; and many of them either succumbed to the privations imposed upon them, or left the service altogether, while of the regular soldiery not a single man had been lost. Those of the volunteers, who remained, had been so wasteful with their provisions, that, only four days' rations remaining in the hands of the commissioner, Gen. Atkinson found it necessary to disperse the troops to obtain provisions, sending Gens. Henry, Dodge, and Alexander, to Fort Winnebago, between the Fox and Wisconsin rivers, whilst he himself, with the regular soldiers, went to Lake Kushkonong to erect a fort, where he could await the return of the volunteers with supplies.

The volunteer generals reached Fort Winnebago within three days, and spent two more in obtaining provisions. Having been informed, on the second day, by the Winnebago chiefs, that Black Hawk, with his war-party, was encamped on Rock river, at the Manitou village, 35 miles north of Gen. Atkinson, they resolved at once to advance upon the enemy; but in the execution of their design, they met with opposition on the part of their officers and men. The officers of Gen. Henry handed to him a written protest, but he, who never wanted presence of mind, even in the most critical situations, ordering the officers to be arrested and escorted to Gen. Atkinson, they at once resumed their duty, and were ever afterwards scrupulous in performing it. Whilst Gen. Alexander, whose men were on the point of mutiny, fell back to Gen. Atkinson, Gen. Henry, who had the chief command of the residue of the troops, marched, on the 15th of July, with two Winnebago guides, in pursuit of the Indians, reaching Rock river after a three days' journey; where three Winnebagoes informed him, that Black Hawk was encamped further up the river. Hoping to be able to overtake the enemy, he despatched two messengers, with an Indian guide, to Gen. Atkinson, to notify him of his intended expedition. After travelling for eight miles, these messengers discovered the fresh trail of the main body of the Indians, and immediately returned. Their Indian guide, who had got the start of them, arrived in the camp a little before them, and was just in the act of communicating the discovery to his treacherous countrymen, who, thunderstruck, attempted to leave, when all of them were arrested and marched off to Gen. Henry, whom, to avoid instant death, they minutely advised of Black Hawk's doings.

On the next morning, July 19th, the troops were ordered to commence their march, leaving their impediments and baggage in the rear. After having made 50 miles, they were overtaken by a terrible thunderstorm, which lasted all night, rendering it impossible for the men to cook a warm supper, or to sleep on dry ground. Nothing cooled, however, in their courage and zeal, they marched again 50 miles the next day, encamping this time near the place where the Indians had encamped the night before. Hurrying along as fast as they could, the infantry keeping up an equal pace with the mounted force, the troops, on the morning of the 21st of July, crossed a river connecting two of the four lakes, by which the Indians had been endeavoring to escape. Finding, on their way, the ground strewn with kettles and articles of baggage, which the hurry of their retreat had obliged the Indians to throw away, the troops, inspired with new ardor, advanced so rapidly, that at noon of the same day they fell in with the rearguard of the Indians, which rallied several times, exchanging shots with the vanguard of the troops, in order to afford the main body of the Indians time enough to escape. The troops, who closely pursued them, were saluted with a sudden fire of musketry, by a body of Indians, who had concealed themselves in the high grass of the prairie. A line of battle being immediately formed, and the centre, which was led on by Gen. Henry himself, having just come up, a most energetic charge was made upon the Indians, who, unable to resist, retreated obliquely, in order to outflank the volunteers on the right. But the latter, reinforced by a detachment sent to their assistance, charged the Indians in their ambush, and expelling them from their thickets at the point of the bayonet, dispersed them along the Wisconsin river. Night having set in, the battle ended, having cost the Indians 68 of their bravest men, whilst the entire loss of the Illinoisians amounted to but 1 killed and 8 wounded.

On the day after the battle, the army retired to the Blue Mounds to obtain a fresh supply of provisions. A few friendly Winnebagoes volunteered their services as guides, which being accepted, the wounded men were placed on litters, and the army, after a march of two days, reached the Blue Mounds, where they were joined by the regular forces, under Gen. Atkinson. Indignant, that the militia should earn the entire glory of the war, Gen. Atkinson, when, provisions having been procured, the pursuit of the Indians was resumed by him, placed the regular soldiers in front, and the division of Gen. Henry in the rear. Pursuit being recommenced, the troops toiled through dense forests and deep muddy ground, finding the road strewn with the corpses of Indians, who, from neglect of the wounds they had received in the Wisconsin river battle, had died on their retreat. The Indians reached the Mississippi some time before Gen. Atkinson's forces came up, but whilst making the necessary arrangements for crossing, happened to fall in with the armed steamboat "Warrior," the commander of which, Capt. Throckmorton, having summoned them in vain to come on board his steamer, greeted them with canister shot, and a brisk fire of musketry, causing the Indians severe losses, and delaying their crossing, so that Gen. Atkinson reached them, before they were able to pass over. Encamped at that time below the Red Axe river, on the Mississippi, the Indians despatched 20 of their men to stop the advance of Gen. Atkinson, and to enable them to gain time for crossing the river. These men concealed themselves in the high grass, opening a sudden fire upon the vanguard of the regular soldiers. Believing that he had the main body of the Indians before him, Gen. Atkinson made a vigorous charge with the regulars upon the concealed Indians, who, giving way at once, were closely pursued by him. But Gen. Henry, on coming up and discovering that the main trail of the enemy was running in a different direction from the one in which Gen. Atkinson pursued them, concluded that Gen. Atkinson had been misled by the wily savages, and resolved to follow up the main trail of the Indians himself. Having left his horses behind him, and formed an advance-guard of eight men to discover the whereabouts of the enemy, he marched forward upon their trail. When these eight men had come within sight of the river, they were suddenly fired upon by some 50 Indians, and five of them killed, the remaining three maintaining their ground, until the main force, under Gen. Henry, had come up, when, in an instant, a line of battle was formed, and the Indians, charged with the bayonet, were obliged to fall back upon their main force, about equal in numbers to Gen. Henry's troops. The battle now became general; the Indians, although taken by surprise, fought with desperate valor, but were furiously assailed by the volunteers with their bayonets, which prevailed in the bloody struggle, cutting many of the Indians to pieces, and driving the rest into the river. Those of the Indians, who escaped being drowned, took refuge on a small island in the river.

On hearing the frequent discharge of musketry, indicating a general engagement, Gen. Atkinson abandoned the pursuit of the twenty

Indians, led by Black Hawk himself, and hurried up as fast as he could to the scene of action, where he arrived too late to take part in the battle. He immediately forded the river with his troops, the water reaching up to their necks, and though not without losing several of his soldiers, who, during the passage of the river, were shot by the Indians from their ambush, effected a landing on the island, where the Indians had secreted themselves. After having once gained a foothold upon the island, the soldiers rushed upon the Indians, killing several of them, taking others prisoners, and chasing the rest into the river, where they were either drowned or shot before reaching the opposite shore. Thus ended the battle, in which the Indian loss amounted to 300 shot, bayoneted, and drowned, besides 50 prisoners, whilst of the soldiers but 17 were killed and 12 wounded.

Black Hawk, with his twenty men, after Gen. Atkinson had ceased to pursue him, retreated up the Wisconsin river. Desirous of securing for themselves the friendship of the whites, whose power they had begun to fear, the Winnebagoes went in pursuit of Black Hawk and his party, and captured and delivered them to Gen. Street, the United States Indian agent. Among the prisoners were also the son of Black Hawk, and the prophet of the tribe, who had been chiefly instrumental in bringing about the war.

Gen. Atkinson, with the soldiers and volunteers, went back to Dixon, where the latter were discharged. Black Hawk, his son, and the prophet, were taken to Jefferson Barracks, where a treaty was concluded, by which the Indians ceded to the United States their lands on the Mississippi, between the Desmoines and Turkey rivers. They were afterwards taken to Washington (D. C.), where Black Hawk is said to have addressed the President as follows: "I am a man, and you are another. We did not expect to conquer the white people. I took up the hatchet to revenge injuries, which could no longer be borne. Had I borne them longer, my people would have said, 'Black Hawk is a squaw; he is too old to be a chief. He is no Sac.' This caused me to raise the war-whoop. I say no more of it. All is known to you. Keokuk once was here; you took him by the hand, and when he wanted to return, you sent him back to his nation. Black Hawk expects, that like Keokuk, he will be permitted to return." The President assured them, that they should return, after which they were delivered to Col. Eustiss, commander of Fort Monroe, with whom Black Hawk became intimately acquainted. On leaving him, Black Hawk presented him with a hunting dress and some feathers of the white eagle, and said: "The memory of your friendship will remain, until the Great Spirit says, that it is time for Black Hawk to sing his death song. Accept these, my brother; I have given one suit like them to the White Beaver (Gen. Atkinson). Accept them from Black Hawk, and when he is far away, they will serve to remind you of him. May the Great Spirit bless you and your children. Farewell."

By order of the President, these Indian prisoners were set free on the 4th day of June, 1833. They made the tour of the Northern States, attracting everywhere great attention; and returned, by way of the Northern lakes, to their people west of the Mississippi. Black Hawk died on the 3d of October, 1840, at the age of 80 years, and was buried on the banks of the Mississippi river, where he had spent his life, and which had been so dear to him.

After the termination of the Indian war, nothing worthy of notice occurred until the month of August, 1834, when Senator Duncan was elected Governor of the State. A new Legislature was also elected, which met at Vandalia in December, 1834. As, in consequence of Gen. Jackson's veto, the United States Bank was then on the eve of being dissolved, the Secretary of the Federal Government, presuming, that a deficiency of currency would be produced by its dissolution, induced the State Banks to discount liberally, in order to avoid such deficiency, thus in a manner creating an impression among the "Jackson men," as if Gen. Jackson's administration was favorable to the establishment of State Banks, wherever the same did not exist. Besides these politicians, there were many others in Illinois, who, from motives of personal interest, would have delighted in seeing the charter of the bank at Shawneetown revived, and a new State Bank created, and were clamorous for their re-establishment. Many of the members of the Legislature, who at first opposed the banks, were, it is probable, won over by bribes, so that, when the "State Bank charter" was brought before the House of Representatives, it was approved and passed, and the banks chartered; the State Bank with a capital of over a million, and the bank at Shawneetown with a capital of three hundred thousand dollars, although the banks were certainly superfluous, if not even dangerous; since, at that time, the commerce of Illinois was still very undeveloped, and, there being no surplus of capital in the State, the capital for banking had to come from, and the stockholders to reside, abroad; in consequence whereof, the management of the affairs of the bank was entrusted to agents, but too apt to provide for their own interests far better than for those of their employers, or of the people. At a subsequent session of the Legislature, the capital of the State Bank was increased two millions of dollars, and the capital of the Illinois Bank, at Shawneetown, one million four hundred thousand dollars. The subscriptions to the stock of the State Bank surpassed by far the amount fixed by its charter, owing, partly, to the extensive arrangements made to induce capitalists of the Eastern States to invest their money in this stock. After the stock had been all taken, the State Bank began to transact business, in 1835, under the chief control of Thomas Mather and Godfrey Gilman & Co., merchants, of Alton. The city of St. Louis having monopolized almost the entire trade of Illinois, inasmuch as nearly the whole of the surplus produce of the State was exported to St. Louis for a market, and the merchants of the State purchased their assortments and their bills of exchange on the Eastern cities in St. Louis, a want was felt by many Illinoisians, of a similar emporium of commerce in their own State, to supply which, and attach, at the same time, Godfrey Gilman & Co. entirely to their own interests, the bank undertook to furnish them, and other Alton merchants, with large sums, to carry on enterprises intended to divert the channels of trade from St. Louis to Alton. The Alton merchants commenced operations by making extensive purchases of lead-mines and smelting establishments in the vicinity of Galena, with a view of monopolizing the lead trade altogether. Whilst they succeeded in raising the price of lead to some sixty per cent. at Galena, being unable to regulate, in a like manner, its price in the Eastern States, to which their lead was destined to be shipped, the Alton merchants were at last compelled to sell at an immense sacrifice, which proved equally ruinous to them and the bank, although the fact of the insolvency of the latter was unknown to the people.

At this session of the Legislature, the first step was taken to carry the project of the Illinois and Michigan Canal into execution. To aid in its construction, Congress, in the year 1826, had donated about 300,000 acres, on the route of the proposed canal, of which a survey had already been made. Nothing was done, however, to carry the work into effect, until this session, when George Forquer, a member of the Senate, in a report remarkable for its sagacious reasoning, as well as the masterly eloquence of its language, proposed the negotiation of a loan of half a million of dollars, to begin the work with. The proposed loan was negotiated on the credit of the State, by Gov. Duncan, in 1836, and the construction of the canal commenced in the same year. During that very year, the mania for speculation in land and town lots, after having rested for several years, broke out anew, and spread all over Illinois. The dazzling example set by the people of Chicago, who, by fostering and advocating this spirit of speculation, had, within less than two years, built up and converted a village of a few houses into an elegant, industrious city of several thousand inhabitants, was well calculated to excite the surprise and amazement of the people, and to revive their old bias for speculation in real estate. Nor could the people of the Eastern States be prevailed upon to stay at home, after it had become known to them, in what a rapid manner fortunes were amassed in Chicago; but looking upon Illinois as a modern El Dorado, large numbers of them immigrated into the State, bringing their money and property with them. The example of Chicago was imitated throughout the State, lots and towns being laid out in every direction. And since the great majority of the speculators had bought far more, than they could hope either to sell or to pay for, it occurring to their minds, that by facilitating immigration, and by attracting wealth and industry from abroad, they would soon transmute the villages into populous cities, and be enabled to sell their lots, either at once, or after a short time, they accordingly commenced agitating, with great ardor, the subject of internal improvements in the State, delivering speeches and holding public meetings, and arguing their cause with such success, that before the next winter a majority of the counties had appointed delegates, who assembled at the same time with the Legislature of 1836–1837, in order to discuss and deliberate thoroughly upon the subject of internal improvements.

and to take good care, that the system to be carried into effect "should be commensurate with the wants of the people." Pressed on all sides, the Legislature passed a law authorizing the construction of about 1300 miles of railroad, commanding, that improvements be made in the navigation of several rivers, and a large sum be paid as indemnification to the counties in which no improvements were to be made. Eight millions, to be raised by a loan, were voted for the execution of the system. A further loan of four millions was negotiated for the completion of the canal from Chicago to Peru, and boards of commissioners, superintending the construction of the works, having been established, to make the folly complete, the works were ordered to be commenced simultaneously on all the roads, at each end. Private interests, intrigues, and corruption, had been actively at work to ensure the adoption of this system. Thus it was, that the friends of the canal were made to give their consent to other improvements, in order to secure the support of their own; and thus politicians would endeavor to obtain the consent of every county in the State, by promises of roads and improvements, allowing the counties which were to be without such, the sum of $200,000 as indemnification: and thus politicians, who were anxious to have the seat of government removed to Springfield from Vandalia, would support or oppose any scheme of improvement, if they could or could not obtain votes in favor of the removal of the seat of government to Springfield in return for it.

In the spring of 1837, the banks throughout the United States suspended specie payments, the banks of Illinois not excepted. Now, since the charters of the Illinois banks, which had been made the fiscal agents for the railroad and canal, and had a large sum of public money on deposit, expressly declared, that the banks, upon refusing specie payments for sixty consecutive days, should be considered as dissolved, it being feared, that such dissolution, whenever it should take place, would necessitate the ruin of the whole improvement system, measures were proposed, and adopted, to have this unavoidable suspension of specie payments duly legalized. The people then firmly believing, that the internal improvement system, which wasted the best energy of the State, was indispensable to her welfare, no modification or alteration was made in it, but, on the contrary, loans were effected, both in Europe and America, large quantities of railroad iron were bought up at an extravagant price, and the work, upon all the improvements, carried on with unabated energy.

In August, 1838, another election came on for Governor; Cyrus Edwards, the whig candidate, openly declaring himself in favor of the improvement system, whilst Thomas Carlin, who had been nominated as the democratic candidate for Governor, by a State convention, upon the principles of the convention system, which, introduced by the immigrants from the Eastern States, to consolidate the strength of party, was then rapidly superseding the hitherto customary election of independent candidates, who had announced themselves as such, cautiously refrained from expressing his opinion, either in favor of, or against the improvement system. Thomas Carlin was elected Governor, and a new Legislature with him, which not only refused to abolish the system, but even authorized new loans for additional works, projected in a style of magnificence far beyond the means of the infant State. Thus, in expectation, that the value of the lands granted by the United States for the construction of the canal, would prove illimitable, a very large and deep canal, to be fed by the waters of Lake Michigan, was proposed to be built, and portions of it were even completed. Thus canal-basins, and other works, for the improvement of navigation on the Illinois river, the execution and completion of which would have absorbed no less than ten millions of dollars, were nevertheless readily provided for. Soon, no more loans could be obtained at par, and the State bonds, notwithstanding the law rigidly enforced their payment in cash at par, were sold on credit, or at a large discount, or deposited for sale with bankers of Europe and America. The firm of Wright & Co., of London, with whom a large amount of them had been left, sold about half a million of dollars worth, and then failed, returning the residue of the bonds; at the division of whose estate, the State being obliged to share with others, received but a few shillings on the pound. In consequence of these calamities, which might have been easily foreseen, the Legislature, at a special session, in 1838–1839, found themselves obliged to discontinue the "internal improvement system." The work on the canal, however, was not wholly abandoned; a million of State bonds having been sold at some 25 per cent. discount in Europe, the fund commissioners were enabled to persevere in it, for some time after the railroads had stopped, but were at last obliged to apply for assistance to the Legislature, in order to pay the interest due in January, 1841. As there was but little time left, until the interest was to be paid, the exigency of the case was such, that the Legislature resorted to the desperate expedient of making a new issue of bonds, to be hypothecated for whatever they would bring, which measure, had it been permanently adopted, would have involved the State in utter bankruptcy. As there were many, who objected to paying interest at all, and especially upon bonds, which had been sold for less than their full value, as expressed on their face, whilst others argued, that if the bonds had passed from the hands of the original into the hands of bona fide holders, who had purchased them at their full price, the State was bound to pay interest to the latter upon the amount of money, which each bond on its face purported to be issued for. Mr. Cavarly, with a view of making a decision on the disputed point unnecessary, introduced a bill empowering the fund commissioner to mortgage 300,000 dollars' worth of internal improvement bonds, making it incumbent upon him to apply the proceeds to the payment of all interest legally due on the debt, and leaving it for him to decide, which would be more legal, to pay interest upon the full amount of the value of the bonds, as shown on their face, or to pay no interest, except on the money, which these bonds had been sold for. Besides providing, that these interest bonds should be sold for their mere market value, the Legislature levied an additional tax of ten cents on every hundred dollars' worth of property to be pledged for the payment of the interest of these bonds, by which devices the difficulty, which the commissioners had experienced in paying the interest, was finally overcome.

In the year 1840, a large majority of the people were democrats, those formerly the so-called Jackson men; whilst their opponent political party, which, before the year 1834, had flourished under the name of "anti-Jackson," and to which many office-holders, and especially most of the Supreme Court Judges, belonged, now adopted the name of "Whigs," attempting to base the same, as did the "Whigs" of the Revolution, upon opposition to the executive power. Two important questions were submitted to the Supreme Court, the first of which was, whether Governor Carlin had a right, as he claimed to have, of appointing a new Secretary of State to supersede the old one. The Supreme Court gave as their opinion, that the Governor had no such right, producing, by their decision, a general dissatisfaction throughout the country, since the democrats, who constituted a majority of the people, very plausibly contended, that the unpopular doctrine of life-officers had been sanctioned by it. The second question was, whether an alien had a right to vote. At that time, the alien vote was about 10,000 strong, full nine-tenths of which belonged to the democratic party. The constitution of the State provided, that all free white inhabitants over the age of twenty-one years, who had resided in the State for six months, were entitled to vote at general, as well as at special elections. The whigs pretended, that the word "inhabitants" did not apply to any but citizens, whilst hitherto aliens, who had been in the State for six months, as well as citizens, had been allowed to vote. This question having already been made the subject of much discussion throughout the State, two whigs undertook to settle it, by agreeing on a fictitious cause, which they brought before the Circuit Court, the judge of which, being himself a whig, of course decided, that the aliens had no right to vote. When this decision became known, the democrats, well aware, that its reversion would be of vital importance to their party, since it would secure them the further support of nearly 10,000 votes, forming the balance of power in the State, carried the case before the Supreme Court, continuing it until December, 1840, after the Presidential election. The defeat, which the democratic party throughout the United States had sustained in the Presidential campaign of 1840, by the election of Gen. Harrison, having added fresh fuel to the irritation of the democrats against the whigs, the former, whilst their case remained suspended, lost no time in introducing a measure, by which the Circuit Courts, created in 1835, were to be abolished, and five additional Judges of the Supreme Court were created, all of whom were required to hold Circuit Courts in place of the Circuit Judges, who had been dismissed from office, which arrangement would have given them a majority of two to one in the Supreme Court. Although the success of the measure was for a long time extremely doubtful, it finally passed in both houses of the Legislature. The result of this democratic victory was, that the appointment of the Secretary of State by the Governor was confirmed, and the democratic party continued to enjoy the support of the alien vote; for nothing could be further from the intention of the new judges, than to concur in the opinion of their whig colleagues on a subject like this.

In July, 1841, payment of the interest on the public debt was stopped. Illinois, for the second time, drew upon herself the censure of the world; people abroad, who had formerly considered Illinois to be a country affording good chances to the industrious settler, no longer entertained the design of emigrating to it, whilst the people at home, could they have found purchasers of their property, would not have hesitated to leave the State, in order to escape the evils of high taxation.

The general distress of the State was rendered complete by the utter failure of the State Bank, which happened in February, 1842; the bank at Shawneetown, after holding out for four months longer, "following in the footsteps of its illustrious predecessor." The banks had first suspended specie payments in the spring of 1837. To save the internal improvement system, this suspension was then legalized, and continued to be made lawful until 1841. This legalized suspension of the banks met with violent opposition from the democrats, which was of itself sufficient to enlist the whigs in their favor, and proved of immense advantage to them, since the business men and capitalists of the State were principally whigs, which party, at the time of Gen. Jackson, in opposition to his policy, had claimed an undue influence in the body politic, whilst the democratic party, in support of Gen. Jackson's administration, had been opposed to the same. In the meantime, the State Bank having been made the depository of the State revenues, which the collectors were required to pay into it as into the public treasury, by the influence it thus acquired over the Legislature, the members of which had to look to the bank for their pay, succeeded in not only obtaining a further privilege of suspension, at the session of the Legislature in 1841, but also a privilege not previously granted, of issuing one, two, and three dollar notes, which must, no doubt, have caused severe disappointment to the democrats The very triumph of the banks, however, accelerated their ruin, because the issue of these small notes, with which they flooded the country, by banishing from circulation the silver dollar, which formed the specie basis of the country, rendered it impossible for them to increase, or even, perhaps, to keep their stock of specie. The continual refusal of the United States to take the money of the State and Shawneetown banks in payment for the public lands, except at a discount, which regularly advanced every year, and the boundless liberality, with which the banks distributed their paper money and advanced loans, to attach the members of the Legislature and administration to their interests, led to their inevitable downfall in 1842, which spread ruin throughout the country, and even some of the neighboring States: leaving the people of Illinois almost wholly without any other circulating medium, for the purpose of trade and commerce, than the "bank rags," printed by the "rag barons," as the presidents of the banks were then called.

Before we go further in the exposition of the civil history of the State, the general character of the people, and the civil commotions and disturbances, which had taken place in earlier times, and which may serve as a proper introduction to the history of the famous Mormon riots, which broke out in 1840, convulsing the State, claim our attention.

CHAPTER V.

THE State of Illinois extends about 150 miles from east to west, by 400 from north to south. Such a disproportion in the geographical figure of a State, is certain to create a separate northern and southern interest, even if the people of such a State were of a common stock, which, not being the case with the people of Iliinois, will sufficiently account for their frequent disinclination to agree upon the adoption of such a policy, and such measures of government, as would have best suited the interests of the State, and aided in relieving her from the calamities, under which she was then suffering. The settlers of the Southern portion of the State were chiefly people from the Slave States, those of the northern section principally New Yorkers and New Englanders. Many of the inhabitants of the neighboring Slave States, who were poor, and did not relish a residence in a slave country, where the very negroes were wont to stigmatize them as the poor white folks, had removed to Illinois, where the immigration of slaveholders was strictly forbidden. The greater part of them were an honest and hospitable people, indifferent to wealth, and fond of social enjoyment.

The settlers of the northern part of the State, on the other hand, were industrious Yankees from the Eastern States, enterprising farmers, manufacturers, or merchants, who, by their restless energy and activity, soon converted the howling wilderness into a region covered with farms, churches, and villages, so that their settlements, though founded at a later period than those of the southern part, were soon ahead of the latter in point of civilization; and their success will sufficiently explain the envy, or rather, the hatred, which the southern people conceived against the Yankee settlers. Never having seen any Yankees, except a few wretched, cheating, pilfering New England pedlars, who perambulated the country with their assortments of wooden clocks or tin-ware, the southerners were led to believe, that the real Yankee was nothing but a most ungenerous, despicable, cheating fellow, whilst the Yankees, in their turn, were not backward in their dislike, presuming the southerner to be fond of dirt and ignorance, and to aspire to nothing beyond the exalted idea of passing his life in a miserable, narrow log-cabin, with a squalid, ragged family around him. Both parties seemed cordially to hate each other, and, on questions affecting the welfare of the whole State, found it, frequently, impossible to agree. Thus, for instance, the southern people for a long time opposed the construction of the canal from Lake Michigan to the Illinois river, supposing such a contrivance to be admirably calculated for flooding the whole country with the obnoxious Yankees.

The politicians of that day had not visibly added to their knowledge of the mysteries of statesmanship, but they were men, who understood exceedingly well how to insinuate themselves in the favor of the people, by a perpetual show of condescending friendship; and, by dint of continual practice, they had acquired the inestimable art of never appearing among the public without a countenance, which, by its cheerful gaiety and congenial mildness, would command universal attention. These politicians were especially remarkable for their genuine horror of passing an unpopular measure, which horror made many of them resort to the ingenious expedient of invariably opposing measures that were introduced, without previous information with regard to the opinion of the people; for if the measure should be passed and become popular, no one would be likely to take much notice of those who had voted against it: but if it should turn out unpopular, then they might triumphantly prove by the journals, that they had voted against it. And should the measure, though not passed, become yet popular, they would excuse themselves by pretending to have been insufficiently informed as to the wishes of their constituents.

This policy originated with one John Grammar, who, notwithstanding his humble pretensions to anything like a refined education, seems to have been a fair type of the politicians of his times. In 1816, he was first elected to the Legislature, of which he managed to remain a member for nearly twenty years. It is reported of him, that when first elected, being utterly destitute of civilised clothing, he gathered immediately, in company with his sons, a large quantity of hazelnuts, which he forwarded to some Ohio settlement, where they were exchanged for some blue strouding, such as the Indians use for breech cloths. The cloth being received, the women of the neighborhood were at once assembled to cut and make it into garments for him; finding it too scant, the women made a very short bob-tailed coat, and a pair of leggins of it. Not at all dismayed, Mr. Grammar put on the coat and the leggins over an old torn garment, intended probably for a pair of breeches, and thus equipped, started for Kaskaskia, then the seat of government, patiently awaiting the day of the passing of the poetry bill, when, having received part of his salary, he set out immediately to procure himself a pair of fashionable "unmentionables."

By the year 1840, the whole State had been settled. Chicago, Alton, Springfield, Quincy, Galena, Nauvoo, and Peoria, were incorporated cities about the year 1842. The benefits conferred upon the State by the immigration from the Eastern States, were not only visible in the improvements made in the agriculture and construction of roads and bridges, but also in the erection of new churches, schools, and even colleges, and in the greater attention, which began to be paid to education, generally. Formerly, the literary efforts of the Illinoisians had not manifested themselves in any sphere except newspaper writing; we now notice the publication, by F. M. Peck, of his Gazetteer of Illinois, of some poetical essays, and the issue of a monthly magazine of high merit, the editor of which, James Hall, gained considerable reputation as a scholar and a writer.

In the years 1816 and 1817, the country was overrun with bands of horse-thieves and counterfeiters, so numerous and so well organized as to care but very little for the authority of the laws. Many of the police, of the sheriffs and justices of the peace, were intimately connected with them, and they had friends among many, who had been considered as very respectable men. So frequent had thefts become, especially in the frontier towns, that at Galena every new comer was asked, whether he would steal or not; and if he answered he would not steal, was looked upon as the model of an honest man. Those of the rogues, who were arrested, either procured the services of some false witnesses, or some of their friends on the jury, and were sure to be acquitted. This so enraged the people, that they organized companies called "Regulators," commanded by officers, and armed as if engaged on a military expedition. The Governor and Judges, who despaired of enforcing the laws in the ordinary way, gave them every possible unofficial encouragement. Such companies would assemble at night, march to the residence of a rogue, arrest him, and after thrashing him soundly, expel him from the State. Although most of the scoundrels were removed in this way, one noted band managed to maintain themselves in some counties on the Ohio, where they built a regular fort, laughing the authority of the State to scorn. But in 1831 the people in the vicinity attacked and stormed the fort, losing one man, and killing three of the rogues in the assault, and taking the rest of them prisoners, who were, however, never convicted.

In the year 1837, a bloody riot occurred at Alton, which, considering the noise it made in the world, cannot be passed over in silence. Rev. Elijah P. Lovejoy, of the Presbyterian Church, had endeavored to publish an abolition paper in St. Louis, but his press was destroyed, and he himself banished from the city. He removed to Alton, where his press was thrown into the river the day it was landed. He then publicly assured the people, that in the paper he was going to start, he would carefully abstain from expressing his opinion about slavery; for none existed in Alton, and it would appear, he said, like cowardice to fly from a place, where the evil existed, to one, where it did not exist, to oppose it. The people then allowed him to establish his "Alton Observer," a paper, which at first was solely devoted to the interests of religion; soon, however, it was changed into a most rabid abolition paper. Not wishing to see the public peace disturbed, a deputation from the people called upon Mr. Lovejoy to make him remember his pledge, when, with most brazen-faced impudence, he denied having given any such pledge; this so enraged the people, that they threw his press at once into the river. Not at all discouraged, but more than ever determined to publish his paper, if necessary, at the point of the bayonet, Lovejoy ordered another press, which arrived from St. Louis at Alton on Monday evening, September 6th. The friends and followers of Mr. Lovejoy, who had formed themselves into a military company, were present, when the press was landed, and safely removed it to a large stone warehouse, where they assembled under arms, threatening to make those, who should attempt its seizure, know the virtue of their cartridges. The excitement now ran high, and on Tuesday evening, September 7th, a mob assembled before the warehouse, demanding, that the press be delivered up to them. The abolitionists within replied, that they were well provided with arms and ammunition, and would sooner die than surrender the press. The mob hurled stones against the house, making preparations for a general assault, when a shot was fired from within, killing one of the crowd almost instantaneously. Ladders were immediately sent for, horns were blown, and the bells of the city rung, armed men arriving from all quarters. A ladder being placed on that side of the house, which was without windows, a man ascended it with a burning torch in his hand. Whilst several shots were exchanged between the crowd and the party within, Mr. Lovejoy twice left the building, firing each time without effect at the crowd, and retreating immediately. The third time, however, he ventured out with one of his party, he was shot, and fell mortally wounded. Whilst the flames were consuming the roof, the multitude continued to fire at the building. Seeing, that if they further persisted in their pretensions, they were doomed to destruction, the men within surrendered the press, and were permitted to make a hasty retreat. The principal instigators of the mob were afterwards arrested, but never convicted. Thus ended the "Alton Tragedy," disgraceful to all concerned, and causing, at the time of its occurrence, an immense excitement throughout the Union.

About the year 1840, many riots occurred in the northern part of the State. People there had settled upon public lands of the United States, and by establishing farms and building villages, had greatly improved them. The settlers had mutually agreed to protect each other in their claims, but there were many, who, with the view of dispossessing the owners and securing the lands for themselves, disputed their right, which was a prolific source of riots and disturbance. The northern portion of the State also, was again infested with organized bands of murderers and horse-thieves, who, in some of the counties, and especially in the county of Ogle, were so numerous as to overawe justice. They would, as formerly, by seating some from their own number on the juries, and hiring crowds of perjured witnesses for their defence, manage to prorogue the trial of their cause from one term to another, and insure to themselves an acquittal. The people, in their turn, formed themselves into companies of "Regulators," as before, seized the most notorious rogues, whipped several of them, and expelled the rest from the country. In one instance, a father and his son, both hardened murderers, were tried, convicted, and summarily executed on the spot; this act of stern justice struck the rogues with terror, rendering them averse to further defiance of the laws of the State.

Nothing else deserving notice happened until the year 1840, when the people generally known by the name of "Mormons," first began to figure conspicuously in the history of the State. They called themselves "The Church of Jesus Christ of Latter-day Saints," and belonged to a sect started and headed by "Joe Smith," for whom they claimed the gift of prophetic power. "Joe Smith" was born at Sharon, Windsor county, Vermont, on the 23d of December, 1805. His parents were so poor as to be unable to give their son even a common education. Thus "Joe Smith" grew up in ignorance, being compensated for his want of knowledge by a naturally crafty and cunning disposition. His parents removed to Palmyra, New York, when he was ten years of age. Here he led an idle, dreaming life, rambled through the woods, exerting himself, in company with his father, to excavate buried treasures, or to indicate, for a valuable consideration, the place, where wells might be dug and water found. During the time he resided in Palmyra, he came in contact with one Sidney Rigdon, who was in possession of a religious romance, written by a clergyman in Ohio, since dead. This being communicated to Joe Smith, he proposed that it should be made the basis of a new religion. They concerted a story to this effect, that golden plates had been dug up somewhere near Palmyra, with inscriptions in miraculous characters, which none but those inspired by God could read; giving an account of the destinies of the ten lost tribes of Israel, their wanderings through Asia, and their settlement in America, where Christ came to preach to them the doctrine of salvation, and was crucified, as he had been in Jerusalem. The plates then continued the history of these early American Christians, until the time, when God, provoked by their great wickedness, determined to exterminate them, by causing the Lamanites, the heathen of America, and the Nephites, the Christians, to make war with each other. A battle was fought between the two parties, in which millions were killed on either side. The Nephites were annihilated, with the exception of Mormon, and Moroni, and a few others, all of them righteous men, who were permitted by the Lord to make good their escape, and afterwards directed by him to inscribe the history of these miraculous events on plates of gold, and bury them in the earth, where they were to remain, until they should be brought to the knowledge of mankind, fourteen centuries afterwards.

At the time he formed an acquaintance with Sidney Rigdon, the prophet, according to his own statements, had profoundly meditated on religious matters, and had especially been very anxious about the salvation of his soul. He had seen innumerable sects and doctrines, all professing to teach the knowledge of the true way to heaven; and this truth had taken hold of his mind with irresistible force, that God could only be the author of one doctrine, and that all the sects he had seen, were very far from following the same. He searched and examined the Scriptures, devoutly believing what he read; and he became aware, that one ought to apply to God himself, who would be willing to diffuse light through the darkness, by revealing unto the true believer his own divine will. He therefore retired from the noise and confusion of the world to a solitary place, near his father's house, where he addressed fervent prayers to the "Most High." Whilst he was praying, suddenly a light began to descend towards him, which, by the time it had reached the tops of the trees, illuminated the whole country around. It then descended towards the earth till it enveloped him, when two brilliant personages stood at once before him, and informed him that his sins were forgiven, that none of the Churches existing on earth followed the doctrine of God, but that he himself, at some future time, would be instructed in the full knowledge of it.

On the 23d of September, 1823, the prophet had another vision. Whilst he was devoutly praying to God, a light purer and more brilliant than the light of day itself, burst into his room, apparently consuming the whole house with fire, and shaking his body as by an ague, causing him to be transported with bliss, and to sink into an unspeakable rapture. On a sudden, a glorious personage appeared before him, in a snow white garment without a seam, diffusing a light around him surpassing in its splendor even that of the first. This supernatural being announced himself as an angel, bringing the glorious tidings unto him, that his prayers had been agreeable to the Lord, that his sins were forgiven, that God's covenant with Israel was about to be fulfilled, and that the millenium of the true Gospel and of universal bliss and happiness had arrived. The angel then told him the history of the Indians, who were the descendants of those ten tribes of Israel settled in America, which had been almost exterminated on account of their awful wickedness; that the holy records of these events had been safely deposited beyond the reach of the wicked, and that he was the chosen servant of God to bring them to light, and to disclose their miraculous contents unto all mankind.

The angel then disappeared, but returned several times afterwards, instructing him, where the holy records were to be found, and telling him to take them away and commence the work of God on earth. The prophet went to the place indicated, and discovered them on a hill, in a stone box, near Palmyra. They consisted of gold plates, inscribed with hieroglyphical characters, the plates being very thin, and fastened together by three rings, composing altogether a volume of six inches in thickness. He also found in the same box two stones of surpassing transparency, the Urim and Thummim, used by ancient seers to discern things past or future.

As the admiring prophet, filled with the Holy Ghost, was about to remove these treasures, the angel appeared again to him, and said, "Look!" and he saw the devil, surrounded by an immense train of his associates.

After receiving further instructions from the angel, he started home, but was attacked on the road by two scoundrels, and barely escaped with his life. He then moved to Pennsylvania, where, with the aid of inspiration and of the Urim and Thummim, he commenced translating the plates, finishing a part of the book of Mormon, which contained the Gospel of Jesus Christ, as he had preached it in America, and was destined to restore pristine Christianity, and to convert the Gentiles, and even the Jews themselves, to the faith. The disciples, who flocked to the prophet, pretended to have the gift of prophecy, and that of tongues, and, as during the times of the early Christian Church, so now were miracles wrought, as, for example, the cure of diseases. Many of the followers of the prophet solemnly certified before the public, to the effect, that they had seen the plates, and the engravings thereon, which were of a curious workmanship; and that these plates had been brought before their eyes by an angel from heaven, as also God had revealed to them, that they were translated by his own divine power.

Within a short time, Joe Smith and his apostles had made many converts, who, on the 6th day of April, 1830, formed themselves into a Church, in Manchester, in the State of New York, whence they removed to Jackson county, Missouri; here they built the town of "Independence." They claimed, that not only the country, but the whole world belonged to *them*, as the saints of the Lord. Such arrogance could not be endured. The Missourians ducked some of these vain pretenders in the river, tarred and feathered several, killed others, and forced the residue to remove to the county of Clay, on the opposite side of the Missouri. The prophet, however, established himself at Kirtland, in Ohio, where, in 1836, a very large assembly of the "Saints" was held, at which it was announced "that the work of God had greatly increased in America, and in England, Scotland, Wales, and the islands of the sea." A bank was started by the prophet, called "The Kirtland Safety Bank," of which he himself was the president. This bank soon failed for a large amount; its failure, the cause of which could be clearly traced to a want of integrity on the part of the prophet, inflamed the people of the town and its vicinity with such a degree of resentment against him, that the prophet, afraid to get himself into trouble, removed, with his apostles, elders, and the saints, to the remotest north-west corner of Missouri, where their arrogance and presumption speedily made them many enemies. Their leaders refused to acknowledge the authority of the government of Missouri. Sidney Rigdon, in a fourth of July speech, delivered before the Mormons, openly proclaimed, that the prophet had resolved no longer to submit to the Missourian Government. Rupture having now become inevitable, both parties determined to settle their differences by the edge of the sword. A battle was fought between the Mormons and a body of Missourians, under Major Bogart, in which the former were totally defeated; this, however, did not prevent them from plundering the towns of their enemies. At last, Gov. Boggs called out the militia, with strict orders to expel the Mormons from the State, at the point of bayonet, if necessary. The Mormons were speedily surrounded, and forced to surrender; all were dismissed, upon giving promise to leave the State, with the exception of their leaders, who were arrested and committed to prison, but managed to escape beyond the boundaries of the State, before they could be brought to trial.

The whole body of the Mormons removed to Illinois in the years 1839 and 1840, being kindly received as sufferers in the cause of their religion, and permitted to settle at a place on the banks of the Mississippi, in the upper part of the county of Hancock, where they soon built a city. To this they gave the name of Nauvoo; it was scattered over some six square miles, part of it being built upon the flat skirting the river side, but the greater part upon the bluffs east of the river, on the brow of which, commanding a view of the country for 20 miles around, in Illinois and Iowa, towered the great temple of the Mormons.

The whig and democratic parties being each of them anxious to conciliate the Mormons to their interests, the latter experienced no difficulty in obtaining from the Legislature charters incorporating Nauvoo under the government of a Mayor, four Aldermen, and nine Councillors, with powers to pass ordinances, provided the same were not repugnant to the Constitution of the United States or Illinois, and incorporating also the militia of Nauvoo into a military legion, called "The Nauvoo Legion," entirely independent of the State militia, and accountable only to the Governor: besides incorporating a great tavern, to be called "The Nauvoo House," in which the prophet and his heirs were to possess a suite of rooms forever. Under these charters, a city government, and the Nauvoo Legion, were promptly organized, Joe Smith being at once elected Mayor, and next to the Governor in the command of the Legion.

In the autumn of the year 1841, the Governor of Missouri made a demand on Gov. Carlin, to deliver up to him Joe Smith, and several other Mormons, as fugitives from justice. Gov. Carlin issued an executive warrant to this effect, which writ, however, was returned without being served. Another such warrant having been issued by him, Joe Smith was arrested and carried before Judge Douglass, who discharged him upon the ground, that the writ, having been once returned before its execution, was "functus officio."

Gov. Carlin issued another writ in 1842. Joe Smith was arrested again, but discharged by his own municipal court by a writ of habeas corpus; the common council of Nauvoo, of which he himself was the presiding member, having passed an ordinance empowering the municipal court of Nauvoo to have jurisdiction in all cases of arrests made in the city, by any process whatever; notwithstanding the charter granted to the municipal court jurisdiction only in cases of arrests for breach of some ordinance.

Early in the year 1842, while the contest for Governor was going on, Adam W. Snyder having been chosen as the democratic candidate, and Joseph Duncan, the former governor, as the whig candidate, Joe Smith issued a proclamation to the saints, exhorting them to vote for Mr. Snyder, and declaring Judge Douglass to be a master spirit. Having hitherto derived considerable support from the Mormon vote, the whig party, at the appearance of this proclamation, which clearly indicated, that they could no longer count upon their former friends, were greatly irritated against the Mormons, their papers abounding with recitals of the atrocities and enormities perpetrated at Nauvoo. They also charged with awful wickedness, the democrats for having admitted such fiends as the Mormons into their ranks, although, by this time, the Mormons had rendered themselves extremely odious to the great body of the people, it being believed, that the Mormons looked upon Illinois as the land promised them by the Lord; their Legion being intended for no other purpose, it was said, than to take possession of the State, whenever it should become strong enough. The excitement throughout the State in regard to the Mormons, soon reached a pitch, which made it evident, that a violent struggle, and perhaps bloodshed, was about to take place.

Adam W. Snyder, the democratic candidate, having died previous to the election, Thomas Ford, one of the Judges of the Supreme Court, at that time engaged in holding a Circuit Court on Fox river, was nominated candidate for Governor in his stead. He was elected Governor by a large majority; at the time he assumed the reins of government, he found the State laboring under the excitement of the

Mormon question. Her finances were in a ruinous condition; the treasury was utterly bankrupt, not containing enough money to pay postage on the usual letters; indebted, moreover, for the customary expenses of government, in the sum of $313,000; whilst the annual revenues provided for the payment of the expenses of government, amounted to but one-third of this sum. The currency of the State was annihilated, in consequence of which no taxes could be paid or collected; a debt of about $14,000,000 had been contracted for carrying out the internal improvement system; and the State, by borrowing beyond her means, had lost her credit. The people were indebted to the merchants: these again to the foreign merchants, or to the banks, and the banks to everybody; and none were able to pay. The confusion of public affairs was, in general, such as to make many despair of the possibility of devising a system of policy, which could relieve the State from the calamities, under which she was then suffering. Many of the whigs were in favor of repudiating the entire State debt, believing this course of proceeding to be acceptable to the great body of the people, and therefore well calculated to increase the power of their party, then smarting under the effects of the defeats they had repeatedly sustained in elections. The two leading organs of the whig party, the Sangamon Journal and the Alton Telegraph, openly contended, that the debt never could nor would be paid, and that everybody ought to acquiesce in this, as a matter of stern necessity, which admitted of no further discussion, and forbade all attempts to charm it away. The great majority, however, of the politicians of the two great parties, observed an ominous silence on the subject, none of them being willing to advocate a measure, which, with a tax-hating people, might have proved in the highest degree injurious to their interests, by destroying their hardly-acquired popularity; so that, but for the energetic action of the Governor in the premises, who boldly took the lead, denouncing with manly firmness all refusals to pay the public debt, Illinois would probably have been made a repudiating State.

The property owned by the State consisted of 42,000 acres, purchased under the internal improvement system; 210,000 acres, granted by the United States under the distribution law of 1841; 230,467 acres of canal lands, besides 3,491 town lots in various towns on the canal; the work done on the canal and railroads, with a large quantity of railroad iron, and the stock in the banks. These were the only resources left, applicable to the liquidation of the whole debt, for the payment of which heavy taxation could not then be resorted to, since it would result in depopulating the country; so that the debt would never be paid.

During the summer of 1842, Justin Butterfield, a distinguished lawyer of Chicago, had several conversations on the subject of the canal with Arthur Bronson, a wealthy New York capitalist, interested in the State stocks of Illinois, and Mr. Michael Ryan: both of whom were acquainted with, and possessed the confidence of capitalists in Europe and America. In consequence of forcible representations on the part of Mr. Butterfield, a plan was devised and adopted by these capitalists and their friends, to the effect, that the owners of canal bonds should advance $1,600,000, the sum reported by the chief engineer to be necessary to complete the canal, to secure which new loan, and provide also for the ultimate payment of the entire canal debt, the State was to convey the canal property to them in trust, and impose a tax sufficient to pay a portion of the interest on the whole debt.

The success of this plan could only have been ensured by the adoption of the right course of policy in regard to the banks, by far the most important subject, that was deliberated upon by the Legislature at their session of 1842; since there were at stake about $3,100,000 worth of State stocks, upon the value of which the completion of the canal depended. The people clamored for some mode of liquidating the bank debts, many of them being in favor of repealing their charters, and appointing commissioners to take charge of their effects, to pay their debts, and collect whatever was due them; whilst by far the greater part of the people declared themselves in favor of a compromise, by which the State would be paid for its stock, and the banks bring their affairs to a close at once. The State Bank held $1,750,000 of State bonds, and $294,000 in Auditor's warrants, together with scrip, amounting in the aggregate to $2,100,000, which it agreed to disgorge at once. The Illinois Bank, at Shawneetown, was willing to deliver at once $500,000, of which $469,998 were in Auditor's warrants; and to pay the residue on a short credit. Those, who advocated the repeal of the bank charters, suggesting, that their effects be placed in the hands of commissioners appointed for that purpose, did not consider that, like all public officers managing money matters, these commissioners would have set their ingenuity at work to devise means, by which to obtain for themselves whatever of the effects would have come in their hands, so that neither creditors nor stockholders would ever have got anything; nor did they consider, that, though the Legislature might repeal, the banks were at liberty to contest their right so to do, involving the case in endless litigation, the result of which might even have been a decision in their favor; whilst, in the meantime, they would not have been at a loss how to remove their assets to a place of safety, beyond the reach of their creditors. They also paid no regard to the fact, that a government, which, yielding to the excitement of the moment, hesitates not to adopt such extreme and violent measures as cannot be justified in point of law, is calculated to excite such distrust in the minds of capitalists as to render them unwilling to subscribe to its stock, or expend their money for the improvements, which it authorizes. On the side of a compromise, it was argued, that the bonds held by the banks could not be suffered to be sold; for the sale of so great an amount of bonds, in addition to those already in the market, would not only still further depreciate their value, but, by impressing people with a belief that the State had wilfully assisted in depressing their value, in order to purchase its own bonds at the largest possible discount, would make them consider, that a State, which felt no repugnance to thus acting like a vulgar swindler, was certainly very far from entertaining any intention to pay a single cent on the public debt.

These reasons prevailing with the people, a majority of them declared themselves in favor of a compromise; accordingly, a bill of compromise with the State Bank was introduced into the House of Representatives, and passed by a vote of 107 to 4. It was at once agreed to by the bank, and Mr. Clernand, the chairman of the finance committee of the Lower House, became its principal advocate. As there existed an old feud between Mr. Clernand and Lyman Trumbull, Secretary of State, the latter threatened, that he would take good care, that the bill should be so altered in the Senate, which body had yet to vote on it, that "the framers, in the House, should not know their own bantling, when it came back to them." On hearing this, the Governor, being of opinion, that the Secretary of State ought to be the confidential adviser and helper of the executive, immediately removed Trumbull from his office. The bill was then passed by a large majority, and approved by the council of revision; and a similar one was passed in regard to the Illinois Bank, at Shawneetown; by which two bills a debt of $2,500,000 was liquidated, and the domestic treasury at once relieved.

The Legislature, at this session, also enacted laws for the sale of State lands and property, for the negotiation of the loan of $1,600,000, which had been proposed to complete the Illinois and Michigan Canal, for the redemption of interest bonds mortgaged to McAlister and Stebbins, and for the reception of the distributive share of the State in the proceeds of the sales of the public lands; by which laws the State debt was reduced to $8,000,000. This reduction could not fail to have a highly beneficial influence upon the condition of the State. Auditor's warrants, which had sold at 50 per cent., at once rose to 90 per cent.; State bonds, which had been selling at 14 cents on the dollar, now sold for 40, the banks paid out their specie, and the currency of the State was restored to a good condition in less than three months.

The negotiation of the canal loan having been already commenced in the year 1842 by Justin Butterfield and Michael Ryan, the latter gentleman, who had been an engineer on the canal himself, and was in possession of much valuable information concerning its progress and statistics, was appointed, with Col. Charles Oakley, agent to bring this business to a conclusion. They proceeded to New York, and wrote a series of articles for the New York newspapers, in which the real condition of the State was truthfully described. Confidence was at once restored among business men and capitalists; and David Leavitt, the distinguished president of the American Exchange Bank, in New York, which held $250,000 of canal bonds, assisted in calling a meeting of the American bondholders, at which it was resolved, that the American creditors should subscribe for their proportion of the loan. Confident of success, Messrs. Oakley and Ryan proceeded to Europe, and had interviews with Baring, Brothers & Co., of London, Hope & Co., of Amsterdam, and Magniac, Jardine & Co., all creditors of the State, and among the wealthiest capitalists in Europe. These gentlemen declared themselves in favor of the loan, but wanted to receive guaranties as to the value of the canal lands, as a security for the money and the ultimate payment of the canal debt ($5,000,000), and to be assured as to the willingness of the people to submit to higher taxation, if necessary. A provisional arrangement was then entered into, during the summer of 1843, in pursuance of which Messrs. Abbott Lawrence, Thomas W. Ward, and William Sturges, of Boston, were directed to appoint two competent persons in America to inquire into the value of the canal lands: $400,000 were promised to be subscribed at once, provided the Governor would pledge himself to urge the necessity of an increased taxation, at the next session of the Legislature; whereupon Messrs. Oakley and Ryan returned, in November, 1843. The choice of the Boston committee fell upon Gov. John Davis, of Massachusetts, and William H. Swift, an eminent engineer and Captain in the U. S. Army. Having examined the canal and canal lands, and satisfied themselves as to the truth of the representations of Messrs. Oakley and Ryan, Gov. Davis and Capt. Swift issued a circular, strongly recommending the loan. Senator Ryan, and afterwards Col. Oakley, returned to London to complete the necessary arrangements for the loan; but the foreign bondholders refusing to meddle any further with it, until the Legislature and the people of the State should have manifested some public regard to their obligations, and made some efforts to pay the interest on the public debt, they were obliged to return without having accomplished anything.

In the fall of 1844, a letter was addressed through the public newspapers to Gov. Thomas Ford, by that faction of the people hostile to increased taxation, in which that measure was bitterly denounced. Although Gov. Ford knew very well, that to advocate increased taxation might render him utterly odious to a tax-hating people, he came up to the question with great resolution and self-devotion to the welfare of his country, publishing an answer to the above letter through the newspapers, which, remarkable as it was for its sound common sense and sagacious views, and the noble spirit of patriotism animating every line of it, not only entirely refuted the arguments set up by the opposite party, but also in due time, when its contents had become known in the Eastern States and London, by convincing the public creditors, that not every man in Illinois was of necessity a hair-brained, rabid demagogue, produced so favorable a change in their minds, as to make them not only at once agree to complete the arrangements for the loan, but also subscribe for a much larger amount, than they had originally intended. Mr. Leavitt, a gentleman of the highest standing and credit in the financial world, and a very able financier, who, by his successful exertions in the arrangement of the loan, to which he himself had very liberally subscribed, had rendered the most essential services to the State, hurried to Illinois, accompanied by Col. Oakley and Gov. Davis. They arrived at Springfield about the middle of February, 1845, during the session of the Legislature. Gov. Davis and Mr. Leavitt submitted the proposition of the public creditors, which was at once communicated to both houses, through the executive. It passed the House by a considerable majority, but was defeated in the Senate, owing to the spirit of hostility engendered in that body by the Ex-Secretary of State and his friends, who, it is probable, from motives of personal resentment, had arrayed themselves in opposition to it. But the friends of the bill procured a reconsideration of the vote, and by dexterously removing and striking out of the canal bill whatever related to, or had the semblance of a public tax, having silenced much of the opposition, secured the concurrence of the Senate in the bill so introduced, and of the House in the bill so amended. Laws were passed perfecting the canal arrangement; two trustees were elected by the bondholders, and one by the Governor: the board was organized, the work on the canal let out to contractors, and the money required for carrying it on was obtained.

The Legislature, at this session of 1845, also fixed the rate of interest on money, at six per cent.; which measure had become necessary, owing to the conduct of a great part of the merchants of the State, who, in the time of bank suspension, having a large stock of goods on hand, in consequence of which competition amongst them, in their retail business, was considerably increased, had found themselves obliged to encourage people to buy on credit, crediting almost any one to the whole amount of his property, and in case he was unable to pay, taking his notes at 12 per cent. interest; so that a majority of the people were soon indebted beyond their means, and compelled to pay a ruinous rate of interest to save themselves from being sued for their debts.

On reviewing again its financial condition, it will be found, that the affairs of the State had been administered with such distinguished skill and integrity by Gov. Thomas Ford, that in December, 1846, when his term of office expired, the domestic debt of the treasury had been reduced from $313,000 to $31,000, Auditor's warrants were at par, the banks had been liquidated in a just and honorable manner, their notes had been banished from circulation, and been replaced by coin currency and the notes of solvent banks of other States, the people had paid their debts, and eight millions of the public debt had been paid, redeemed, or otherwise provided for: and the State itself, which but a short time before had been in a most ruinous condition, discredited throughout the world, had yet been able to borrow the further sum of $1,600,000 for the completion of the work on the canal. Confidence in the prospects of the State was at once revived, and the tide of emigration once more directed to Illinois, the population of which in 1845, according to the census of that year, amounted to 662,150 souls, and was rapidly increasing.

CHAPTER VI.

HAVING, in the last chapter, brought down the civil history of the State to the end of the year 1846, we now prosecute again the history of the State as connected with the Mormons. This people had settled in Hancock county, and in the year 1842 had increased their numbers to nearly 20,000 souls. The warrant of Gov. Carlin for the arrest of Joe Smith, their prophet, as a fugitive from justice in Missouri, which had not been executed, and was still impending at the time Gov. Ford came into office, had been annulled and rendered void of effect by the writ of habeas corpus, made out by Judge Pope, of the Federal Court, who belonged to the whig party; in consequence of which proceeding the prophet had been discharged. But an accusation being vamped up in Missouri against Joe Smith, for having attempted the murder of the Governor of Missouri, on the 5th of June, 1843, another demand was made by the Missourian governor for the arrest of the prophet, and a warrant accordingly issued by Gov. Thomas Ford; in pursuance of which Joe Smith was arrested while absent from Nauvoo, on a visit to Rock river. The Missourian agent started with the holy prophet in his safe keeping, on his way to Missouri; but on the road was waylaid by a number of armed Mormons, who captured the whole party, and conducted their sacred prophet in triumph back to Nauvoo, the Zion of the modern age. The prophet was immediately taken before the Municipal Court, the members of which, being his intimate friends, did not fail to discharge him.

About that time, an election for Congress was to take place in the Mormon district. The whigs expected, that the essential services they had rendered to the Mormons, by procuring the discharge of their prophet, would secure them the support of the Mormon vote for their own candidate, Cyrus Walker, but they were outgeneraled by the democrats, who terrified the saints with the prospect of the militia being sent against them, in case they voted for the whig candidate;

which was, without doubt, the cause of the vision of Hiram Smith, patriarch in the Mormon Church, and brother of the prophet; in which God had revealed to him, that the Mormons must support Mr. Hoge, the democratic candidate. This vision, after the prophet himself had attested it to be a genuine one, decided the contest in favor of Mr. Hoge, who, having received 3000 votes in Nauvoo, was elected to Congress by 800 majority. Awful was the consternation of the whigs at this unexpected defeat: they again gave vent to their anger and boiling rage through the newspapers, which now, as formerly, teemed with accounts of the enormities and atrocities committed at Nauvoo; charging the democrats, who could consent to receive the votes of such miscreants, with horrible wickedness, well worthy of the fire of eternal damnation.

No further demand having been made by the Missourians for delivering up the prophet, the latter, together with his saints, continued in their usual course of arrogance and insolence. They published ordinances proclaiming, that no person in Nauvoo should be arrested on a foreign writ, without the approval of the Mayor, endorsed on the same; and that any person attempting to serve any foreign writ without any such approval, would be imprisoned for life. They also conceived the absurd idea of petitioning Congress to establish a separate territorial government for them in Nauvoo, thus rendering it morally certain, that they contemplated to erect an "imperium in imperio." Nay, to fill the measure of their arrogance, Joe Smith, in the spring of 1844, was announced by them as a candidate for the Presidency of the United States, and 3000 missionaries were despatched in every direction, to electioneer for their prophet, and to reveal the "fullness of the gospel" to the astonished multitude. The ridicule, with which these devoted missionaries were overwhelmed by all sensible men, was but the just reward of this crowning piece of Mormon folly.

About this time, the prophet instituted a new and select order of the priesthood, who were to be his nobility, and the defenders of his throne. He also instituted an order called the Danite Band, who were to be his chosen body-guard. He then caused himself to be anointed priest and king, claiming to descend, in direct line, from Joseph, the son of Jacob, and prescribing the form of the oath of allegiance to himself which every one of his followers was to take.

10

He also instituted a female order, called "Spiritual Wives;" revealing this doctrine, that no woman could be "sealed up to eternal life," except by selecting a Mormon elder, with whom she was to share at least once her bed; and that any man was allowed to have one wife, and yet, at the same time, in a mystical, spiritual way, might enjoy the possession of many others; the truth of which doctrines he demonstrated, by referring to the examples of Abraham, Jacob, David, and Solomon, the favorites of God; and was one of the first to illustrate their practical working, by seducing a number of women, and endeavoring to make the wife of William Law, one of his most talented disciples, his spiritual mistress. Such corrupt despotism could not be endured. William Law, an eloquent preacher, and five other leaders of the Mormons, resolved to set at naught the authority of the prophet, by establishing a newspaper in Nauvoo, intended to enlighten their brethren on their real condition, for which daring offence they were immediately tried by the Common Council, and having been abundantly convicted of innumerable crimes and misdemeanors, were ejected from the Mormon Church; their press, by order of the prophet, was scattered to the four winds. The expelled Mormons retired to Carthage, the county seat of Hancock county, and took out warrants against the Mayor and members of the Common Council, and others, who had been engaged in the outrage; these were, however, immediately taken before the Municipal Court, on a writ of habeas corpus, and discharged; upon which the seceding Mormons despatched a committee to the Governor, requesting him to call out the militia to assist them in arresting the offenders and bringing them to punishment. That high-handed proceeding, on the part of the prophet and his saints, by which the liberty of the press, one of the most sacred rights of a republican people, had been so rudely assailed, produced an immense excitement among a people already so much embittered against the Mormons, on account of their practice of voting in a body, so that none could aspire to the honors and offices of the county without the consent and approbation of the Mormons, who constituted the balance of power; as also on account of their apparent determination to establish a separate government, independent of the State; and, lastly, on account of their numerous robberies and petty larcenies. The militia of the county having been called out by the constables, to serve as a "posse comitatus," to assist in the execution of the process, the Governor, who, on receiving the complaints of the rejected Mormons, had resolved to visit in person that section of the country, in order to inquire, on the spot, into the particulars of the whole affair, arriving at Carthage on the 21st of June, 1844, found a large military force assembled, which was hourly increasing. Having placed the whole force then assembled at Carthage under the command of their proper officers, he called them together, explaining to them what he could do and was willing to do, and exhorting them to keep strict order and discipline, and not to violate the authority of the laws: to all these charges they cheerfully assented. Having received these assurances, the Governor despatched a force of ten men, with the constable, to Nauvoo, to make the necessary arrests, and escort the prisoners to head-quarters: to the culprits protection was to be extended, in case they should voluntarily submit.

In the meantime, Joe Smith, as Lieutenant-General of the Nauvoo Legion, had declared martial law in the city; the Mormons in the neighborhood of Nauvoo had marched to his assistance, the Legion had assembled under arms, and the city seemed one great military camp, all avenues to which were strictly guarded and watched. Upon the arrival of the constable and guard, the Mayor and Common Council at once agreed to surrender, and to proceed to Carthage early on the morning of the next day; but the constable and guard, who belonged to a faction of daring, violent spirits, who had secretly conspired to bring matters with the Mormons to extremities, made no effort to arrest them, nor would he stay one minute beyond the time allotted him, but immediately returned with the report, that the accused had fled, and could not be found.

Gov. Thomas Ford, who was soon informed of this base conduct of the constable and guard, reflecting that the season had just become suitable for the harvest, a delay of two weeks in the gathering of which might produce a general famine, and considering, also, that the terrible freshets at that time liable in all the rivers of the western country (one of which, the Mississippi, had risen several feet higher than was known before, overflowing the whole American bottom from eight to twenty feet deep, washing away houses, fences, and cattle, and nearly ruining the time-honored village of Kaskaskia; the other rivers, in proportion to the dimensions of their beds, causing as much damage as the Mississippi), would render all efforts to procure provisions, in case an expedition should be undertaken, totally unavailing, resolved to postpone the general calling out of the militia, giving, in the meantime, another opportunity to the accused to surrender. He therefore made a demand upon the officers of the Mormon Legion to surrender the arms, with which the Legion, at the time of their incorporation, had been furnished by the State, and required, that the prophet-mayor of Nauvoo, together with his brother Hiram, and other conspicuous Mormon leaders, be delivered up. The arms, consisting of 3 pieces of cannon and 220 stand of small arms, were immediately given up, and on the 24th day of June, the illustrious prophet and his brother, together with those of his associates, who had been summoned by the warrant, entered Carthage, surrendering themselves as prisoners to the constable, on an indictment of riot. Having given such pledges as the justice of the peace deemed necessary, that they would appear at court to answer the charge, they were all of them released, save the prophet and his brother, who were detained on a charge of treason. There being no witnesses present at the time, the justice of the peace postponed the examination, meanwhile committing the illustrious prisoners for safe keeping to the county jail, a massive stone building. The Governor then despatched a company of militia, under the command of Capt. Singleton, to Nauvoo, to guard the town and take command of the Legion.

The force assembled at Carthage consisted of about 1200 men, some 500 more being stationed at Warsaw. Nearly all of those, who resided in Hancock county were clamorous for marching into Nauvoo, pleading, that this measure was indispensable, to strike terror into the Mormons, and to seize some apparatus supposed to be there for the manufacture of bogus coin, together with the counterfeit money itself. The Governor yielding to their entreaties, the 27th of June was appointed for the march, and Golden's Point, near the Mississippi, about equi-distant from Nauvoo and Warsaw, designated as the place of rendezvous. Whilst preparations were making for the expedition, the Governor learned, that a plan had been set on foot by some of his own party, to fire, under the cover of night, upon the troops, on the day of their arrival in Nauvoo, accusing the Mormons of the deed:

for which they were to be massacred by the troops. Justly incensed at the barbarity of this plan, which would have cost the lives of thousands of inoffensive women and children, that a city like Nauvoo, then numbering 15,000 inhabitants, must necessarily contain; and irritated at the absurdity of the idea of taking the field against 3000 well-armed men, with a force of but 1700, scantily provisioned for two days, Gov. Ford, at a council of officers, convened on the morning of the 27th of June, strongly urged them to desist from their sanguinary designs; but seeing, that a majority of the council were even more anxious than before to march into Nauvoo, being fearful, lest a collision might take place, he ordered the troops to be disbanded, both at Carthage and Warsaw, with the exception of three companies, two of which were appointed to guard the jail, while with the third he proposed to march to Nauvoo himself, to intimidate the Mormons, and search for the bogus coin and the apparatus for manufacturing it, about which the officers were so much troubled. Having left Gen. Deming in command of Carthage, and entrusted to two companies, under the command of Capt. R. F. Smith, of the Carthage Grays, the keeping of the jail, they promising to discharge their duty strictly according to law, Gov. Ford proceeded to Nauvoo, accompanied by Col. Buckmaster and Capt. Dunn's company of dragoons. Whilst on his march, having been notified, that an attack upon the jail was meditated, he ordered, that the baggage-wagons return to Carthage, and hurried with the utmost speed to Nauvoo, where he immediately convoked an assembly of the citizens, to whom he stated, in what particular the laws had been violated by their leaders; also the excitement and hatred prevailing everywhere against them, and the causes of it, calling on them to keep the public peace; after which, having received a unanimous vote from the Mormons, that they would abide the laws and strictly observe their provisions, he returned on the evening of the same day, with the utmost despatch, to Carthage. He had scarcely proceeded two miles, when he was met by a Mormon, who told him, that the Smiths had been assassinated in jail early in the morning of that day. Anticipating the worst consequences from such a treacherous act, which was only too well calculated to rouse the fanatical, revengeful spirit of the Mormons, making them determined to wage a war of extermination, the Governor, in order to prepare for any emergency, lost no time in getting to Warsaw, where he found the people in the highest state of excitement, owing to some ridiculous and exaggerated reports, that he and his party had been furiously assailed by the Mormon Legion, and unless assistance was rendered in two days, would be cut up without mercy; which rumors had been circulated by the anti-Mormon party, to influence the public to take vengeance upon the Mormons. Such was the agitation of the public mind, that knowing himself to be distrusted by the anti-Mormon ultraists, both of the democratic and whig party, and finding his influence and command to be at an end, the Governor made application to the United States for 500 men of the regular army, which being refused, he made the best arrangements, that circumstances permitted, for the pacification and defence of the country. He also studiously inquired into the details of the assassination of the Smiths, and was informed, that the order to disband had reached the Warsaw force whilst on their march to Golden Point; when some two hundred of them, having disguised themselves by blackening their faces with powder and mud, hastened immediately to Carthage, where, of the two companies of the Carthage Grays appointed to guard the jail, but one remained, the other having disbanded and returned home. Having entered into communication with the remaining company, and made an arrangement, that the guard should fire at them with blank cartridges, when they stormed the jail, the conspirators rushed on to the assault, jumped over the fence, were fired upon by the guard, which, according to agreement, made no attempt to resist, and entered the prison, making their way at once to the room, where the prisoners, with two of their friends, who voluntarily bore them company, were confined. When the door was burst open, shots were immediately exchanged between the conspirators and the company in the room; Hiram Smith was instantly killed, and the prophet, who, after shooting down three of his assailants, with a six-barrelled pistol given him by his friends, had jumped out of the window, stunning himself so severely in his fall as to be unable to pursue his flight, was despatched by the conspirators below with four balls through his body.

Thus fell Joe Smith, the holy prophet of the Mormons; the most daring impostor in modern times, and by many of the Puritanic stock believed to have been the very incarnation of Satan. Totally ignorant of almost every fact in science, as well as in law, he made up in constructiveness and natural cunning, whatever in him was wanting of instruction. The animal nature largely preponderating in the man, he had not the genius to form any vast and comprehensive plans for the future; but whatever he did, was merely intended for present convenience, and gratification of his beastly lusts and desires. He was possessed of some qualities, which would have eminently fitted him for the stage, being always able to change his external appearance and conduct according to circumstances; at times affecting the deepest humiliation for his sins, suffering the most unspeakable tortures, as if burning already in the terrible fire of eternal damnation, and calling for the prayers of the brethren in his behalf, with a fearful, soul-stirring energy, and heart-rending earnestness; then again being exceedingly soft and gentle in his behavior; then again, loud and furious as "a highway robber," "swearing like a pirate and drinking like a sailor." He bore in his profile a strong resemblance to that of a boar; he was full six feet high, and endowed with a frame of uncommon vigor, to the superior strength of which he was no doubt much indebted for the influence he exercised over an ignorant people. Those of his followers, who aided and supported him in the administration of his government, were mostly unprincipled and bankrupt, but talented men, who claimed to have a right to teach to, or impose upon mankind a new religion, which might afford them a living, or some cheap glory. This class of men constituted the leaders, whilst their deluded followers were principally men of a weak and unstable character; this made them easily subject to the power of designing machinators; and of a dreamy and wandering disposition, and a ready belief in wonderful and supernatural matters. Many of the Mormons were notorious rogues; but the greater part of them were pitiable victims of a religious imposture, sincere and fanatical in their faith.

When the news of the death of their revered leaders reached the Mormons at Nauvoo, they were so stupefied by it as to remain quiet, much to the astonishment of every one. Many of them at first refused to believe the dire intelligence; others published revelations, that the prophet, in imitation of the Saviour, was to rise from the dead; and many maintained, by solemn oath, that they had seen him at the head of a celestial army, coursing the air on a magnificent white steed.

After the holy prophet had thus met with an untimely fate, Sidney Rigdon, who had been a member of the first presidency of the Church, composed of Joe and Hiram Smith and the twelve apostles, claimed the government of the Church, alleging a will of the prophet in his favor. Perhaps he might have succeeded in his pretensions, had he not, unfortunately, published a revelation imparted him from heaven, directing the Mormons to abandon the holy city of Nauvoo, and to remove to Pittsburgh; which at once destroyed his influence with the Mormons, who now confided the government of the Church to the twelve apostles, with Brigham Young, a cunning rascal, at their head.

Another election for members of Congress and for the Legislature, was to take place in August, 1844, and a presidential election was pending throughout the nation. The contest was carried on by the various parties with the most fierce and determined spirit, and as the Mormons participated in this contest, it being feared, that they would, as usual, cast their votes as a unit, thereby compelling every office-seeker to court the favors of that despised people, the hatred of the people against the Mormons soon rose to a terrible pitch of excitement; to allay this the Governor strongly recommended the Mormons not to vote. But a dexterous politician went to their city a few days before the election, and by artful representations and liberal promises of the support of the democratic party, induced the Mormons, who were foolish enough to believe him authorized to make such assurances, to vote the whole democratic ticket. This vote of the Mormons, the whig leaders, and many democrats desirous of making political capital, laid to the Governor's charge; which made the anti-Mormon ultraists more than ever determined to expel this body.

In the fall of 1844, the leaders of the anti-Mormons sent printed circulars to all the militia captains in Hancock and the neighboring counties of Missouri, inviting them to be present at a great wolf-hunt in Hancock. Arrangements were made for assembling several thousand men, provisioned for six days, the anti-Mormon press simultaneously renewing their crusade against the Mormons, whom they charged with the most horrible murders, thefts, rapes, and villanies of every kind.

In this state of affairs, the Governor applied to the chief officers of the State militia, who, uniting their exertions with his own, succeeded in raising a force of 500 volunteers, under command of Brigadier-General Hardin; with these the Governor proceeded to Hancock. He arrived in Hancock county on the 25th of October. The conspirators dispersed at his approach, and their leaders fled to Missouri. During his stay in the county, the Governor found out, that his officers and men were so much infected with anti-Mormon prejudices as to make it utterly impossible for him to control them. Determined to make the assassins of the Smiths, for whose protection in jail he had pledged his word, which had been so shamefully violated, feel the utmost rigor of the law, the Governor prepared to cross with a small force to Missouri, at Churchville, to seize three anti-Mormon leaders, accused of that murder; but had the mortification to see, that one of his own officers frustrated his design, by advising all against joining the expedition, and arranging privately the terms of surrender for the accused, whereupon two of them came forth and delivered themselves up. They were tried before Judge Young, in the summer of 1845, but although the Governor, being resolved to make the offenders pay the utmost penalty of the law, employed the most able lawyers in their prosecution, such was the influence of party faction, that the accused were all acquitted. At the next term, the leading Mormons were tried for the destruction of the heretical press; but the Mormons having, in their turn, impanelled a jury favorable to them, these accused were also acquitted. The result of these trials made it evident, that no one could be convicted of any crime in Hancock; which for a time rendered it impossible to administer the criminal law in that unhappy county, unless, indeed, by force of arms; so that, while the early French settlers seemed to have verified the assertion, that a virtuous and contented people do not only not require the paternal care of any kind of government, but are most happy without such, the people in Hancock county, on the other hand, seemed to establish the fact, that a corrupt and lawless people are fit objects to be ruled over by the iron hand of a despot, whose government is peremptorily demanded by their happiness and welfare.

During the course of the summer and fall of 1845, the hatred between the Mormons and anti-Mormons reached a higher degree of intensity, than ever before. The anti-Mormons, as usual, loaded their papers with startling descriptions of the awful wickedness and enormities of Nauvoo, loudly complaining of the thefts and robberies of the Mormons, and calling upon the people to rise and exterminate the miscreants. About this time, the deputy marshal went to Nauvoo to arrest some of the twelve apostles, against whom a suit had been commenced in the United States Circuit Court, on a note given in Ohio. He was threatened and abused for attempting to serve a process of law, and in a public assembly of the Mormons, after sanguinary addresses had been delivered by their leaders, it was unanimously resolved and agreed, that no process should be served in Nauvoo.

Not long after this, in the fall of 1845, the anti-Mormons of Lima and Green Plains held a meeting to plan a scheme for the expulsion of the Mormons. They agreed between themselves, that several of their own number should fire at the meeting-house, taking good care not to hurt any one. This was done, the house was fired at without any one being hurt, whereupon the anti-Mormons immediately broke up their meeting, and travelling over the country in every direction, spread the rumor, that the Mormons had commenced the work of death and extermination. Such intelligence was sure to gather a mob in a county like Hancock, many of the inhabitants of which had acquired a reputation for their desperate character, being always ready to indulge in their love of free fights, whenever a suitable occasion presented itself. A mob of anti-Mormons soon assembled at Lima, and proceeded to the settlements of some very poor Mormons in their neighborhood, threatening them with fire and sword, if they did not leave at once. The Mormons refusing to remove, the mob burnt down their houses, or rather hovels, compelling their wretched inmates to fly, in a state of utter destitution, to Nauvoo. Terrible was the wrath of the saints at Nauvoo, when they saw their brethren arrive in so pitiful a condition. The sheriff of the county, Jacob B. Backinstos, whom the Mormons had just succeeded in electing, immediately proceeded to Nauvoo, where he raised a posse of several hundred Mormons, with which he scoured the country, driving everything before him, occupied Carthage, and established a permanent Mormon garrison there. Afraid to be dealt with by the same measure, with which they had accommodated the Mormons, the anti-Mormons fled everywhere before the sheriff; some to Iowa and Missouri, others to the neighboring counties in Illinois. The anti-Mormons having left, by their flight, the sheriff and his Mormon friends undisputed masters of the country, the Mormons, whose houses had been burnt, sallied forth in their turn, destroying the habitations of their adversaries, laying waste the country with fire and sword, and plundering and carrying off, whatever admitted of any transportation. Upon receiving intelligence of these proceedings, the Governor hastened to Jacksonville, where, in a conference with Gen. Hardin, Major Warren, Judge Douglass, and Attorney-General McDougall, it was agreed, that these gentlemen should proceed to Hancock with whatever forces had been raised, to restore order in that distracted county. Having raised about 400 volunteers, Gen. Hardin lost no time in getting to Carthage, where he dispersed the Mormon garrison and put an end to the ravages of the Mormons, recalling the anti-Mormons, and prohibiting the assemblage of parties above four in number, either of Mormons or anti-Mormons.

The twelve apostles and the other leaders of the Mormons, satisfied by this time, that it would not do for the Mormons to remain any longer in the State, made arrangements with their enemies, through the intervention of the Governor and Gen. Hardin, for the unmolested removal of their people in the spring of 1846. The force of Gen. Hardin was diminished to 100 men, and Major W. B. Warren appointed their commander; he managed this force with such efficiency and skill as to render both parties afraid to set the laws at defiance during the winter.

In the meantime, the Mormons made the most enormous efforts for removal; all the houses in Nauvoo, not even excepting the temple, having been converted into workshops, so that before spring more than 12,000 wagons were in readiness for removing their families and effects. By the middle of May, about 16,000 Mormons had crossed the Mississippi on their march to California, leaving but a thousand of their number behind in Nauvoo, such as, having no money, or property which they might convert into money, were without the means of removing.

During the same month, the President called for four regiments of volunteers from Illinois for the Mexican war; this was no sooner known in Illinois, than nine regiments, numbering 8370 men, answered the call, though only four of them, amounting to 3720 men, could be taken. These regiments, as well as their officers, were everywhere foremost in the American ranks, and distinguished themselves by their matchless valor in the bloodiest battles fought throughout the campaign. Gen. Hardin, at the battle of Buena Vista, attacked and routed a body of Mexican infantry and lancers five times the number of his own, deciding, by his gallant charge, the victory for the Americans, which was won at the expense of his own life and that of many of his bravest men. At the same battle, Lieutenant-Colonel Weatherford, with his men, during the whole day stood the fire of the Mexican artillery, without being allowed to advance near enough to return it. Warren, Trail, Bissel, and Morrison, distinguished themselves by their intrepid valor at the same battle; Shields, Baker, Harris, and Coffey, are illustrious names, indissolubly connected with the glorious capture of Vera Cruz, and the not less famous storming of Cerro Gordo. In this latter action, when, after the valiant Gen. Shields had been placed hors du combat, the command of his force, consisting of two Illinois and one New York regiment, devolved upon Col. Baker, this officer with his men stormed with unheard-of prowess the last stronghold of the Mexicans, sweeping everything before them, and scattering the Mexican forces to the four winds. Such, indeed, was the intrepid valor and daring courage exhibited by the Illinoisian volunteers during the Mexican war, that their deeds will live in the memory of their countrymen until those latest times, when the very name of America shall have been forgotten.

After this slight digression, due to the memory of the Illinoisian heroes in the Mexican war, we return again to the Mormons. Although after June, 1846, but few of that people remained behind, their enemies, fearing, that enough of them had been left to control the elections, commenced again harassing and annoying them, until they had extorted the promise from the Mormon leaders, that their people should not vote at the next election. When this election, however, came off (August, 1846), the Mormons, without exception, voted the democratic ticket, which act terribly enraged the people against them. An outbreak of hostilities being looked for as unavoidable, whilst both parties were collecting their forces, the trustees of Nauvoo, belonging to the number of the new citizens, who had purchased the houses and property of the Mormons, who had removed, applied to the Governor for a force to protect them. A force of militia was raised, and Mayor Parker appointed their commander; but the abuse heaped upon this officer by the whig party, rendered it impossible for him to assist them effectually. As this force was about to march into the city, information reached the Governor, that the new citizens of Nauvoo were divided in two parties, one of which was friendly to the Mormons, whilst the other, being hostile to them, had been threatened with death by them, if they did not join in the defence of the city. The Governor lost no time, but sent M. Brayman, Esq., a distinguished citizen of Springfield, to Nauvoo, with strict orders, forbidding the Mormons to force the new citizens to join them against their will. Mr. Brayman went to Nauvoo, where it was agreed between him and the Mormons, that the latter should leave the State in two months, their arms to remain in custody of the State during the meantime, which treaty was agreed to by Gen. Singleton, Col. Chittenden, and others, on the part of the anti-Mormon forces, and Mayor Parker and some Mormon leaders, on the other side. But when the treaty was submitted to the anti-Mormon forces for ratification, it was rejected by them, whereupon Gen. Singleton and Col. Chittenden immediately retired from the command, which was at once assumed by Thomas S. Brockman, an ignorant, rough and uncouth Campbellite preacher, who was bitterly opposed to the Mormons, on account of their immoral practices; although he fully equalled, if he did not eclipse them in these, having been defaulter to a large amount, while collector of taxes, and having committed various other rogueries. With a force of 800 men, and five cannon, belonging to the State, he proceeded to Nauvoo, where an engagement in the suburbs was fought between his troops and about 150 Mormons, together with some of the new citizens, as their allies; in which, owing to the very safe distance at which both parties kept from each other, but one man was killed, and some three or four wounded on either side, although the battle raged with unabated fury the whole day, 9000 cannon-balls and an infinite number of bullets being fired on each side.

After this sanguinary battle, through the intervention of an anti-Mormon committee from Quincy, the remaining Mormons at last agreed to remove from the State. In the midst of the sickly season they were hurried in the boats and thrown upon the Iowa shore, without shelter or provisions; in consequence whereof, great numbers of them miserably perished. The new citizens, who had joined the Mormons in their defence of the city, were many of them ducked and "baptized" in the river, and the rest of them driven, at the point of the bayonet, across the river, by the horde of armed scoundrels under the command of the villanous Campbellite preacher, the professed servant of the meek and lowly Jesus.

Some of the new citizens returned several times to look after their property, but were brutally driven off each time. A reaction now took place, however, in the minds of the people, in favor of the oppressed; which the Governor no sooner perceived, than he started with about 200 men, raised in Springfield, to Hancock, in order to reinstate sixty families of the unfortunate new citizens in their homes, which had been unmercifully plundered in the meantime. Having succeeded in this, and having made diligent, but unsuccessful search, for the five pieces of cannon belonging to the State, he disbanded the principal part of his force, leaving Major Jackson and Capt. Connelly, with a force of 50 men, to stay in the county until the 15th of December, 1846, by which time the cold of winter was expected to put an end to the anti-Mormon disturbances; which expectation was realized.

While this bloody war was waged in Hancock county, between the followers of the prophet and their adversaries, an equally violent rebellion, though upon a smaller scale, broke out in the county of Massac, on the Ohio, the ancient settlement of horse-thieves, robbers, and counterfeiters, who had again become so numerous and well organized as to set the laws at defiance, by committing horrible murders and depredations. The honest portion of the people formed themselves into companies of regulators, and were about to order the rogues from the country, when the latter, in the election for county officers, which came off in August, 1846, voted all one way, thereby causing the election of a sheriff and other officers, who at once arrayed themselves in open hostility to the regulators, allowing some of the rogues, who had already been arrested, to escape from jail; wherefore, they were ordered by the regulators to leave the country at once.

In this state of things, the Governor issued an order to Brigadier-General John T. Davis, to examine into the disturbances and the causes thereof, calling out the militia, if order could not be restored by peaceable means. Gen. Davis proceeded to Massac, assembling the parties and settling their differences, as he supposed; he had, however, no sooner left the county, than new disturbances broke out, many of the regulators coming, this time, as far as from Kentucky, expelling the sheriff, with other officers, and some of the rogues; and summarily punishing every one, whether rogue or honest man, who dared to interfere with their violent proceedings.

Judge Scates, at the Circuit Court, not long afterwards held in Massac county, strongly urged the grand jury to inquire into the outrageous conduct of the regulators, whereupon indictments were found and warrants issued against a number of them, who were arrested by the sheriff and committed to jail. The regulators assembled from Kentucky and the neighboring counties of Illinois, threatening to lynch Judge Scates, if he ever returned to hold a court, and liberating their friends confined in the jail, expelling the sheriff and his friends from the country. The sheriff went to the Governor, then at Nauvoo, to apply to him for aid and protection. But the Governor, whose term of office was about to expire, refused to meddle with the affair, contenting himself with charging Dr. William J. Gibbs to call out the militia for the protection of the sheriff and other county officers, and the honest portion of the community. The militia, however, refused to turn out, and the regulators exercising uncontested sway over the county, caught a number of suspicious characters and tried them by committee, whipping and tarring and feathering those, who had been convicted, and taking many of them away as prisoners, of whom several were afterwards reported to "have gone to Arkansas:" by which was understood, that they had been drowned in the Ohio, and left to swim with the current of that river in the direction of Arkansas. On the 23d of December, 1846, a convention of regulators from the counties of Johnson, Massac, and Pope, assembled at Golconda, ordering the sheriff and the clerk of the county court of Massac, together with many other citizens, to leave the country within thirty days. The sheriff and many others accordingly left the country, remaining absent all winter. This was the last act of violence on the part of the regulators; the disturbances afterwards gradually passing away, being destined, like everything else, to come to an end.

CHAPTER VII.

THE term of office of Governor Thomas Ford, under whose administration, as already mentioned, the condition of the State had been very materially ameliorated, having expired in December, 1846, Augustus C. French was elected Governor of the State of Illinois; he assumed the reins of government the same month, delivering, on the 8th of December, 1846, an inaugural address to the Legislature, wherein he recommends, that all the available means of the State be brought into such a condition, that they might be applied to the final payment of her public debt. Although during his administration the debt was not further reduced, but even considerably enlarged, it was while he was Governor, that Illinois entered, with gigantic strides, upon the road of industry and prosperity, recovering entirely from her sunken position, rapidly increasing in population, and so wonderfully developing her immense resources, that in point of wealth, industry, and enterprise, Illinois now acknowledgedly ranks one of the first States of the Union; her debt is larger than before; but when we consider her population, nearly trebled, and her resources, in so short a time increased a hundred fold, it no longer excites the slightest apprehension in the mind of any sensible man intending to make Illinois his future home, aware, as he must be, that Illinois, having successfully opposed and combatted the hideous monster of repudiation, is just now reaping the reward due to the restless energy, activity, and intelligence of her citizens, enjoying the very highest standing and credit throughout the civilized world: whereas, but a few years since, she was discredited in every portion of the globe.

In the years 1846 and 1847, a movement was made for bringing together a large mass meeting, to deliberate upon the interests of the Western States; and this resulted in the assembling of the great "Harbor and River Convention," held at Chicago in the first week of July, 1847, which was a most important event in the history of Illinois, and had a very beneficial effect upon its destiny.

The attention of the citizens of Illinois having, for several years been turned to the necessity of revising the State Constitution, on August 31, 1847, a convention held for that purpose adopted the present constitution, which was ratified by the people, March 7, 1848, and went into operation on the 1st of April ensuing. Under the new constitution, Governor Augustus C. French was re-elected Governor of Illinois for the next four years, commencing with January, 1849. Upon comparing the old constitution, adopted in 1818, with the new one, it will be found that the latter is much more complete, having received many additions, besides several alterations, of which the following are the most important:

In the first place, while the old constitution, as will fully appear on reference to its third and fourth articles, made the appointment of most of the State officers, including even the Judges of the Supreme Court and inferior Courts, chiefly dependent upon the General Assembly, the new constitution renders the same officers, including the said Judges, eligible by the people, those only excepted, the right of whose appointment is vested in the Governor, as from the following parallel provisions of the new constitution, in whose fourth and fifth articles they are contained, will be circumstantially seen, to wit:

The Governor (in whom, by virtue of Section 1 of Article IV., the executive power of the State is vested, and who, according to Section 2 and 3 of Article IV. is to be elected once in four years, on the Tuesday next after the first Monday of November, and to enter upon the duties of his office on the second Monday of January succeeding—the first election of Governor, under the new constitution, having been held on the Tuesday next after the first Monday in November, 1848), by virtue of the 12th Section of the same Article, shall nominate, and by and with the advice and consent of the Senate (a majority of all the Senators concurring), appoint all officers, whose offices are established by the constitution, or which may be created by law, and whose appointments are not otherwise provided for; and no such officer shall be appointed or elected by the General Assembly.

According to the 14th Section of the same Article (IV.), a Lieu tenant-Governor shall be chosen at every election of Governor, in the same manner, continue in office for the same time, and possess the same qualifications; and shall, by virtue of his office, be Speaker of the Senate, have a right, when in committee of the whole, to debate and vote on all subjects, give the casting vote when the Senate are equally divided, and administer the government, whenever the Governor is unable to attend to his duties.

According to the 22d Section of the same Article (IV.), there shall be elected by the qualified electors of this State, at the same time with the election for Governor, a Secretary of State, whose term of office shall be the same as that of the Governor, who shall keep a fair register of the official acts of the Governor, and, when required, shall lay the same, and all papers, minutes, and vouchers, relative thereto, before either branch of the General Assembly, and shall perform such other duties as shall be assigned him by law; and shall receive a salary of eight hundred dollars per annum, and no more, except fees: Provided, that if the office of Secretary of State should be vacated by death, resignation, or otherwise, it shall be the duty of the Governor to appoint another, who shall hold his office until another Secretary shall be elected and qualified.

The 23d Section of the same Article (IV.) ordains, that there shall be chosen, by the qualified electors throughout the State, an Auditor of Public Accounts, who shall hold his office for the term of four years, and until his successor is qualified, and whose duties shall be regulated by law, and who shall receive a salary, exclusive of clerk hire, of one thousand dollars per annum for his services, and no more.

The 24th Section of the same Article (IV.) provides, that there shall be elected, by the qualified electors throughout the State, a State Treasurer, who shall hold his office for two years, and until his successor is qualified, whose duties may be regulated by law, and who shall receive a salary of eight hundred dollars per annum, and no more.

Regarding the Judiciary Department, Sections 2 and 3 of Article V. provide, that the Supreme Court shall consist of three judges, two of whom shall form a quorum, whose concurrence shall in all cases be necessary, and that the State shall be divided into three grand districts, as nearly equal as may be, and the qualified electors of each division shall elect one of the said judges for the term of nine years;

another of the said judges to be elected for six, and the third for three years.

The 7th Section of the same Article (V.) provides, that the State shall be divided into nine judicial districts, in each of which one Circuit Judge shall be elected by the qualified electors thereof; he shall hold his office for the term of six years, and until his successor shall be commissioned and qualified.

The 13th Section of the same Article (V.) ordains, that the first election for Justices of the Supreme Court, and Judges of the Circuit Court, should be held on the first Monday of September, 1848.

The 14th Section, that the second election for one Judge of the Supreme Court, should be held on the first Monday of June, 1852, and every three years thereafter an election for one Justice of the Supreme Court.

The 15th Section, that on the first Monday of June, 1853, and every sixth year thereafter, an election shall be held for Judges of the Circuit Courts: Provided, that whenever an additional circuit is created, provision may be made to hold the second election of such additional judge at the regular elections herein provided.

The 17th Section, that one County Judge shall be elected by the qualified voters of each county, who shall hold his office for four years, and until his successor is elected and qualified.

The 21st Section provides, that the Clerks of the Supreme and Circuit Courts, and State Attorneys, shall be elected at the first special election for judges, and the second election for Clerks of the Supreme Court on the first Monday of June, 1855, and every sixth year thereafter: the second election for Clerks of the Circuit Courts, and State Attorneys, shall be held on the Tuesday next after the first Monday of November, 1852, and every fourth year thereafter.

The 23d Section provides, that the election of all officers, and the filling of all vacancies that may occur by death, resignation, or removal, not otherwise directed or provided for by the constitution, shall be made in such a manner as the General Assembly shall direct: Provided, that no such officers shall be elected by the General Assembly.

The 27th Section, that there shall be elected, in each county in this State, in such districts as the General Assembly may direct, by the qualified electors thereof, a competent number of Justices of the

STATE CAPITOL, SPRINGFIELD.

Peace, who shall hold their offices for the term of four years, and until their successors shall have been elected and qualified; and they shall perform such duties, receive such compensation, and exercise such jurisdiction as may be prescribed by law.

The 28th Section, that there shall be elected, in each of the judicial circuits of the State, by the qualified electors thereof, one State's Attorney, who shall hold office for the term of four years, and until his successor shall be commissioned and qualified; who shall perform such duties, and receive such compensation, as may be prescribed by law: Provided, that the General Assembly may hereafter provide by law for the election, by the qualified voters of each county in the State, of one County Attorney for each county, in lieu of the State's Attorneys provided for in this Section; the term of office, duties, and compensation of which County Attorneys shall be regulated by law.

And the 29th Section of the same Article (V.) provides, that the qualified electors of each county shall elect a Clerk of the Circuit Court, who shall hold his office for the term of four years, and until his successor shall have been elected and qualified: who shall perform such duties and receive such compensation as may be prescribed by law. The Clerks of the Supreme Court shall be elected in each division, by the qualified voters thereof, for the term of six years, and until their successors shall have been elected and qualified; whose duties and compensation shall be provided by law.

In the second place, the third Section of the second Article, which, according to the old constitution, read thus: "No person shall be a representative, who shall not have attained the age of twenty-one years, who shall not be a citizen of the United States, and an inhabitant of this State;" has been so far changed in the new constitution, that now an age of twenty five years, and in addition to a United States citizenship, a residence of three years within the limits of the State, are required of a person before he can be elected a representative. The above ordinance, thus altered, constitutes the third Section of the third Article in the present constitution.

Thirdly, Section 6th, Article 2d, which, in the old constitution, was conceived in the following terms: "No person shall be a Senator, who has not arrived at the age of twenty-five years, who shall not be a citizen of the United States, and who shall not have resided one year in the county;" &c., has, in the new constitution, been so far altered, that at present an age of thirty years, a United States citizenship, a residence of five years in the State, and of one year within the electing county, are required to render a person eligible to the office of Senator. Thus altered, does the above law form the fourth Section of the third Article in the present constitution.

Fourthly, the fifth Section of Article 2d, which, in the old constitution, was couched in the following language: "The number of representatives shall not be less than twenty-seven nor more than thirty-six, until the number of inhabitants within this State shall amount to 100,000; and the number of Senators shall never be less than one-third, nor more than one-half of the number of representatives;" has thus been amended in the present constitution, the sixth Section of the third Article of which it forms, that the Senate is to consist of twenty-five, and the House of Representatives of seventy-five members, until the population of the State shall amount to one million. The population already exceeding this number, an additional amendment of the constitution will no doubt shortly become necessary.

Fifthly, the third Section of the third Article, which, in the old constitution, is thus expressed: "The Governor shall be at least thirty years of age, and have been a citizen of the United States thirty years, and resided for two years within the limits of this State;" has thus been amended in the present constitution, the fourth Section of the fourth Article of which it forms, that a candidate for the office of Governor must have attained his thirty-fifth year, and been ten years a resident of the State, and fourteen years a citizen of the United States.

Sixthly, the eighteenth Section of the second Article of the old constitution, fixing, by law, the yearly salary of the Governor at one thousand dollars, has been made the fifth Section of the fourth Article of the present constitution; granting the Governor an annual income of fifteen hundred dollars.

Lastly, the nineteenth Section of the third Article of the old constitution, which, determining by law the veto power on the part of the executive, has the following provisions in the old constitution: "The Governor for the time being, and the Judges of the Supreme Court, or a majority of them, together with the Governor, shall be and are hereby constituted a Council, to revise all bills about to be passed into laws by the General Assembly; and for that purpose shall assemble themselves from time to time, when the General Assembly shall be convened; for which service, nevertheless, they shall not receive any salary or consideration, under any pretence whatever; and all bills, which have passed the Senate and House of Representatives, shall, before they become laws, be presented to the said Council, for their revisal and consideration; and if, upon such revisal and consideration, it should appear improper to the said Council, or a majority of them, that the bill should become a law of this State, they shall return the same, together with their objections thereto, in writing, to the Senate or House of Representatives (in whichever the same shall have originated), who shall enter the objections set down by the Council at large in their minutes, and proceed to reconsider the said bill. But if, after such reconsideration, the Senate or House of Representatives shall, notwithstanding the said objections, agree to pass the same by a majority of the whole number of members elected, it shall, together with the said objections, be sent to the other branch of the General Assembly, where it shall also be reconsidered, and if approved by a majority of all the members elected, it shall become a law;" is thus shaped in the new constitution, the twenty-first section of the fourth Article of which it forms: "Every bill, which shall have passed the Senate and House of Representatives, shall, before it becomes a law, be presented to the Governor: if he approve, he shall sign it, but if not, he shall return it, with his objections, to the House in which it shall have originated; and the said House shall enter the objections at large on their journal, and proceed to reconsider it. If, after such reconsideration, a majority of the members elected shall agree to pass the bill, it shall be sent, together with the objections, to the other House, by which it shall likewise be reconsidered, and if approved by a majority of the members elected, it shall become a law, notwithstanding the objections of the Governor; but in all such cases, the votes of both Houses shall be determined by yeas and nays, to be entered on the journal of each House respectively."

Both constitutions, the old and the new one, here require the Governor to return any bill presented to him within ten days (Sundays, and the days intervening between the adjournment and the re-assembling of the General Assembly, in case the latter should adjourn previous to the expiration of the ten days, not being counted), otherwise the bill so presented shall become a law. In the new constitution, it will be observed, the Judges of the Supreme Court are excluded from sharing with the Governor in the privilege of exercising the veto power.

These being the principal alterations in the old constitution of the State, we now turn again to her history.

Here, it is worthy of special remark, that when the new constitution was formed, in 1847, a clause was introduced in it by which, if approved by the people, a special tax of two mills upon the dollar was levied, and was to be applied to extinguish the principal of the State debt. The people, in 1848, voted upon this provision separately, and adopted it by ten thousand majority. This, so far as we know, is the first instance, in which the people of a State deliberately taxed themselves, in order to pay an old and burthensome debt. It is a fine exhibition of the integrity of the citizens of Illinois, and has contributed much towards establishing the character and reputation she now enjoys in commercial circles, both in this country and in Europe.

The Illinois and Michigan Canal, which, for so long a time, remained in an unfinished condition, and for which so many fruitless struggles were made, was at length completed and opened for navigation, in the spring of 1848. Connecting Lake Michigan, at Chicago, with La Salle, the head of navigation on the Illinois river, it forms an uninterrupted water communication between the Lakes and the Mississippi, being 100 miles long, navigable for boats of the largest class, and in every respect one of the finest canals in the Union.

Upon inquiring, whether, besides the canal, other works of improvement had been proposed and carried out, we shall find, that since the State trusted to individual enterprise, what she herself, under the "internal improvement system," had failed to accomplish, railroads were projected, the rapid progress and completion of so many of which, within the short space of four years, must excite our just surprise. While, previous to February, 1852, there were but 95 miles of railroad in operation throughout the whole State, within the following four years 2315 additional miles of railroad were completed and put in operation, intersecting the State in every direction. The fact, that 2315 miles of railroad were completed in Illinois in four years, we leave as an achievement for future ages to emulate, and, if possible, excel.

The best part of the whole affair is, that they are all doing a fine business, and as they were so cheaply built over the beautiful prairies of the State, there is hardly room for doubt, but that they will pay handsome dividends to their enterprising stockholders; the Galena Road has paid as high as twenty-one per cent. in a single year. Of these various railroads, the one called "Illinois Central Railroad," being one of the most magnificent works in this or any other country, deserves particular notice. Its main track extends from Dunleith, a new town on the Mississippi, opposite Dubuque, Iowa, directly through the heart of the State, to Cairo, at the mouth of the Ohio. At Centralia, 112 miles north of Cairo, the Chicago branch leaves the main line, pursuing a direct course, a little east of the centre of the State, to Chicago. The distance from Chicago to Centralia is 251, and from Cairo to Dubuque 453 miles, making the total length of the road 704 miles.

The road owes its rapid completion to the generous grant made, in 1850, by Congress, to the State of Illinois, of 2,595,000 acres of land to aid in its construction, and on the 10th of February, 1851, the Legislature gave a charter to the present company, granting it all the land given by Congress to the State, on condition, that the road should be completed by 1857, and that after it was finished, seven per cent. of its gross receipts should be paid into the treasury of the State. The lands belonging to the road are worth, and will sell for far more than the road has cost; part has already been sold; the quality of the residue, now in the market, justifies the assertion, that so good an opportunity for men in moderate circumstances to secure a farm and a competency, will not be likely to occur again for many years.

Of the advantages bestowed by this great work upon the State, we need not speak. It runs through a country as rich in agricultural and mineral resources as any other sublunary region: it connects the Upper Mississippi and the Great Lakes with the Mississippi at Cairo, below which that majestic river is navigable for large steamers at all seasons of the year; giving Chicago a perpetual communication with the Southern States. A single glance upon the map, and its relations to the prosperity of the entire State will at once be understood. The completion of the road will involve an expenditure of nearly twenty millions of dollars.

In 1850, the national census returned the population at 851,470, an increase of about 80 per cent. since 1840, which, though less than that in previous decades, owing to the fact that emigrants had then just begun to locate in Wisconsin, Iowa, and Minnesota, a large portion of whom, it is known, went from Illinois, was yet a most rapid growth.

In 1851, the General Assembly, by an Act approved February 17, authorized a geological survey of the State, which is yet in progress, under the direction of J. G. Norwood, who, on the 5th of February, 1853, sent in a report, showing, how far he had succeeded in his labors, and establishing the fact, that large as the natural resources of the State of Illinois were already then estimated to be, they were yet very far underrated. Mr. Norwood is still engaged on his work; no further account of the results of his investigations have been published as yet.

At the election in November of that year, the people ratified the General Banking Law, the professed object of which, at the time of its adoption, was to furnish a well-regulated and well-secured paper currency, thereby driving from among the people worthless foreign paper money, and equally worthless domestic issues.

Governor Augustus C. French, who, in conformity with a plan of his, the adoption of which he earnestly urged upon the Legislature, to ascertain the true extent and condition of the State debt, by re-funding the various bonds and scrips into one uniform transferable stock, reducing thereby the motley mass of forms, of which the debt consisted, into a clear and tangible shape — had, by an Act of the General Assembly, passed February 28, 1847, been authorized to cause to be received from the holders, and cancelled, all the various kinds of State indebtedness (canal alone excepted); and to substitute therefor an issue of certificates of stock, or stock-bonds of a character uniform and transferable; those issued on account of the principal debt, to be allowed to bear like interest with those originally surrendered up, and those issued for overdue interest, or interest in arrear, to be forbidden to draw interest for ten years, or until after A. D. 1857: delivered, on the 3d of January, 1853, when his term of office was about to expire, to the eighteenth Assembly, a message, wherein, after reviewing the general condition of the State, and pointing out for correction some defects in the working of the General Banking Law, he proceeds to state, that the portion of the public debt required by law to be re-funded or exchanged for other and uniform securities, had been principally exchanged; that the small amount yet outstanding would soon be brought forward, which being done, the whole subject of the State debt would appear upon record in a shape easily to be understood by all. In the same message, he estimates the entire State debt at $16,724,177.41; the principal debt, exclusive of interest, of the canal, the affairs of which were, and, we presume, still are, managed by three trustees, acting for the stockholders and the State, amounting to five millions, which would be fully met and liquidated from the proceeds of the sales of land granted by Congress (alternate sections, five miles from each side of the canal), amounting to 230,000 acres, 70,000 of which had already been sold, up to the spring of 1851. Governor Augustus C. French retired from his office, which he had filled for six consecutive years, universally esteemed for the prudent discretion, integrity, and distinguished ability, with which he had administered the affairs of the State.

Joel A. Mattison was elected governor in his stead, and Gustavus Kœrner, a German by birth, Lieutenant-Governor of the State, at the same time. Joel A. Mattison assumed the reins of government, delivering, on the 10th of January, 1853, his inaugural message to the Legislature, wherein he speaks thus: "Our public debt, that for a time seemed almost to be a burden sufficient to prevent immigration to our State, has increased in amount until it now (January, 1853) reaches the large sum, principal and interest, of $16,724,177.41; but while this amount has been increasing at the rate of six per cent. per annum, our State has increased at the rate of over ten per cent. for the past few years on her taxable property, continually developing our resources, and adding largely to our population. What seemed almost a burden twelve years ago, is now looked upon as requiring no great effort on the part of the people to fully pay without any increase of taxation." He estimates its probable amount on January 1, 1857, at $10,275,262.41, and thinks it probable, that it would be entirely paid before 1865. These expectations of the Governor seem to be on the eve of being realized; for after pressing upon the Legislature the subject of improvement of the navigable rivers and lake harbors of the Western States by the General Government, and wisely recommending the adoption of a system of education, whereby every child in the State might be furnished with an education, that would fit them for every station and condition of life, in a message placed before the Legislature on the 1st of January, 1855, he estimates the entire State debt, inclusive of interest up to that date, at $17,944,652.89, whereupon he proceeds to speak thus:

"Besides paying enough to pay the entire interest upon the State debt each year, for the past two years, there has been paid and applied upon the arrearage of interest, and the principal of the debt, the sum of $2,750,037.96, being the sum of $1,375,018.98 each year, over and above the accruing interest, making, in all, paid on principal and interest during the past two years, the sum of $3,951,037.96. During the next two years, I confidently expect, that the amount from all sources derived from the available assets of the State, and the revenue applicable to the liquidation of the State debt, will be increased at least twenty per cent., which will render the calculation certain, that the views entertained two years ago will be more than realized in ten years, and I might say still sooner, but prefer to give full time. The past two years have realized over $750,037.96 more than enough to meet the calculation, that the debt would be paid, all but $74,080.62, in eleven years. It will be perceived, that a large amount has been paid at this time, more than enough to meet the calculation referred to, during the past two years; and that the principal and the interest of the debt is being absorbed and cancelled each year, while the revenue is rapidly increasing, and swelling the means of the State to pay."

Before concluding, the fact appears still worthy of being noticed, that, from 1853 to the spring of 1855, an immense excitement prevailed throughout the State, concerning the temperance question: which resulted in the repudiation, by 15,000 majority, of the Prohibitory Liquor Law, previously passed by the Legislature, on February 12th, 1855.

The advancement of the State of Illinois for the last few years, is best shown by the startling increase of her population, returned, by the census of 1855, at 1,300,251 souls; the rapid development of her agricultural and mineral resources — the State having, in one single year, produced 170,000,000 bushels of corn, wheat, and oats — an amount which no other State in the Union ever yielded in a year; her gigantic system of internal improvements, and the regard paid by her to thorough universal education, as well as the untiring energy, enterprise, and intelligence of her citizens, warrant the belief we fondly indulge, that ere three lustres shall have rolled by, the State of Illinois, in point of population, business facilities, wealth and intelligence, will proudly assume her well-deserved position as the Empire State of the West.

CONSTITUTION OF THE STATE.

PREAMBLE.

We, the people of the state of Illinois—grateful to Almighty God for the civil, political, and religious liberty, which he hath so long permitted us to enjoy, and looking to him for a blessing upon our endeavors to secure and transmit the same unimpaired to succeeding generations—in order to form a more perfect government, establish justice, insure domestic tranquillity, provide for the common defence, promote the general welfare, and secure the blessings of liberty to ourselves and our posterity, do ordain and establish this constitution for the state of Illinois.

Article I.—*Boundaries.*

Sec. 1. The boundaries and jurisdiction of the state shall be as follows, to wit: beginning at the mouth of the Wabash river; thence up the same, and with the line of Indiana, to the north-west corner of said state; thence east, with the line of the same state, to the middle of Lake Michigan; thence north, along the middle of said lake, to north latitude forty-two degrees and thirty minutes; thence west to the middle of the Mississippi river, and thence down, along the middle of that river, to its confluence with the Ohio river; and thence up the latter river, along its north-western shore, to the place of beginning: *Provided,* that this state shall exercise such jurisdiction upon the Ohio river as she is now entitled to, or such as may hereafter be agreed upon by this state and the state of Kentucky.

Article II.—*Concerning the Distribution of the Powers of Government.*

Sec. 1. The powers of the government of the state of Illinois shall be divided into three distinct departments, and each of them be confided to a separate body of magistracy, to wit: those which are legislative, to one; those which are executive, to another; and those which are judicial, to another.

2. No person, or collection of persons, being one of these departments, shall exercise any power properly belonging to either of the others, except as hereinafter expressly directed or permitted, and all acts in contravention of this section shall be void.

ARTICLE III.—*Of the Legislative Department.*

SEC. 1. The legislative authority of this state shall be vested in a general assembly, which shall consist of a senate and house of representatives, both to be elected by the people.

2. The first election for senators and representatives shall be held on the Tuesday after the first Monday in November, one thousand eight hundred and forty-eight; and thereafter, elections for members of the general assembly shall be held once in two years, on the Tuesday next after the first Monday in November, in each and every county, at such places therein as may be provided by law.

3. No person shall be a representative who shall not have attained the age of twenty-five years; who shall not be a citizen of the United States, and three years an inhabitant of this state; who shall not have resided within the limits of the county or district in which he shall be chosen twelve months next preceding his election, if such county or district shall have been so long erected, but, if not, then within the limits of the county or counties, district or districts, out of which the same shall have been taken, unless he shall have been absent on the public business of the United States or of this state; and who, moreover, shall not have paid a state or county tax.

4. No person shall be a senator who shall not have attained the age of thirty years; who shall not be a citizen of the United States, five years an inhabitant of this state, and one year in the county or district in which he shall be chosen immediately preceding his election, if such county or district shall have been so long erected, but, if not, then within the limits of the county or counties, district or districts, out of which the same shall have been taken, unless he shall have been absent on the public business of the United States or of this state, and shall not, moreover, have paid a state or county tax.

5. The senators at their first session, herein provided for, shall be divided by lot, as near as can be, into two classes. The seats of the first class shall be vacated at the expiration of the second year, and those of the second class at the expiration of the fourth year; so that one half thereof, as near as possible, may be biennially chosen for ever thereafter.

6. The senate shall consist of twenty-five members, and the house of representatives shall consist of seventy-five members, until the population of the state shall amount to one million of souls, when five members may be added to the house, and five additional members for every five hundred thousand inhabitants thereafter, until the whole number of representatives shall amount to one hundred; after which the number shall be neither increased nor diminished; to be apportioned among the several counties according to the number of white inhabitants. In all future apportionments, where more than one county shall be thrown into a representative district, all the representatives to which said counties may be entitled shall be elected by the entire district.

7. No person elected to the general assembly shall receive any civil appoint-

ment within this state, or to the senate of the United States, from the governor, the governor and senate, or from the general assembly, during the term for which he shall have been elected; and all such appointments, and all votes given for any such member for any such office or appointment, shall be void; nor shall any member of the general assembly be interested, either directly or indirectly, in any contract with the state, or any county thereof, authorised by any law passed during the time for which he shall have been elected, or during one year after the expiration thereof.

8. In the year one thousand eight hundred and fifty-five, and every tenth year thereafter, an enumeration of all the inhabitants of this state shall be made in such manner as shall be directed by law; and in the year eighteen hundred and fifty, and every tenth year thereafter, the census taken by authority of the government of the United States, shall be adopted by the general assembly as the enumeration of this state; and the number of senators and representatives shall, at the first regular session holden after the returns herein provided for are made, be apportioned among the several counties or districts to be established by law, according to the number of white inhabitants.

9. Senatorial and representative districts shall be composed of contiguous territory, bounded by county lines; and only one senator allowed to each senatorial, and not more than three representatives to any representative district: *Provided*, that cities and towns, containing the requisite population, may be erected into separate districts.

10. In forming senatorial and representative districts, counties containing a population of not more than one-fourth over the existing ratio, shall form separate districts, and the excess shall be given to the nearest county or counties not having a senator or representative, as the case may be, which has the largest white population.

11. The first session of the general assembly shall commence on the first Monday of January, one thousand eight hundred and forty-nine; and for ever after the general assembly shall meet on the first Monday of January next ensuing the election of the members thereof, and at no other period, unless as provided by this constitution.

12. The senate and house of representatives, when assembled, shall each choose a speaker and other officers (the speaker of the senate excepted). Each house shall judge of the qualifications and election of its members, and sit upon its own adjournments. Two-thirds of each house shall constitute a quorum; but a smaller number may adjourn from day to day, and compel the attendance of absent members.

13. Each house shall keep a journal of its proceedings, and publish them. The yeas and nays of the members on any question shall, at the desire of any two of them, be entered on the journals.

14. Any two members of either house shall have liberty to dissent and

protest against any act or resolution, which they may think injurious to the public, or to any individual, and have the reasons of their dissent entered on the journals.

15. Each house may determine the rules of its proceedings, punish its members for disorderly behavior, and, with the concurrence of two-thirds of all the members elected, expel a member, but not a second time for the same cause; and the reason for such expulsion shall be entered upon the journal, with the names of the members voting on the question.

16. When vacancies happen in either house, the governor, or the person exercising the powers of governor, shall issue writs of election to fill such vacancies.

17. Senators and representatives shall in all cases, except treason, felony, or breach of the peace, be privileged from arrest during the session of the general assembly, and in going to and returning from the same; and for any speech or debate in either house, they shall not be questioned in any other place.

18. Each house may punish by imprisonment, during its session, any person, not a member, who shall be guilty of disrespect to the house, by any disorderly or contemptuous behavior in their presence: *Provided*, such imprisonment shall not, at any one time, exceed twenty-four hours.

19. The doors of each house, and of committees of the whole, shall be kept open, except in such cases as, in the opinion of the house, require secresy. Neither house shall, without the consent of the other, adjourn for more than two days, nor to any other place than that in which the two houses shall be sitting.

20. The style of the laws of this state shall be: "*Be it enacted by the people of the state of Illinois, represented in the general assembly.*"

21. Bills may originate in either house, but may be altered, amended, or rejected by the other; and on the final passage of all bills, the vote shall be by ayes and noes, and shall be entered on the journal; and no bill shall become a law without the concurrence of a majority of all the members elect in each house.

22. Bills making appropriations for the pay of the members and officers of the general assembly, and for the salaries of the officers of the government, shall not contain any provision on any other subject.

23. Every bill shall be read on three different days in each house, unless, in case of urgency, three-fourths of the house, where such bill is so depending, shall deem it expedient to dispense with this rule; and every bill, having passed both houses, shall be signed by the speakers of their respective houses; and no private or local law which may be passed by the general assembly, shall embrace more than one subject, and that shall be expressed in the title. And no public act of the general assembly shall take effect or be in force, until the expiration of sixty days from the end of the session at which the same

may be passed, unless, in case of emergency, the general assembly shall otherwise direct.

24. The sum of two dollars per day, for the first forty-two days' attendance, and one dollar per day for each day's attendance thereafter, and ten cents for each necessary mile's travel, going to and returning from the seat of government, shall be allowed to the members of the general assembly, as a compensation for their services, and no more. The speaker of the house of representatives shall be allowed the sum of one dollar per day, in addition to his per diem as a member.

25. The per diem and mileage allowed to each member of the general assembly, shall be certified by the speakers of their respective houses, and entered on the journals, and published at the close of each session.

26. No money shall be drawn from the treasury, but in consequence of appropriations made by law; and an accurate statement of the receipts and expenditures of the public money shall be attached to, and published with, the laws at the rising of each session of the general assembly. And no person, who has been or may be a collector or holder of public moneys, shall be eligible to a seat in either house of the general assembly, nor be eligible to any office of profit or trust in this state, until such person shall have accounted for, and paid into the treasury, all sums for which he may be accountable.

27. The house of representatives shall have the sole power of impeaching; but a majority of all the members elected, must concur in an impeachment. All impeachments shall be tried by the senate; and when sitting for that purpose, the senators shall be upon oath, or affirmation, to do justice according to law and evidence. No person shall be convicted without the concurrence of two-thirds of the senators elected.

28. The governor, and other civil officers under this state, shall be liable to impeachment for any misdemeanor in office; but judgment in such cases shall not extend further than to removal from office, and disqualification to hold any office of honor, profit, or trust, under this state. The party, whether convicted or acquitted, shall, nevertheless, be liable to indictment, trial, judgment, and punishment, according to law.

29. No judge of any court of law or equity, secretary of state, attorney general, attorney for the state, recorder, clerk of any court of record, sheriff or collector, member of either house of Congress, or person holding any lucrative office under the United States or of this state — provided, that appointments in the militia, or justices of the peace, shall not be considered lucrative offices — shall have a seat in the general assembly; nor shall any person, holding any office of honor or profit under the government of the United States, hold any office of honor or profit under the authority of this state.

30. Every person who shall be chosen or appointed to any office of trust or profit shall, before entering upon the duties thereof, take an oath to support the constitution of the United States, and of this state, and also an oath of office.

31. The general assembly shall have full power to exclude from the privilege of electing, or being elected, any person convicted of bribery, perjury, or other infamous crime.

32. The general assembly shall have no power to grant divorces, but may authorize the courts of justice to grant them for such causes as may be specified by law: *Provided,* that such laws be general and uniform in their operation.

33. The general assembly shall never grant or authorize extra compensation to any public officer, agent, servant, or contractor, after the service shall have been rendered, or the contract entered into.

34. The general assembly shall direct by law in what manner suits may be brought against the state.

35. The general assembly shall have no power to authorize lotteries for any purpose, nor to revive or extend the charter of the State bank, or the charter of any other bank heretofore existing in this state, and shall pass laws to prohibit the sale of lottery-tickets in this state.

36. The general assembly shall have no power to authorize, by private or special law, the sale of any lands or other real estate belonging in whole or in part to any individual or individuals.

37. Each general assembly shall provide for all the appropriations necessary for the ordinary and contingent expenses of the government until the adjournment of the next regular session, the aggregate amount of which shall not be increased without a vote of two-thirds of each house, nor exceed the amount of revenue authorized by law to be raised in such time: *Provided,* the state may, to meet casual deficits or failures in revenues, contract debts, never to exceed in the aggregate, fifty thousand dollars; and the moneys thus borrowed shall be applied to the purpose for which they were obtained, or to repay the debt thus made, and to no other purpose; and no other debt, except for the purpose of repelling invasion, suppressing insurrection, or defending the state in war (for payment of which the faith of the state shall be pledged), shall be contracted, unless the law authorizing the same shall, at a general election, have been submitted to the people, and have received a majority of all the votes cast for members of the general assembly at such election. The general assembly shall provide for the publication of said law for three months, at least, before the vote of the people shall be taken upon the same; and provision shall be made, at the time, for the payment of the interest annually, as it shall accrue, by a tax levied for the purpose, or from other sources of revenue; which law, providing for the payment of such interest by such tax, shall be irrepealable until such debt be paid: *And provided, further,* that the law levying the tax shall be submitted to the people with the law authorizing the debt to be contracted.

38. The credit of the state shall not, in any manner, be given to, or in aid of, any individual, association, or corporation.

39. The general assembly shall provide, by law, that the fuel and stationery furnished for the use of the state, the copying, printing, binding, and distributing the laws and journals, and all other printing ordered by the general assembly, shall be let, by contract, to the lowest responsible bidder; and that no member of the general assembly, or other officer of the state, shall be interested, either directly or indirectly, in any such contract: *Provided*, that the general assembly may fix a maximum price.

40. Until there shall be a new apportionment of senators and representatives, the state shall be divided into senatorial and representative districts; and the senators and representatives shall be apportioned among the several districts as follows, viz:—

Senatorial Districts.

1. The counties of Alexander, Union, Pulaski, Johnson, Massac, Pope, and Hardin, shall constitute the first senatorial district, and shall be entitled to one senator.

2. The counties of Gallatin, Saline, Williamson, Franklin, and White, shall constitute the second senatorial district, and be entitled to one senator.

3. The counties of Jefferson, Wayne, Marion, and Hamilton, shall constitute the third senatorial district, and be entitled to one senator.

4. The counties of Washington, Perry, Randolph, and Jackson, shall constitute the fourth senatorial district, and be entitled to one senator.

5. The counties of St. Clair and Monroe, shall constitute the fifth senatorial district, and be entitled to one senator.

6. The counties of Madison and Clinton, shall constitute the sixth senatorial district, and be entitled to one senator.

7. The counties of Christian, Shelby, Montgomery, Bond, and Fayette, shall constitute the seventh senatorial district, and be entitled to one senator.

8. The counties of Effingham, Jasper, Clay, Richland, Lawrence, Edwards, and Wabash, shall constitute the eighth senatorial district, and be entitled to one senator.

9. The counties of Edgar, Clark, and Crawford, shall constitute the ninth senatorial district, and be entitled to one senator.

10. The counties of Vermilion, Champaign, Piatt, Moultrie, Coles, and Cumberland, shall constitute the tenth senatorial district, and be entitled to one senator.

11. The counties of Tazewell, McLean, Logan, De Witt, and Macon, shall constitute the eleventh senatorial district, and be entitled to one senator.

12. The counties of Sangamon, Menard, and Mason, shall constitute the twelfth senatorial district, and be entitled to one senator.

13. The counties of Macoupin, Jersey, Greene, and Calhoun, shall constitute the thirteenth senatorial district, and be entitled to one senator.

14. The counties of Morgan, Scott, and Cass, shall constitute the fourteenth senatorial district, and be entitled to one senator.

15. The counties of Adams and Pike shall constitute the fifteenth senatorial district, and be entitled to one senator.

16. The counties of McDonough, Schuyler, Brown, and Highland, shall constitute the sixteenth senatorial district, and be entitled to one senator.

17. The counties of Hancock and Henderson shall constitute the seventeenth senatorial district, and be entitled to one senator.

18. The counties of Fulton and Peoria shall constitute the eighteenth senatorial district, and be entitled to one senator.

19. The counties of Rock Island, Henry, Mercer, Warren, Knox, and Stark, shall constitute the nineteenth senatorial district, and be entitled to one senator.

20. The counties of La Salle, Bureau, Putnam, Marshall, Woodford, Livingston, and Grundy, shall constitute the twentieth senatorial district, and be entitled to one senator.

21. The counties of Du Page, Kendall, Will, and Iroquois, shall constitute the twenty-first senatorial district, and be entitled to one senator.

22. The counties of Ogle, Lee, De Kalb, and Kane, shall constitute the twenty-second senatorial district, and be entitled to one senator.

23. The counties of Jo Daviess, Stephenson, Carroll, and Whiteside, shall constitute the twenty-third senatorial district, and be entitled to one senator.

24. The counties of McHenry, Boone, and Winnebago, shall constitute the twenty-fourth senatorial district, and be entitled to one senator.

25. The counties of Cook and Lake shall constitute the twenty-fifth senatorial district, and be entitled to one senator.

Representative Districts.

1. The counties of Union, Alexander, and Pulaski, shall constitute the first representative district, and be entitled to one representative.

2. The counties of Massac, Pope, and Hardin, shall constitute the second representative district, and be entitled to one representative.

3. The counties of Gallatin and Saline shall constitute the third representative district, and be entitled to one representative.

4. The counties of Johnson and Williamson shall constitute the fourth representative district, and be entitled to one representative.

5. The counties of Jackson and Franklin shall constitute the fifth representative district, and be entitled to one representative.

6. The counties of Marion, Jefferson, Wayne, and Hamilton, shall constitute the sixth representative district, and be entitled to three representatives: *Provided*, that no county in said district shall have more than one of said representatives, and the county from which a senator shall be selected, shall not be entitled to a representative residing in said county.

7. The county of White shall constitute the seventh representative district, and be entitled to one representative.

8. The counties of Wabash and Edwards shall constitute the eighth representative district, and be entitled to one representative.

9. The counties of Lawrence and Richland shall constitute the ninth representative district, and be entitled to one representative.

10. The counties of Crawford and Jasper shall constitute the tenth representative district, and be entitled to one representative.

11. The county of Coles shall constitute the eleventh representative district, and be entitled to one representative.

12. The county of Clark shall constitute the twelfth representative district, and be entitled to one representative.

13. The counties of Cumberland, Effingham, and Clay, shall constitute the thirteenth representative district, and be entitled to one representative.

14. The county of Fayette shall constitute the fourteenth representative district, and be entitled to one representative.

15. The counties of Montgomery, Bond, and Clinton, shall constitute the fifteenth representative district, and be entitled to two representatives.

16. The counties of Washington and Perry shall constitute the sixteenth representative district, and be entitled to one representative.

17. The county of Randolph shall constitute the seventeenth representative district, and be entitled to one representative.

18. The county of Monroe shall constitute the eighteenth representative district, and be entitled to one representative.

19. The county of St. Clair shall constitute the nineteenth representative district, and be entitled to two representatives.

20. The county of Madison shall constitute the twentieth representative district, and be entitled to two representatives.

21. The county of Macoupin shall constitute the twenty-first representative district, and be entitled to one representative.

22. The counties of Jersey and Greene shall constitute the twenty-second representative district, and be entitled to two representatives.

23. The county of Scott shall constitute the twenty-third representative district, and be entitled to one representative.

24. The county of Morgan shall constitute the twenty-fourth representative district, and be entitled to two representatives.

25. The counties of Cass and Menard shall constitute the twenty-fifth representative district, and be entitled to one representative.

26. The county of Sangamon shall constitute the twenty-sixth representative district, and be entitled to two representatives.

27. The counties of Mason and Logan shall constitute the twenty-seventh representative district, and be entitled to one representative.

28. The county of Tazewell shall constitute the twenty-eighth representative district, and be entitled to one representative.

29. The counties of McLean and De Witt shall constitute the twenty-ninth representative district, and be entitled to one representative.

30. The county of Vermilion shall constitute the thirtieth representative district, and be entitled to one representative.

31. The county of Edgar shall constitute the thirty-first representative district, and be entitled to one representative.

32. The counties of Champaign, Platt, Moultrie, and Macon, shall constitute the thirty-second representative district, and be entitled to one representative.

33. The counties of Shelby and Christian shall constitute the thirty-third representative district, and be entitled to one representative.

34. The counties of Pike and Calhoun shall constitute the thirty-fourth representative district, and be entitled to two representatives.

35. The counties of Adams, Highland, and Brown, shall constitute the thirty-fifth representative district, and be entitled to three representatives.

36. The county of Schuyler shall constitute the thirty-sixth representative district, and be entitled to one representative.

37. The county of Hancock shall constitute the thirty-seventh representative district, and be entitled to two representatives.

38. The county of McDonough shall constitute the thirty-eighth representative district, and be entitled to one representative.

39. The county of Fulton shall constitute the thirty-ninth representative district, and be entitled to two representatives.

40. The county of Peoria shall constitute the fortieth representative district, and be entitled to one representative.

41. The county of Knox shall constitute the forty-first representative district, and be entitled to one representative.

42. The counties of Mercer, Warren, and Henderson, shall constitute the forty-second representative district, and be entitled to two representatives.

43. The counties of Rock Island, Henry, and Stark, shall constitute the forty-third representative district, and be entitled to one representative.

44. The counties of Whiteside and Lee shall constitute the forty-fourth representative district, and be entitled to one representative.

45. The counties of Carroll and Ogle shall constitute the forty-fifth representative district, and be entitled to one representative.

46. The counties of Jo Daviess and Stephenson shall constitute the forty-sixth representative district, and be entitled to two representatives.

47. The county of Winnebago shall constitute the forty-seventh representative district, and be entitled to one representative.

48. The counties of Putnam, Marshall, and Woodford, shall constitute the forty-eighth representative district, and be entitled to one representative.

49 The counties of La Salle, Grundy, Livingston, and Bureau, shall constitute the forty-ninth representative district, and be entitled to two representatives.

50. The counties of Du Page, Kendall, Will, and Iroquois, shall constitute the fiftieth representative district, and be entitled to three representatives.

51. The counties of Kane and De Kalb shall constitute the fifty-first representative district, and be entitled to two representatives.

52. The counties of Boone and McHenry shall constitute the fifty-second representative district, and be entitled to two representatives.

53. The county of Lake shall constitute the fifty-third representative district, and be entitled to one representative.

54. The county of Cook shall constitute the fifty-fourth representative district, and be entitled to two representatives.

SEC. 41. Until the general assembly shall otherwise provide, the clerks of the county commissioners' courts, in each of the aforesaid senatorial districts, and in such of the representative districts as may be composed of more than one county, shall meet at the county seat of the oldest county in said district, within thirty days next after any election for senator or representative therein, for the purpose of comparing and canvassing the votes given at such election; and the said clerks shall, in all other respects, conform to the laws on the subject in force at the time of the adoption of this constitution.

ARTICLE IV.—*Of the Executive Department.*

SEC. 1. The executive power of the state shall be vested in a governor.

2. The first election of governor shall be held on Tuesday next after the first Monday in November, A. D. 1848; and the next election shall be held on Tuesday next after the first Monday of November, A. D. 1852; and thereafter an election for governor shall be held once in four years, on Tuesday next after the first Monday of November. The governor shall be chosen by the electors of the members of the general assembly, at the same places and in the same manner that they shall, respectively, vote for members thereof. The returns for every election of governor shall be sealed up, and transmitted to the seat of government, by the returning officers, directed to the speaker of the house of representatives, who shall open and publish them in the presence of a majority of the members of each house of the general assembly. The person having the highest number of votes shall be governor; but if two or more be equal and highest in votes, then one of them shall be chosen governor by joint ballot of both houses of the general assembly. Contested elections shall be determined by both houses of the general assembly, in such manner as shall be prescribed by law.

3. The first governor shall enter upon the duties of his office on the second Monday of January, A. D. 1849, and shall hold his office until the second Monday of January, A. D. 1853, and until his successor shall have been elected and qualified; and thereafter the governor shall hold his office for the term of four years, and until his successor shall have been elected and qualified; but he shall not be eligible to such office more than four years in any term of eight years, nor to any other office until after the expiration of the term for which he was elected.

4. No person, except a citizen of the United States, shall be eligible to the office of governor; nor shall any person be eligible to that office, who shall not have attained the age of thirty-five years, and been ten years a resident of this state, and fourteen years a citizen of the United States.

5. The governor shall reside at the seat of government, and receive a salary of fifteen hundred dollars per annum, which shall not be increased or diminished; and he shall not, during the time for which he shall have been elected, receive any emolument from the United States, or either of them.

6. Before he enters upon the duties of his office, he shall take the following oath or affirmation, to wit: "I do solemnly swear [or affirm], that I will faithfully execute the duties appertaining to the office of governor of the state of Illinois; and will, to the best of my ability, preserve, protect, and defend the constitution of this state; and will, also, support the constitution of the United States."

7. He shall, from time to time, give the general assembly information of the state of the government, and recommend to their consideration, such measures as he shall deem expedient.

8. The governor shall have power to grant reprieves, commutations, and pardons, after conviction, for all offences, except treason and cases of impeachment, upon such conditions and with such restrictions and limitations as he may think proper, subject to such regulations as may be provided by law, relative to the manner of applying for pardons. Upon conviction for treason, he shall have power to suspend the execution of the sentence, until the case shall be reported to the general assembly at its next meeting, when the general assembly shall pardon the convict, commute the sentence, direct the execution thereof, or grant a further reprieve. He shall, biennially, communicate to the general assembly each case of reprieve, commutation, or pardon granted, stating the name of the convict, the crime for which he was convicted, the sentence and its date, and the date of commutation, pardon, or reprieve.

9. He may require information in writing from the officers in the executive department, upon any subject relating to the duties of their respective offices, and shall take care, that the laws be faithfully executed.

10. He may, on extraordinary occasions, convene the general assembly by proclamation, and shall state, in said proclamation, the purpose for which they are to convene; and the general assembly shall enter on no legislative business, except that for which they were specially called together.

11. He shall be commander-in-chief of the army and navy of this state, and of the militia, except when they shall be called into the service of the United States.

12. The governor shall nominate, and, by and with the advice and consent of the senate (a majority of all the senators concurring), appoint all officers whose offices are established by this constitution, or which may be created by

law, and whose appointments are not otherwise provided for; and no such officer shall be appointed or elected by the general assembly.

13. In case of disagreement between the two houses with respect to the time of adjournment, the governor shall have power to adjourn the general assembly to such time as he thinks proper, provided it be not to a period beyond the next constitutional meeting of the same.

14. A lieutenant-governor shall be chosen at every election of governor, in the same manner, continue in office for the same time, and possess the same qualifications. In voting for governor and lieutenant-governor, the electors shall distinguish whom they vote for as governor, and whom as lieutenant-governor.

15. The lieutenant-governor shall, by virtue of his office, be speaker of the senate, have a right, when in committee of the whole, to debate and vote on all subjects, and, whenever the senate are equally divided, to give the casting vote.

16. Whenever the government shall be administered by the lieutenant-governor, or he shall be unable to attend as speaker of the senate, the senators shall elect one of their own number as speaker for that occasion; and if, during the vacancy of the office of governor, the lieutenant-governor shall be impeached, removed from office, refuse to qualify, or resign, or die, or be absent from the state, the speaker of the senate shall, in like manner, administer the government.

17. The lieutenant-governor, while he acts as speaker of the senate, shall receive for his services the same compensation which shall, for the same period, be allowed to the speaker of the house of representatives, and no more.

18. If the lieutenant governor shall be called upon to administer the government, and shall, while in such administration, resign, die, or be absent from the state, during the recess of the general assembly, it shall be the duty of the secretary of state, for the time being, to convene the senate for the purpose of choosing a speaker.

19. In case of the impeachment of the governor, his absence from the state, or inability to discharge the duties of his office, the powers, duties, and emoluments of the office shall devolve upon the lieutenant-governor; and in case of his death, resignation, or removal, then upon the speaker of the senate for the time being, until the governer, absent or impeached, shall return or be acquitted; or until the disqualification or inability shall cease; or until a new governor shall be elected and qualified.

20. In case of a vacancy in the office of governor, for any other cause than those herein enumerated, or in case of the death of the governor elect before he is qualified, the powers, duties, and emoluments of the office shall devolve upon the lieutenant-governor, or speaker of the senate, as above provided, until a new governor be elected and qualified.

21. Every bill which shall have passed the senate and house of representatives, shall, before it becomes a law, be presented to the governor; if he approve, he shall sign it; but if not, he shall return it, with his objections, to the house in which it shall have originated; and the said house shall enter the objections at large on their journal, and proceed to reconsider it. If, after such reconsideration, a majority of the members elected shall agree to pass the bill, it shall be sent, together with the objections, to the other house, by which it shall likewise be reconsidered; and if approved by a majority of the members elected, it shall become a law, notwithstanding the objections of the governor; but in all such cases, the votes of both houses shall be determined by yeas and nays, to be entered on the journal of each house respectively. If any bill shall not be returned by the governor within ten days (Sundays excepted) after it shall have been presented to him, the same shall be a law, in like manner as if he had signed it, unless the general assembly shall, by their adjournment, prevent its return, in which case the said bill shall be returned on the first day of the meeting of the general assembly, after the expiration of said ten days, or be a law.

22. There shall be elected by the qualified electors of this state, at the same time of the election for governor, a secretary of state, whose term of office shall be the same as that of the governor, who shall keep a fair register of the official acts of the governor, and, when required, shall lay the same, and all papers, minutes, and vouchers, relative thereto, before either branch of the general assembly, and shall perform such other duties as shall be assigned him by law, and shall receive a salary of eight hundred dollars per annum, and no more, except fees: *Provided*, that if the office of secretary of state should be vacated by death, resignation, or otherwise, it shall be the duty of the governor to appoint another, who shall hold his office until another secretary shall be elected and qualified.

23. There shall be chosen, by the qualified electors throughout the state, an auditor of public accounts, who shall hold his office for the term of four years, and until his successor is qualified, and whose duties shall be regulated by law, and who shall receive a salary, exclusive of clerk hire, of one thousand dollars per annum for his services, and no more.

24. There shall be elected, by the qualified electors throughout the state, a state treasurer, who shall hold his office for two years, and until his successor is qualified; whose duties may be regulated by law, and who shall receive a salary of eight hundred dollars per annum, and no more.

25. All grants and commissions shall be sealed with the great seal of state, signed by the governor or person administering the government, and countersigned by the secretary of state.

26. The governor and all other civil officers shall be liable to impeachment for misdemeanor in office, during their continuance in office, and for two years thereafter.

ARTICLE V.—*Of the Judiciary Department.*

SEC. 1. The judicial power of this state shall be, and is hereby, vested in one supreme court, in circuit courts, in county courts, and in justices of the peace: *Provided,* that inferior local courts, of civil and criminal jurisdiction, may be established by the general assembly in the cities of this state, but such courts shall have a uniform organization and jurisdiction in such cities.

2. The supreme court shall consist of three judges, two of whom shall form a quorum; and the concurrence of two of said judges shall, in all cases, be necessary to a decision.

3. The state shall be divided into three grand divisions, as nearly equal as may be, and the qualified electors of each division shall elect one of the said judges for the term of nine years: *Provided,* that after the first election of such judges, the general assembly may have the power to provide by law for their election by the whole state, or by divisions, as they may deem most expedient.

4. The office of one of said judges shall be vacated, after the first election held under this article, in three years; of one, in six years; and of one, in nine years; to be decided by lot, so that one of said judges shall be elected once in every three years. The judge having the longest term to serve shall be the first chief-justice; after which, the judge having the oldest commission shall be chief-justice.

5. The supreme court may have original jurisdiction in cases relative to the revenue, in cases of *mandamus, habeas corpus,* and in such cases of impeachment as may be by law directed to be tried before it, and shall have appellate jurisdiction in all other cases.

6. The supreme court shall hold one term annually in each of the aforesaid grand divisions, at such time and place, in each of said divisions, as may be provided for by law.

7. The state shall be divided into nine judicial districts; in each of which one circuit judge shall be elected by the qualified electors thereof, who shall hold his office for the term of six years, and until his successor shall be commissioned and qualified: *Provided,* that the general assembly may increase the number of circuits to meet the future exigencies of the state.

8. There shall be two or more terms of the circuit court held, annually, in each county of this state, at such times as shall be provided by law; and said courts shall have jurisdiction in all cases at law and equity, and in all cases of appeals from all inferior courts.

9. All vacancies in the supreme and circuit courts shall be filled by election as aforesaid: *Provided, however,* that if the unexpired term does not exceed one year, such vacancy may be filled by executive appointment.

10. The judges of the supreme court shall receive a salary of twelve hundred dollars per annum, payable quarterly, and no more. The judges of the circuit courts shall receive a salary of one thousand dollars per annum, payable

quarterly, and no more. The judges of the supreme and circuit courts shall not be eligible to any other office or public trust, of profit, in this state or the United States, during the term for which they are elected, nor for one year thereafter. All votes for either of them for any elective office (except that of judge of the supreme or circuit court), given by the general assembly, or the people, shall be void.

11. No person shall be eligible to the office of judge of any court of this state, who is not a citizen of the United States, and who shall not have resided in this state five years next preceding his election, and who shall not, for two years next preceding his election, have resided in the division, circuit, or county, in which he shall be elected; nor shall any person be elected judge of the supreme court, who shall be, at the time of his election, under the age of thirty-five years; and no person shall be eligible to the office of judge of the circuit court until he shall have attained the age of thirty years.

12. For any reasonable cause, to be entered on the journals of each house, which shall not be sufficient ground for impeachment, both justices of the supreme court, and judges of the circuit court, shall be removed from office, on the vote of two-thirds of the members elected to each branch of the general assembly: *Provided, always,* that no member of either house of the general assembly shall be eligible to fill the vacancy occasioned by such removal: *Provided, also,* that no removal shall be made unless the justice or judge complained of shall have been served with a copy of the complaint against him, and shall have an opportunity of being heard in his defence.

13. The first election for justices of the supreme court, and judges of the circuit courts, shall be held on the first Monday of September, 1848.

14. The second election for one justice of the supreme court shall be held on the first Monday of June, 1852; and every three years thereafter an election shall be held for one justice of the supreme court.

15. On the first Monday of June, 1855, and every sixth year thereafter, an election shall be held for judges of the circuit courts: *Provided,* whenever an additional circuit is created, such provision may be made as to hold the second election of such additional judge at the regular elections herein provided.

16. There shall be, in each county, a court, to be called a county court.

17. One county judge shall be elected by the qualified voters of each county, who shall hold his office for four years, and until his successor is elected and qualified.

18. The jurisdiction of said court shall extend to all probate and such other jurisdiction as the general assembly may confer in civil cases, and such criminal cases as may be prescribed by law, where the punishment is by fine only, not exceeding one hundred dollars.

19. The county judge, with such justices of the peace in each county as may be designated by law, shall hold terms for the transaction of county business, and shall perform such other duties as the general assembly shall prescribe:

Provided, the general assembly may require, that two justices, to be chosen by the qualified electors of each county, shall sit with the county judge in all cases; and there shall be elected, quadrennially, in each county, a clerk of the county court, who shall be *ex officio* recorder, whose compensation shall be fees: *Provided*, the general assembly may, by law, make the clerk of the circuit court *ex officio* recorder, in lieu of the county clerk.

20. The general assembly shall provide for the compensation of the county judge.

21. The clerks of the supreme and circuit courts, and state's attorneys, shall be elected at the first special election for judges. The second election for clerks of the supreme court shall be held on the first Monday of June, 1855, and every sixth year thereafter. The second election for clerks of the circuit courts, and state's attorneys, shall be held on the Tuesday next after the first Monday of November, 1852, and every fourth year thereafter.

22. All judges and state's attorneys shall be commissioned by the governor.

23. The election of all officers, and the filling of all vacancies that may happen by death, resignation, or removal, not otherwise directed or provided for by this constitution, shall be made in such manner as the general assembly shall direct: *Provided*, that no such officer shall be elected by the general assembly.

24. The general assembly may authorize the judgments, decrees, and decisions, of any local, inferior court of record, of original civil or criminal jurisdiction, established in a city, to be removed, for revision, directly into the supreme court.

25. County judges, clerks, sheriffs, and other county officers, for wilful neglect of duty, or misdemeanor in office, shall be liable to presentment or indictment by a grand jury, and trial by a petit jury; and, upon conviction, shall be removed from office.

26. All process, writs, and other proceedings, shall run in the name of "*The people of the State of Illinois.*" All prosecutions shall be carried on "*In the name and by the authority of the people of the State of Illinois,*" and conclude, "*Against the peace and dignity of the same.*"

27. There shall be elected in each county in this state, in such districts as the general assembly may direct, by the qualified electors thereof, a competent number of justices of the peace, who shall hold their offices for the term of four years, and until their successors shall have been elected and qualified, and who shall perform such duties, receive such compensation, and exercise such jurisdiction, as may be prescribed by law.

28. There shall be elected, in each of the judicial circuits of this state, by the qualified electors thereof, one state's attorney, who shall hold his office for the term of four years, and until his successor shall be commissioned and qualified; who shall perform such duties and receive such compensation as may be prescribed by law: *Provided*, that the general assembly may hereafter

provide by law for the election, by the qualified voters of each county in this state, of one county attorney for each county, in lieu of the state's attorneys provided for in this section; the term of office, duties, and compensation of which county attorneys, shall be regulated by law.

29. The qualified electors of each county in this state shall elect a clerk of the circuit court, who shall hold his office for the term of four years, and until his successor shall have been elected and qualified, who shall perform such duties and receive such compensation as may be prescribed by law. The clerks of the supreme court shall be elected, in each division, by the qualified electors thereof, for the term of six years, and until their successors shall have been elected and qualified; whose duties and compensation shall be provided by law.

30. The first grand division, for the election of judges of the supreme court, shall consist of the counties of Alexander, Pulaski, Massac, Pope, Hardin, Gallatin, Saline, Williamson, Johnson, Union, Jackson, Randolph, Perry, Franklin, Hamilton, White, Wabash, Edwards, Wayne, Jefferson, Washington, Monroe, St. Clair, Clinton, Marion, Clay, Richland, Lawrence, Crawford, Jasper, Effingham, Fayette, Bond, Madison, Jersey, and Calhoun.

The second grand division shall consist of the counties of Edgar, Coles, Moultrie, Shelby, Montgomery, Macoupin, Greene, Pike, Adams, Highland, Hancock, McDonough, Schuyler, Brown, Fulton, Mason, Cass, Morgan, Scott, Sangamon, Christian, Macon, Piatt, Champaign, Vermilion, De Witt, Logan, Menard, Cumberland, and Clark.

The third grand division shall consist of the counties of Henderson, Warren, Knox, Peoria, Tazewell, Woodford, McLean, Livingston, Iroquois, Will, Grundy, Kendall, La Salle, Putnam, Marshall, Stark, Bureau, Henry, Mercer, Rock Island, Whiteside, Lee, Carroll, Jo Daviess, Stephenson, Winnebago, Ogle, De Kalb, Boone, Kane, McHenry, Lake, Cook, and Du Page.

31. The terms of the supreme court for the first division, shall be held at Mount Vernon, in Jefferson county; for the second division, at Springfield, in Sangamon county; for the third division, at Ottawa, in La Salle county; until some other place, in either division, is fixed by law.

32. Appeals and writs of error may be taken from the circuit court of any county to the supreme court held in the division which includes such county, or, with the consent of all the parties in the cause, to the supreme court in the next adjoining division.

33. The foregoing districts may, after the taking of each census by the state, be altered, if necessary, to equalize the said districts in population; but such alteration shall be made by adding to such district such adjacent county or counties as will make said district nearest equal in population: *Provided*, no such alteration shall affect the office of any judge then in office

ARTICLE VI.—*On Elections and the Right of Suffrage.*

SEC. 1. In all elections, every white male citizen above the age of twenty-one years, having resided in the state one year next preceding any election, shall be entitled to vote at such election; and every white male inhabitant of the age aforesaid, who may be a resident of the state at the time of the adoption of this constitution, shall have the right of voting as aforesaid; but no such citizen or inhabitant shall be entitled to vote, except in the district or county in which he shall actually reside at the time of such election.

2. All votes shall be given by ballot.

3. Electors shall in all cases, except treason, felony, or breach of the peace, be privileged from arrest during their attendance at elections, and in going to and returning from the same.

4. No elector shall be obliged to do militia duty on the days of election, except in time of war or public danger.

5. No elector shall be deemed to have lost his residence in this state by reason of his absence on the business of the United States or of this state.

6. No soldier, seaman, or marine, in the army or navy of the United States, shall be deemed a resident of this state, in consequence of being stationed at any military or naval place within the state.

7. No person shall be elected or appointed to any office in this state, civil or military, who is not a citizen of the United States, and who shall not have resided in this state one year next before the election or appointment.

8. The general assembly shall have full power to pass laws excluding from the right of suffrage persons convicted of infamous crimes.

9. The general elections shall be held on the Tuesday next after the first Monday of November, biennially, until otherwise provided by law.

ARTICLE VII.—*Of Counties.*

SEC. 1. No new county shall be formed or established by the general assembly, which will reduce the county or counties, or either of them, from which it shall be taken, to less contents than four hundred square miles; nor shall any county be formed of less contents; nor shall any line thereof pass within less than ten miles of any county seat of the county or counties proposed to be divided.

2. No county shall be divided, or have any part stricken therefrom, without submitting the question to a vote of the people of the county, nor unless a majority of all the legal voters of the county voting on the question shall vote for the same.

3. All territory which has been, or may be stricken off, by legislative enactment, from any organized county or counties, for the purpose of forming a new county, and which shall remain unorganized after the period provided for such organization, shall be and remain a part of the county or counties from

which it was originally taken, for all purposes of county and state government, until otherwise provided by law.

4. There shall be no territory stricken from any county unless a majority of the voters living in such territory shall petition for such division; and no territory shall be added to any county without the consent of a majority of the voters of the county to which it is proposed to be added.

5. No county seat shall be removed until the point to which it is proposed to be removed shall be fixed by law, and a majority of the voters of the county shall have voted in favor of its removal to such point.

6. The general assembly shall provide, by a general law, for a township organization, under which any county may organize whenever a majority of the voters of such county, at any general election, shall so determine; and whenever any county shall adopt a township organization, so much of this constitution as provides for the management of the fiscal concerns of the said county by the county court, may be dispensed with, and the affairs of said county may be transacted in such manner as the general assembly may provide.

7. There shall be elected in each county in this state, by the qualified electors thereof, a sheriff, who shall hold his office for the term of two years, and until his successor shall have been elected and qualified: *Provided*, no person shall be eligible to the said office more than once in four years.

Article VIII.—*Militia.*

Sec. 1. The militia of the state of Illinois shall consist of all free male able-bodied persons (negroes, mulattoes, and Indians excepted), residents of the state, between the ages of eighteen and forty-five years, except such persons as now are or hereafter may be exempted by the laws of the United States or of this state, and shall be armed, equipped, and trained, as the general assembly may provide by law.

2. No person or persons, conscientiously scrupulous of bearing arms, shall be compelled to do militia duty in time of peace, provided such person or persons shall pay an equivalent for such exemption.

3. Company, battalion, and regimental officers, staff officers excepted, shall be elected by the persons composing their several companies, battalions, and regiments.

4. Brigadier and major-generals shall be elected by the officers of their brigades and divisions, respectively.

5. All militia officers shall be commissioned by the governor, and may hold their commissions for such time as the legislature may provide.

6. The militia shall, in all cases, except treason, felony, or breach of the peace, be privileged from arrest during their attendance at musters and elections of officers, and in going to and returning from the same.

ARTICLE IX.—*Of the Revenue.*

SEC. 1. The general assembly may, whenever they shall deem it necessary, cause to be collected from all able-bodied, free white male inhabitants of this state, over the age of twenty-one years, and under the age of sixty years, who are entitled to the right of suffrage, a capitation tax of not less than fifty cents, nor more than one dollar each.

2. The general assembly shall provide for levying a tax by valuation, so that every person and corporation shall pay a tax in proportion to the value of his or her property; such value to be ascertained by some person or persons to be elected or appointed in such manner as the general assembly shall direct, and not otherwise; but the general assembly shall have power to tax pedlars, auctioneers, brokers, hawkers, merchants, commission merchants, showmen, jugglers, inn-keepers, grocery-keepers, toll bridges and ferries, and persons using and exercising franchises and privileges, in such manner as they shall from time to time direct.

3. The property of the state and counties, both real and personal, and such other property as the general assembly may deem necessary for school, religious, and charitable purposes, may be exempted from taxation.

4. Hereafter, no purchaser of any land or town lot, at any sale of lands or town lots for taxes due either to this state, or any county, or incorporated town or city within the same; or at any sale for taxes or levies authorized by the laws of this state, shall be entitled to a deed for the lands or town lot so purchased, until he or she shall have complied with the following conditions, to wit: Such purchaser shall serve, or cause to be served, a written notice of such purchase, on every person in possession of such land or town lot, three months before the expiration of the time of redemption on such sale; in which notice he shall state when he purchased the land or town lot, the description of the land or lot he has purchased, and when the time of redemption will expire. In like manner he shall serve on the person or persons in whose name or names such land or lot is taxed, a similar written notice, if such person or persons shall reside in the county where such land or lot shall be situated; and in the event that the person or persons in whose name or names the land or lot is taxed, do not reside in the county, such purchaser shall publish such notice in some newspaper printed in such county; and if no newspaper is printed in the county, then in the nearest newspaper that is published in this state to the county in which such lot or land is situated; which notice shall be inserted three times, the last time not less than three months before the time of redemption shall expire. Every such purchaser, by himself or agent, shall, before he shall be entitled to a deed, make an affidavit of his having complied with the conditions of this section, stating particularly the facts relied on as such compliance; which affidavit shall be delivered to the person authorized by law to execute such tax deed, and which shall by him be filed with the officer having custody of the records of lands and lots sold for taxes and entries

of redemption, in the county where such land or lot shall lie, to be by such officer entered on the records of his office, and carefully preserved among the files of his office; and which record or affidavit shall be *prima facie* evidence that such notice has been given. Any person swearing falsely in such affidavit shall be deemed guilty of perjury, and punished accordingly. In case any person shall be compelled, under this section, to publish a notice in a newspaper, then, before any person, who may have a right to redeem such land or lot from tax sale, shall be permitted to redeem, he or she shall pay the officer or person who by law is authorized to receive such redemption-money, the printer's fee for publishing such notice, and the expenses of swearing or affirming to the affidavit, and filing the same.

5. The corporate authorities of counties, townships, school districts, cities, towns, and villages, may be vested with power to assess and collect taxes for corporate purposes; such taxes to be uniform in respect to persons and property within the jurisdiction of the body imposing the same. And the general assembly shall require that all the property within the limits of municipal corporations, belonging to individuals, shall be taxed for the payment of debts contracted under authority of law.

6. The specification of the objects and subjects of taxation shall not deprive the general assembly of the power to require other objects or subjects to be taxed in such manner as may be consistent with the principles of taxation fixed in this constitution.

Article X.—*Corporations.*

Sec. 1. Corporations, not possessing banking powers or privileges, may be formed under general laws, but shall not be created by special acts, except for municipal purposes, and in cases where, in the judgment of the general assembly, the objects of the corporation cannot be attained under general laws.

2. Dues from corporations, not possessing banking powers or privileges, shall be secured by such individual liabilities of the corporators, or other means, as may be prescribed by law.

3. No state bank shall hereafter be created, nor shall the state own or be liable for any stock in any corporation or joint stock association for banking purposes, to be hereafter created.

4. The stockholders in every corporation or joint stock association, for banking purposes, issuing bank notes, or any kind of paper credits to circulate as money, shall be individually responsible, to the amount of their respective share or shares of stock in any such corporation or association, for all its debts and liabilities of every kind.

5. No act of the general assembly, authorizing corporations or associations with banking powers, shall go into effect, or in any manner be in force, unless the same shall be submitted to the people at the general election next succeeding the passage of the same, and be approved by a majority of all the votes cast at such election for and against such law.

6. The general assembly shall encourage internal improvements, by passing liberal general laws of incorporation for that purpose.

Article XI.—*Commons.*

All lands which have been granted, as a "common," to the inhabitants of any town, hamlet, village, or corporation, by any person, body politic or corporate, or by any government having power to make such grant, shall for ever remain common to the inhabitants of such town, hamlet, village, or corporation; but the said commons, or any of them, or any part thereof, may be divided, leased, or granted, in such manner as may hereafter be provided by law, on petition of a majority of the qualified voters interested in such commons, or any of them.

Article XII.—*Amendments to the Constitution.*

Sec. 1. Whenever two-thirds of all the members elected to each branch of the general assembly shall think it necessary to alter or amend this constitution, they shall recommend to the electors at the next election of members of the general assembly, to vote for or against a convention; and if it shall appear that a majority of all the electors of the state voting for representatives have voted for a convention, the general assembly shall, at their next session, call a convention, to consist of as many members as the house of representatives at the time of making said call, to be chosen in the same manner, at the same place, and by the same electors, in the same districts that chose the members of the house of representatives; and which convention shall meet within three months after the said election, for the purpose of revising, altering, or amending this constitution.

2. Any amendment or amendments to this constitution may be proposed in either branch of the general assembly; and if the same shall be agreed to by two-thirds of all the members elect in each of the two houses, such proposed amendment or amendments shall be referred to the next regular session of the general assembly, and shall be published at least three months previous to the time of holding the next election for members of the house of representatives; and if, at the next regular session of the general assembly after said election, a majority of all the members elect, in each branch of the general assembly, shall agree to said amendment or amendments, then it shall be their duty to submit the same to the people at the next general election, for their adoption or rejection, in such manner as may be prescribed by law; and if a majority of all the electors voting at such election for members of the house of representatives, shall vote for such amendment or amendments, the same shall become a part of the constitution. But the general assembly shall not have power to propose an amendment or amendments to more than one article of the constitution at the same session.

ARTICLE XIII.—*Declaration of Rights.*

That the general, great, and essential principles of liberty and free government may be recognised and unalterably established, WE DECLARE:—

SEC. 1. That all men are born equally free and independent, and have certain inherent and indefeasible rights; among which are those of enjoying and defending life and liberty, and of acquiring, possessing, and protecting property and reputation, and of pursuing their own happiness.

2. That all power is inherent in the people, and all free governments are founded on their authority, and instituted for their peace, safety, and happiness.

3. That all men have a natural and indefeasible right to worship Almighty God according to the dictates of their own consciences; that no man can of right be compelled to attend, erect, or support any place of worship, or to maintain any ministry, against his consent; that no human authority can, in any case whatever, control or interfere with the rights of conscience; and that no preference shall ever be given by law to any religious establishments or modes of worship.

4. That no religious test shall ever be required as a qualification to any office of public trust under this state.

5. That all elections shall be free and equal.

6. That the right of trial by jury shall remain inviolate; and shall extend to all cases at law, without regard to the amount in controversy.

7. That the people shall be secure in their persons, houses, papers, and possessions, from unreasonable searches and seizures: and that general warrants, whereby an officer may be commanded to search suspected places without evidence of the fact committed, or to seize any person or persons not named, whose offences are not particularly described and supported by evidence, are dangerous to liberty, and ought not to be granted.

8. That no freeman shall be imprisoned, or disseized of his freehold, liberties, or privileges, or outlawed or exiled, or in any manner deprived of his life, liberty, or property, but by the judgment of his peers, or the law of the land.

9. That in all criminal prosecutions, the accused hath a right to be heard by himself and counsel; to demand the nature and cause of the accusation against him; to meet the witnesses face to face; to have compulsory process to compel the attendance of witnesses in his favor; and in prosecutions by indictment or information, a speedy public trial by an impartial jury of the county or district wherein the offence shall have been committed, which county or district shall have been previously ascertained by law; and that he shall not be compelled to give evidence against himself.

10. No person shall be held to answer for a criminal offence unless on the presentment or indictment of a grand jury, except in cases of impeachment, or in cases cognizable by justices of the peace, or arising in the army or navy, or in the militia when in actual service in time of war or public danger: *Pro-*

vided, that justices of the peace shall try no person, except as a court of inquiry, for any offence punishable with imprisonment or death, or fine above one hundred dollars.

11. No person shall, for the same offence, be twice put in jeopardy of his life or limb; nor shall any man's property be taken or applied to public use without the consent of his representatives in the general assembly, nor without just compensation being made to him.

12. Every person within this state ought to find a certain remedy in the laws for all injuries or wrongs which he may receive in his person, property, or character; he ought to obtain right and justice freely, and without being obliged to purchase it, completely and without denial, promptly and without delay, conformably to the laws.

13. That all persons shall be bailable by sufficient sureties, unless for capital offences where the proof is evident or the presumption great; and the privilege of the writ of *habeas corpus* shall not be suspended, unless, when in cases of rebellion or invasion, the public safety may require it.

14. All penalties shall be proportioned to the nature of the offence; the true design of all punishment being to reform, not to exterminate mankind.

15. No person shall be imprisoned for debt, unless upon refusal to deliver up his estate for the benefit of his creditors, in such manner as shall be prescribed by law, or in cases where there is strong presumption of fraud.

16. There shall be neither slavery nor involuntary servitude in this state, except as a punishment for crime, whereof the party shall have been duly convicted.

17. No *ex post facto* law, nor any law impairing the obligation of contracts, shall ever be made: and no conviction shall work corruption of blood or forfeiture of estate.

18. That no person shall be liable to be transported out of this state for any offence committed within the same.

19. That a frequent recurrence to the fundamental principles of civil government is absolutely necessary to preserve the blessings of liberty.

20. The military shall be in strict subordination to the civil power.

21. That the people have a right to assemble together in a peaceable manner to consult for their common good, to instruct their representatives, and to apply to the general assembly for redress of grievances.

22. No soldier shall, in time of peace, be quartered in any house without the consent of the owner; nor in time of war, except in manner prescribed by law.

23. The printing-presses shall be free to every person who undertakes to examine the proceedings of the general assembly, or of any branch of government; and no law shall ever be made to restrain the right thereof. The free communication of thoughts and opinions is one of the invaluable rights of man; and every citizen may freely speak, write, and print, on any subject, being responsible for the abuse of that liberty.

24. In prosecutions for the publication of papers investigating the official conduct of officers, or of men acting in a public capacity, or when the matter published is proper for public information, the truth thereof may be given in evidence; and in all indictments for libels, the jury shall have the right of determining both the law and the fact, under the direction of the court, as in other cases.

25. Any person who shall, after the adoption of this constitution, fight a duel, or send or accept a challenge for that purpose, or be aider or abettor in fighting a duel, shall be deprived of the right of holding any office of honor or profit in this state, and shall be punished otherwise, in such manner as is or may be prescribed by law.

26. That from and after the adoption of this constitution, every person who shall be elected or appointed to any office of profit, trust, or emolument, civil or military, legislative, executive, or judicial, under the government of this state, shall, before he enters upon the duties of his office, in addition to the oath prescribed in this constitution, take the following oath: "I do solemnly swear [or affirm, as the case may be] that I have not fought a duel, nor sent or accepted a challenge to fight a duel, the probable issue of which might have been the death of either party, nor been a second to either party, nor in any manner aided or assisted in such duel, nor been knowingly the bearer of such challenge or acceptance, since the adoption of the constitution; and that I will not be so engaged or concerned, directly or indirectly, in or about any such duel, during my continuance in office. So help me, God."

ARTICLE XIV.—*Public Debt.*

There shall be annually assessed and collected, in the same manner as other state revenue may be assessed and collected, a tax of two mills upon each dollar's worth of taxable property, in addition to all other taxes, to be applied as follows, to wit: The fund so created shall be kept separate, and shall annually, on the first day of January, be apportioned and paid over, *pro rata*, upon all such state indebtedness, other than the canal and school indebtedness, as may, for that purpose, be presented by the holders of the same, to be entered as credits upon, and, to that extent, in extinguishment of the principal of said indebtedness.

GOVERNMENT JUDICIARY, AND FINANCES.

GOVERNMENT.

Joel A. Mattison (manufacturer), of Will county, Governor, and ex officio Land Commissioner. Term ends, second Monday in January, 1857. Salary, $1500.

Gustavus Kœrner (lawyer), of St. Clair county, Lieutenant-Governor. Salary, $3 a day during session, and 10 cents a mile travel.

Alexander Starne (merchant), of Pike county, Secretary of State. Term ends, January, 1857. Salary, fees and $800.*

Thomas H. Campbell (lawyer), of Springfield, Auditor. Term ends, January, 1857. Salary, $1000.*

John Moore (farmer), of Randolph's Grove, Treasurer. Term ends, January, 1857. Salary, $800.*

Ninian W. Edwards, of Sangamon county, State Superintendent of Common Schools. Term ends, January, 1857. Salary, $1500.

J. G. Norwood, M. D., of Sangamon county, State Geologist.

Moses K. Anderson, of Sangamon county, Adjutant-General.

Thomas J. Turner, of Stephenson, Speaker of the House. Salary, $3 a day during the session.

E. T. Bridges, of La Salle, Clerk.

George T. Brown, of Madison, Secretary of Senate.

The sessions of the Legislature are biennial. The nineteenth session commenced in January, 1855.

JUDICIARY.

Supreme Court.

First Division.—Walter B. Scates, of Jefferson county, Chief Justice. Term ends, June, 1861. Salary, $1200. Noah Johnson, of Jefferson county, Clerk. Fees.

Second Division.—Onias C. Skinner, of Quincy, Judge. Term ends, June, 1858. Salary, $1200. Wm. A. Turney, of Springfield, Clerk. Term ends, June, 1861. Fees.

---

* Exclusive of clerk hire.

Third Division.—J. Deane Catton, of Ottawa, Judge. Term ends, June, 1864. Salary, $1200. Lorenzo Leland, of Ottawa, Clerk. Term ends, June, 1861. Fees.

Ebenezer Peck, of Chicago, Reporter.

This Court holds one session in each division of the State each year. The terms are: first division, at Mt. Vernon, Jefferson county, on the second Monday in November; second division, at Springfield, on the third Monday in December; third division, at Ottawa, La Salle county, on the first Monday in February.

CIRCUIT COURTS.*

CIRCUIT.	NAME OF JUDGE.	RESIDENCE.	SAL'RY.	PROS. ATTORNEY.	RESIDENCE.	SALARY.
1.	D. M. Woodson,	Greene co.	$1000	Cyrus Epley,	Morgan co.	$500 & fees.
2.	Sidney Breese,	St. Clair co.	"	Wm. H. Snyder,	St. Clair co.	"
3.	Wm. K. Parish,	Franklin co.	"	Jno. A. Logan,	Jackson co.	"
4.	Justin Harlan,	Clarke co.	"	A. Kitchell,	Richland co.	"
5.	P. H. Walker,	Schuyler co.	"	Jno. S. Bailey,	McDonough co.	"
6.	J. W. Drury,	Rock Island co.	"	Wm. T. Miller,	Carroll co.	"
7.	Geo. Mainerre,	Cook co.	"	Daniel McIlroy,	Cook co.	"
8.	David Davis,	McLean co.	"	A. M. Williams,	Sangamon co.	"
9.	M. E. Hollister,	La Salle co.	"	W. H. L. Wallace,	La Salle co.	"
10.	J. I. Thompson,	Mercer co.	"	Wm. C. Grudy,	Fulton co.	"
11.	S. W. Randall,	Will co.	"	S. W. Bowen,	Will co.	"
12.	Edwin Beecher,	Wayne co.	"	J. S. Robinson,	White co.	"
13.	Isaac G. Wilson,	Kane co.	"	M. W. Boyce,	Boone co.	"
14.	B. R. Sheldon,	Jo Daviess co.	"	Wm. Brown,	Winnebago co.	"
15.	Jos. Sibley,	Hancock co.	"	C. A. Warren,	Adams co.	"
16.	Onslow Peters,	Peoria co.	"	E. G. Johnson,	Peoria co.	"
17.	Chas. Emerson,	Macon co.	"	G. Rust,	Macon co.	"

Cook County Common Pleas.—John M. Wilson, Judge. Term ends, 1857. Salary, $1000 and fees. Walter Kimball, Clerk.

Recorder's Court of the City of Chicago.—Robert S. Wilson, Judge. Term ends, 1858. Salary, $2200 and fees. Daniel McIlroy, Prosecuting Attorney. Term ends, 1856. Salary, $500 and fees. Philip A. Hoyne, Clerk. Term ends, 1858. Fees.

These Courts have concurrent jurisdiction in the county and city, respectively, with the Circuit Court and Common Pleas, in all civil cases, and in all criminal cases, except murder and treason. Each county has a County Court, with jurisdiction to the same amount as Justices of the Peace, but their business is chiefly probate matters.

* The term of office of the several judges ends in June. 1861; of the prosecuting attorneys, November, 1856.

FINANCES.

The debt of the State, principal and interest, was, January 1, 1855, $13,994,615. During the two years ending November 30, 1854, there has been paid of the public debt, in addition to $1,200,000 paid on account of accruing interest, the sum of $2,750,038, making a total of $3,950,038 paid during this time, on account of the public debt. If the present rate of taxation is continued, and the present method of reducing the State debt followed, it will be eventually extinguished in 1866.

The receipts into the treasury for ordinary revenue, for the two years ending November 30, 1854,* chiefly from taxes, were	$408,529 77	
Add balance in the treasury, Dec. 1, 1852,	146,372 36	
		$554,902 13
The expenditures for the same period, were:		
Ordinary expenses,	$255,195 31	
Special appropriations and expenditures,	269,720 85	
Old warrants and miscellaneous,	961 13	
		525,877 29
Balance in the treasury, Dec. 1, 1854,		$29,024 84
Amount of interest fund tax received for the same period, including balance, was		592,972 08
Amount of warrants issued for payment of interest cancelled,		528,294 66
Amount received for liquidation of State debt, including balance,		963,708 37
Warrants for pro rata payments of State indebtedness cancelled,		544,555 50

The total assessed value of property in the State in 1852, was $149,294,805; in 1853, $225,159,633. Rate of taxation on each $100: in 1852, 60⅓ cents; in 1853, 49⅓ cents. During the two

* The following letter of the State Treasurer to the Chicago Tribune, gives the total amount paid by the people into the treasury in 1855:

TREASURER'S OFFICE, Springfield, Dec. 14, 1855.

Editors of the Tribune:—Agreeably to your request, I send you the amount of payments into the treasury, from 1st January to 30th November, 1855, upon the assessment of 1854, alone, as follows:

Revenue purposes,	$288,586 78
State debt (2 mills tax),	478,753 56
Interest fund,	358,757 32
Total receipts for 1855,	$1,126,077 56

Very respectfully, &c., JOHN MOORE,
Treasurer of the State of Illinois.

years $280,894.06 were received from the sale of 80,126.04 acres of land belonging to the State, and 48,598.15 acres remained unsold, December 1, 1854.

Amount of funds devoted to Common Schools, December 10, 1854:

Three per cent. on net proceeds of public lands (except one-sixth),	$463,490 93	
Surplus revenue from the United States,	335,592 32	
		$799,083 25
There are, besides:		
The College Fund, being one-sixth of the three per cent. fund,	$92,682 10	
The Seminary Fund, i. e. proceeds of sales of seminary lands,	59,738 72	
		152,420 82
Making, devoted to purposes of education,		$951,504 07

The whole of this sum has been borrowed or appropriated by the State, and devoted to pay the current expenses of the government. The State pays six per cent. interest on the amount. The interest of the Common School Fund for 1853, was $57,090.25, which, except one-fourth of one per cent. ($2,378.76) paid to the Deaf and Dumb Asylum, was divided among the several counties, in proportion to the number of white children under the age of 21.

Besides this State fund, there are county and township funds. The value of the county funds is estimated at $50,000; of the township funds, $1,952,090.51; which would make a total principal of $2,953,594.58. The interest on the State fund is at 6 per cent.; on county and township funds, at 10 per cent.; total net proceeds of interest, $196,281.54.

LAWS.

LAND TITLES.

The following are the provisions of the Revised Statutes concerning the regulation of estates and land: —

Livery of seisin shall in no case be necessary for the conveyance of real property; but every deed, mortgage, or other conveyance in writing, signed and sealed by the party making the same (the maker or makers being of full age, sound mind, discovert, at large, and not in duress), shall be sufficient, without livery of seisin, for the giving, granting, selling, mortgaging, leasing, or otherwise conveying or transferring any lands, tenements, or hereditaments in this state, so as, to all intents and purposes, absolutely and fully to vest in every donee, grantee, bargainee, mortgagee, lessee, or purchaser, all such estate or estates as shall be specified in any such deed, mortgage, lease, or other conveyance. Nothing herein contained shall be so construed as to divest or defeat the older or better estate or right of any person or persons not a party to any such deed, mortgage, lease, or other conveyance. (R. S. 102, Sec. 1.)

Every estate, feoffment, gift, grant, deed, mortgage, lease, release, or confirmation of lands, tenements, rents, services, or hereditaments, made or had, or hereafter to be made or had, by any person or persons, being of full age, sound mind, discovert, at large, and not in duress, to any person or persons, and all recoveries, judgments, and executions had or made, or to be had or made, shall be good and effectual to him, her, or them, to whom it is or shall be made, had, or given, and to all others; to his, her, or their use, against the judgment-debtor, seller, feoffor, donor, grantor, mortgagor, lessor, releasor, or confirmer, and against his, her, or their heirs or heir claiming the same only as heir or heirs, and every of them, and against all others having or claiming any title or interest in the same only to the use of the same judgment-debtor, seller, feoffor, donor, grantor, mortgagor, lessor, releasor, or confirmer, or his, her, or their said heirs, at the time of the judgment, execution, bargain, sale, mortgage, covenant, lease, release, gift, or grant made. (R. S., page 103, Sec. 2.)

Where any person or persons stand or be seized, or at any time hereafter shall stand or be seized, of and in any messuages, lands, tenements, rents, services, reversions, remainder, or other hereditaments, to the use, confidence, or trust of any other person or persons, or of any body politic, by reason of any bargain, sale, feoffment, fine, recovery, covenant, contract, agreement, will, or otherwise, by any manner of means whatsoever; in every such case, all and every such person or persons and bodies politic that have, or hereafter shall have, any such use, confidence, or trust in fee simple, for terms of life, or for years, or otherwise, or any use, confidence, or trust in remainder or reversion, shall from thenceforth stand and be seized, deemed, and adjudged in lawful seisin, estate, and possession of and in the same messuages, lands, tenements, rents, services, reversions, remainders, and hereditaments, with their appurtenances, to all intents, constructions, and purposes in law, of and in such like estates as they had or shall have in use, confidence, or trust of or in the same; and that the estate, right, title, and possession that was or shall be in such person or persons that was or hereafter shall be seized of any lands, tenements, or hereditaments to the use, confidence, or trust of any person or persons, or of any body politic, be from henceforth clearly deemed and adjudged to be in him, her, or them that have or hereafter shall have such use, confidence, or trust, after such quality, manner, form, and condition as they had before in or to the use, confidence, or trust that was or shall be in them. (R. S., p. 103, Sec. 3.)

Any person claiming right or title to lands, tenements, or hereditaments, although he, she, or they may be out of possession, and notwithstanding there may be an adverse possession thereof, may sell, convey and tranfer his or her interest in and to the same in as full and complete a manner as if he or she were in the actual possession of the lands and premises intended to be conveyed, and the grantee or grantees shall have the same right of action for the recovery thereof, and shall in all respects derive the same benefits and advantages therefrom, as if the grantor or grantors had been in the actual possession at the time of executing the conveyance. (R. S., p. 103, Sec. 4.)

No estate in joint tenancy in any lands, tenements, or hereditaments shall be held or claimed under any grant, devise, or conveyance whatsoever heretofore or hereafter made, other than to executors and trustees, unless the premises therein mentioned shall expressly be thereby declared to pass, not in tenancy in common, but in joint tenancy; and every such estate, other than to executors or trustees, (unless otherwise expressly declared, as aforesaid,) shall be deemed to be in tenancy in common. (R. S., p. 103, Sec. 5.)

In cases where by the common law any person or persons might hereafter become seized in fee tail of any lands, tenements or hereditaments by virtue of any devise, gift, grant, or other conveyance hereafter to be made, or by any other means whatsoever, such person or persons, instead of being or becoming seized thereof in fee tail, shall be deemed and adjudged to be and become seized thereof for his or her natural life only, and the remainder shall pass in fee simple absolute to the person or persons to whom the estate tail would, on

15

the death of the first grantee, devisee, or donee in tail, first pass according to the course of the common law by virtue of such devise, gift, grant, or conveyance. (R. S., p. 104, Sec. 6.)

If any person shall sell and convey to another by deed or conveyance purporting to convey an estate in fee simple absolute in any tract of land or real estate lying and being in this state, not then being possessed of the legal estate or interest therein at the time of the sale and conveyance, but after such sale and conveyance the vendor shall become possessed of and confirmed in the legal estate to the land or real estate so sold and conveyed, it shall be taken and held to be in trust and for the use of the grantee or vendee, and the conveyance aforesaid shall be held and taken, and shall be as valid as if the grantor or vendor had the legal estate or interest at the time of said sale or conveyance. (R. S., p. 104, Sec. 7.)

Every person in the actual possession of lands or tenements under claim and color of title made in good faith, and who shall for seven successive years continue in such possession, and shall also during said time pay all taxes legally assessed on such lands or tenements, shall be held and adjudged to be the legal owner of said lands or tenements to the extent and according to the purport of his or her paper title. All persons holding under such possession by purchase, devise, or descent before said seven years shall have expired, and who shall continue such possession, and continue to pay the taxes as aforesaid, so as to complete the possession and payment of taxes for the term aforesaid, shall be entitled to the benefit of this section. (R. S., p. 104, Sec. 8.)

Whenever a person having color of title, made in good faith, to vacant and unoccupied land, shall pay all taxes legally assessed thereon for seven successive years, he or she shall be deemed and adjudged to be the legal owner of said vacant and unoccupied land, to the extent and according to the purport of his or her paper title. All persons holding under such tax payer by purchase, devise, or descent before said seven years shall have expired, and who shall continue to pay the taxes as aforesaid, so as to complete the payment of taxes for the term aforesaid, shall be entitled to the benefit of this section: *Provided*, however, if any person having a better paper title to said vacant and unoccupied land shall, during the said term of seven years, pay the taxes assessed on said land for any one or more years of the said term of seven years, then and in that case such tax payer, his heirs and assigns, shall not be entitled to the benefit of this section.* (R. S., p. 104, Sec. 9.)

---

* The Supreme Court of the United States did, not long ago, decide a case, which refers to the above, and regarding which the Chicago Democratic Press, dated Feb. 16, 1856, contains the following letter: —

QUINCY, *February* 5, 1856.

Dear Sir: — I have just received the opinion of the Supreme Court of the United States in the case of Wright *vs.* Matteson.

The two preceding sections shall not extend to lands or tenements owned by the United States or this State, nor to school and seminary lands, nor to lands held for the use of religious societies, nor to lands held for any public purpose, nor shall they extend to lands or tenements when there shall be an adverse title to such lands or tenements, and the holder of such adverse title is under the age of twenty-one years, insane, imprisoned, femme covert, out of the limits of the United States, and in the employment of the United States or of this State: provided such person shall commence an action to recover such lands or tenements so possessed as aforesaid within three years after the several disabilities herein enumerated shall cease to exist, and shall prosecute such action to judgment, or in case of vacant and unoccupied land shall within the time last aforesaid pay to the person or persons who have paid the same all the taxes, with interest thereon at the rate of twelve per cent. per annum, that have been paid on said vacant and unoccupied land. (R. S., p. 104, Sec. 10.)

All deeds whereby any estate of inheritance in fee simple shall hereafter be limited to the grantee and his heirs or other legal representatives, the words "grant," "bargain," "sell," shall be adjudged an express covenant to the grantee, his heirs and other legal representatives, to wit: that the grantor was seized of an indefeasible estate in fee simple, free from encumbrances done or suffered from the grantor, except the rents and services that may be reserved, as also for quiet enjoyment against the grantor, his heirs and assigns, unless limited by express words contained in such deed. And the grantee, his heirs, executors, administrators, and assigns, may in any action assign breaches as if such covenants were expressly inserted: *Provided, always*, that this law shall not extend to lease at rack rent, or leases not exceeding twenty-one years, where the actual possession goes with the lease. (R. S., p. 105, Sec. 10.)

Every deed conveying real estate which by any thing therein contained

---

It is decided in my favor — that is, for Wright — and is full, satisfactory, and conclusive Under this decision, all persons who have had possession of land for seven years, and have paid taxes during that time, under any of our tax titles, from 1823 down to the present time inclusive, will be fully and completely protected.

The Court say, that however inadequate the deed may be to carry the true title to the property, and however incompetent may have been the power of the grantor, yet a claim asserted under such deed is strictly a claim under color of title, and one which will draw to the possession of the grantee the protection of the statutes of limitations. No matter whether the sale was regular or irregular, or on the right or wrong day, it is still color of title, and so it is if the party were in possession of the land when he purchased at the tax sale and acquired his deed. Nor is it necessary that he shall connect with any source of title.

If he possesses in good order a deed from one having no pretence to title, it is the same thing. It is color of title, and protected by the statute.

O. H. BROWNING.

shall appear to have been intended only as a security in the nature of a mortgage, though it be an absolute conveyance in terms, shall be considered as a mortgage. (R. S., p. 105, Sec. 12).

Every estate in lands which shall be granted, conveyed, or devised to one, although words heretofore necessary to tranfer an estate of inheritance be not added, shall be deemed a fee simple estate of inheritance, if a less estate be not limited by express words, or do not appear to have been granted, conveyed, or devised by construction or operation of law. (R. S., p. 105. Sec. 13.)

When an estate hath been or shall be by any conveyance limited in remainder to the son or daughter, or to the use of the son or daughter, of any person, to be begotten, such son or daughter, born after the decease of his or her father, shall take the estate in the same manner as if he or she had been born in the lifetime of the father, although no estate shall have been conveyed to support the contingent remainder after his death. (R. S., p. 105, Sec. 14.)

All aliens residing in this State may take by deed, will, or otherwise, lands and tenements, and any interest therein, and alienate, sell, assign, and transmit the same to their heirs or any other persons, whether such heirs or other persons be citizens of the United States or not, in the same manner as natural born citizens of the United States or of this State might do; and upon the decease of any alien having title to or interest in any lands or tenements, such lands and tenements shall pass and descend in the same manner as if such alien were a citizen of the United States; but all such persons shall have the same rights and remedies, and in all things be placed on the same footing, as natural born citizens and actual residents of the United States. (R. S., p. 47, Sec. 1.)

Execution of Deeds and Mortgages.

The execution of Deeds and Mortgages is regulated by the following provisions of the Revised Statutes:

Conveyances may be written or printed, must set forth the residence and the name of the parties, the land, and the terms of the grant, must be legible, and upon some material susceptible of delivery and record.

They must be signed by the party or parties thereto. The provisions of the Statutes, however, permit the subscribing of a deed by an attorney of the grantor, if he should have been thereunto authorized by an instrument in writing, executed and acknowledged by his principals, with all the formalities required in the execution of a deed, and not otherwise.

They should be attested by two subscribing witnesses, unless acknowledged previous to their delivery.

They must be sealed. A scrawl of the pen may be used as a seal. It is usual to flourish an intended circle at the right of the signature, with the initials L. S. inserted in it.

FORM OF ACKNOWLEDGMENT.

STATE OF ILLINOIS, }
COUNTY OF } ss.

Be it remembered, that on this first day of , one thousand eight hundred and , before me, John Hancock, a notary public, personally appeared John Walker and Mary his wife, to me known to be the real persons whose names are subscribed to the foregoing conveyance, and severally acknowledged that they executed the same, and the said Mary, on an examination separate and apart from her husband, having had the contents thereof fully made known to her by me, acknowledged that she executed the same, and relinquished her dower to the lands and tenements therein mentioned, voluntarily, freely, and without any compulsion of her said husband.

In witness whereof, I have hereunto set my hand and notarial seal of office, the day and year first above written.

(Seal of office.) JOHN HANCOCK, Notary Public.

All persons of full age, except femmes covert, idiots, and lunatics, are entitled to convey real estate, subject to the provisions of the Statute. When any married woman shall join her husband in the execution of a deed or mortgage of his real estate, and acknowledge the same as mentioned below, she may relinquish her right of dower. (R. S. 106, Sec. 17.)

Deeds containing the words "grant," "bargain," "sell," are adjudged to express a covenant to the grantee and his heirs and representatives, that the grantor was seized of an indefeasible estate in fee simple, free from incumbrances done or suffered by the grantor, except the rents and devises that may be reserved, and also for quiet enjoyment against the grantor, his heirs and assigns, unless limited by express words contained in such deed. (R. S. 105, Sec. 11.)

Every deed conveying real estate, which, by anything therein contained, shall appear to have been intended only as a security in the nature of a mortgage, though it be an absolute conveyance in terms, shall be considered as a mortgage. (R. S., Sec. 12.)

PROVISIONS OF THE STATUTES CONCERNING PROOF AND ACKNOWLEDGMENT OF DEEDS AND MORTGAGES, IN ILLINOIS.

All instruments for the conveyance of real estate in this State, or any interest therein, affecting the rights of any person in law or equity, must be acknowledged or proved before one of the following officers, viz.: When acknowledged or proven in Illinois, before any Judge, Justice, or Clerk of any Court of Record therein, having a seal, or before any Mayor of a city, Notary Public, or Commissioner authorized to take the acknowledgment of deeds, having a seal, or any Justice of the Peace. When acknowledged or proved without the State of Illinois, and within the United States or their territories, or the District of Columbia, before an officer commissioned for the purpose by the Governor of Illinois, in conformity with the laws of such State, Territory, or District; provided, that any Clerk of a Court of Record within such State, Territory, or District, shall, under his hand and the seal of such Court, certify that such deed or instrument is executed and acknowledged, or proved, in conformity with the laws of such State, Territory, or District. When acknowledged or proven without the United States, before any Court of any Republic, State, Kingdom, or Empire, having a seal, or any Mayor or chief officer of any city or town, having a seal, or before any officer authorized, by the laws of such foreign country, to take acknowledgments of conveyances of real estate, if he have a seal, such deed to be attested by the official seal of such Court or officer; and in case such acknowledgment is taken other than before a Court of Record, or Mayor, or chief officer of a town, having a seal, proof that the officer taking such acknowledgment was duly authorized by the laws of his country to do so, shall accompany the certificate of such acknowledgment. (R. S. 105, Sec. 16.)

The officer taking the acknowledgment must certify, that the person offering to make such acknowledgment is personally known to him to be the real person whose name is subscribed to the deed as having executed the same, or that he was proved to be such by a credible witness (naming him). (R. S. 107, Sec. 20.)

In case of married women, in addition to the above, he shall acquaint her with the contents of the deed, and shall examine her separately and apart from her husband, whether she executed the same, and relinquished her dower to the lands and tenements therein mentioned, voluntarily, freely, and without compulsion of her said husband, and shall certify the same on or annexed to the deed. (R. S., Sec. 17.)

Recording of Deeds and Mortgages, and the effect thereof.

All instruments relating to or affecting the title to real estate in this State, must be recorded in the county in which such real estate is situated. (R. S. 108, Sec. 22.)

All deeds, mortgages, and other instruments of writing, which are required to be recorded, shall take effect and be in force from and after the time of filing the same for record, and not before, as to all creditors and subsequent purchasers, without notice, and all such deeds and title papers shall be adjudged void as to all such creditors and subsequent purchasers, without notice, until the same shall be filed for record. (R. S., Sec. 23.)

All powers of attorney to convey lands are required to be recorded before any deed, executed under the authority contained in the power, goes upon record. (R. S., Sec. 24.)

The County Recorder,* biennially elected, commissioned by the Governor, and required to reside at the county seat, and to keep the books of record, is also required to give a receipt to the person bringing any deed or writing to be recorded, bearing date on the same day as the entry, and containing the abstract aforesaid, and for which entry and receipt he is entitled to no fees (R. S. 432, Sec. 7), but for the recording he is entitled to fifteen cents per hundred words, and twenty-five cents for a certificate, that the same has been recorded. (R. S. 248, Sec. 23.)

All conveyances acknowledged or proven in the State before any Judge, Justice of the Supreme or Circuit Court, or before any Court or officer, having a seal, and attested by such seal, are entitled to record without further attestation. But when acknowledged or proven before a Justice of the Peace residing within the State, the certificate of the Clerk of the County Commissioners' Court of the proper county, under his seal of office, that the person taking such proof or acknowledgment was a Justice of the Peace at the time of taking the same, must be produced to the Recorder; and when acknowledged or proved out of the State, before an officer other than Commissioner of this State residing there, the certificate of acknowledgment or proof must be accompanied with a certificate of a Clerk of a Court of Record within the State, Territory, or District, where the acknowledging officer resides, under the hand of such clerk and the seal of his Court, setting forth that the deed or instrument is executed, acknowledged, or proved, in conformity with the laws of such State, Territory, or District.

The conveyance, certificate of acknowledgment or proof, and the certificate of authentication, go upon record together, and for recording the whole thereof the Recorder is entitled to be paid.

Satisfaction of mortgages may be entered upon record, by the mortgagees, in the Recorder's office, and the record will thereby be effectually cancelled. If not so done, the cancellation may be effected by the mortgagees signing and sealing, in the presence of an attesting witness, and acknowledging in form, satisfaction thereof in writing; which instrument, on being produced to the Recorder, is sufficient authority for him to discharge the record. (R. S. 110, Sec. 37.)

Wills of Real Estate.

The Statutes of Illinois provide, that every person aged twenty-one years, if a male, or eighteen years, if a female, or upwards, and not married, being of sound mind and memory, shall have power to devise all the estate, right,

* The Clerk of the Circuit Court is now Recorder of Deeds, and performs all the duties formerly required to be performed by the County Recorder, which office was abolished by act of the Legislature of 1849. (Laws of 1849, page 64, Sec. 12.)

title, and interest, in possession, reversion, or remainder, which he or she hath, or at the time of his or her death shall have, of, in, and to any lands, tenements, hereditaments, annuities, or rents charged upon or issuing out of them, or goods and chattels, or personal estate of every description whatsoever, by will or testament; all persons of the age of seventeen years, and of sound mind and memory (married women excepted), have power to dispose of their personal estate, by will or testament; and married women have power to dispose of their separate estate, both real and personal, by will or testament, in the same manner as other persons. (R. S. 536, Sec. 1.)

Wills, testaments, and codicils, by which any lands, tenements, hereditaments, annuities, rents, or goods and chattels are devised, shall be reduced to writing, and signed by the testator or testatrix, or by some person in his or her presence, or by his or her direction, and attested in the presence of the testator or testatrix, by two or more credible witnesses. If the testator be unable to write, his mark affixed will suffice for a signature, if accompanied with the declaration, that the same is his mark; if another write his name by his direction, the same must be done in his presence, otherwise such signature will be invalid. (R. S., Sec. 2.)

Wills may or may not contain a provision for the appointment of executors thereof. If they contain no appointment, the Court which admits them to probate has the power to supply the omission, by appointing an administrator, with the will annexed.

In no case, where any testator or testatrix shall, by his or her will, appoint his or her debtor to be his or her executor or executrix, shall such appointment operate as a release or extinguishment of any debt due from such executor or executrix to such testator or testatrix, unless the testator or testatrix shall, in such will, expressly declare his or her intention to devise or release such debt; nor even in that case, unless the estate of such testator or testatrix is sufficient to discharge the whole of his or her just debts, over and above the debt due from such executor or executrix. (R. S., Sec. 12.)

If, after making a last will and testament, a child or children shall be born to any testator or testatrix, and no provision be made in such will for such child or children, the will shall not, on that account, be revoked, but unless it shall appear by such will, that it was the intention of the testator or testatrix to disinherit such child or children, the devises and legacies by such will granted and given shall be abated in equal proportions, to raise a portion for such child or children, equal to that which such child or children would have been entitled to receive out of the estate of such testator or testatrix, if he or she had died intestate. (R. S., Sec. 13.)

Whenever a devisee or legatee in any last will and testament, being a child or grandchild of the testator or testatrix, shall die before such testator or testatrix, and no provision shall be made for such contingency, the issue of such devisee or legatee shall take the estate devised and bequeathed, and if there be no such issue at the time of the death of such testator or testatrix, the estate disposed of by such devise or legacy shall be considered and treated in all respects as intestate estate. (R. S., Sec. 14.)

Codicils must be executed in the same manner as wills, and no will, testament, or codicil, shall be revoked otherwise than by burning, cancelling, tearing, or obliterating the same by the testator himself, or in his presence, by his direction or consent, or by some other will, testament, or codicil in writing, declaring the same, signed by the testator or testatrix, in the presence of two or more witnesses, and by them attested in his or her presence, and no words spoken shall revoke or annul any will, testament, or codicil in writing, executed as aforesaid, in due form of law. (R. S., Sec. 15.)

Every devise of land or any estate therein, by a married man, shall bar his surviving widow's right of dower therein, unless otherwise expressed in the will, but she may elect whether she will take such devise or bequest, or whether she will renounce the benefit of such devise or bequest, and take her dower in the lands. And she will be deemed to have elected to such jointure or devise, unless within one year after the authentication or probate of the will, she shall deliver or transmit to the Court of Probate of the proper county, a written renunciation. (R. S. 199, Sec. 11.)

The Probate and Recording of Wills.

When any will, testament, or codicil shall be exhibited in the Court of Probate* for probate thereof, it shall be the duty of the court to receive the probate of the same without delay, and to grant letters testamentary thereon to the person or persons entitled, and to do all other needful acts to enable the parties concerned to make settlement of the estate at as early a day as shall be consistent with the rights of the respective persons interested therein: provided, however, that if any person interested shall within five years after the probate of any such will, testament, or codicil, in the Court of Probate as aforesaid, appear, and by his or her bill in chancery contest the validity of the same, an issue at law shall be made up, whether the writing produced be the will of the testator or testatrix or not; which shall be tried by a jury, in the Circuit Court of the county wherein such will, testament, or codicil shall have been proved and recorded as aforesaid, according to the practice in courts of

* The County Court is invested with all of the powers and jurisdiction formerly exercised by the Probate Court, which is now abolished. (Laws of Ill., p. 65, Sec. 13.)

The County Court was created by the same act by which the Probate Court was abolished and holds its sessions for the transaction of business at the Court-house, or usual place of holding courts in the several counties, on the first Monday of each month, except the months of December, March, June, and September, and on the third Mondays of said months, and continues open day by day, until all the business before it be disposed of.

chancery in similar cases; but if no such person shall appear within the time aforesaid, the probate as aforesaid shall be forever binding and conclusive on all the parties concerned, saving to infants, femmes covert, persons not *compos mentis* or absent from the State, the like period after the removal of their respective disabilities. And in all such trials by jury, as aforesaid, the certificate of the oaths of the witnesses at the time of the first probate shall be admitted as evidence, and to have such weight as the jury shall think it may deserve. (R. S., p. 537, Sec. 6.)

On the probate of any will at least two credible attesting witnesses are required to be sworn and examined, and before the same can be admitted to record such witnesses must have declared, on oath or affirmation, that they were present and saw the testator or testatrix sign said will, testament, or codicil in their presence, and heard him or her acknowledge the same to be his or her act and deed; and they believed the testator or testatrix to be of sound mind and memory at the time of signing or acknowledging the same. (R. S., p. 536, Sec. 2.)

It shall be the duty of each and every witness to any will, testament, or codicil, made and executed in this State as aforesaid, to be and appear before the Court of Probate on the regular day for probate of such will, testament, or codicil, to testify of and concerning the execution and validity of the same, and the said Court of Probate shall have power and authority to attach and punish by fine and imprisonment, or either, any witness who shall, without a reasonable excuse, fail to appear when duly summoned for the purpose aforesaid; provided the said punishment by imprisonment shall in no case exceed the space of twenty days, nor shall a greater fine be assessed for any such default than the sum of fifty dollars.

When any will, testament, or codicil shall be produced to the Court of Probate for probate of the same, and any witness attesting such will, testament, or codicil shall reside without the limits of this State, it shall be lawful for the Probate Justice to issue a *dedimus potestatem*, or commission annexed to such will, testament, or codicil, directed to some judge, justice of the peace, mayor, or other chief magistrate of the city, town, or corporation, or county where such witness may be found, authorizing the taking and certifying of his or her attestation in due form of law. And if the person to whom any such commission shall be directed, shall certify in the manner that such acts are usually authenticated, that the witness personally appeared before him and made oath or affirmation that the testator or testatrix signed and published the writing annexed to such commission as his or her last will and testament; or, that some other person signed it by his or her direction, that he or she subscribed his or her name as a witness thereto in the presence of the testator or testatrix, and at his or her request; such oath or affirmation shall have the same operation, and the will shall be admitted to probate in like manner, as if such oath or affirmation had been made in the Court of Probate from whence such commission issued. (R. S., p. 537, Sec. 4.)

Any will, testament, and codicil, or authenticated copies thereof, proven according to the laws of any of the United States or Territories thereof, or of any country out of the limits of the United States, and touching or concerning estates within this State, accompanied with a certificate of the proper officer or officers that such will, testament, codicil, or copy thereof, was duly executed and proved agreeebly to the laws and usages of that State or country in which the same was executed, shall be recorded as aforesaid, and shall be good and available in law, in like manner as wills made and executed in this State. (R. S., p. 538, Sec. 8.)

Form of Attestation.

Signed, sealed, published, and declared, by the said John Warren, as and for his last will and testament, in the presence of us, who, at the request of the said John Warren, and in his presence, and in the presence of each other, have hereunto subscribed our names, and respective places of residence, as witnesses.

(Names.)	*(Residences.)*
JOHN WALTER,	....
JOHN GRIFFITH,	....

Title to Real Estate by Inheritance.

The Statutes provide that the estates, both real and personal, of resident or non-resident proprietors dying intestate, or whose estates or any part thereof shall be deemed and taken as intestate estate, and after all just debts and claims against such estates shall be paid as aforesaid, shall descend to and be distributed to his or her children and their descendants in equal parts: the descendants of a deceased child or grandchild taking the share of their deceased parent in equal parts among them; and when there shall be no children of the intestate, nor descendants of such children, and no widows, then to the parents, brothers and sisters of the deceased person and their descendants in equal parts among them, allowing to each of the parents, if living, a child's part, or to the survivor of them, if one be dead, a double portion; and if there be no parent living, then to the brothers and sisters of the intestate and their descendants. When there shall be a widow and no child or children, or descendants of a child or children of the intestate, then the one-half of the real estate and the whole of the personal estate shall go to such widow as her exclusive estate forever, subject to her absolute disposition and control, to be governed in all respects by the same rules and regulations as are or may be provided in case of estates of femme sole: if there be no children of the intestate, or descendants of such children, and no parents, brothers or sisters, or descendants of brothers and sisters, and no widow, then such estate shall descend in equal parts to the next of kin to the intestate in equal degree, computing by the rules of the civil law; and there shall be no representation among collaterals, except with the descendants of the brothers and sisters of the intestate; and in no case shall there be a distinction between the kindred of the whole and the half blood: saving to the widow in all cases her dower, as provided by law. (R. S., p. 545, Sec. 46.)

When any femme covert shall die intestate, leaving no child or children, or descendants of a child or children, then the one-half of the real estate of the decedent shall descend and go to her husband, as his exclusive estate forever. (R. S., p. 546, Sec. 47.)

Upon the decease of any alien, having title to or interest in any lands or tenements, such lands and tenements shall pass and descend in the same manner as if such alien were a citizen of the United States; and it shall be no objection to any person having an interest in such estate, that they are not citizens of the United States, but all such persons shall have the same rights and remedies, and in all things be placed on the same footing as natural born citizens and actual residents of the United States. (R. S., p. 48, Sec. 1.)

It is further provided, that if any person shall die seized of any real estate, without having devised the same, and leaving no heirs or representatives capable of inheriting the same, or the devisees thereof capable of holding the same, such estate shall escheat to and vest in the State. (R. S., p. 225, Sec. 1.)

The Levy and Collection of Land Taxes.

All real estate within the State is liable to taxation, except such as belongs to the State or to the United States; lands sold by the United States within the preceding five years; lands belonging to township school-funds; lands whereon any school-house, court-house, or jail, shall have been erected; lands not exceeding five acres, whereon any county buildings are situated; not exceeding ten acres, whereon any church shall have been erected; burial grounds, not exceeding ten acres, and grounds on which any building belonging to any literary, religious, benevolent, charitable, or scientific institution, shall be situated, not exceeding ten acres.

The Statutes invest the County Commissioners' Court with the power to levy taxes in their respective counties for county purposes, under the restrictions that they shall not, unless specially authorized by law, levy a tax that shall exceed four mills on each dollar's worth of property.

The Treasurer, in the capacity of Assessor, upon the receipt of such transcript and list, is required to prepare a list of all taxable property within his county, and to proceed to assess the value thereof by going to the place of residence of such owner of taxable property within his county. And if he shall deem it necessary, he may require every owner of taxable property "to give in under oath, either by himself or agent, a list and description of all his taxable lands, by townships, ranges, quarter sections, tracts, lots, or parts thereof, and the number in each tract, with the improvements thereon; all town lots, with the improvements thereon; all pleasure carriages, whether with two or four wheels; all horses, mares, jacks, jennies, mules, indentured servants, neat cattle, ships and vessels, stocks, money on hand and at interest, household furniture, and every other description of personal property; all capital employed each year in merchandising, adopting as a criterion the value of the greatest amount of goods on hand at any time in the year: and he (the Assessor) shall, in the presence of such person, enter the same in his book, and value each tract or lot separately, and each species of personal property separately, placing the description and value in figures opposite the name of the person owning or listing the same; provided, that unimproved town-lots may be listed and assessed in blocks. (R. S., p. 439, Sec. 16.)

The minimum value of all lands in this State, for the purposes of taxation, is three dollars per acre.

If any Assessor shall be unable to find the owner of any lands or lots contained in his list, he shall value the same according to the best information he can procure, and enter the same on his list in the name of the patentee or present owner, if known. (R. S., p. 440, Sec. 17.)

If any person shall give a false or fraudulent list, or refuse to deliver to the Assessor, when called on for that purpose, a list of his or her taxable property as required by law, the said Assessor, as a penalty therefor, shall assess the property of such person at double its value. (R. S., Sec. 18.)

Lands and town-lots owned by non-residents of the country, when once correctly listed for taxation by their owners, shall not be required to be listed again by them, till a subdivion or change of ownership takes place. (R. S., Sec. 20.)

Any person feeling himself aggrieved by the assessment of his property must apply to the County Commissioners' Court, at the September term thereof next succeeding the assessment; and if it shall be made to appear by credible proof, that the valuation of the Assessor was too high, such court in its discretion may order a reduction; but if he does not apply at the said term, he will be concluded by the assessment as made by the Assessor.

The Sheriff of each county in Illinois is *ex officio* Collector of Taxes levied therein. After having given a bond to the people of the State for the faithful performance of his duty as Collector of Taxes, it is his duty to receive from the County Commissioners' Clerk the assessed list, and to proceed to collect the taxes charged on said list by calling on each person residing in his county, at his or her usual place of residence, and requiring payment thereof.

Upon the receipt of the list by the Sheriff, a lien upon the property assessed attaches for the tax, and no sale or transfer of the same after that time can defeat or affect such lien. The property may be seized by the Collector, and by him sold to discharge the taxes and the costs and expenses of collection. (R. S., Sec. 33.)

The statute further provides, that in case any person shall refuse or neglect to pay his or her taxes when demanded, or within ten days thereafter, it shall be the duty of the Collector to levy the same, together with the costs and charges that may accrue, by distress and sale of the personal property of such person as ought to pay the same, wherever the same may be found in the county. No real estate can be legally sold for taxes whilst personal property can be found by the Collector. But no sale is valid, unless by advertisement posted in at least three public places in the precinct where such sale shall take place, at least ten days previous to the day of sale, the Collector shall have notified the public of the time and place thereof and the property to be sold. (R. S., Sec. 35, 36.)

The sale is required to be at public auction, and if practicable no more property than is sufficient to pay the tax, costs, and charges due, should be sold. "Land shall, if convenient, be sold in parcels, and if sold for more than the amount of the tax, costs, and charges, the surplus shall be returned to the owner of such property." (R. S., Sec. 37.)

State taxes are required to be collected in gold and silver coin and Auditor's warrants, and county taxes in gold and silver coin, Auditor's warrants, or jury certificates.

The statute further provides, that when any person owning lands in any county shall fail to pay the taxes assessed thereon, and the Collector shall be unable to find any personal property of such person in his county whereon to levy, of a value sufficient to pay the taxes and costs, it is made the duty of the Collector to make report thereof to the Circuit Court of his county, at the first term thereof in each year. (R. S., p. 444, Sec. 46.)

At least six weeks' notice of such report and application, however, is necessary to be published in some newspaper printed in the said county, if any such there be, or if there be none, then in the nearest newspaper in the State; which notice is required to contain the names of the owner or owners, if known, the amount of the delinquent tax, interest, and costs due thereon, and the year or years for which the same are due; and to mention his intended application to the court for judgment against said lands, and for an order to sell the same for the satisfaction of such taxes, interest, and costs; and that on the fourth Tuesday next succeeding the day fixed by law for the commencement of the said term of the said Circuit Court, all the lands against which judgment shall be pronounced, and for the sale of which such order is required to be made, will be exposed to public sale, at the Court-house of the said county, for the amount of said taxes, interest, and costs due thereon. (R. S., Sec. 47.)

Such Circuit Court, at the term aforesaid, is required to call the docket of such cases, and if upon such calling any defence be offered by any of the owners of lands delinquent and reported, or by any person having a claim or interest therein, it shall hear and determine the same in a summary way, without pleadings; and if no defence be made, to pronounce judgment against the said lands, and direct the Clerk to issue an order for their sale. (R. S., p. 445, Sec. 58.)

On the day specified in the Collector's notice, it is the duty of that officer to attend at the Court-house in his county, and then and there, at the hour of ten o'clock in the forenoon, to proceed to offer for sale, separately, each tract of land in the said list on which the taxes and costs have not then been paid, and the person offering to pay the taxes and costs for the least quantity of land becomes the purchaser of such quantity, to be taken from the east side of the tract. (R. S., Sec. 51.)

Any person or persons owning or claiming lands advertised for sale as aforesaid, may pay the taxes, interest, and costs due thereon, to the collector of the county in which the same are situated, at any time before the sale thereof. (R. S. 446, Sec. 61.)

When purchasers fail to pay the taxes assessed on lands designated and known as Illinois and Michigan Canal lands, sold upon a credit, it is the duty of the collector to report such failure to the acting commissioner of the said canal, and thenceforth all right, interest, and title of the said purchaser ceases, and said lands are not permitted, in any case, to be sold for the non-payment of taxes, and any sale, if made, is declared to be absolutely void. (R. S. 450, Sec. 94.)

If taxes assessed upon property as aforesaid shall not be paid according to law, and it shall be necessary to sell the same for taxes, such sales shall extend to the interest paid and all improvements thereon, the simple title to said property still remaining in the State. (R. S. 590, Sec. 2.)

Every tract of land offered for sale by any collector, as hereinbefore provided, and not sold for want of bidders, is considered as forfeit to the people, and the claims thereto of the former owner or owners utterly transferred to and vested in the State of Illinois; yet lands thus forfeited may be redeemed at any time within two years, by paying to the Clerk of the County Commissioners' Court of the county in which said lands may be situated, double the amount for which such real estate was forfeited, and all taxes accruing thereon to the time of redemption, with interest on each year's tax at the rate of six per cent. from the first Monday of May in each year to the time of redemption. Infants, femmes covert, and lunatics, may redeem at any time within one year after the removal of such disability or disabilities. (R. S. 449, Sec. 78.)

Concerning these lands, it is provided, that every two years from the first Monday of September, eighteen hundred and forty-five, the Clerks of the County Commissioners' Courts of the several counties, respectively, shall cause them to be sold at public auction. When any sale of any lot thus forfeited shall be effected, it is the duty of such clerk to deliver to the purchaser a certificate of purchase, which, on being presented to the auditor, entitles the holder thereof to a deed, conveying all the right, title, interest, and claim of the State, to the tracts or lots described in said certificate. (R. S. 450, Sec. 87.)

Land Tax, Forfeitures, and Redemptions.

The Statute provides, that real estate sold for delinquent taxes may be redeemed at any time before the expiration of two years from the date of sale, by the payment, in specie, to the Clerk of the County Commissioners' Court of the proper county, of double the amount for which the same was sold, and all taxes accruing after such sale, unless such subsequent taxes have been paid to the collector, as may be shown by the collector's receipt, by the person redeeming, with six per cent. interest thereon from the first day of May in each year up to the time of payment; *provided*, that if the real estate of any infant, femme covert, or lunatic, be sold for taxes, the same may be redeemed at any time within one year after such disability shall be removed, upon the terms specified in this section. (R. S. 447, Sec. 69.)

At any time after the expiration of two years from the sale of any real estate for taxes, if the same shall not have been redeemed, the collector, on request, and on the production of the certificate of purchase, shall execute and deliver to the purchaser, his heirs or assigns, a deed of conveyance for the real estate described in such certificate. (R. S., Sec. 71.)

The deed so made by the collector shall be acknowledged and recorded in the same manner as other conveyances of real estate, and shall vest in the grantee, his heirs or assigns, the title of the property therein described. (R. S., Sec. 72.)

Where purchasers of land sold for taxes shall neglect to pay the taxes thereon, and such land shall be again sold for taxes before the expiration of two years from the date of his or her purchase, such purchaser is not entitled to a deed for the land until the expiration of two years from the date of the second sale, during which time the land is subject to redemption upon the usual terms, except that the person redeeming is only required to pay for the use of such purchaser, the amount paid for the land, and double the amount paid by the second purchaser. (R. S. 451, Sec. 97.)

Limitation of Actions.

All actions of trespass quare clausum fregit, trespass detinue, trover, and replevin, for taking away goods and chattels, all actions for arrearages of rent due on a parole demise, and all actions of account and upon the case, except actions for slander and malicious prosecution, and such as concern the trade of merchandise between merchant and merchant, their factors or agents, shall be commenced within five years next after the cause of action accrued.

Actions of trespass for assault, battery, wounding, and imprisonment, shall be commenced within two years next after the cause of action accrued.

Actions on the case for words shall be commenced within one year, and for malicious prosecution shall be commenced within two years.

Every action of debt, or covenant for rent, or arrearages of rent, founded upon any lease under seal, and of debt or covenant, founded upon any single or penal bill, promissory note, or writing obligatory for the direct payment of money, or the delivery of property, or the performance of covenants, or upon any award under the hands and seals of arbitrators for the payment of money only, shall be commenced within sixteen years after the cause of action accrued, and when any payment has been made upon such instrument, then within sixteen years from the time of such payment.

Judgments of any Court of Record of the State may be revived by action of scire facias, or action of debt, within twenty years after the rendition of the same.

Right of entry and actions to recover lands are barred by the lapse of twenty years.

Infants, married women, persons insane and absent from this State, may make such entry and bring such actions within the times respectively limited, after the removal of their disability.

The absence of a defendant from the State is not to be computed in the limitation.

Limitation of Actions for the Recovery of Real Estate.

The Statutes provide, that no person having any right of entry into any lands, tenements, or hereditaments, shall make an entry therein but within twenty years after such right shall have accrued, and that such person shall be barred from any entry afterwards. (R. S. 349, Sec. 6.)

That every real, possessory, ancestral, or mixed action, or writ of right, brought for the recovery of any lands, tenements, or hereditaments, shall be brought within twenty years next after the right or title thereto, or cause of such action accrued, and not after. (R. S., Sec. 7.)

That every real, possessory, ancestral, or mixed action, or writ of right, brought for the recovery of any lands, tenements, or hereditaments, of which any person may be possessed by actual residence thereon, having a connected title in law or equity deducible of record, from this State or the United States, or from any public officer or other person authorized by the laws of this State to sell such land for the nonpayment of taxes, or from any sheriff, marshal, or other person authorized to sell such land on execution, or under any order, judgment, or decree of any Court of Record, shall be brought within seven years next after possession being taken as aforesaid, but when the possessor shall acquire such title after taking such possession, the limitation shall begin to run from the time of acquiring title. (R. S., Sec. 8.)

But possession to bar such rights, actions, and suits, must have been continued in manner aforesaid for the term of seven years next preceding the time of asserting the right of entry, or the commencement of any suit or action. (R. S., Sec. 9.)

No person who has, or may have, any right of entry into any lands, tenements, or hereditaments, of which any person may be possessed by actual residence thereon, having a connected title in law or equity deducible of record from this State or the United States, or from any public officer or other person authorized by the laws of this State to sell such lands for the nonpayment of taxes, or from any sheriff, marshal, or other person authorized to sell such land on execution, or under any order, judgment, or decree of any Court of Record, shall make any entry therein, except within seven years from the time of such possession being taken; but when the possessor shall acquire such title after the time of taking such possession, the limitation shall begin to run from the time of acquiring title.

In all the foregoing cases, in which the person or persons who shall have any right of entry, title, or cause of action, shall be, at the time of such right of entry, title, or cause of action, under the age of twenty-one years, insane, or femme covert, such person or persons may make such entry, or institute such action, so that the same may be done within such time as is within the time limited, after his or her becoming of full age, sane, or femme sole.

Exemptions.

The necessary wearing apparel of every person shall be exempt from sale on execution, writ of attachment, or distress for rent.

The following property, when owned by any person being the head of a family and residing with the same, shall be exempt from levy and sale on any execution, writ of attachment, or distress for rent, and such articles of property shall continue so exempt while the family of such person, or any of them, are removing from one place of residence to another in this State, viz.:

1. Necessary beds, bedsteads, and bedding, the necessary utensils for cooking, necessary household furniture, not exceeding in value fifteen dollars, one pair of cards, two spinning wheels, one weaving loom and appendage, one stove, and the necessary pipe therefor, being in use, or put up for ready use, in any house occupied by such family.

2. One milch cow and calf, two sheep for each member of the family, and the fleeces of two sheep for each member of the family, which may have been purchased by any debtor not owning sheep, and the yarn and cloth that may be manufactured from the same, and sixty dollars' worth of property suited to his or her condition or occupation in life, to be selected by the debtor.

3. The necessary provisions and fuel for the use of the family for three months, and necessary food for the stock hereinbefore exempted from sale, or that may be held under the provisions of this act.

When any lot not exceeding ten acres shall be appropriated and used as a burying ground, and shall be recorded as such in the Recorder's office of the county, it shall be exempt from all taxes, and when sold in lots for burying the dead, the said lots shall not be subject to execution or attachment; provided, that no person shall hold more than one-eighth of an acre exempt from execution.

When, in any case, the head of a family dies, deserts, or ceases to reside with the same, the said family shall be entitled to retain the property above exempted free from levy and sale on execution.

In cases of fines for assault, assault and battery, and frays, the property of the party, having a family, reserved from execution, is one bed and bedding, one cow, and ten dollars' worth of household kitchen furniture.

Homestead Exemption.

In addition to the property now exempt by law from sale under execution, there shall be exempt from levy and forced sale, under the process or order from any court of law or equity in this State, for debts contracted from and after the fourth day of July, 1851, the lot of ground and the buildings thereon, occupied as a residence and owned by the debtor, being a householder and having a family, to the value of one thousand dollars. Such exemption shall continue after the death of such householder for the benefit of the widow and family, some or one of them continuing to occupy such homestead until the youngest child shall become twenty-one years of age, and until the death of such widow, and no release or waiver of such exemption shall be valid, unless the same shall be in writing, subscribed by such householder, and acknowledged in the same manner as conveyances of real estate are by law required to be acknowledged.

No property shall, by virtue of this act, be exempt from sale for nonpayment of taxes on assessments, or for a debt or liability incurred for the purchase or improvement thereof, or prior to the recording of the aforesaid conveyance or notice.

If, in the opinion of the creditors or officer holding an execution against such householder, the premises claimed by him or her as exempt, are worth more than one thousand dollars, such officer shall summon six qualified jurors of his county, who shall, upon oath, to be administered to them by the officer, appraise said premises, and if, in their opinion, the property may be divided without injury to the parties, they shall set off so much of said premises, including the dwelling-house, as in their opinion shall be worth one thousand dollars, and the residue of said premises be advertised and sold by such officer.

In case such surplus, or the amount due on said execution, shall not be paid within the said sixty days, it shall be lawful for the officer to advertise and sell the said premises, and out of the proceeds of such sale to pay to such execution debtor the said sum of one thousand dollars, which shall be exempt from execution for one year thereafter, and apply the balance on such execution; *provided*, that no sale shall be made unless a greater sum than one thousand dollars shall be bid therefor, in which case the officer may return the execution for want of property.

The costs and expenses of setting off such property, as provided herein, shall be charged and included in the officer's bill of costs upon such execution.

Lien Law.

Boats and vessels of all descriptions, built, repaired, or equipped, or running upon any of the navigable waters within the jurisdiction of this State, shall be liable for all debts contracted by the owner or owners, masters, supercargoes, or consignees thereof, on account of all work done, supplies or materials furnished by mechanics, tradesmen, and others, for or on account of the building, repairing, furnishing or equipping such boats and vessels, and such debts shall have the preference of all other debts due from the owners or proprietors, except the wages of mariners, boatmen, and others, employed in the service of such boat and vessels, which shall be first paid.

All engineers, pilots, mariners, boatmen, and others, employed in any capacity in or about the service of any such boat or vessel, who may be entitled to arrearages of wages in consequence of such service, shall have a lien as above. No creditor shall be allowed to enforce the lien created as specified, unless such lien be enforced within three months after the indebtedness accrues.

All judgments rendered in any court of record for any debt, or damages, costs, or other sum of money, shall cease to be a lien upon the lands, tenements, and real estate of the persons against whom it is rendered, after the lapse of seven years.

The time during which any person in whose favor any such judgment shall have been entered, shall be restrained by injunction out of chancery, or order of any judge or court, from issuing execution or selling thereon, shall not be deemed as part of the seven years.

Every landlord shall have a lien upon the crops growing or grown upon demised premises, in any year, for rent that shall accrue for such year.

Any person who shall furnish labor or materials toward the erecting or repairing any building, or the appurtenances of any building, shall have a lien upon the same, and upon the land on which such building stands, for the amount due him for such labor or materials, whether the kind or quantity of work or amount to be paid be specified or not, *provided* the time of completing the contract be not extended beyond the period of three years, nor the time of payment beyond the period of one year from the time stipulated for the completion thereof.

Persons furnishing labor or materials in repairing or erecting any building, in order to enforce their lien as above stated, must bring suit within six months from the time that the last payment should have been made.

Chattel Mortgages.

No mortgage on personal property hereafter executed shall be valid as against the rights and interests of third persons, unless possession of the property shall be delivered to and remain with the mortgagee, or the said mortgage be acknowledged and recorded in the office of the recorder of the county in which the mortgagor shall reside.

Any mortgagor must first acknowledge before any justice of the peace, in the justice's district in which he may reside, such mortgage, and the said justice must certify to such acknowledgement, and enter the same upon his docket.

It shall then be valid for two years, provided that such mortgage shall provide for the possession of the property so to remain with the mortgagor.

Contracts.

No action shall be brought whereby to charge any executor or administrator upon any special promise to answer any debt or damages out of his own estate, or whereby to charge the defendant upon any special promise to answer for the debt, default, or miscarriage of another person, or to charge any person upon any agreement made upon any consideration of marriage, or upon any contract for the sale of lands, tenements, or hereditaments, or any interest in or concerning them for a longer term than one year, or upon any agreement that is not to be performed within the space of one year from the making thereof, unless the promise or agreement upon which such action shall be brought, or some memorandum or note thereof, shall be in writing, and signed by the party to be charged therewith, or some other person thereunto by him lawfully authorized.

Collection of Debts.

Arrest.

When any debtor shall refuse to surrender his estate, lands, goods, or chattels, for the satisfaction of any execution which may be issued against the property of any such debtor, it shall and may be lawful for the plaintiff or his attorney or agent to make affidavit of such fact before any justice of the peace of the county, and upon filing such affidavit with the clerk of the court from which the execution issued, or with the justice of the peace who issued such execution, it shall be lawful for such clerk or justice of the peace, as the case may be, to issue a *capias ad satisfaciendum* against the body of such defendant in execution.

In all actions to be commenced in any court of record in the state, founded on any specialty, judgment, or contract, in which the plaintiff or other credible person can ascertain the sum due or damages sustained, and will make affidavit before the clerk of the court from which process issues, or a justice of the peace, or if the plaintiff resides out of the state, before any person who may be authorized to administer an oath in the state or kingdom in which he resides, that the same is in danger of being lost, or that the benefit of any judgment which may be rendered will be lost, unless the defendant be held to bail, and such affidavit be delivered to the clerk of the court, the clerk must issue a writ against the body of the defendant, with directions to the sheriff endorsed to take bail.

When damages are unliquidated, the affidavit must state facts, and the nature and cause of action, and the clerk must fix the amount of bail.

When any person is arrested for debt on execution, or on original process, for the purpose of being held to bail, it is the duty of the officer having the custody of the debtor, at his request, to convey him before the judge of the county in which the arrest is made. The county judge must require of the debtor a complete schedule of his property, of whatever description, with an account of the debts owing by the debtor at the time. The debtor may then take the oath prescribed by statute, and if no fraud appears upon examination of the debtor, or of the witnesses produced, and the debtor assign the property named in the schedule, not exempt, and produce the receipt of the assignee to the court, he is discharged.

The plaintiff in execution may, after the defendant has taken the oath prescribed, pay the sheriff the jail fees on the Monday of each week, and keep the defendant in jail until the debt is paid, at the rate of one dollar and fifty cents per day, upon the happening of which event the sheriff returns the exection satisfied by imprisonment.

Attachment.

If any creditor or his agent shall make complaint, on oath or affirmation, to the clerk of the Circuit Court of any county in this state, that his debtor is about to depart from this state, or has departed from this state, with the intention, in either case, of having his effects and personal estate removed without the limits of this state, to the injury of such creditor, or stands in defiance of any officer to arrest him on civil process, so that the ordinary process of law can not be served on such debtor, and that the debtor is indebted to him in a sum exceeding twenty dollars, specifying the amount and nature of such indebtedness, such creditor may sue out a writ of attachment against the debtor's lands and tenements, goods and chattels, rights and credits, moneys and effects, of what nature soever, or so much as will satisfy the debt sworn to, with interest and costs.

When any creditor, his agent or attorney, shall make oath or affirmation before any justice of the peace in the state, that any person being a nonresident of this state is indebted to such creditor in a sum not exceeding fifty dollars, such justice may issue an attachment against his personal estate.

Attachment may issue in the case of a non-resident against all his property, for a sum exceeding twenty dollars, from the clerk of the Circuit Court of any county.

Imprisonment for debt is forbidden by the Constitution, except in case of the debtor's refusal to deliver up his estate for the benefit of creditors, as prescribed by law, or when there is strong evidence of intentional fraud.

Rate of Interest.

From and after January 30, 1849, money may be loaned at such rate of interest, not exceeding ten per cent. per annum on each hundred dollars, as the parties may agree upon. In the trial of any action brought upon a promissory note or writing obligatory, in any of the courts of this state, wherein is reserved a higher rate of interest than six per cent. per annum, it shall be lawful for the defendant to set up and plead, as a defence in any such suit, that the consideration of said note or writing obligatory, upon which such suit is brought, was not "money loaned"; upon which issue it shall be lawful for the debtor, the creditor being alive, to become a witness, and his testimony shall be received as evidence; and the creditor, if he shall offer his testimony, shall be received as a witness, together with any other legal evidence that may be introduced by either party; and if upon the trial of the said issue it shall be found that the said note or writing obligatory, upon which such suit is brought, was not given for money loaned, then the said court shall render judgment for the principal sum in said promissory note or writing obligatory, and six per cent interest thereon.

Landlord and Tenant.

Tenants who hold over after the expiration of their term, and after demand made and notice in writing given for the possession thereof, by the landlord, must pay at the rate of double the yearly value of the land for the time such landlord is so kept out of possession.

Every tenant, who shall be sued in ejectment by any person other than his landlord, shall forthwith give notice thereof to his landlord or his attorney, under the penalty of forfeiting two years' rent of the premises in question.

In all cases of distress for rent, the landlord may by himself, or his attorney, seize for rent any personal property of his tenant, that may be found in the county where such tenant shall reside, and in no case shall the property of any other person, though the same shall be found on the premises, be liable to seizure for rent due from such tenant.

The person making the distress shall immediately file with some justice of the peace, in case the amount claimed does not exceed one hundred dollars, or with the clerk of the Circuit Court in case it exceeds that sum, a copy of the distress warrant, together with the inventory of the property levied upon, and thereupon the tenant shall be summoned, and the amount due from him assessed and entered upon the records of the Court. The Court shall certify to the person or officer making the distress, the amount found due, together with the costs of the Court, and the officer shall proceed to sell the property distrained, and return the certificate, with an endorsement thereon of his proceedings, which return and certificate shall be filed in the proper court.

If the tenant does not, within five days after notice of such distress and the cause of taking, replevy the goods so taken, the person distraining may, with the sheriff or constable of the county, cause the goods to be appraised by two reputable freeholders under oath, and the landlord may then sell the goods at public auction, on giving ten days' notice.

The landlord has a lien upon the growing or grown crops for rent that shall accrue during the year of their growth.

If any person makes an illegal or forcible entry into lands, or holds over after the expiration of the time for which such lands were let to him, after demand made in writing for possession thereof, such person shall be adjudged guilty of a forcible entry and detinue, and may be removed from such possession by an action before a justice of the peace.

Form of Demand for Possession.

To A. B., of M., in the County of H.

Take notice, that you are hereby required to quit, and deliver up to me, on the day of next (or immediately), the possession of the dwelling house (or rooms and apartments, or lands and premises), with the appurtenances, which you now hold or claim to hold of me, situate in M., in the County of H., known as No. 12, on E. street.

May 4th, 185 . J. L.

Affidavit of Service (written on a copy).

I certify, that on the day of , 185 , I gave to A. B. above named (or left at the usual place of abode of A. B. above named), an original notice, of which the within is a true copy.

H., May 4th, 185 . [Seal.]

Personally appeared T. W., and made oath, that the above affidavit, by him subscribed, is true.

Before me, N. M., Justice of the Peace.

Warrant to Distrain.

To C. D.

I hereby authorize and require you to distrain the goods and chattels in the dwelling house (or rooms and apartments, or on the lands and premises) now in the possession of A. B., situate in M., in the County of A., known as No

12, on E. street, for six months' rent, due to me under a lease of the same, and to proceed thereon for the recovery of the said rent, as the law directs.

Witness my hand, this day of , 185 .

E. F.

[*Note.* — This warrant may be addressed to any agent or attorney of the landlord.]

Notice to Tenant of Distress for Rent.

To A. B.

Take notice, that by the authority and on behalf of your landlord, E. F., I have this day distrained the several goods and chattels specified in the inventory hereto attached, in your house, in M., in the County of H., known as No. 12, on E. street, for eighty dollars arrearages of rent due to him, the said E. F. Now, therefore, if you do not pay the rent so due, or replevy the said goods and chattels according to law, within five days from the date hereafter, I shall cause the said goods and chattels to be appraised and sold, according to the statute in such case made and provided.

May 10th, 185 . C. D.

[*Note.* — The inventory must be attached to the foregoing, and left with the tenant, in presence of some one, who should certify to that fact.]

Promissory Notes and Bills of Exchange.

Foreign bills of exchange, expressed that the value has been received, protested for non-acceptance, or non-payment, are entitled to ten per cent. damages, together with legal interest and costs, and charges of protest.

A foreign bill is one drawn on a party out of the United States.

When an inland bill of exchange, expressed that the value has been received, is protested for non-acceptance or non-payment, the drawer or endorser shall pay legal interest from the time such bill ought to have been paid, and five per cent. damages, together with costs and charges of protest.

All promissory notes, bonds, due bills, and other instruments in writing, for the payment of money or articles of personal property, are assignable by endorsement, in the same manner as bills of exchange, so as absolutely to vest the property thereof in the assignee.

The assignee cannot sue the assignor on such endorsement, until he has first instituted and prosecuted a suit against the maker of such note, bond, &c., for the recovery of the money due thereon; provided, that if the institution of such suit would have been unavailing, or the maker had absconded or left the State when such note became due, such assignee may at once sue on the endorsement.

Apprentices.

All children under the age of fourteen years may be bound without their consent, and all minors above that age with their consent, males until they are twenty-one, and females until they are eighteen. Such minors may be bound with the consent of the father, or if he be incompetent, then with the consent of the mother, or if she be incompetent, then with that of the guardian of the minor, or if there be no guardian, then with the approbation of the Judge of the County Court, or by any two justices of the peace of the county in which such minor resides, endorsed on the indenture.

The fact of such incompetence to consent shall be tried and found by a jury in the County Court.

Any minor who shall be likely to become a public charge may be bound by the County Court, or by any two overseers of the poor, or by any two justices of the peace of the county in which such minor may reside, with the approval of the Judge of the County Court.

The indenture must be signed and sealed by the parties, whose consent is required by law, but the approval of the Judge of the County Court may be endorsed on the indenture, attested by his seal of office.

The age and time of service of the minor shall be inserted in the indenture. It must be provided in the indenture, that the apprentice shall be taught to read, write, and the cardinal rules of arithmetic.

The Judge of the County Court, or any two justices of the peace, excepting the justices who may have bound the apprentice complaining, shall hear complaints of apprentices against their masters, and may discharge the indenture.

Indentures not in conformity with this law are void.

Rights of Married Women and Widows.

Widows shall be allowed, in all cases, in exclusion of creditors, as their sole property for ever, necessary beds, bedsteads and bedding for themselves and families, necessary household and kitchen furniture, one spinning wheel, one loom and its appendages, one pair of cards, one stove, and the necessary pipe therefor, the wearing apparel of themselves and families, one milch cow and calf for every four persons in the family, one horse at the value of forty dollars, one woman's saddle and bridle of the value of fifteen dollars, provisions for themselves and families one year, two sheep for each member of the family, and the fleeces taken from the same, food for the stock above described for six months, fuel for themselves and families for three months, and sixty dollars' worth of other property.

The appraisers certify to the County Court an estimate of the value of each article allowed to the widow, and she may take other property in lieu of that above specified, at the value affixed by the appraisers.

In addition to the above, widows of persons who may die intestate shall be entitled to one-third of the personal estate of their deceased husbands, after the payment of debts, as their property for ever.

If the estate be intestate, and there shall be a widow, and no child or descendants of the intestate, then the one-half of the real estate, and the whole of the personal estate, shall go to such widow, as her exclusive estate for ever.

A widow is endowed of a third part of all the lands whereof her husband was seized of an estate of inheritance at any time during the marriage.

Every devise of land bars her dower, unless otherwise expressed in the will, but she may elect, at any time within a year, whether she will take her dower or take under the will.

Dower may be barred by a jointure created before marriage, with the assent of the intended wife, evinced by her becoming a party to the conveyance, by which it shall be settled, if she be of full age, or if she be an infant, by her joining with her father or guardian in such conveyance.

A married woman may relinquish her right of dower in any of the real estate of her husband, by joining him in a deed of conveyance, and acknowledging the same, separate and apart from the husband.

The real estate of the wife may be conveyed by her joining with her husband in the deed, if she be above the age of eighteen years, and by her acknowledging the same, separate and apart from her husband.

Married women have power to dispose of their separate estate, both real and personal, by will, in the same manner as other persons.

A married woman, residing out of the State, may relinquish dower, if above eighteen years of age.

ESTRAYS.

Sec. 1. Every person who shall take up any estray horse, mare, colt, mule, or ass, after having given not less than ten nor more than fifteen days' notice, by posting up notices in three of the most public places in the justice's district in which he resides, shall take the same before some justice of the peace of the county where such estray shall be taken up, and make oath before such justice, that the same was taken up at his or her plantation or place of residence, in said county, and that the marks or brands have not been altered since the taking up.

Sec. 2. The said justice shall then summon three disinterested householders of the neighborhood, to appraise said estray, under oath, which appraisement, together with the brands, marks, stature, color, and age of such animal, shall be entered in a book to be kept by said justice, and transmitted to the clerk of the County Court within fifteen days after the same is taken up.

Sec. 3. No such animal shall be taken up and posted between the first day of April and first day of November, unless the same be found out of the range of the proper owner, or within the lawful fence or enclosure of the taker up, having broken in the same, or manifestly running away from the owner.

Sec. 4. No person not a householder of the county shall take up or post such animal.

Sec. 5. Any person who shall take up any neat cattle, sheep, hogs, or goats, shall give the notice required in Sec. 1, and shall go with some householder before a justice of the peace of the county, and make the oath required in the same section, and then such justice shall take from the householder a particular description of the animal, and cause the same to be appraised as in Sec. 2d, which description and valuation to be entered and transmitted to the clerk of the County Court, as before directed. In case the value of such animal does not exceed five dollars, the justice need not make such return to the clerk, but shall enter the description and value in his estray book, and advertise the same in three of the most public places in his neighborhood.

Sec. 6. The clerk shall cause a copy of such return to be affixed to the court-house door, within five days after the same shall be transmitted to him.

Sec. 7. No neat cattle, sheep, hogs, or goats, shall be taken up between the month of April and the first day of November, unless the same be found in the lawful fence or enclosure of the taker up, having broken the same, and for the reward of the taker up there shall be paid by the owner one dollar for every horse, mare, colt, mule, or ass, and for every head of neat cattle fifty cents, and for every hog, sheep, or goat, twenty-five cents, with all reasonable charges.

Sec. 8. If the owner shall prove and take away such animals before appraisement, he shall pay all reasonable charges of the taker up. It is not lawful for the takers up to use estrays previous to advertising them.

Sec. 9. It is the duty of the clerk of the County Court to publish the justice's return in some paper, to be designated by the governor, at the end of ten days after the same is transmitted to him, and the printer must transmit a copy of his paper to the clerks of the County Court of the several counties of the State.

Sec. 10. If no owner appears within one year after such publication, the property shall be vested in the taker up; but the former may, at any time thereafter, by proving his property, recover the valuation money, upon payment of costs and all reasonable charges.

Sec. 11. If any person shall sell or dispose of such estray within the year, he shall be liable to indictment, and shall be fined double the value of the property.

Sec. 12. When the estray is worth less than five dollars, the property vests in the taker up in one year from the time the description and value have been published at the court-house door.

Sec. 13. It is lawful for any person taking up an estray hog between the first day of November and the first day of March, after complying with the provisions of Sec. 1 and Sec. 3, and making oath that he believes said estray has strayed from some drove, if no owner shall appear to prove said estray within the time specified in said notice, to sell said estray to the highest bidder, after giving public notice of said sale ten days previous thereto, the proceeds, after paying reasonable charges, to be paid to the county.

The Game Law.

Section 1. *Be it enacted by the People of the State of Illinois represented in the General Assembly,* That it shall be unlawful for any person to kill, ensnare, or trap, any deer, fawn, wild turkey, grouse, prairie hens or chickens, or quail, between the fifteenth day of January and the first of August of each and every year.

Sec. 2. That it shall be unlawful for any person to buy, sell, or have in possession, any of the above-mentioned animals or birds, which shall have been killed, ensnared, trapped, or taken, between the first day of January and the first day of August of each and every year, as aforesaid; and that having or being in possession of any of the above-mentioned animals or birds aforesaid by any person or persons between the said first day of January and the first day of August aforesaid, shall be deemed and taken as *prima facie* evidence that the same was ensnared, trapped, or killed, by the person having possession of the same, in violation of the provisions of this act.

Sec. 3. Any person who shall go upon the premises of any person or persons, or corporation, whether the same be enclosed or not, with intention to hunt, or to be found hunting, entrapping, or ensnaring any of the above-mentioned animals or birds, at or within the time aforesaid shall be deemed guilty of trespass, and may be prosecuted before any justice of the peace in the county wherein the said premises may lie, by the owner or person in possession of the same, in action of trespass, and fined in any sum not less than five nor more than twenty dollars, to go to the owner or occupant of said premises: *Provided, however,* that a judgment obtained against any person for a violation of this act, under the fourth section thereof, shall be a bar to any suit under the third section of this act.

Sec. 4. Any person who shall wilfully violate any of the provisions of this act, shall forfeit and pay a fine of fifteen dollars for each deer or fawn thus killed, ensnared, entrapped, bought, sold, or held in possession; and for any other wild game, animals, or birds enumerated, either killed, ensnared, entrapped, bought, sold, or held in possession, as aforesaid, the sum of five dollars shall be paid; to be sued for and recovered before any justice of the peace of the county in which the act shall have been violated, in an action of debt, or before any court having jurisdiction thereof; one-half of said penalty shall go to the complainant, and the other half to the school trustees of the township in which the act shall have been violated, to be added to the school fund of said township; the action to be brought in the name of said county.

Sec. 5. Provided that nothing in this act shall apply to the counties of

White, Wabash, Clay, Richland, Jasper, Lawrence, Crawford, Clark, Edgar, Coles, Moultrie, Effingham, Fayette, Bond, Cass, Menard, Pike, Schuyler, Brown, Scott, Washington, Jefferson, Marion, Hamilton, Clinton, Jackson, Franklin, Wayne, Edwards, McDonough, Alexander, Pulaski, Union, Hardin, Massac, Warren, Henderson, Monroe, Perry, Shelby, Cumberland, Jersey, Calhoun, Randolph, Pope, McLean, Knox, Fulton, Hancock, Adams, Stark, Vermilion, Montgomery, and Christian.

Sec. 6. This act shall be in force from and after its passage.

Approved, February 15, 1855.

GEOGRAPHY.

SITUATED in the centre of the United States, the state of Illinois extends from 37° to 42° 30′ latitude North, and from 87° 49′ to 91° 28′ longitude West of Greenwich, or from 10° 47′ to 14° 26′ longitude West of Washington. Illinois is bounded on the North-east by Lake Michigan; on the East by Indiana, from a part of which it is separated by the Wabash river; on the South by Kentucky and Missouri, being separated from Kentucky by the Ohio, and from Missouri by the Mississippi; on the West by Missouri, from which it is also separated by the Mississippi; on the North-west by Iowa, the Mississippi constituting the common boundary of both states, and on the North by Wisconsin.

The whole length of the Illinoisian frontier amounts to 1160 miles, 855 of which are formed by navigable waters, as Lake Michigan, the Wabash, Ohio, and Mississippi. The greatest length of the state, from South to North, from Cairo to Wisconsin, amounts to 378 miles; its greatest breadth to 212 miles. The area of the state is computed at 55,405 square miles, or 35,459,200 acres,—1,833,412 of which are so-called swamp-lands; the residue, 33,625,788 acres, being tillable, and the most part of them having a soil of unsurpassed fertility.

Illinois communicates by means of the St. Lawrence with the Atlantic ocean, and by the Mississippi with the Gulf of Mexico.

The state of Illinois forms the lower part of that slope in which is embraced the greater part of the state of Indiana, and of which Lake Michigan, with its shores, constitutes the upper part. The lowest point of this slope and of the state is the city of Cairo, situated about 350 feet above the level of the Gulf of Mexico, at the conflux of the Ohio and Mississippi, in the extreme southern portion of the state; hence, the highest place in Illinois being situated only 800 feet above the level of the sea, it will appear, that the whole state, though containing several hilly sections, is a very level plain; being, with the sole exception of Delaware and Louisiana, the flattest country in the Union.

Illinois is more than forty times as great as the state of Rhode Island in its area, containing but 10,720 square miles less than the entire New England states. None but the following states possess a greater area — Virginia having 61,852, Georgia 58,000, Florida 59,268, Missouri 67,380, Michigan 56,243, California 188,981, and Texas 237,321 square miles; but if California shall yet be divided into Upper and Lower California, Michigan into the state of Superior and Michigan proper, and Texas, as at the time of its annexation was provided for, into five different states, then Illinois, as far as regards its area, will rank fifth among the states of the Union. Illinois seems to be destined, within a short time, to play a great role in the United States, being entitled to this not only by the vastness of its area and its excellent geographical position, but also by the fertility of its easily culivated soil, the multitude of its rivers and fine railroads, and the rapid increase of its population, together with the enterprise and intelligence of its citizens.

The principal rivers of the state of Illinois are —

The *Illinois river*, which, formed by the conflux of the Kankakee and Des Moines about fifty miles south-west of Chicago, during a course of 500 miles, receives several other rivers, as the Fox river, the Spoon river, the Crooked Creek, Mackinaw, Sangamon, and the Vermilion, from the south, besides several others. The Illinois river is deep and broad, extending at several places, as at Peoria, where it forms a basin called then Peoria Lake, to such a breadth as to present the appearance of a sea. It was first navigated in the year 1828 by a steamboat.

Rock River, rising in Wisconsin, pursues a course of 300 miles, being navigable to some extent; there are, however, several rapids in the upper part of its course. A great part of the country through which Rock River runs is an undulating prairie, with a rich soil, though with but few forests.

The *Kaskaskia*, a navigable river, rising in Champaign county, after a run to the south-west of more than 300 miles, empties its waters into the Mississippi, about 120 miles above the mouth of the

Ohio. Kaskaskia River was already, in the year 1837, navigated by steamboats as far as Carlisle. Its banks, for an extent varying from two to ten miles, are richly garnished with woods and forests of oaks, hickory, ash, maple, elm, and acacia trees. The country through which the river winds its course is undulating and fertile.

The *Big Muddy river*, in the south-western portion of the state, has various sources, constituting at their conflux the river above named, which, after a run to the south-west, discharges its waters into the Mississippi. The country through which it runs is undulating and wooded, offering great advantages to agriculture and the breeding of cattle,

Embarras River, in the eastern part of the state, takes its rise near the source of the Kaskaskia, and runs southerly, discharging its waters into the Wabash about six miles below Vincennes. The land along Embarras River is not everywhere of the same good quality, consisting at the origin of the river chiefly of prairie lands, and further north of Charleston, of forests garlanding the banks of the river at a breadth varying between two and six miles, extending even to ten miles below that place.

Little Wabash River, rising also near the source of the Kaskaskia, runs south, emptying its waters into the Great Wabash, in Gallatin county. Its banks, for an extent of several miles, are garnished with good and heavy timber; at intervals poplars can be found. The country adjacent to this river is fertile, exposed however to inundations from the river.

Sangamon River, rising in McLean county, runs south-west, constituting during the latter part of its course the boundary line between Monroe and Cass counties, and emptying its waters into Illinois River. The country watered by the Sangamon is one of the richest, being quite level, and having excellent soil.

Apple River, rising in Jo Daviess county, near the Wisconsin frontier, has a rocky bed, and is very rapid, running south-west, and flowing into the Mississippi about twenty miles below Galena. The adjacent bottom-lands have excellent soil; the more elevated country in its vicinity being hilly, its banks woody, and the country around its springs undulating.

Chicago River, consisting of two branches, the more considerable one of which is that running North, and both of them flowing together within the city of Chicago, empties its waters into Lake Michigan.

Des Plaines River, rising in Wisconsin, at the distance of a few miles from Lake Michigan, runs South, and is a tributary of Illinois River by the union of its waters with those of the Kaukakee. Its banks are tufted with frequent groves, the country around it being well watered, and the soil very rich.

Du Page River, in the north-eastern section of the state, consists of two branches, emptying their united waters into the Des Plaines river, three miles above the confluence of the latter with the Kaukakee.

The *Cash river,* in the southern portion of the state, formed by the union of several small streams, flows into the Ohio, six miles above the junction of the latter with the Mississippi. The alluvial land along Cash River, wherever it is not exposed to inundation, possesses a rich soil and heavy timber.

The *Edwards river,* rising in the midst of the prairies of Henry county, runs Westward, through Mercer county, to the Mississippi. The country around it consists of undulating prairie-lands, intersected by shady groves, and well supplied with water.

The *Fever river,* rising in Jo Daviess county, consists of two branches, and empties its waters into the Mississippi, about seven miles south of Galena. Its channel is rocky, and its course very rapid. On the eastern branch there is little wood, but excellent prairies, and mines yielding an abundant supply of lead. There is more wood on the western branch, the alluvial country around which has a rich soil. The name of the river has been derived from the fevers said to prevail in the vicinity of its banks; whilst others have called it Bean River (in French, Rivière à la Fève), either of which is incorrect, the river having been named by a Frenchman of the name of Le Fèvre, who at an early period settled at the mouth of the stream.

Fox River, on the banks of which fine forests may be found, rises in Wisconsin, flowing, near Ottawa, into the Illinois.

Another river of the *same name* runs south, a tributary of the

Little Wabash, into which it empties its waters. The land along its banks is not very excellent.

A *third* river of the *same name*, in White county, runs, after a short course, into the Great Wabash.

Green River, rising in the swamps of the northern counties, runs west, through Henry county, into Rock River. The country below the swamps is good, consisting of both woods and prairies.

Henderson River, rising in Knox county, runs south-west, receiving during its course several small streams, and flowing into the Mississippi. Fine forests grow on its banks, the country around which is among the most fertile in Illinois.

Iroquois River, rising in the north-western section of Indiana, runs North-West, becoming a tributary of the Illinois by discharging its waters into the Kankakee. The country through which the Iroquois runs is undulating; the soil a little sandy, but rich; timber to be found in sufficient quantity.

The *Kankakee*, one of the principal tributary rivers of the Illinois, rising in Indiana, runs west, receiving the Iroquois and Des Plaines rivers. Woods are but rarely to be met with on its banks, the prairies around which are slightly undulating, having a rich soil.

The *Kickapoo* consists of two branches, after the conflux of which it pursues a southerly direction, discharging its waters into the Illinois, two miles below Peoria. On both its branches there is much excellent land, intersected with groups of forests, the ground being rather hilly.

The *Kishwaukee*, or Sycamore, formed by the junction of several small waters, some of which rise in Wisconsin, others in the northern counties of Illinois, discharges the waters of its three principal branches, after their combination, in Rock River. Its banks have but little wood; the prairie along the eastern branch is flat and fertile; and the country along the southern and northern branches undulating, and remarkable for its very rich, deep, black soil, and its beds of lime and coal.

The *Kite river*, in Ogle county, runs west, flowing into Rock river, about two miles below Oregon. The country is very level, and the soil very fine; woods, among which are many poplars, can be found at intervals.

The *Leaf river*, in Ogle county, also empties its waters into Rock River. The land adjoining its banks is rich, calcareous, and woody at intervals.

Little Rock River, rising in Jo Daviess county, flows into Rock River. On its banks there is much excellent soil.

The *Mackinaw* (Michilimackinac), rising in the prairies of McLean county, and receiving several small brooks, runs through Tazewell county into the Illinois river, three miles below Pekin. The adjacent bottom-lands have a rich soil. Timber, especially white oak and cedar, may be found. The prairies of the country are undulating and dry. Towards the sources of the river, the number of species of woods increases, whilst the soil is very good.

The *Mauvaise Terre*, in Morgan county, runs west, meeting Illinois River about two miles below Naples. Although from the name of the river (Mauvaise Terre, "poor land") one might infer that the soil of the adjacent country is of a very bad quality, this is not the case; the country, on the contrary, surpassing many other sections in fertility, and has the advantage of having a just proportion between prairie and forest, as also a remarkable salubrity of waters.

The *Peek-a-ton-o-kee* rises in Wisconsin, in two separate branches, which, after their conflux, flows into Illinois to meet Rock River.

The *Plum river*, the country surrounding the banks of which has a fine soil, with both wood and prairie, runs through Jo Daviess county into the Mississippi.

Pope's River, rising in the great prairies in the southern part of Henry county, runs west through Mercer county, discharging its waters into the Mississippi a few miles below the mouth of Edwards' River. The adjacent country is very good, but destitute of forests; on the banks of the river, towards the end of its course, there are, however, some extensive woods, while its upper banks are surrounded by prairies.

Saline River, in Saline and Gallatin counties, consists of three branches, discharging their united waters into the Ohio, twelve miles below Shawneetown.

Senatchwine River, on the banks of which there is much good land, both wood and prairie, runs through Peoria county into Illinois River, about twenty miles above Peoria.

The *Sinsinaway*, rising in Wisconsin, runs south-west into the Mississippi, about six miles above Fever River. Timber on its banks is very rare; only now and then some cedars and pines may be found.

Small-pox River, rising south-east of Galena, runs west into the Mississippi, close by the mouth of Fever River. On its banks, near the place where it flows into the Mississippi, much valuable timber may be found.

The *Snycartee*, a branch of the Mississippi, whence it flows, in the southern portion of Adams county, running for about fifty miles parallel with, and five miles from, the Mississippi, to meet it again in Calhoun county, forms, with the Mississippi, an island, consisting of alluvial land, not destitute either of forest or prairie, but frequently exposed to inundations.

Spoon River consists of an eastern and western branch, both of which having received a multitude of creeks, unite; whereupon the river takes a southern direction to meet the Illinois, opposite Havana. On its banks there are many extensive woody tracts; the soil of the adjoining country is of unsurpassed excellence. The prairies near by the river are undulating, dry, and fertile.

St. Mary's River, rising in Perry county, discharges its waters into the Mississippi six miles below the mouth of the Kaskaskia.

The *Sugar river*, rising in Wisconsin, runs southerly to meet the Peek-a-ton-o-kee. The land upon its banks is of good quality; the country between Rock and Sugar rivers very humid.

Turtle River, rising in Wisconsin, flows near the boundary into Rock River.

Vermilion River, rising in Livingston county, runs through La Salle county, emptying into Illinois River. Towards its springs the country is nearly level, having a rich soil and vast prairies, but very little wood. In the vicinity of the river, and near the bluffs, are many extensive coal mines, of which those situated in the direction of the Illinois river reach a depth of 100 feet; also beds of sand, and lime, and a kind of stone used as whetstone, may here be found.

Big Vermilion River, proceeding in three different branches through Champaign and Vermilion counties, falls, in Indiana, into the Wabash. Its banks are garnished with a wood from one to two miles broad; the adjacent prairies are dry, rolling, and fertile.

Little Vermilion River, rising in the southern part of Vermilion county, runs also into the Wabash in Indiana. On its banks fine forests may be found.

Wood River, rising in Macoupin county, runs through Madison county, discharging its waters nearly opposite the mouth of the Missouri, into the Mississippi. The land through which it runs is of superior quality.

Illinois has, besides these streams, a multitude of rivulets, the banks of which, as well as those of the rivers mentioned above, consist of alluvial, and consequently very fertile soil, so that neither in the Union, nor anywhere else on earth, could be found a State of equal size with Illinois rivalling the latter in the fertility and superior quality of its soil.

Of lakes, none can be found in Illinois; that portion of Lake Michigan* bounding the State being comparatively but small, so that this lake, the navigation of which has contributed so much to the advancement of Illinois, cannot be properly considered as belonging to the State.

The only sheet of water, that in a measure might lay claim to the name of a lake, is Peoria Lake, which, however, as was mentioned when Illinois River was spoken of, is nothing but an enlargement of this river; none of the other waters deserve this name at all, but should rather be called ponds.

An artificial aqueduct, that has likewise considerably accelerated the advancement of Illinois, is yet to be mentioned. The Illinois and Michigan Canal extends from Chicago to Peru, a distance of one hundred miles, connecting thus the Lake of Michigan with the Illinois: it is 6 feet deep, 70 feet broad at the top, and 36 at the bottom.

What distinguish the State of Illinois from all the other States of the Union, are its immense prairies, from which it has been exclusively called the "Prairie State." We do not intend to give in this geographical sketch a detailed description of the nature of a prairie, but setting apart a special chapter for this, we shall here only mention the principal prairies — those known under peculiar names.

* The greatest length of Lake Michigan is 360 miles; its greatest breadth, 108 miles; mean depth, 300 feet; elevation, 587 feet; area, 23,000 square miles.

The most considerable of these prairies is the *Grand Prairie*, comprehending all prairie-lands between the rivers flowing into the Mississippi and those meeting the Wabash. The prairie itself does not consist of one single continuous extensive tract of land, but of many different prairies, separated one from the other by a range of woods, while the prairies, in their turn, stretch between the usually woody banks of the rivers and creeks. The most southerly portion of the great prairie is situated in the north-east section of Jackson county, extending north-easterly from the Mississippi, with a breadth varying from two to ten and more miles, through Perry, Washington, Jefferson, Marion, Fayette, Clay, Effingham, Shelby, Moultrie, Cumberland, Coles, Champaign, Vermilion, and Iroquois counties; here it meets the prairies stretching easterly from Illinois River and its tributaries. That portion of these prairie-lands lying in Marion county, between Crooked Creek and the eastern branch of the Kaskaskia, intersected by the Ohio and Mississippi Railroad, is often exclusively named the Grand Prairie.

The greater portion of the Grand Prairie is slightly undulating, its southern part quite level, having many tracts of land of but inferior quality. At the distance of ten or twelve miles around, timber is sure to be found; coal almost everywhere, at no great depth.

Another prairie, also called *Grand Prairie*, commences in Crawford county, extending north through Clark and Edgar counties to Vermilion. It is not very broad, and at frequent intervals is intersected by forest-bordered rivers.

The soil of the southern and eastern is not as good as that of the northern and western portion of these prairies, which, with the exception of those adjacent to the Wabash, have a thin and nearly level washy humus.

Allen's Prairie, in Greene county, twelve miles north-east of Carrollton, is fertile, and wooded on the banks of the rivers running through it.

Alison's Prairie, in Lawrence county, five miles easterly from Lawrenceville, is some five miles by ten. That portion of it adjacent to the Wabash, is humid; by far the greater portion of it, however is dry and fertile.

Apple-Creek Prairie, in Greene county, north of Apple Creek, is from three to four miles by ten in extent. Its soil is good.

Barney's Prairie, in Wabash county, north of Mount Carmel. Fertile.

Bear Prairie, in Wayne county, east of Fairfield.

Bellevue Prairie, in Calhoun county, at the foot of the bluffs, ten miles in extent, has a dry and fertile soil.

Big Mound Prairie, Wayne county, west of Fairfield, three miles long, rolling, with a thin surface of humus.

Big Prairie, in White county, three miles square, much mixed with sand, but fertile.

Boltinghouse Prairie, in Edwards county, south of Albion, extending four miles by three, has an undulating, fertile soil.

Bonpas Prairie, in the same county, north-east of Albion, and about two miles in diameter. Soil good.

Brown's Prairie, twelve miles north of Alton, runs through the corners of Macoupin, Jersey, and Madison counties, which border upon each other. The soil is dry and fertile.

Brushy Prairie, in Wayne county, eleven miles east of Fairfield.

Buckheart Prairie, in Fulton county, north-east of Lewistown, about seven miles long.

Buck Prairie, in Edwards county, six miles north-east of Albion, two and a half miles broad.

Buckhorn Prairie, in Morgan county, about seven miles south of Jacksonville. The soil is rich, a little humid, and very level.

Bullard's Prairie, in Lawrence county, west of Lawrenceville, is ten miles by two in extent, having a second-rate soil.

Burnt Prairie extends from the north-western section of White into Wayne county. Its circumference is not very great; its soil at intervals good.

Another prairie of the *same name,* situate in Edwards county, north-west of Albion, extends two miles by six, interspersed with many small groves. Soil good.

Canton Prairie, in Fulton county, commencing in the vicinity of Spoon River, extends northerly till it meets Grand Prairie, near Rock River; it is rolling, dry, and very fertile, with the exception of its northern section, which is of inferior quality.

Casey's Prairie, in Jefferson county, five miles by two, nearly level; second-rate soil.

Christy's Prairie, in Lawrence county, ten miles west of Lawrenceville, rolling, and of good average soil.

Clay's Prairie, in Clark county, eight miles south-west of Darwin.

Cold Prairie, in St. Clair county, between Belleville and Illinoistown.

Compston's Prairie, in Wabash county, twelve miles west of Mount Carmel, is level, fertile, but somewhat humid.

Cotton Hill Prairie, in Sangamon county, twelve miles south of Springfield.

Cox's Prairie, in Jackson county, north-east of Brownsville; good rolling prairie.

Crow Prairie, in Putnam county, twelve miles below Hennepin, six miles by three; fertile, and bounded by forests.

Another prairie of the *same name* extends, four miles by twelve, along the western bank of Illinois River from Putnam into Bureau county; soil dry and productive.

Decker's Prairie, in Wabash county, twelve miles north-east of Mount Carmel.

Diamond Grove Prairie, in Morgan county, south of Jacksonville, containing about sixteen square miles, is dry, undulating, and productive.

Dolson's Prairie, in the western section of Clark county, containing about seventy square miles, has a level, humid, clayish soil.

Dutch Prairie, in the south-western part of St. Clair county.

Edmonson's Prairie, in McDonough county, six miles south-west of Macomb, ten miles by two.

Eight-mile Prairie, in Williamson county, eighteen miles south-west of Frankfort; very flat.

Elk Prairie, in Perry county, five miles long, dry and nearly level; second-rate soil.

Ester's Prairie, in Franklin county, fourteen miles north of Frankfort; level and dry.

Flat Prairie, in Randolph county, twenty miles east of Kaskaskia.

Fork Prairie, in Bond county, north of Greenville; gently undulating.

Four-mile Prairie, in Perry county, four miles by seven; dry, rolling, and productive.

Fourteen-mile Prairie, in Effingham county, east of Livingston; nearly level, for the most part dry, interspersed with groups of forests.

Garden Prairie, in Sangamon county, fourteen miles north-west of Springfield, two miles by eight; first-rate soil.

Granger's Prairie, in the north-western section of Adams county, three miles square; possesses very productive soil.

Gun Prairie, in Jefferson county, six miles south of Mount Vernon, has a considerable circuit, and a fertile soil.

Hancock Prairie, commencing in Adams county, runs, with a breadth varying between ten and twenty miles, far north, through Hancock, Henderson, and Warren counties, between Henderson and Spoon rivers, being nearly level, and very productive.

Hargrave's Prairie, in Wayne county, seven miles by two, is undulating, having but a thin surface of humus.

Hawkins' Prairie, in Greene county, nine miles south-east of Carrollton.

Herron's Prairie is situated in Williamson county.

Herrington's Prairie, in Wayne county, eleven miles north-west of Fairfield, eight miles by four; has an undulating surface, and second-rate soil.

High Prairie, in St. Clair county, eight miles from Belleville; very productive.

Hog Prairie, in Hamilton county, situated westerly from McLeansburg; has a small circumference, and a level, humid soil.

Horse Prairie, in Randolph county; soil rolling and fertile.

Illinois Prairie, in Calhoun county, commencing near the mouth of Illinois River, runs, twenty miles by two, along the bluffs, having a fertile soil.

Indian Prairie, in Wayne county, ten miles north-west of Fairfield; is level, and its soil of indifferent quality.

Jersey Prairie, in Morgan county, ten miles north of Jacksonville, has a rich soil, and is bounded by fine timber.

Jordan's Prairie, in Jefferson county, six miles north of Mount Vernon, five miles by two, has a second rate soil.

Knight's Prairie, in Hamilton county, west of McLeansboro'.

Knob Prairie, in Franklin county, north-west of Frankfort, is low and humid.

La Motte Prairie, in Crawford county, eight miles long, of a breadth which greatly varies; has a somewhat sandy, but rich soil.

La Salle Prairie, in Peoria county, adjacent to Peoria Lake; the southern section is rolling and fertile, though a little sandy; the northern being more clayish.

Lemarde Prairie, in Wayne county, seven miles north-west of Fairfield, is three miles by six in extent, having an indifferent soil.

Little Mount Prairie, in the same county, three miles south-west of Fairfield; not very large.

There are four prairies in the state bearing the name of *Long Prairie,* of which —

The *first* is in Wabash county, thirteen miles north-west of Mount Carmel; undulating, and of but inferior quality.

The *second,* in Edwards county, north of Albion, is nine miles by two in extent, interspersed with many groves.

The *third,* in Clay county, runs into Wayne county, nine miles by three; being, properly speaking, a branch of Twelve-mile Prairie. It is level, and has but a poor soil.

The *fourth,* in Jefferson county, five miles west of Mount Vernon, is four miles by two in extent, having a sufficiently good soil.

Looking-glass Prairie, in St. Clair county, twenty miles long, and from six to ten miles wide; undulating, and very productive, runs into Madison county.

Lorton's Prairie, in the northern part of Greene county, has excellent soil and fine forests.

Lost Prairie, in Perry county, seven miles west of Pinckneyville, one and a half miles broad and double that length, is high, rolling, and very productive.

Loup Prairie, in St. Clair county.

Luckons' Prairie, in the southern part of Lawrence county.

Macon County Prairie, situated north of Decatur, extends between the northern branch of the Sangamon river and Salt Creek, with a breadth varying from fifteen to twenty miles; some parts of it are level and humid, others rolling and dry.

Macoupin Prairie, in Greene county, reaches into Jersey county; gently rolling, having a rich soil and stately forests near the Illinois river and the Macoupin creek.

Marshall's Prairie, in Jackson county, fourteen miles north-east of Brownsville, has a rolling and fertile surface.

Mason's Prairie, in the southern section of Richland county.

Mill's Prairie, in Edwards county, eleven miles north-east of Albion, is four miles long, about two broad; quite fertile.

Moore's Prairie, in Jefferson county, south-east of Mount Vernon, eight miles by about two. Some parts of it are flat and humid, others dry and gently undulating.

Another prairie of the *same name,* situated in St. Clair county, five miles east of Belleville, has a diameter of about five miles; it is nearly level, and fertile.

Mud Prairie, in Washington county, reaches into Perry county, north-east of Pinckneyville; it is level and humid.

Another prairie of the *same name* lies in Wayne county, north-west of Fairfield; also low and humid.

A *third* prairie of the *same name* (Mud Prairie) is situated in the south-eastern portion of St. Clair county.

Nine-mile Prairie, in Perry county, ten miles east of Pinckneyville.

North Arm Prairie, in Edgar county, six miles east of Paris, is three miles broad, running along the frontier of Indiana, until it meets the grand prairie. Its soil is good.

North Prairie, in Morgan county, twelve miles north-east of Jacksonville, is dry, undulating, and very productive.

Another prairie of the *same name,* in the same county, runs along Walnut Creek, and is level.

Ogle Prairie, in St. Clair county, five miles north of Belleville, extending one and a half miles by five, is rolling and very fertile.

Ox-bow Prairie, in Putnam county, ten miles south of Hennepin, five miles by one and a half, surrounded by fine forests, and very productive.

Parker's Prairie, in the western section of Clark county, has a level, humid soil, of inferior quality.

Philo's Prairie, in Williamson county, twelve miles south of Frankfort; gently undulating, and fertile.

Plum Creek Prairie reaches from St. Clair into Randolph county, and is ten miles by three in extent. Its soil is good.

Prairie du Long, in the south of St. Clair county.

Pratt's Prairie, in Greene county, fifteen miles north-west of Carrollton.

Rattan's Prairie, in Madison county, seven miles north-west of Edwardsville; is level, and at intervals washy.

Ridge Prairie, in Madison county, is eight miles by eight, running from near by Edwardsville to St. Clair county; gently undulating, and very productive.

Rollins' Prairie, in Franklin county, north of Frankfort, is six miles long by four broad; it is level and fertile.

Five different prairies in the State of Illinois bear the name of *Round Prairie*, of which —

The *first* is in Schuyler county, four miles in diameter; dry, fertile, and surrounded by woods.

The *second* is in Wabash county, north-east of Mount Carmel, with a diameter of four miles: has an excellent soil.

The *third* is in Bond county, six miles north-west of Greenville, with a diameter of nearly two miles: is rolling, very fertile, and surrounded by forests.

The *fourth* is in Perry county, about eight miles from Pinckneyville: it has but a small circumference.

The *fifth* is in Sangamon county, seven miles south-east of Springfield: it is very productive.

Salt Prairie, in Calhoun county, forms a small strip, half a mile broad and six miles long: it is dry and fertile.

Sand Prairie, in Tazewell county, four miles south of Pekin, has a sandy, good soil.

Seven-mile Prairie, in White county, seven miles west of Carmi.

Shipley's Prairie, in Wayne county, five miles south-east of Fairfield.

Shoal-Creek Prairie runs from Clinton through Bond into Montgomery county, with an average breadth of eight miles, gently undulating, and containing much good land.

Six's Prairie, in Brown county, seventeen miles south-west of Rushville, is ten miles by three in extent, undulating, dry, productive, and surrounded by woods.

Six-mile Prairie, in the south-western section of Madison county, consisting of alluvial ground, is enclosed by woods.

Another prairie of the *same name* is situated in Perry county, nine miles south of Pinckneyville, nine miles long by six broad, with tolerably good soil.

Smooth Prairie, in Madison county, eight miles east of Alton, is three miles by two in extent, being level and somewhat humid.

South Prairie, in Morgan county, on the southern side of Walnut Creek.

Squaw Prairie, in Boone county, is level and fertile, containing about ten square miles.

String Prairie, in Greene county, commences four miles west of Carrollton, running fifteen miles east, with a breadth of from one to three miles; is level, and a good tract of land upon the whole.

Sweet's Prairie, in Scott county, three miles west of Manchester, is level and washy.

Swett's Prairie, in Madison county, four miles north-east of Edwardsville.

Three-mile Prairie, in Washington county, eight miles south of Nashville, is undulating.

Tonis Prairie, in Wayne county, six miles north-east of Fairfield, has second-rate soil.

Totten's Prairie, in Fulton county, seven miles north-west of Lewistown, is ten miles long and of varying breadth. The soil is good.

Turney's Prairie, in Wayne county, eight miles south of Fairfield, has a small circumference and a good soil.

Twelve-mile Prairie, in Effingham county, reaches into Clay county; level and humid at intervals.

Another "Twelve-mile Prairie," situated in St. Clair county, is somewhat rolling, having a good soil.

Union Prairie, in the south-eastern section of Clark county, is five miles long by three broad.

Another prairie bearing the *same name* (Union Prairie), lies in Schuyler county, four miles west of Rushville.

Village Prairie, in Edwards county, two miles north of Albion, is about three miles long.

Walnut Hill Prairie reaches from Jefferson into Marion county; it is four miles by three, some parts of it being fertile, others humid and level.

Walnut Prairie, in Clark county, extends five miles by two, having a fertile, though somewhat sandy soil.

Webb's Prairie, in Franklin county, fifteen miles north-east of Frankfort, has a fertile soil.

Wood's Prairie, in Wabash county, ten miles distant from Mount Carmel, is very productive.

Having enumerated above the prairies which are known by their own proper names, we cannot leave it unmentioned, that there are many others bearing indifferent names; Illinois having in general such an abundance of prairies, that nearly two-thirds of its area consist of them.

In order to enable the reader to inform himself regarding the manner in which prairie and forest are distributed over the area of the State, we subjoin a prairie and forest map, wherein the counties are marked and designated. We repeat them here, in alphabetical order:

1. Adams.
2. Alexander.
3. Bond.
4. Boone.
5. Brown.
6. Bureau.
7. Calhoun.
8. Carroll.
9. Cass.
10. Champaign.
11. Christian.
12. Clark.
13. Clay.
14. Clinton.
15. Coles.
16. Cook.
17. Crawford.
18. Cumberland.
19. De Kalb.
20. De Witt.
21. Du Page.
22. Edgar.
23. Edwards.
24. Effingham.
25. Fayette.
26. Franklin.
27. Fulton.
28. Gallatin.
29. Greene.
30. Grundy.
31. Hamilton.
32. Hancock.
33. Hardin.
34. Henderson.
35. Henry.
36. Iroquois.
37. Jackson.
38. Jasper.
39. Jefferson.
40. Jersey.
41. Jo Daviess.
42. Johnson.
43. Kane.
44. Kankakee.
45. Kendall.
46. Knox.
47. Lake.
48. La Salle.

49. Lawrence.
50. Lee.
51. Livingston.
52. Logan.
53. Macon.
54. Macoupin.
55. Madison.
56. Marion.
57. Marshall.
58. Mason.
59. Massac.
60. McDonough.
61. McHenry.
62. McLean.
63. Menard.
64. Mercer.
65. Monroe.
66. Montgomery.
67. Morgan.
68. Moultrie.
69. Ogle.
70. Peoria.
71. Perry.
72. Piatt.
73. Pike.
74. Pope.
75. Pulaski.
76. Putnam.
77. Randolph.
78. Richland.
79. Rock Island.
80. Saline.
81. St. Clair.
82. Sangamon.
83. Scott.
84. Shelby.
85. Schuyler.
86. Stark.
87. Stephenson.
88. Tazewell.
89. Union.
90. Vermillion.
91. Wabash.
92. Warren.
93. Washington.
94. Wayne.
95. White.
96. Whitesides.
97. Will.
98. Williamson.
99. Winnebago.
100. Woodford.

There are no mountains in Illinois; in the southern, as well as in the northern part of the State, there are a few hills; near the banks of the Illinois, Mississippi, and several other rivers, the ground is elevated, forming the so-called bluffs, on which, at the present day, may be found, uneffaced by the hand of Time, the marks and traces left by the water, which was formerly much higher, and gradually lowered; whence it may be safe to conclude, that where now the fertile prairies of Illinois extend, and the rich soil of the country yields its golden harvests, must have once been a vast sheet of water, the mud deposited by which formed the soil, thus accounting for the present great fertility of the country.

In relation to the quality of its soils, Illinois is generally divided as follows:

First, the alluvial land on the margins of the rivers, and extending with a breadth varying from half a mile or a mile to seven or eight miles. Wherever it is elevated, this country is of an extraordinary fertility; at those places where it is low, and consequently exposed to inundations, it is a very unsafe matter to attempt cultivating it. The most extensive tract of alluvial land is the so-called American Bottom, which was thus named at the time it formed the western boundary

of the United States; it stretches from the junction of the Kaskaskia with the Mississippi, along the latter to the mouth of the Missouri, containing about 450 square miles, or 288,000 acres.

Secondly, the table-land, fifty to a hundred feet higher than the alluvial land; this commences at the slopes, by which the latter is encompassed; it consists principally of prairies, which, according to their respectively higher or lower situations, are either dry, or humid and marshy.

Thirdly, the somewhat hilly sections of the State, which, alternately consisting of wood and prairie, are on the whole not as fertile as either the alluvial or the table land.

The soil of Illinois is unsurpassed in fertility by that of any other State, there being no room for doubt, that at the time it shall have been settled throughout its entire extent, the produce of its harvests will surpass that of many other States together. Where in the world could a fertility be found equal to that of the American Bottom, which, ever since it was settled by the French, about 150 years ago, has, without any manuring whatever, yielded, year after year, the most abundant crops of Indian corn?

STATISTICS.

THE population of Illinois is returned, by the Census of 1855, at 1,300,251 souls; having, since the year 1810, increased as follows:—

In the year 1810 it amounted to	12,282	inhabitants.
" 1820 "	55,211	"
" 1830 "	157,445	"
" 1835 "	272,427	"
" 1840 "	476,183	"
" 1845 "	662,125	"
" 1850 "	851,470	"
" 1855 "	1,300,251	"

Thus increasing—

From 1810 to 1820 by	42,929	inhabitants.
" 1820 " 1830 "	102,234	"
" 1830 " 1835 "	114,982	"
" 1835 " 1840 "	203,756	"
" 1840 " 1845 "	185,942	"
" 1845 " 1850 "	189,345	"
" 1850 " 1855 "	448,781	"

What distinguishes the state of Illinois from the other states of the Union, is its gigantic growth in numbers, as upon instituting a comparison with those states, the ratio of the increase in the population of which has also been very considerable, will be placed beyond a doubt.

The United States' Census returns the population of Indiana, Maine, Massachusetts, Michigan, New Jersey, New York, Ohio, and Pennsylvania, as follows:—

Indiana,	in 1800	4,875	inhabitants.
	1810	24,520	"
	1820	147,178	"
	1830	343,031	"
	1840	685,866	"
	1850	988,416	"

Maine, ... in	1790	96,540	inhabitants.
	1800	151,719	"
	1810	228,705	"
	1820	298,335	"
	1830	399,455	"
	1840	501,793	"
	1850	583,169	"
Massachusetts, in	1790	378,717	"
	1800	423,245	"
	1810	472,040	"
	1820	523,287	"
	1830	610,408	"
	1840	737,699	"
	1850	994,514	"
Michigan, ... in	1810	4,762	"
	1820	8,896	"
	1830	31,639	"
	1840	212,267	"
	1850	397,654	"
New Jersey, ... in	1790	184,139	"
	1800	211,949	"
	1810	245,555	"
	1820	277,575	"
	1830	320,823	"
	1840	373,306	"
	1850	489,555	"
New York, ... in	1790	340,120	"
	1800	586,756	"
	1810	959,049	"
	1820	1,372,812	"
	1830	1,918,608	"
	1840	2,428,921	"
	1850	3,097,394	"
Ohio, ... in	1800	45,365	"
	1810	230,760	"
	1820	581,434	"
	1830	937,903	"
	1840	1,519,467	"
	1850	1,980,329	"
Pennsylvania, in	1790	434,373	"
	1800	602,361	"
	1810	810,091	"

Pennsylvania,	in 1820	1,049,458	inhabitants.
	1830	1,348,233	"
	1840	1,724,033	"
	1850	2,311,786	"

Thus the increase of the population of the before-mentioned states, in which census returns were made since 1810, for the forty years, from 1810 to 1850, must be calculated as follows: —

Indiana	3,931	per cent.
Maine	155	"
Massachusetts	110	"
Michigan	8,250	"
New Jersey	99	"
New York	316	"
Ohio	758	"
Pennsylvania	185	"
Illinois	6,832	"

Although from the above it would appear, that Michigan surpasses the state of Illinois in the rapid increase of its population, on considering that in the year 1850 Michigan possessed a much smaller population than Illinois, having but 397,654 inhabitants to set off against the 851,470 of the latter; that the immigration to Michigan, during the years 1850 — 1855, was considerably less than that to Illinois; further, that the population of Illinois, during the five years, 1850—1855, has increased by about 52 per cent., or more than one-half; and during the forty-five years, 1810—1855, by about 10,486 per cent.; we can only regret that we are not in possession of the returns of the census of Michigan for 1855; by placing the statement given by these with regard to the increase of the population of Michigan up to that year before the reader, we would be enabled to prove, that the state of Illinois, far from being inferior in rapidity of the growth of its population, for the last forty years, to the other states, is in reality superior not only to them, but also to Michigan.

Iowa and Wisconsin, which states have also prodigiously advanced, could not be well compared with the above states, for the last forty years, they being of too recent date.

Illinois consists of one hundred counties, the population of which, for the years 1840, 1850, and 1855, was, respectively, the following: —

COUNTIES.	1840.	1850.	1855.
Adams	14,476	26,598	34,311
Alexander	3,313	2,484	2,927
Bond	5,060	6,144	7,511
Boone	1,705	7,624	10,994
Brown	4,183	7,198	7,940
Bureau	3,067	8,841	19,518
Calhoun	1,741	3,231	3,768
Carroll	1,023	4,586	7,610
Cass	2,981	7,253	8,946
Champaign	1,475	2,649	6,565
Christian	1,878	3,203	7,041
Clark	7,453	9,532	13,863
Clay	3,228	4,289	7,076
Clinton	3,718	5,139	6,823
*Coles	9,616	9,335	14,937
Cook	10,201	43,385	103,960
Crawford	4,422	7,135	10,152
Cumberland	——	3,718	6,099
De Kalb	1,697	7,540	13,636
De Witt	3,247	5,002	8,508
Du Page	3,535	9,290	12,307
Edgar	8,225	10,692	13,920
Edwards	3,070	3,524	4,598
Effingham	1,675	3,799	6,226
Fayette	6,328	8,075	9,592
Franklin	3,682	5,081	7,182
Fulton	13,142	22,508	27,968
*Gallatin	10,760	5,448	6,723
Greene	11,951	12,429	13,092
*Grundy	——	3,023	7,021
Hamilton	3,945	6,362	7,212
Hancock	9,946	14,652	22,158
Hardin	1,378	2,887	3,920
Henderson	——	4,612	7,128
Henry	1,260	3,807	9,218
†Iroquois	1,695	4,149	6,788
Jackson	3,566	5,862	7,834
Jasper	1,472	3,220	6,842

* The counties marked * were, during the years 1840—1850, subdivided into new counties.

† From the counties Will and Iroquois, denoted by †, sections were taken since 1850, and made to constitute Kankakee county.

COUNTIES.	1840.	1850.	1855.
Jefferson	5,762	8,109	10,258
Jersey	4,535	7,354	8,771
Jo Daviess	6,180	18,604	24,104
*Johnson	3,626	4,114	4,966
Kane	6,501	16,703	26,665
Kankakee	——	——	10,110
Kendall	——	7,730	10,145
Knox	7,060	13,279	22,847
Lake	2,634	14,226	17,630
*La Salle	9,348	17,815	35,563
*Lawrence	7,092	6,121	8,160
Lee	2,035	5,292	11,618
Livingston	759	1,552	4,606
Logan	2,333	5,128	8,324
McDonough	5,308	7,610	12,886
McHenry	2,578	14,978	19,285
McLean	6,565	10,163	19,578
*Macon	3,039	3,998	8,365
Macoupin	7,826	12,355	17,403
Madison	14,433	20,441	31,556
Marion	4,742	6,720	10,139
Marshall	1,849	5,180	9,900
Mason	——	5,921	7,775
Massac	——	4,092	5,692
Menard	4,431	6,349	8,029
Mercer	2,352	5,246	9,660
Monroe	4,481	7,629	10,285
Montgomery	4,490	6,277	9,041
Morgan	19,549	16,064	17,735
Moultrie	——	3,234	4,435
Ogle	3,479	10,120	16,456
Peoria	6,153	17,547	30,134
Perry	3,222	5,278	6,858
Platt	——	1,605	3,052
Pike	11,728	18,819	23,351
*Pope	4,094	3,975	6,835
Pulaski	——	2,265	2,462
Putnam	2,131	3,024	5,100
Randolph	7,944	11,879	12,601
Richland	——	4,012	7,049
Rock Island	2,010	6,937	16,217
St. Clair	13,631	20,180	28,554

COUNTIES.	1840.	1850.	1855.
Saline	——	5,588	6,776
*Sangamon	14,716	19,224	25,604
Schuyler	6,972	10,573	12,296
Scott	6,215	7,914	7,937
*Shelby	6,659	7,807	11,270
Stark	1,573	3,710	6,293
Stephenson	2,800	11,666	13,316
*Tazewell	7,222	12,052	17,371
Union	5,524	7,615	10,106
Vermillion	9,303	11,492	15,893
Wabash	4,240	4,692	6,233
*Warren	6,739	8,176	12,209
Washington	4,810	6,953	10,059
Wayne	5,133	6,825	9,902
White	7,119	8,925	10,387
Whitesides	2,514	5,361	13,416
†Will	10,167	16,703	24,468
*Williamson	4,457	7,216	9,430
Winnebago	4,609	11,775	20,826
Woodford	——	4,415	8,400

Illinois has, besides, a county called Cook county, which numbers more than 100,000 inhabitants, and in which Chicago, that city of unparalleled growth, is situated; another county (La Salle), with more than 35,000; three (Adams, Madison, and Peoria), with from 30,000 to 35,000; four (Fulton, Kane, St. Clair, Sangamon), with from 25,000 to 30,000; six (Hancock, Jo Daviess, Knox, Pike, Will, Winnebago), with from 20,000 to 25,000; ten (Bureau, Lake, McHenry, McLean, Macoupin, Morgan, Ogle, Rock Island, Tazewell, and Vermilion), with from 15,000 to 20,000; twenty-four with from 10,000 to 15,000; forty-two with from 5000 to 10,000: and nine with less than 5000 inhabitants. The counties having the fewest inhabitants are Pulaski and Alexander, the former with 2462, the latter with 2927 inhabitants, contiguous to each other, and being situated in the most southern section of the State.

In order to enable the reader with one glance to survey the comparatively smaller or greater density of the population of the various parts and counties of the State, we here subjoin a population-map of it, wherein the counties are marked and designated, the following columns corresponding to which contain a statement of the number of inhabitants residing on a geographical square mile in every single county, according to the census of the State returned in 1855:

1. Cook	2396	41. McDonough	475
2. Kane	1049	42. Edwards	466
3. Peoria	1031	43. Williamson	464
4. Adams	937	44. Johnson	456
5. Madison	918	45. White	456
6. St. Clair	916	46. Ogle	452
7. McHenry	878	47. De Kalb	449
8. Rock Island	862	48. Hardin	447
9. Knox	843	49. Bureau	432
10. Winnebago	830	50. De Witt	432
11. Jo Daviess	822	51. Macoupin	430
12. Morgan	820	52. Coles	426
13. Lake	816	53. Menard	413
14. Boone	805	54. Henderson	409
15. Clark	782	55. Bond	404
16. Scott	782	56. Whitesides	404
17. La Salle	714	57. McLean	394
18. Fulton	684	58. Kankakee	386
19. Wabash	682	59. Cumberland	385
20. Kendall	666	60. Pope	384
21. Pike	643	61. Richland	383
22. Schuyler	639	62. Saline	383
23. Will	639	63. Stark	383
24. Du Page	630	64. Jefferson	379
25. Monroe	628	65. Putnam	377
26. Hancock	624	66. Washington	377
27. Edgar	588	67. Lawrence	377
28. Sangamon	588	68. Marion	375
29. Tazewell	586	69. Mercer	366
30. Brown	554	70. Carroll	362
31. Union	553	71. Franklin	353
32. Jersey	537	72. Hamilton	353
33. Greene	528	73. Lee	349
34. Marshall	526	74. Grundy	345
35. Randolph	511	75. Woodford	341
36. Cass	511	76. Perry	337
37. Massac	505	77. Shelby	336
38. Stephenson	503	78. Gallatin	330
39. Crawford	490	79. Pulaski	327
40. Warren	482	80. Macon	319

81. Mason	319	91. Montgomery	273
82. Calhoun	315	92. Alexander	260
83. Clay	313	93. Effingham	256
84. Clinton	302	94. Henry	251
85. Fayette	298	95. Christian	213
86. Jasper	292	96. Vermillion	202
87. Wayne	292	97. Pyatt	164
88. Moultrie	292	98. Champaign	138
89. Logan	290	99. Iroquois	134
90. Jackson	277	100. Livingston	94

The entire number of dwellings in the State, was, in the year 1850,* 146,544; the number of families 149,153, with 851,470 members, 846,104 of whom were whites, and 5,366 free colored persons. Of the whites 445,644 belonged to the male and 400,460 to the female sex; of the colored population 2756 to the male and 2610 to the female sex. Among the 851,470 inhabitants, there were 475 deaf and dumb, 257 blind, 249 maniacs, and 371 idiots.

Of the inhabitants, 736,931 were born in the United States, including also the descendants of the earlier European settlers and the later immigrants; 110,593 in foreign countries; while the birth-place of 3946 could not be ascertained. Of those born in America, 3693 were from Maine, 4288 from New Hampshire, 1381 from Vermont, 9230 from Massachusetts, 1051 from Rhode Island, 6899 from Connecticut, 67,180 from New York, 6848 from New Jersey, 37,979 from Pennsylvania, 1397 from Delaware, 6898 from Maryland, 226 from the District of Columbia, 24,697 from Virginia, 13,851 from North Carolina, 4162 from South Carolina, 1341 from Georgia, 23 from Florida, 1335 from Alabama, 490 from Mississippi, 480 from Louisiana, 63 from Texas, 727 from Arkansas, 32,303 from Ten-

* Owing to the fact, that in the year 1855 an incomplete and very imperfect census, which does not enter into details as did the census of 1850, was returned, most of the amounts could only be stated according to the census of 1850. Had a complete census, that besides stating the number of inhabitants, would have paid due regard to the agricultural, manufacturing, commercial, industrial, and social interests of the State, been published, the picture of Illinois this book is intended to place before the eyes of the reader, would no doubt have been a much more complete one; for in this very period of 1850–1855, the brilliant progress of Illinois has been such as no former period ever witnessed.

nessee, 49,508 from Kentucky, 64,219 from Ohio, 2158 from Michigan, 30,953 from Indiana, 7288 from Missouri, 1511 from Iowa, 1095 from Wisconsin, 3 from California, 16 from the Territories, and 343,618 were natives of Illinois.

Of those born in foreign countries, 18,628 were natives of England, 27,786 of Ireland, 4661 of Scotland, 572 of Wales, 38,511 of Germany, inclusive of Austria, 3396 of France, 70 of Spain, 42 of Portugal, 33 of Belgium, 220 of Holland, 43 of Italy, 1635 of Switzerland, 27 of Russia, 93 of Denmark, 2415 of Norway, 1123 of Sweden, 4 of Greece, 3 of Asia, 11 of Africa, 10,699 of British America, 30 of Mexico, 12 of South America, 75 of the West Indies, 9 of the Sandwich Islands, and 495 from various other countries.

Farming lands. — In the year 1850, Illinois had 76,208 farms, containing 12,037,412 acres, making an average of 158 acres to each farm, 5,039,545 of which were improved, and 6,997,867 still uncultivated. The value of these 76,208 farms was estimated at $96,133,290; hence the average value of each farm was $1261. The value of the agricultural implements amounted to $6,405,561.

The live stock, of cattle, was estimated at $24,209,258; of horses, $267,653; of asses and mules, $10,573: making an aggregate of $278,226, against $199,235 in 1840; of milk cows, $294,671; of oxen, $76,156; of bulls, heifers, and cattle fit for slaughter, $541,209; neat cattle in the aggregate, $912,036, against $626,274 in 1840; of sheep, $894,043, against $395,672 in 1840; of hogs, $1,915,907, against $1,495,254 in 1840. The value of the slaughtered cattle in the year 1850, amounted to $4,972,286; and the value of the live stock of cattle in 1850, to $30,000,000.

The following were the crops in 1850: — 9,414,575 bushels of wheat, against 3,335,393 in the year 1840; 83,364 bushels of rye, against 88,197 in 1840; 10,087,241 bushels of oats, against 4,988,008 in 1840; 57,646,984 bushels of Indian corn, against 22,634,211 in 1840; 2,514,861 bushels of Irish, and 157,433 bushels of sweet potatoes — making an aggregate of 2,672,294 bushels of potatoes, against 2,025,520 bushels in 1840; 110,795 bushels of barley, against 82,251 in 1840; 184,504 bushels of buckwheat, against 57,884 in 1840; 601,952 tons of hay, against 164,932 in 1840. Hence it follows, that of the produce of the fields, rye alone has decreased, all the other species of corn having increased, and that wheat and Indian corn have advanced by the highest ratio.

The harvest of 1855 is roughly estimated at 20,000,000 bushels of wheat, 20,000,000 bushels of oats, 130,000,000 bushels of Indian corn, and 1,000,000 tons of hay.

Other farm produces in the year 1850, were: — 3551 lbs. of hops, against 17,742* in 1840; 3427 lbs. of cloverseed; 14,380 lbs. of seeds of other species of grass; 12,526,543 lbs. of butter; 1,278,225 lbs. of cheese — making an aggregate of 13,804,768 lbs., against 428,175 lbs. in 1840; 82,814 bushels of peas and beans. The value of the produce of the market-gardens amounted to $127,494; fruitery, etc., $1,146,049, against $126,756 in 1840; wax and honey, to 869,444 lbs., against 29,173 in 1840; articles of produce for domestic use, to $1,155,902; flaxseed, to 10,787 bushels; flax, to 160,063 lbs.; maple sugars, to 248,904 lbs.; molasses, to 8,354 gallons; tobacco, to 841,394 lbs., versus 564,326 in 1840; wool, to 2,150,113 lbs., versus 650,007 in 1840; silk cocoons, to 47 lbs., versus 1150 in 1840; wine, to 2997 gallons, versus 474 in 1840.

Of manufactories, Illinois, in the year 1850, had 3164 establishments, doing business with a capital of $6,385,387, consuming $8,915,173 worth of raw materials, employing 11,632 men and 433 women, paying wages to the amount of $3,286,249, and manufacturing goods to the value of $17,236,073.

Of manufactories of woollen articles, Illinois, in the year 1850, had 16, operating with a capital of $154,500, consuming of raw materials 396,964 lbs. of wool and 987 tons of coal, valued in the aggregate at $115,367; employing 124 men and 54 women, and manufacturing goods to the value of $206,572.

Of manufactories of pig iron, there were but two, having a capital of $65,000. These consumed 5500 tons of ore, estimated at $15,500, and while employing 150 laborers, manufactured 2700 tons of pig iron, valued at $70,200.

---

* This statement, though, like all the preceding, taken from the United States census, appears to us erroneous; for as, during the last few years, a remarkable increase has taken place, both in the brewing and consumption of beer, it seems scarcely credible, that the cultivation of hops should have so considerably fallen off.

Of iron foundries, there were 29, doing business with a capital of $260,400. These expended $172,330 for 4818 tons of pig iron, 50 tons of old iron, besides fuel, &c.; employing 332 laborers, and manufacturing goods to the value of $441,185.

Of breweries and distilleries, there were 52, having a business capital of $303,400, consuming 98,000 bushels of barley, 48,700 bushels of rye, and 703,500 bushels of Indian corn, occupying 274 hands, and furnishing a supply of 27,925 barrels of beer, &c., and 2,315,000 gallons of whiskey, and various other spirits.

Lastly, Illinois possesses a salt manufactory, operating with a capital of $2500, consuming $2000 worth of raw material, employing 3 hands, and producing 20,000 bushels of salt, estimated at $6000.

Of churches, there are 1223 in the State, having 486,576 members, and appertaining to the various denominations, as follows: The Baptists have 282 churches, with 94,130 members; the Christians, 69 churches, with 30,864 members; the Congregationalists, 46 churches, with 15,626 members; Dutch Reformed, 2 churches, with 875 members; Episcopalians, 27 churches, with 14,000 members; Free, 2 churches, with 750 members; Friends, 6 churches, with 1550 members; German Reformed, 3 churches, with 280 members; Lutherans, 42 churches, with 16,640 members; Methodists, 405 churches, with 178,452 members; Moravians, 2 churches, with 400 members; Presbyterians, 206 churches, with 83,129 members; Roman Catholics, 59 churches, with 29,100 members; Swedenborgians, 2 churches, with 140 members; Tunkers, 4 churches, with 1225 members; Unionists, 30 churches, with 8625 members; Unitarians, 4 churches, with 1050 members; Universalists, 2 churches, with 2000 members; various other small sects, 25 churches, with 7740 members. The whole church property amounted to $1,482,182.

Of places for education there were:—4052 public schools, with 4248 teachers, 125,725 pupils, and a yearly revenue of $349,712; 83 academies and private schools, with 160 teachers, 4244 scholars, and a yearly income of $40,488; 4 colleges, with 29 professors, and 223 students. Whole amount of lands appropriated by the Federal Government for educational purposes, up to 1st of January, 1854: for schools, 978,755 acres; for universities, 23,040 acres; making an aggregate of 1,001,795 acres.

According to the army register for 1851, the militia of Illinois numbered 170,359, in all the departments, 4168 of whom were commissioned officers, the residue (165,741) being non-commissioned officers, privates, and musicians. Among the commissioned officers there were 30 general officers, 79 general staff officers, 1297 field officers, and 3192 company officers.

Of libraries, Illinois, in 1850, possessed 152, with 62,486 volumes, 33 of which, with 35,982 volumes, were public libraries; 29 school libraries, with 5875 volumes; 86 Sunday-school libraries, with 12,829 volumes; 4 college libraries, with 7800 volumes.

In the year 1828, 4 newspapers were edited; in 1840, 52; in the year 1850, 107; among which were 7 monthly and 1 quarterly periodical. These 107 newspapers, &c., issued, in the year 1850, 5,102,276 numbers, and may be classified as follows: literary and miscellaneous, 22; neutral, 1; political, 73; religious, 8; scientific, 3.

In 1850, 797 paupers were in the State, who were either wholly or to some extent provided for and relieved.

Of criminals, 316 were condemned during the year expiring June 1st, 1850; on that day the number of those imprisoned for crime, &c., amounted to 252.

Of the 851,470 inhabitants of the State in 1850, 41,283 were unable to read or write; 35,336 of these were born in the United States, and 5947 in foreign countries; 40,054 of them were whites, to wit: 16,633 males and 23,421 females; and 1229 were colored people, to wit: 605 males and 624 females.

CLIMATE, SOIL, PLANTS, AND ANIMALS.*

Upon looking at the map of the Upper Mississippi, we have before us that very extensive net of streams and rivers which is bounded in the west, below the junction of the Ohio and Mississippi, by the Ozark Mountains, through which the Arkansas and Red Rivers have forced their passage; and in the east, by the projecting ridge of the Alleghany Mountains. High lands, elevated 2000 feet above the level of the sea, divide this district in the north from the Arctic river-district, together with which it was undoubtedly covered by a vast sheet of water, at an early period of the formation of the earth; the hills separating it from Lake Superior, which is situated 600 feet above the level of the sea, do not rise more than 1000 feet above it, and the boundary line dividing it from the river-district of the St. Lawrence, runs along the shores of the other great lakes. No chain of moun-

* Dr. Fred. Brendel, of Peoria, to whom we are indebted for many valuable contributions to this chapter, has for several years pursued with great zeal the study of the natural history of Illinois, and would be very happy, could he meet with fellow-laborers in this work; for which reason we take the liberty of calling the attention of those of our readers, who take an interest in Natural Sciences, to the following lines:—

"A thorough examination of such an extensive State as Illinois, with respect to all the various branches of natural science, is a difficult undertaking for a single man, but might be easily accomplished by a number of scientific men, co-operating in the different parts of the country. Meteorological observations, catalogues of the plants, animals, and petrifactions found in the various districts, it would be advisable to publish in one annual collective report; specimens contributed from every district would form a State Museum; and naturalists, residing at distances from each other, would much more enhance and accelerate the advancement of knowledge by mutual correspondence, than by pursuing separate studies, each one for himself. Any person who is willing thus to promote the interests of science, will find me ready to assist him." Frederick Brendel, M. D., Peoria, Illinois.

tains, therefore, properly speaking, separates in the north this enormous territory, a small portion of which constitutes the State of Illinois, from the plateaux projecting to the north, which circumstance must necessarily exercise a decisive influence upon the climate of the State, situated as it is between the 43d and 37th degrees of north latitude, and separated by seven degrees from the Gulf of Mexico.

A sea open at all times of the year separates Europe from the North Pole; and the Mediterranean Sea washes between it and Africa; this will sufficiently account for her moderate climate. A frozen region sending during winter its icy blasts after the flying sun, bounds North America on the north, while her southern coast, penetrated in the summer by the almost perpendicular rays of a burning sun, radiates its accumulated heat to the north. This will explain why a country situated within the same degrees of latitude with Spain and Italy, has cold winters and hot summers.

Illinois has an average temperature, which, if compared with that of Europe, equals that of Middle Germany; its winter is more severe than that at Copenhagen, and her summer as warm as those of Milan or Palermo. Compared with the other States of the Union, Northern Illinois possesses a temperature similar to that of Northern Pennsylvania or Southern New York, while the temperature of Southern Illinois will not differ much from that of Kentucky or Virginia.

As far as we know, exact observations of the state of the weather have not yet been published in Illinois; we, therefore, confine ourselves to the observations of the celebrated Dr. Engelmann, at St. Louis, which at least serve for *one* part of Illinois. From his observations of 20 years we infer, that at a middle height of the barometer, of 29·477, (105′ above the lowest height of water in the Mississippi), the greatest difference in a year (1852) amounted to 1″ 5‴, and that at a middle temperature of + 54° 8 F. (= + 13° 79 C. = + 10° 13 R.), very great fluctuations prevailed.

At the coldest day, (Feb. 8, 1835,) the thermometer stood — 25° F. (= — 31° 6 C. = — 25° 3 R.), while during the hottest days in July, 1833, '34, '38, and '41, and in August, 1834, the mercury indicated a little more than + 100° F., (= + 38° C. = + 30° R.), making a difference of 125° F., (= 69° 4 C. = 55° 5 R.) Very great and rapid changes often take place in the temperature; thus, the temperature from the 16th to the 17th day of March, 1852, fell, within 17 hours, about 51° F., (= 28° 3 C. = 22° 5 R.) As for the rest, the thermometer very rarely falls below 0 F. (= — 17° 7 C. = — 14° 2 R.); on Jan. 19th, 1852,* the coldest day for 20 consecutive years, the mercury ranged — 12° F. (= — 24° 4 C. = — 19° 5 R.) The lowest temperature is generally above 0 F., and on an average ranges highest in July; then follow June and August; January being the coldest month. The first frost generally appears on the 26th of October, the last on the 6th of April, 203 days thus intervening between the first frost in autumn and the last in spring. The earliest frost appeared on Oct. 4th, 1836, and the latest, May 2d, 1851.†

The prevailing winds are either western or south-eastern. Storms generally come from the west or north-west, in the summer sometimes from the south. The severest storms are those coming from the west, as, on considering that they traverse the entire space between the Rocky Mountains and the Mississippi, within 24 hours, and reach the Atlantic coast within the next 24 hours, will be placed beyond a doubt. A clear sky and dry air prevail while they sweep over the Mississippi Valley, and not before having reached the east, will they be accompa-

---

* The winter of 1855–6 alone, which reigned with almost unexampled rigour throughout the United States, makes an exception; we here subjoin a report of the state of the thermometer on the coldest days of the winter, in the following places in Illinois:—

On January 4th, 1856, at Aurora, Kane Co., 22 degrees below zero; at Sterling, Whiteside Co., 26°; at Dixon, Lee Co., 23°; at Sycamore, De Kalb Co., 24°; at Waukegan, Lake Co., 21°; at Moline, Rock Island Co., 18°. On January 5th, at Elgin, Kane Co., 26°; at Moline, 14°; January 6th, at Moline, 30°; January 8th, at Sterling, 21°; at Springfield, Sangamon Co., 20°; at Rock Island, 22°; at Bloomington, McLean Co., 18°; at Belvidere, Boone Co., 22°; at Macomb, McDonough Co., 17°; at Elgin, 18°; at Moline, 20°; at Oquawka, Henderson Co., 25°; at Peoria, 14°. January 9th, at Springfield, 24°; at Chicago, 24°; Alton, Madison Co., 22°; at Aurora, 30°; at Geneseo, Henry Co., 29°; at Jerseyville, Jersey Co., 20°; at Macomb, 20°; at Mendota, La Salle Co., 28°; at Monmouth, Warren Co., 28°; at Morris, Grundy Co., 20°; at Paris, Edgar Co., 30°; at Peoria, 20°; and at Sterling, 21°.

† In the summer of 1850, while the temperature of St. Louis ranged very high, that of St. Clair Co. was continually lower, by about 2° R., than the former, which difference was probably in consequence of the calcareous soil of the city.

nied with heavy showers of rain; which latter fact we may account for by the condensation of the vapours abstracted by them from the Mississippi Valley, coming in contact with the Alleghany Mountains.

Rainy days there were in 1838 but 78; in 1836, however, 115; there are, on an average, 89 in every year, with a quantity of rain amounting to 42 inches, the smallest portion of which (2″) falls in January; the quantity of rain falling increasing with every succeeding month, until in June it reaches the height of 6″. More than 4 inches of rain fell within 24 hours, June 23, 1852.

The first fall of snow generally takes place in November, often, however, not before December; the last, in March, it occurring but very rarely in April. The greatest quantity of snow which fell in a single month, (December, 1839, and December, 1846,) amounted to scarcely 1″ 5. Thunderstorms there were on an average 49; beautiful days, 137; changeable days, 180; days without sunshine, 45.

Upon comparing these results with the observations made in 1852, in Wisconsin, at eight different places, the observation made at one of which, to wit, at Beloit, near the Illinoisian frontier, half way between the Mississippi and Lake Michigan, may be considered as valid for the northern part of Illinois also; we find the thermometer ranging between 29·597 and 28·665, being a difference of 0·932, while in the south the same amounted to 1·584; an average temperature reigns there of + 47° 421 F. (= + 8° 1 C. = + 6° 5 R.), being 7° 1 F. (= 4° C. = 3° 1 R.) less than in the south. On the coldest day the mercury indicated — 18° F. (= — 27° 7 C. = — 22° 1 R.), and therefore 6° F., (= 3° 3 C. = 2° 6 R.) less than at the south; and on the hottest day + 93° F. (= + 34° C. = + 27° R.) and therefore only 2° F. (= 1° 1 C. = 0° 9 R.) less than in the south. Here we must remark that the winter at that place was unusually cold. It rained 40 inches, 2 inches less than at the south, which difference, as already observed, was created by a single day's rain. The prevailing winds were north-west by north, and south-west.

From the direction of its hills and rivers, which generally run from north-east to south-west, a plain forms, gently sloping to the south-west; in this plain the rivers have worn channels from 60 to 200 feet deep; being dammed up at one side by a terrace-like, rising bank, they inundate the opposite plain to a considerable depth, overflowing

20*

it from winter to summer, and producing a luxuriant growth of grass; causing also the intermittent fever, the principal sickness of the country, which, however, only seizes the incautious settler, at places near the river; and never, except in very rainy years, visits the settlers on the ocean-like, undulating prairies.*

That the channels have gradually sunken we may distinctly see, on the shores of the Upper Mississippi, walls of rock rising perpendicularly, upon the sloping banks of which extend from Lake Pepin to below the junction of the Wisconsin with the Mississippi, as if they were walls built of equal height by the hand of men. Wherever the river describes a curve, walls may be found on the convex side of the latter. Here, the force of the river, ere it had yet excavated its channel, was broken, and the river, tired of being resisted, turned against the other side; not, however, without causing some damage to the rock which it washed; just as at the present day the river may be seen undermining its steep, rocky bank, above and below St. Paul, in Minnesota.

The upper coal formation occupies three-fifths of the State; commencing at 41° 12′ north latitude, where, as also along the Mississippi, whose banks it touches between the places of junction of the Illinois and Missouri Rivers, it is enclosed by a narrow layer of calcareous coal. This immense coal-field extends south-easterly beyond the Wabash and Ohio Rivers, far into the States of Kentucky and Ohio. The shores of Lake Michigan, and that narrow strip of land, which, commencing near them, runs along the northern bank of the Illinois, towards its south-western bend, until it meets Rock River, at its junction with the Mississippi, belongs to the Devonian system; the residue of the northern territory consists of Silurian strata, which, containing the rich lead mines of Galena, in the north-western corner of the State, rise at intervals in conical hills, thus giving the landscape a character different from that of the middle or southern portion of the State.

Over these various geological formations, underlaid at intervals by beds of sand, a process of putrefaction, which, for thousands of years

* The attention of those readers wishing more minute information regarding the state of health in Illinois, is called to the chapter treating of that subject in particular.

continued uninterrupted, has spread the richest humus, that, rather too luxurious for other grains, yields the most abundant harvests of Indian corn, the staple commodity of agriculture.

Remarkable are also those large blocks of granite and other primitive rocks, which are scattered along the banks. Since the nearest beds of primitive rocks first appear in Minnesota, and the northern part of Wisconsin, their presence can only be accounted for by assuming, that at the time the State of Illinois was covered with water, they were floated down from the north, enclosed and supported by masses of ice, which no sooner melted than the rocks sunk to the bottom, maintaining, as old settlers, their present position, whilst the work of excavation of the valleys, ravines, and channels by the water, was going on; whereas the lighter masses of earth, driven down the river, were deposited at the southern corner of the State, near the mouth of the Ohio, or contributed to the formation of the Mississippi Delta; since, in fact, the later alluvial land of the Lower Mississippi Valley reaches up the river to that point.

On the banks of the Illinois River, the pebbles rounded by the water may be found covered with a yellowish crust, as if they were baked together. These are the later fresh water calcareous strata, continually deposited before our eyes by the water.

The vegetation of the State forms the connecting link between the Flora of the northeastern States, and those of the Upper Missisippi, exhibiting, besides the plants common to all States lying between the Mississippi and Atlantic Ocean, such as are, properly speaking, natives of the western prairies; not being found east of the Alleghany Mountains. Immense prairies of grass, interlaced with groves, and stretching, principally, along the water-courses, cover two-thirds of the entire area of the State in the north, while her southern part is garnished with tufts of massive thickets, greatly diversifying the otherwise somewhat monotonous landscape.

In order to obtain a view of the variety of the vegetable creation of the State, we invite the reader to accompany us on a summer excursion.

The large, scattered, village-like formation of the smaller and middle towns, and the want of a pavement, render it possible for us to herbalise in the very town, from the moment we have stepped outside our house. Lo! close to the door is the round-leaved mallow, Malva rotundifolia, L.), next to it the swine-grass, (Polygonum aviculare, L.), here the cass-weed, (Capsella bursa pastoris, Mœnch), there the pseudo-camomile, (Anthemis arvensis, L.), covers entire tracts; a neglected garden adjoining the house is entirely overspread with the fleshy leaves of the purslain, (Portulaca), among which rises the white orache (Chenopodium album, L.), to an unusual height. But do they belong to the American, and particularly the Illinoisian Flora? No, they are immigrants; the vegetable immigration from the old world.*

* Whether the various species of a genus are of common origin, and have formed themselves under external influences, having sprung from a single individual, and spread from a single place of nativity, are questions regarding which opinions are divided. Of many cultivated plants in Europe, one could not tell whence they came thither, and of many that grow wild, whether they occupied their present domicile from primeval times, or only lately emigrated to it. That the plants do migrate, nay, that they even leave a country altogether, when the conditions indispensable to their growth are no longer found in the country, has been historically proven. Mr. Fraas, in a little work published in Germany, entitled "The Plant in Time and Climate," (Die Pflanze in Zeit und Klima") has quoted from ancient Greek authors many passages mentioning plants of Greece identical with certain ones existing at this present day in Germany, which therefore must at that time have been indigenous in the Grecian groves, but which have now disappeared together with the groves. The wooded country having assumed the character of a mere heath, other plants have taken their place, which may also be found in Syria and Egypt, whence they probably emigrated into Greece, and being rather remarkable, would certainly have been noticed and mentioned by the ancient authors, had they existed in Greece. Although the fact of the immigration, which by the agency of man took place, of plants from the old to the new continent, is within the reach of modern history, so that similar investigations might be instituted with the greatest success here, the American botanists have in regard to many plants not yet been able to agree, whether they are of native or foreign origin. In his "Principles of Geology," Lyon speaks of an old author by the name of "Jocelyn," as having drawn up a catalogue of the plants that, since the colonization of New England, came to these shores. The common nettle (Urtica), he says, was the first which the settlers noticed, and the plantain, (Plantago major, L.), received the name of the "Englishman's Foot," by the Indians: by which the latter understood, that it appeared to have grown up under the very footsteps of the English. The total number of those plants was estimated to be 22; it has, however, enormously increased since. These emigrants have of course not spread equally. Thus, although many species have penetrated to

In the same manner in which the immigrating races of the human family do in this country prosper and increase, becoming as numerous as the sands on the sea-shore, prosper and grow up also the plants accompanying the immigrant. Thus the rather inodorous thorn-apple (Datura stramonium, L.), occupies in our land so large a space as to make one doubt, whether it is to be considered a native of the old or new world.* And as the immigrant on his arrival finds many a countryman whom he is by no means overjoyed to meet again, he salutes on the other hand many an old acquaintance among the vegetable world, with the exclamation, "You here, too?"

Where once the prairie stretched along the banks of the river, or skirted the forest, and the wigwam of the Indian was standing, there the stately mansions of modern civilisation may now be found—and near them many a foreign plant. Brick walls not being congenial to them, the flowers of the prairie and forest unfold their charms under the airy canopy of heaven; and the few left behind of the various vervains (Verbena), ambrosias (Ambrosias), the prickly lidas (Lida spinosa L.), and the Pennsylvanian polygonies (Polygonum Pennsylvanicum), and others, are peaceable neighbors of the immigrated burdock (Arctium lappa, Gaertn.), the so-called "Leonurus cardiaca," the common marum (Marubium vulgare, L.), the marsh-mallow of Vincennes (Abutilon avicennæ, Gaertn.), the yellow lion's mouth (Linaria vulgaris, Mill.), the black mustard (Sinapis nigra, L.), and the rue (Sisym-

---

the Mississippi, we have not yet been able to discover in Illinois, that primitive settler, the nettle (Urtica), nor the knot-grass (Triticum repens), which has already become the plague of the eastern farmer. Most of the herbs known to have immigrated are of European origin; but a few belong to other countries, as the prickly amaranth (Amaranthus spinosus, L.), from East India; the Indian eleusine (Eleusine Indica, Gaertn.), a tropical plant, a native probably of the West Indies; the Mexican poppy (Argemone Mexicana, L.), from the south-western States; as also the so called martynia proboscidea, Glox. Whether the catalpa (Catalpa bignonioides), which you may frequently find planted in the streets, is peculiar to the Southern States, or was introduced by the natives, remains uncertain.

* It is singular, that, while the stramonium is sure to be encountered wherever the white man has fixed his domicile, again, at places where the wigwam of the red man is still standing, you would search in vain for this poisonous plant; thus, in a manner is it intimated, that nature's pure state is corrupted by civilisation.

brium officinale, Scop). Unlike their human prototypes, these plants do not deny to others, because immigrated, the right of settling at any place they may have chosen, but stand peaceably side by side, deriving their nourishment from the same parent, imbibing the dew of the heavens, and enjoying the light equally diffused over them, of the glorious sun of Deity.

Before we finally turn our backs on the last scattered houses of the city, we find both sides of the road lined with ugly worm-fences, which are overtopped by the various species of helianthus (Helianthus), thistles (Cirsium Virginianum, Mich. and C. altissimum, Spr.), biennial gaura (Gaura biennis, L., Greek γαῦρα = proud, superb), with the vermilion, and the Illinoisian bell-flower (Campanula Illinoisiensis, Fresen.), with cerulean blossoms, and other tall weeds. Here may also be found the coarse-haired Asclepias tuberosa, L., with fiery-red umbels, the strong-scented Monarda fistulosa L. var. mollis, and an umbelliferous plant, the grass-like, spiculated leaves of which recall to mind the southern agaves, the eryngo (Eryngium aquaticum, L.) Among these untutored children of nature rises the civilised plant, the Indian corn, with its stalks nearly twelve feet high, and its green, succulent leaves and swelling knots.

Next to Indian corn, wheat is most cultivated; oats next, and, since, in consequence of the extensive German immigration, rye-bread and beer are in great demand, also barley and rye. The broom-corn (Sorghum saccharatum Pers.), is raised for the manufacturing of brooms. Potatoes being a rather expensive luxury, are little cultivated, and that little chiefly in the north-western part of the State, near Galena, on meagre soil. The sweet potato (the tuber of a convolvulacea, of the Batatas edulis, Choisy), the water-melon, sweet melon, various pumpkins and tomatoes (Lycopersicum esculentum, Mill.), are common products of the fields. In the south the castor-oil plant (Ricinus communis, L.), is also cultivated.

Having now arrived at the end of the cultivated lands, we enter upon the dry prairies extending up the bluffs, where we are saluted by the small vermilion sorrel (Rumex acetosella, L.), and mouse-ear (Myosotis stricta, Link.), which, however, do not reside here as foreigners, but as natives,* like many other plants that remind the European of

* Of such plants as are equally diffused over the entire north-temperate

his native country, as for instance the dandelion (Taraxacum officinale, Wig.), a kind of rose (Rosa lucida), with its sweet-scented blossoms, has a great predilection for this dry soil. With surprise we meet here also many plants with hairy greenish-gray leaves and stalk-covers; as, for instance, the Onosmodium melle, Mich., Hieracium longipilum, Torr., Pycnanthemum pilosum, Nutt., Chrysopsis villosa, Nutt., Amorpha canescens, Nutt., Dalea alopecuroides, Willd., Tephrosia Virginiana, Pers., Lithospermum canescens, Lehm.; between which the immigrated mullein (Verbascum thapsus, L.), may be found. The pebbly fragments of the entire slope, which, during spring-time were sparingly covered with dwarfish herbs, such as the Androsace occidentalis, Pursh., Draba Caroliniana, Walt., Antennaria plantaginifolia, Hook., plantain (Plantago Virginica, L.), Scutellaria parvula, Mich., are now crowded with plants of taller growth and variegated blossoms. Rudbeckia herta, L., with its numerous radiating blossoms of a lively yellow colour, and the closely allied Echinacea purpurea (Moench), whose long purple rays hang down from a ruddy hemispherical disc, are the most remarkable among plants belonging to the genus "compositæ," which blossom early in summer; in the latter part of summer follow innumerable plants of the different species Liatris, Vernonia, Aster, Solidago, Helianthus, &c., Tephrosia Virginiana, Pers., with numerous great pink and yellow-coloured blossoms; the violet Psoralea floribunda, Nutt., and Psor. Onobrychis, Nutt.; Petalostemon violaceum, Mich., and Petalostemon candidum, Mich., belonging all of them to the family of the leguminous plants, blossom here, together with the Linum Virginianum, L., and the Polygala incarnata, L., with rosy, pretty little blossoms on a tall stalk.

We approach a sinuous chasm of the bluffs, having better soil and underwood, which, thin at first, increases gradually in density. Low bushes, hardly a foot high, are formed by the American thistle (Ceanothus Americanus, L.), a plant whose leaves were used instead of tea, after the English tea had been thrown in the sea, at Boston, during the revolution; the flower being very beautiful may be used for ornamental purposes. Next follow the hazel-bush (Corylus Americana, Walt.), the fiery-red Castilleja coccinea, Spreng., and the yellow

---

zone, there are many, especially ranunculæ, cruciferæ, aquatic plants of every kind, and reed-grasses.

Canadian lousewort (Pedicularis Canadensis, L.); the Diptera, canthus strepens Nees (Ruellia, L.), with great blue funnel-shaped blossoms, and the Gerardia pedicularia, L., are fond of such places; and where the bushes grow higher, and the Rhus glabra, L., Zanthoxylum Americanum, Mill., Ptelea trifoliata, L., Staphylea trifolia, L., together with Ribes-Rubus Pyrus, dogwood (cornus), and hawthorn (Cratægus), form an almost impenetrable thicket, surrounded and garlanded by the round-leaved, rough bind-weed (Smilax rotundifolia), and herbacea L., Dioscorea villosa, L., the blooming, everywhere-climbing, bristling rose (Rosa setigera, L.), the Celastrus scandens, L., remarkable for its beautiful red fruits, the Clematis Virginiana, L., the polygony of the brakes (Polygonum dumetorum, L.), the bindweed (Convolvulus panduratus, L.), and other vines, these weedy herbs attempt to over-top the bushes. Developing their young shoots under the protection of the shade, they exert themselves to gain the open air, and unfold in the sunshine the splendours of their brilliant blossoms. Baptisia leucantha, Torr & Gr., with its delicate pale hue, the Canadian tragacanth (Astragalus canadensis, L.), which grows to an extraordinary size, the goat's beard (Spiræa Arancus, L.), the Canadian elder-bush (Lambucus Canadensis), the purple liver-wort (Eupatorium purpureum, L.), and the gigantic Composituræ Silphium perfoliatum, L., the Rudbeckia laciniata, L., Lepachys pinnata, Torr. & Gr., finally the deep blue Tradescantia Virginica, L., stand beside the purple swallow-wort (Asclepias purpurascens, L.); and the carmine calix of the Lilium superbum, L., among which those beautiful grasses, Melica speciosa, Muhl., Tricuspis seslerioides, Torr., Stipa Avenacea, L., Andropogon Virginicus, L., elevate their heads.

Having reached the table land, we wander through a little grove, consisting of small-sized trees, stunted oak and hickory, which on better soil attain a good height, since in the forests you may find white oaks a hundred feet high, and of considerable thickness; with hickory, and maple trees, cotton—poplars, and sycamores 80 feet high, besides at least twenty different species of trees, attaining or even surpassing the height of 60 feet.

We now enter upon the illimitable prairie which lies before us; not upon that dry sandy prairie, with its temporary herbaceous dress, but the fertile prairie, in whose undulating surface the moisture is retained; this waits for cultivation, and will soon be deprived of its flowery attire, and bear plain, but for man's nourishment indispensable, grain. Those who have not yet seen such a prairie, should not imagine it like a cultivated meadow, but rather a heaving sea of tall herbs and plants, decking it with every variety of colour.

In the summer the yellow of the large compositæ will predominate here and there, intermingled with the blue of the tradescantias, the fiery red of the lilies (Lilium Philadelphium, and Lilium Canadense, L.), the purple of the Phlox glaberrima, L., the white of the Cacalia tuberosa, Nutt., the pepper-wort (Melanthium Virginicum, L.), and the umbelliferous plants. In spring, small sized plants bloom here, such as the anemone (Anemone Caroliniana, Walt.), with its blue and white blossoms, the palmated violet (Viola palmata), the ranunculus (Ranunculus fascicularis, Muhl.), which are the first ornament of the prairies in spring; then follow the esculent sea-onion (Scilla esculenta, Ker.), Pentalophus longiflorus, D. C., the grummel (Lithospermum hirtum, Lehm.), the Cynthia virginica, Don., Echinacea angustifolia, D. C., and Baptisia leucophæa, Nutt. As far as the eye reaches no house nor tree can be seen; but where civilization has come, the farmer has planted small rows of the quickly-growing black acacia (Robinia pseudacacia, L.), which affords shelter from the sun to his feeding cattle, and fuel for his hearth in the winter. We find the greatest prairies in the northeastern part of the State, stretching from the Illinois River to the State of Indiana, at intervals intersected by the shaded course of a river, but entirely destitute of trees on its highest points, whence in all directions flow little brooks to meet the Illinois and Wabash.

"There one breathes more freely," are the words of an old hunter, for whom the daily increasing fences proved too confining; "as far as the eye can reach, nothing but the skies and an ocean of grass." Taste, however, varying greatly, many would prefer a limited view, changing by turns and affording to the eye points of rest; such a view as may be had from Prospect Hill, four miles north of Peoria. Having approached the margin of the table-land, we look down upon a delightful valley, through which flows the Illinois River, enlarged to the breadth of a sea. Fifteen miles further up, we perceive the cloud of smoke following a steamer sailing upward, and stopping at the white houses of yonder little town just built, from which a long railroad train hurries across the gently rising prairie, disappearing behind the projecting wooded bluff. Bushes rise prominent above the sheet of water which inundates the country, adjacent to the other bank, beyond which in the distant background may be seen a cultivated plain, destitute of trees, covered with corn fields, which wave around the isolated farms enclosed by groves; close to our feet, however, and distinctly indicating the broken, rolling formation of the slope, is a vast forest, which, assuming in autumn all varieties of colour, from the most lively carmine to the darkest green, presents a most striking appearance.

Here in rocky places may be found the Aquilegia Canadensis, L., fostered in the gardens of Europe, and remarkable for its yellow and red coloured blossoms, curiously shaped in the form of a bell; the violet wood-sorel (Oxalis violacea, L.), that, together with the Dodecatheon meadia, L., is fond of the prairie; the well known strawberry (Fragaria vescat. and Virginiana, Ehrh.), the Senega milk-tare (Polygala Senega, L.), the Comandra umbellata, of the order of the santalaceæ, Heuchera Americana, L., one of the few saxifragas growing here, the shrub-like Hydrangea arborescens, L., with its white tufts; the Rhus aromatica, with its irregularly indented leaves, and scarlet-red fruits, flourishing at the feet of old trunks of trees; and various rock cresses. On descending below the shadowy canopy of mighty oaks, walnut trees, linden, maple, elm, ash, mulberry, sassafras, and chesnut trees, we find the ground strewn with beautiful grasses, (belonging to the orders of the Muhlenbergia, Glyceria, Uniola, Leersia, Cinna and Panicum), and numerous ferns, among which the pedate venus grass (Adiantum pedatum, L.), excels by its delicate fan-form and purple-black stalk, and the Claytonian onoclea (onoclea Claytoniana), Polystichum acrostichoides, Schott., and the Pteris aquilina, well known in Germany by its exuberant growth. Among these rises the Desmodium acuminatum, D. C., on its broad-leaved basis, the rosy-red Paniela, adorned with papilionaceous blossoms, together with the tall white anemones (Anemone Pennsylvanica, L., and Anemone Virginiana, L.), the beautiful blue Delphinium exaltatum, Ait., the American bell-flower, (Campanula Americana), with long stalks covered with sky-blue blossoms, the Aralia racemosa, L., Triosteum perfoliatum, L., and the Agrimonia Eupatoria, L., are rarely wanting. Following the course of a spring, which bubbles down, we find at its margin the Circaca lutetiana, L., also indigenous in Germany, the marsh wolf's milk (Lathyris palustris, L.), the asper horse-mint (Stachys aspera, Mich.), the meadow rue (Thalietrum Cornuti L.), the clustered rough bind-weed (Smilacina racemosa, Desf.), and the high-growing Polygonatum canaliculatum Pursh. We now enter the level part of the forest, which has a rich black soil. Great sarmentous plants climb here up to the tops of the trees, wild grapes, the climbing poisonous sumac (Rhus toxicodendron, L., var. radicans), and the vine-like quinquefoil (Ampelopsis quinquefolia, Mich.), which transforms withered naked trunks into green columns, Tecoma radicans Juss (Bignonia, L.), with their brilliant, scarlet, trumpet flowers, are the most remarkable. Imposing are also the draperies of the green dome of foliage, the contemplation of which delights the eye of the spectator; but you would search in vain here for the evergreen pine-tree, with its strong smell of resin. The Thuja occidentalis, L., which may be met with in European gardens, stands in mournful solitude on the margins of pools; here and there an isolated cedar (Juniperus Virginiana, L.), and the low box-tree (Taxus Canadensis), on the rocky slopes of the Mississippi Valley, are in Illinois the only representatives of the evergreens, forests of which first appear in the northern part of Wisconsin and Minnesota.

Gerardias, with purple and yellow monkey-flowers, Mimulus ringens, L., and Mimulus alatus, Ait., Chelone glabra, L., Blephilia hirsuta, Benth., and the common prunel (Prunella vulgaris, L.), blossom here; of the compositæ, the beautiful Rudbeckia triloba, L., excels by its black purple disc, and fiery yellow spoke-flowers, and among the delicate little plants, the Anychia dichotoma, Mich., Cerastium nutans, Raf., Stellaria longifolia, Muhl., and various galia, are deserving of particular notice. On wet and shaded places an exuberance of Impatiens fulva, Nutt. and pallida, Nutt., may be found united with urticaceas.

While the forest is resplendent in summer with a dazzling array of colours, in spring it is adorned with lovely plants of delicate succulent structure. The first child of spring is the blue liverwort (Hepatica triloba., D. C.), which unfolds its brilliant blossoms about the middle of March; then follows, on wet places, the buttercup (Caltha palustris, L.), and in the midst of April, we see among the naked trees, of which the yellow winter-oak (Æsculus flava, Ait.), first shoots forth its leaves, a multitude of most beautiful flowers, most of them of the purest white, or imperceptibly changing from white into a tender rose colour, among them that lovely anemone-like meadow rue (Thalictrum anemonoides, Mich.), the Canadian blood-wort (Sanguinaria canadensis, L.), the broad-leaved Podophyllum peltatum, L., the round-leaved Cardamine (Cardamina rotundifolia, Mich.), Mitella diphylla, L., the Trillium cernuum, L., Dicentra canadensis, D. C., a delicate fumariacea, with a flesh-coloured stalk, and pale green leaves, which, on account of the peculiar form of its blossoms, that in a manner resemble short, spread-out leather breeches, is called "Dutchman's breeches," the Dentaria lanciniata Muhl., Claytonia Virginica, L., and Ellisia nyctelaea, L. The blue tint is peculiar to the Mertensia Virginica D. C., which covers entire wooded tracts, the capon's tail, Polemonia reptans, L., or Polemonia pilosa L., and the crested violet (Viola cucullata, Ait.), the Violet Pedanthus hesperides, Torr. & Gr., the red Geranium maculatum, L., the Trillium sessile, L., with a brownish flower enclosed in three leaves, the yellow ranunculus (Ranunculus repens, L.), Cypripedium pubescens, Willd., with pedate flowers, almost two inches long, and the Uvularia grandiflora, Smith. All these species are represented by numerous individuals. Less frequently are seen the purple violet rag-wort, Orchis spectabilis, L.), with white labiated flowers, Leontice thalietroides, L., Aralia medicinalis, L., &c.

The trees are also clad in other colours besides green. The inflexible branches of the Cercis canadensis are covered with peach-coloured blossoms, the Pyrus coronaria, L., exhibits rosy-red blossoms, the Sassafras officinale Nees, yellow ones, and different species of hawthorn (Cratægus), and dogwood (Cornu).

The pawpaw tree (Asimina triloba, Dunal), a small tree, with large oval leaves, developes still sooner its brown-red blossoms, and bears in autumn great, fleshy, dirty-yellow fruits, which taste like stale dough; the Euonymus atropurpureus Jacq., has smaller, brownish-red blossoms. Of large trees, there are also the wild-cherry tree, (Cerasus serotina, D. C.), the prickly Gleditschia triacanthos L., with its fine coronate leaves, and another cisalpinia, the Gymnocladus cana densis, Lam., with thick pulpous pods; rarer to be seen is the Virginian persimmon (Diospyros Virginiana, L.), whose orange-coloured fruits are eatable only after the first frost in late autumn, and the Cornus Florida, L., with its great snow-white husks, both of them being more frequent in the southern part of the State. On the margin of the forest we also perceive the American plum-tree, a small tree bearing an orange-coloured fruit; yonder on the bank of the river stand mighty trunks, indigenous to a wet soil, and stretching forth their branches far beyond the edge of the water; perhaps the flowery Echinocystis lobata, Torr. & Gr., clasps itself around them; there you may find also the Platanus occidentalis, L., here called sycamore, with its glistening bark and deeply-indented leaves, and the Populus monilifera, L., called cotton-wood, because its fruits, which are strung together like beads, on bursting cover the surrounding earth with its wool-like capsules.

Flowers of the most brilliant hues bedeck the rivers' banks; above all the Lobelia cardinalis, L., and the Lobelia syphilitica, of the deepest carmine and cerulean tinge, the yellow Cassia Marilandica, L., whose leaves serve for the affusion of the senna, and the delicate Cassia chamæcrista, L., with sensitive elder-leaves, then the delicate Rosa blanda, L., a rose without thorns, also the Scrophularia nodosa, L.

The sandy parts of the banks have their own particular Flora. Dwarfish cyperoids, and the frequent Mollugo verticillata, L., Lespedeza repens, Torr. & Gr., Eragrostis reptans Nees, Euphorbia maculata L., and other creepers partly cover the gravelly sand; among them rises the deep-rooted Allionia nyctaginea, Mich., Euphorbia Cyathiphora Mich., Darlingtonia brachyloba, D. C., the only species of mimosa, Crotalaria sagittalis, L., amsonia salicifolia Pursh, and Clematis pitcher., Torr. & Gr., with procumbent violet-colored stalks, and thick reflexed tips of the calix, finally, Polanisia graveolens, Raf., an isolated apparidacea, of repulsive smell.

The banks flattening, the marshy ground commences, upon which thrive the Iris versicolor, L., Cephalanthus occidentalis, L., Asclepias incarnata, L., the primrose-tree (Lysimachia), liver-wort (Eupatoria), most frequent, however, are the tall Physostegia Virginiana, Beuth, with rosy-red blossoms, and the Helenium auctumnale, L., in which the yellow color predominates. In spring, the dark violet blossom of the Amorpha fructicosa, L., diffuses its fragrance.

Let us now jump in the boat and row to the opposite flat bank, where a branch of the river joins a swamp, and at the end of our excursion examine the aquatic vegetation.

Already where we cannot touch the bottom with the oar, we perceive a little white flower, waving to and fro, supported by long spiral halms between straight grass-like leaves. This is the valisneria spiralis, L., a remarkable plant, which may also be met with in Southern Europe, especially in the canal of Languedoc, and regarding the fructification of which different opinions prevail. This plant has two different blossoms, a male and a female one, the latter are situated on spiral pedicals, which, lengthened at the time of blooming, elevate the flower above the surface of the water to reach the female blossom without separating; though this was heretofore supposed, it was believed that the male flower, after separating, rose to swim round the female, delivering the pollen it was bearing at the time. As, however, no such male flower was ever observed to separate and swim freely about, but the particles of pollen have been observed, the latter are presumed solely to reach the surface and fecundate the female flowers.

Already, nearer to the land, we observe similar grass-like leaves, but with little, yellow, stellated flowers; these belong to the order of the Schollera graminea Willd, which also vegetate on the banks, but then in diminished size. Other larger leaves belong to the amphibious Polygony (polygonium amphibium), and different species of the potamogeton, the ears of whose blossoms rise curious above the surface of the water. We can already look down upon the bottom of the river. Ceratophyllum echinatum Gray, predominates; at intervals charas and utriculareas may be found. Clearing our way through a row of tall swamp weeds (rye-grass, zizania aquatica, L., rush-grass, Scirpus lacustris, L., Scirpus pungens Vahl.), among which the white flowers of the bur reed (Sparganium ramosum Huds., Sagittaria variabilis Engelm.), and Echinodorus subulatus Engelm., are conspicuous, we steer into a large inlet entirely covered with the broad leaves of the odoriferous seagarland (Nymphaea odorata, Ait.), but little differing from the European water lily, and the Nelumbium luteum, Willd., of which the former modestly waves its beautiful flower on the surface of the river, whilst the latter, the queen, in fact, of the waters, proudly raises her magnificent crown upon a perpendicular foot-stalk; yonder, on the opposite bank, the evening breeze lifts the triangular leaves, and rosy-red flowers of the marsh-mallow (Hibiscus militaris Cav.), overhung by gray willows and the silver-leaved maple (Acer dasycarpum, Ehrh., and acer rubrum, L.,) on which a multitude of white herons have alighted. A profound silence reigns everywhere, scarcely interrupted by a few dragon-flies, buzzing about, and over the entire scene the parting sun diffuses his rosy, faint, trembling light. It is a solemn, sublime scene; an hour thus passed, within nature's bosom, is an hour of consecration; an hour of true edification and devotion. Nature, indeed, is the most sublime temple of God.

At the termination of our excursion, let us throw a glance over the whole, and consider how man turns to advantage the wealth of the vegetable creation.

The species of corn that are cultivated have already been mentioned at length, with the exception of a species used for nourishment by the Indians, to wit, the wild maize (Zizania aquatica L.), which has been slightly noticed. This plant, six feet high, or more, has a panicle but below male, another above, female flowers. In autumn, when the grains are ripe, the Indian, or rather his squaw, rows in a canoe to this aquatic harvest, the tops of which he bends over the gunwale of his boat, beating out the grain with a stick; the rice is so loosely enclosed between the bearded husks as to fall out at the slightest puff of wind, by reason whereof this harvest can only be continued for a few days after the maturity of the crop. Many prefer this wild to the ordinary rice, and cattle feed with avidity on its succulent leaves.* The timothy grass (phleum pratense L.), was imported almost a century since from Europe, and has been cultivated until now, as also the Dactylis glomerata, L., Poa pratensis, L., Festuca pratensis, Huds., and other European grasses for fodder, for which purpose the indigenous herbs command an inferior value, with hardly the exception of the Calamagrostis canadensis, Beauv., and several glycerias, one of which Glyceria fluitans, R. Br., produces the "manna seed," that is often mixed as groats with the soup. A gigantic grass attaining the height of forty feet, the Arundinaria macrosperma, Mich., thrives in the south

* The Indians have a wild-growing succedaneum for the potato, to wit: the mealy, bulbous roots of the nelumbium luteum, and paint themselves yellow with the root of hydrastis canadensis, L.

on the banks of the Mississippi, and along the Ohio as far as to its falls, near Louisville, Kentucky. Its stalks are frequently sold for fishing-rods in the market.

The forest furnishes of eatable fruits, strawberries, blackberries, raspberries, gooseberries, mulberries, grapes, wild plums and cherries, wild apples and hips, the Amelanchier canadensis, Torr. & Gr., the persimmon, the pawpaw, hickory, hazel, and walnuts. Many other fruits are greedily devoured by "pigs and boys," as Asa Gray remarks, when speaking of the May-apple, the fruit of the Podophyllum peltatum.

The sugar maple, besides the sugar gathered from its sap, furnishes also firewood of very superior quality; the white oak (Quercus alba L., Quercus macrocarpa Mich.), and the hickories, especially Carya alba Nutt., and Carya tomentosa Nutt., yield also excellent fuel; the Carya amara Nutt., however, to a less degree.

The bark of the dying oak (Quercus tinctoria, Bartr.), furnishes the famous color for the home-made woollen fabrics of the farmer. From the wood, which may be easily split, of the Quercus imbricaria Mich., with not lobated, but laurel-like, leaves, roof-shingles are made. Oak, linden, ash, walnut, cherry, hickory, and maple trees, furnish the wood required by wheelwrights and cabinet-makers, for their work; the hardest is the iron-wood (Carpinus Americanus Mich., and Ostrya Virginica, Willd.); the wood of the sycamore and the cotton-wood is almost useless.

Next follow the plants used for medicinal purposes. It is well known, that the medical profession has usurped almost every thing having either taste or smell, in the vegetable creation, in order to prepare those infallible remedies and specifics, mixtures, pills, and drugs, so abundantly praised and recommended in the newspapers, and at every street corner; although it can hardly be doubted that they prove much more frequently injurious than beneficial, their healing properties being at best very indifferent. Too much time would be taken up, should we enumerate every herb and root. How many emetics besides the phytolacea decandra do they not substitute for ipecacuanha! how many drastics besides the Radix Podophylli for jalap! And what specifics against the bite of serpents, and fevers! We confine ourselves to a few wild growing drugs, most frequently met in the trade; the blood-wort, Sanguinaria canadensis, L.; milk-tare, Polygala senega L.; Cassia Marilandica L.; Lobelia inflata L.; Menyanthes trifoliata L.; Sassafras officinale Nees. We shall, however, not exhibit ingratitude towards some popular remedies, whose virtues entitle them to mention here, for example, the slippery elm (ulmus fulva Mich.), and the oriental sesame, frequently growing in our gardens (sesamum orientale L.); the interior bark of the former and the leaves of the latter, may be recommended as mucilaginous remedies, the latter, especially, for summer complaints; and an infusion of water-melon seeds may be drunk in case of dropsy, after intermitting fevers.

We shall conclude with the best and most efficient medicinal herb. Various species of the vine grow here, they climb the highest trees, and separate themselves from the trunk, so that the bunches of grapes hang down from the twigs as big as one's arm; the grapes are small, of good flavour, and are much used by housewives for preserves; if cultivated this grape attains a larger size, and is most succulent. The American vine, less influenced by the weather than the European, admits of more successful cultivation than the latter. The fox-grape (Vitis labrusca L.), is the most improvable variety, and furnishes various brands; Isabella, &c. The tilling of vines makes rapid progress in the Western States, and is already commenced in Illinois. St. Clair and Monroe Counties in the south produce an excellent Catawba wine, which may be safely compared to good Rhine-wine, and is nearly equal in strength to the Hungarian wines. Also in the environs of Peoria and Nauvoo, the cultivation of the vine has been commenced, and that with a success which bids fair to be lasting. Let us hope, that at no distant time many counties of the fertile Prairie State will be clothed in the green dress of this noble plant.

The times have long since passed when herds of buffaloes were feeding in the prairies of Illinois, and the beaver built her dwellings here, and the elk (Elaphus canadensis Ray), bounded through the forests. The latter must now be hunted up, far away in Minnesota. The last beaver was killed in Wisconsin, in 1819, and the last buffalo (Bison Americanus, Gm.), on this side of the Mississippi, was seen in 1832. Also the black bear (ursus Americanus Pall.), has become very rare. Civilization has driven all these beasts, together with the Indians, to the north and west. Nevertheless the hunter cannot complain of want of occupation. The largest animal of the forest is the Virginian stag, midway in size between the European stag and roe. Of carnivorous animals may be found the red fox (Vulpes fulvus Desm.), the gray fox (Vulpes Virginianus Dekay), the prairie wolf (Canis latrans Say), the common wolf (Lupus Occidentalis Richardson), the wild cat (Lyncus rufus, Temm,); but scarcely a single specimen of the panther (Felis concolor L.); the otter (Lutra Canadensis Sabine), the mink (Putorius visor L.), the marten (Mustela Canadensis L.), the pole-cat (Mephitis Americana Desm.), the badger (Meles Labradoria Sabine); lastly, the raccoon (Procyon lotor, L.), (Waschbär, in German), which can be easily tamed, and runs freely about the dwellings; he has received his Latin and German names probably on account of his rubbing every object with his forepaws, and splashing about in the water. That he immerses every morsel of food in the water before devouring it, is a mere fable, which, however, may still be found in many treatises on zoology. The farmer is his sworn enemy, since the raccoon not only steals away his poultry, but entering the maize-fields at a time when the grains are just milky, commits great devastation, by spoiling more than twenty times the amount he devours. The opossum (Didelphys Virginiana Pennant), with his naked rat-like tail, looks extremely ugly, but furnishes excellent roast-meat, for which reason he is not skinned, but, like the hog, dipped in boiling water. This animal brings forth eleven young ones, which she carries about in a pouch in her belly.

We have besides, the red, gray, black, and mottled, together with the flying squirrel (Pteromys volucella Harl), the American marmot (Arctomys monax Gm.), the muskrat (Fibes Zibethicus L.), and two species of rabbits, to wit: Lepus nanus Schreb., and Lepus Americanus Erzl.; an infinite number of rats, mice, &c.

The largest bird of prey is the white-headed eagle (Haliætus leucocephalus L.), which the Union has chosen for its emblem. With his wings spread he measures more than seven feet. The Washington eagle (Haliætus Washingtonii, And.), is by many believed to be identical with the white-headed eagle, although, while both head and tail of the latter are white, those of the former on the contrary are black, and further, while the beak of the white-headed eagle is yellow, that of the Washington eagle is of an entirely different dusky hue.

The Washington eagle is believed first to get the white plumage of his head and tail, and his yellow beak when three or four years old, a change of colors being not unusual in the case of birds of prey. A certain naturalist has embraced this opinion because the birds have the same manner of living, and are frequently seen together. They subsist like the smaller Pandion Haliætus, L., on fish. The royal eagle (Aquila Chrysætos, L.), is said to build its nest here, on high trees, in the absence of rocks, as do also from fifteen to twenty smaller species of falcons. The only kind of vulture to be met with here (Cathartes Aura, L.), is called the turkey-buzzard, because of his resemblance to the turkey: he feeds on carrion.

The larger among the ten or twelve different species of owls are, the snowy owl (Lurnia Lyctia, L.), and the great horned owl (Bubo Virginianus, Gm.), which last is quite similar to the European eagle-owl.

Numerous species of smaller birds* belonging to the order of the Oscines Clamatores and Scansores, populate the forest and prairie.

The plumage of many is resplendent with lively colors, thus Pyranga rubra, Wils., is scarlet-red, but has black wings; Agelajus Phœniceus, L., the notorious corn-thief, better known by the name of blackbird, whole swarms of which pounce upon the maize-fields, picking the grains out of the germs on the soil, has a shining black hue, but scarlet-red wing-shell feathers; the various wood-peckers are most of them carmine, black and white; the Blue Jay (Garrulus cristatus, L.), and

---

* A complete list of all the birds of Illinois has not yet been compiled; Mr. Lapham, however, has published such a catalogue for Wisconsin,—which may answer for Illinois also — wherein 290 species are enumerated; to wit: — 34 different birds of prey; 9 fowls; 49 swamp-birds (the Canadian crane, Grus Canadensis, is wanting here); 50 swimming birds; 12 climbing birds (to which the woodpeckers, parrots, and cuckoos belong); 4 clamatores (halcyon, colibri, and goat-suckers); lastly, 132 warblers, birds, the heads of whose windpipes are furnished with the song-muscle apparatus; though some, like the ravens, which belong to this class, are unable to sing. The families of the finches and sylviades are most numerously represented by them; these by 36, those by 33 species; then follow 14 species of gnat-snappers; 10 of the throttles, and 10 of the starlings; 6 of the swallows and vireoninæ, respectively; 5 of the ravens and certhiadæ; 3 of the shrikes, and but 2 of the larks and ampelides, respectively. One of the larks 'Alauda alpestris,' L., may be met with anywhere from Texas to Labrador; the other, Otocoris rufa, And., is more frequently seen farther west.

Sialia Wilsonii, Sw., are beautifully blue—the latter has a brownish-red breast; Icterus Baltimore, L., which bears a striking resemblance to the European oriole, is black and yellow; Sturnella Ludoviciana, L., improperly called tit-lark, has a tawny breast. Of the species Fringilla Sylvia, and Muscicapa, there are a great many varieties. The throttles excel in song; we count eight different species; most worthy of mention is the mocking-bird (Mimus polyglottus, Lath.), which closely imitates the voice of every other bird. The southern orders of birds are represented by single species; the parrots, by the Psittacus Carovinensis, Bon.; the humming-bird, by the Trochilus colubris, L., which can be seen every summer, buzzing about the flowers, and is often confounded with a butterfly.

The hunter takes but little notice of these birds, while looking for richer booty, especially in spring and autumn, when the waters are crowded with ducks, geese, or other aquatic birds. The duck most frequently met, is the so-called Anas Borchas, L., then follows the Anas Strepera, L.; Anas Obscura, Gm.; A. americana, Gm.; A. discors, L.; the fen duck (A. crecca, Bon.), the shoveler (A. clypeata, L.), A. acuta, L., and the wood-duck (A. sponsa, L.), the most beautiful of them all, which lays and sets on trees, remaining here all summer. Of divers, there may be frequently met with the scaup-duck, Fuligula Marila, L., Fuligula Valisneria, Bonap., F. rufitorques, Bon., the red-headed duck, (F. ferina, L.), the golden eye L., (F. clangula), the buffalo-headed duck, Fuligula albeola, L., and Fuligula glacialis, L. Rarer to be seen is the Fuligula Histrionica, L., and Fuligula rubida, Bon. Of geese there are six different species, of which the Canadian goose (Anser Canadensis, L.), the white-fronted goose (Anser albifrons, Bechst), the ring-goose (A. berniclea, L.), and the snow-goose (Anser hyperborea, Gm.), most frequently occur.

Of swans we distinguish two different species, Cygnus Americanus, And., and Cygnus buccinator, Rich. The mergansers, Mergus merganser, L., Mergus serrator, L., and Mergus cucullatus, L., have a very fishy taste, and are therefore not eaten.

Among the marsh birds that can be hunted there are the cranes, which are good roasted, and of which there are three species: the American crane (Grus Americana, Bon.), the Canadian crane (Grus Canadensis, Temm.), and Grus cinerea, L.; then many gold-breasted trumpeters and plovers (Tringa, Charadrino), the common snipe (Scolopax Wilsonii, Temm.), and the wood-snipe (Scolopax minor, Bon.)

In autumn and spring millions of migratory pigeons (Ectopistes migratoria, And.), arrive; immediately everybody hurries into the field to exact a tribute from the passing flights, so that all day long nothing but continuous discharges are heard. Highly interesting is the description by Audubon, of the enormous flights, which he observed on the Ohio, in the fall of 1813; they obscured the day-light, and lasted three days without interruption. According to a very moderate estimate of his, each flight contained the stupendous number of one billion, one hundred and fifteen thousand millions, one hundred and thirty-six thousand pigeons. These flights caused a general commotion among the entire rural population. Desirous of booty, and anxious lest their crops should be spoiled, the farmers, arming themselves with rifles, clubs, poles, torches, and iron pots filled with sulphur, proceeded to the resting places of the birds, in order to shoot the pigeons, or knock them down from the trees, or kill them by sulphurous exhalations, expedients which were rendered necessary by their numbers; since the birds were so numerous on the trees that their excrements covered the ground several inches deep. The work of slaughter being accomplished, everybody sat down amongst mountains of dead pigeons and barrels, busying himself with plucking and salting the birds which they selected, abandoning the rest to the foxes, wolves, raccoons, opossums, and hogs, whole herds of which were driven to the battle-field. Also flocks of eagles, hawks, buzzards, and vultures came thither, having scented the prey from afar.

The turtle-dove (Ectopistes Carolinensis, Aud.), is the permanent resident of the forests, as is also the partridge (Ortyx Virginiana, L.), and the Tetrao umbell., L. The prairie-fowl (Tetrao cupidus, L.), never enters the forest, but stays in the prairies, and approaches in winter so near to the habitations of man, that it may often be seen sitting on the fences.* It is as large as the domestic fowl; the greatest, however, among the game-birds is the turkey, the same which can be

* The sportsman presents a very curious appearance, who, on a fine winter's day, when the earth is covered with snow, turns out to shoot wild fowl. Dressed entirely in white, with his face also painted white, save two great spots below the eyes, which are painted black to absorb the rays of the sun,

found among the tame poultry, but in a wild state, and always with brown-red plumage, playing from one color into another.

Among the birds not hunted, those worth remarking are the various herons, of which the smallest (Ardea exilis, Bon.), measures but one foot from the end of his beak to the tip of his tail, and the largest (Ardea herodias, L.), more than four feet. Besides these, there are the Ardea nycticorax, L., also existing in Europe; the freckled heron (Ardea lentiginosa, Swains.); the Ardea vircocens, L.; the western heron (Ardea occidentalis, And.), the Ardea candidissima, Gmel.; the Ardea egretta, Gmel. The three latter are white. Of pelicans there are Phalacrocorax dilophus, Swains., and the Pelicanus Americanus, And., Colymbus glacialis, Bon., several gulls and sea-swallows, among which is the Sterna hirundo, L., with scarlet-red feet and beak.

Of the reptilia, numerous species of serpents exist, only three of which are venomous, to wit: the striped rattlesnake (Crotalus durissus, L.), the prairie rattlesnake, or Massasauga (Crotalophorus tergeminus, Say.), and the copper-head (Agkistroton contortrix, Baird & Girard, Boa contortrix, L.) The largest snakes are the black serpent (Bascanion constrictor, B. & G., Coluber constrictor, L.), five feet long, and the Pituophis malansleucus, Holbr., which measures six feet.

Among the batrachii, the bull-frog (Rana pipiens), is most deserving of notice, who, with his feet spread, attains a length of nearly two feet, and raises at night a hideous clamor. The wood-frog (Rana silvatica), and the marsh-frog (Rana palustris), are much smaller. Of toads there is but one species, the American toad (Bufo Americanus); of green frogs, two species, Hyla versicolor, and Hyla lateralis. Of the lizards, we notice Triton dorsalis, Necturus lateralis, Ambystoma punctata, and Menopoma Alleghaniensis, the greatest species, which often attains the length of two feet. Of the numerous Saurii peculiar to the Southern States, there are either few or none in Illinois; of turtles, however, quite a large number. Of the twenty species which belong to the genus of the fresh-water turtles (Emys), Illinois has several, among which are the beautiful Emys picta, and the Chelonura serpentina, which presents a grim aspect, and is wont to snap with his sharp beak at the intruder. The lower shell of the Cistuda clausa is subdivided

---

he manages to advance stealthily within a short distance of the prairie fowls, sitting on the hedges.

into three parts, the anterior as well as the posterior of which it may draw up at pleasure, wholly enclosing itself in the shell. The soft-shell species, which is often used for soups, belong to the genus Trionyx.

The waters of Illinois teem with fish, but few of which have been properly examined or classified.

The perch (Perca), the Centrarchus, Pomotis, Pimelodus, Leuciscus, salmon (Salmo), Corregonus, Lepidosteus, Pike (Esox), eel (Anguilla), tunny-fish (Anica), Noturus and Corvina, are the chief species, the largest of which is the Lepidosteus osseus,* here called Alligator gar, because of the resemblance of his head to that of the real alligator. In the Peoria Lake one was once captured, which was fifteen feet long. A singular cartilaginous fish is a species of sturgeon called the paddle-fish (Polyodon folium), whose upper gill is horizontally compressed, projecting about half the length of the whole body. This fish also attains a considerable size.

Besides these the waters contain crabs, and many molluskas; among the snails, the Heliceæ and Lymneaceæ predominate; among the the shell-fishes, the Najads.

The greatest variety, however, prevails among the spiders and insects. Among the Scarabees, the family of the Cerambides has many different species excelling by their size and beauty, as, for instance, the Clytus pictus, which measures nearly 1¾ inches. Another Scarabee, belonging to the family of the spring beetles, or Elaterides (Alaus oculatus), is 1⅓ inches in length. We have yet to notice many beautiful Cicindelæ, and the shining lantern-flies, myriads of which, in warm summer nights, alight on the flowers, or buzzing about, produce the most brilliant illumination of the forest. The scarabeus first noticed by everybody, is the Canthon læve, which belongs

* The Ganoides populated the waters in the earliest times of animal formation; most of the genus disappeared in the course of time, and are now only to be found in a petrified state; few belong to the present animal creation. Of the Holosteæ, with bony skeletons, the species Lepidosteus and Amia belong to North America; the Polypterus, however, to Africa. Of the Chondrosteæ, with cartilaginous skeletons, the sturgeon (Scaphichynchus platyrhynchus), and the paddle fish (Polyodon folium), may be found in the waters of the Mississippi.

to the family of the Carabaides; these animals busy themselves with removing globules an inch in thickness from the excrements of the cows, on the roads, at which work two are invariably engaged, one of which, leaning on its fore feet, pushes the load with its hind feet, whilst the other climbs the front part of the globule, and draws it down by its weight. After depositing their eggs in these globules, these ingenious animals bury them on a place where the ground can be easily scratched up. The prairie teems with grasshoppers and crickets, and many a dwelling is pestered with mill-moths (Blatta). The most remarkable species of the Orthopteræ is the "wandering leaf," (Mantis Carolina), here called "devil's horse," because of its adventurous figure. Of the Heteropteræ, an insect of the class of the Nepides, nearly three inches long, known as the Belostoma grandis, which lives in the water, subsisting on small fishes and frogs, deserves to be mentioned, as also a small but terrible insect, immense numbers of which are found in the beds, the Acanthia lectularia, or bed-bug; of the Homopteræ, many Cercopedes, and the improperly so-called locust (Cicada septemdecim). The mate of this noxious hardy insect, which at first sight resembles a great hornet, and attains the length of one and a half inches, deposits her eggs in the fresh twigs of trees, after having perforated their bark with her feeling saw. The twig soon withers, so that the tops of the trees of entire forests often appear as if desolated by fire. Within 52 days, the larva creeps out, falls down to the ground, and bores its way through the same to the roots, whose sap it greedily sucks, causing new damage even then. After this it changes into a chrysalis, that, toward the end of May, leaves the earth, so that the empty cases can be seen everywhere on trees and fences. In many seasons thousands of this plump animal can be seen flirting about, and clinging to the wheat-grains, which it bites off, thus destroying on many a corn-field, the crop which the farmer was all along so anxiously expecting. Another sworn enemy of the crops, fortunately not very frequent here, is the so-called "Hessian fly," a Cecidomyia, of the family of the Tipulidæ (class Diptera). To these and the Culcides, the various species of the notorious musquitoes belong, which, if we are to assume that everything has been created on account of man, must have been created to teaze and torment him; but only the female is the real tormentor; the male, whom you may easily tell by his feathery feelers, is harmless, and never stings. High, airy dwellings, are little frequented by these terrible guests, which usually visit those which are low, or situated in the vicinity of waters. They harass people generally only at night, commissioning the house-fly to vex him in day-time.

On walls and underneath roofs, cells may be frequently seen, constructed of mud, in the same fashion in which bees use to build their own—a wasp-like insect, marked black and yellow, flies to and fro, fearless and undisturbed, for it fetches forward the building materials it wants without molesting men any further. The posterior part of the body is connected by a very long isthmus of muscles with the breast; the name of this industrious little animal is Pelopæus flavipes; it belongs to the Sphegides (class: Hymenoptera), as also the genera of Ammophila and Pompilus, whose species may often be seen bearing the former company. Xylocopa victima, which belongs to the bees, is another domestic resident; she selects wooden buildings, whose frame-walls she perforates to deposit her eggs therein; the honey-bee, however, builds her mellifluous cells in hollow trees, to the great joy of the raccoon. The nests of the paper-wasps, which belong to the Polistes fuscata, can be often seen on bushes. The greater, hornet-like wasp (Vespa maculata), frequently enters houses to hunt after flies. Of the ants, the large yellow ones enslave the smaller, black ones, so that we can only wonder why the human slave-holders have not yet adduced this fact in proof and evidence of slavery being instituted by nature herself.

Among the Neuropteras, numerous Libellas, part of which are of very vivid colors, a light green Hemerobide, and the ephemerides claim our attention. In summer, millions of the latter appear suddenly, especially in the vicinity of rivers; on houses, hedges and everywhere, the first dress can be seen hanging, which they cast off in the first night. They float about in so dense swarms as to resemble a shower of snow, whenever their glassy wings gleam in the sun. Eight or ten days after their first appearance they all vanish again.

We conclude with the Papilios, the most beautiful and most admired of all insects. Among the Bombicides there is a magnificent Saturnia; among the "Spanners," a light-green Acæna. The genus Papilio here has many different species and varieties, among which is the Papilio turnus, very similar to his European brother. Of swallow-tails, there are a great many varieties; the yellow color of the one is almost entirely superseded by black. Many European species are indigenous here, among other, many Vanessa species, the admiral (V. Atalanta), the morio (V. Antiopa), the great and small brownish-red Papilio (V. polychlorus and V. urticæ), and the C. bird (V. C. album). Very frequent is the painted lady (V. Cardui), which rocks on flowers in all parts of the globe.

The view of such a Papilio flying from flower to flower, and parading in the most magnificent colors, reconciles us with many of its troublesome fellow-creatures. An image of the fickleness of beauty and a symbol of transitoriness, he inculcates high wisdom, and while exhorting us, during the short span of our mortal life, to enjoy what God's beautiful world proffers us, he admonishes us that the end of our earthly career is not very far off.

STATE OF HEALTH AND DISEASES.

WHEN people in the Eastern States speak admiringly of the extraordinary fertility of the soil of Illinois, they will often add some remark, expressing their fears in regard to the fever and ague said to prevail there, just as though the state of health in Illinois was so miserable as to counterbalance all the great advantages that a residence in the State offers to the industrious settler. Were this really the condition of things, how could the population of the State increase at such an enormous rate as it does now, and would not many of the families, after a residence of a few years in Illinois, leave the State in order to select a more healthy residence? Just the contrary is the case, as will at once appear from the fact, that the tide of immigration from the Eastern States to Illinois, swells enormously every year, and but very few families residing in the State are known to remove beyond its limits.

Everybody knows that of all diseases the ague occurs most frequently in Illinois, but they will know also, that while new ground is annually subjugated to culture, the disease is confined to more and more narrow limits; and further, that it depends very much upon the particular plan of abode, and manner of living, whether the fever is to visit a family or not. Whosoever resides in the bottoms, or close by swamps, or in districts where the water—owing to the ground being rather too level, cannot rapidly flow off, will be more exposed to the fever, than one who resides on the high, rolling prairie. Moreover it is perfectly safe to presume that one-half of those who are down with this fever, have to ascribe this to nothing but their own imprudence, and the use of improper food.

To the latter cause must be added, drinking of stagnant water, or a too immoderate use of fruits, lard, eggs, or fish; and, further, nobody should needlessly expose himself to the night air, but live in substantially-built dwellings and sleep in well-ventilated rooms; wearing by day thin clothing, and in the evening, when exposed to the night air, warm, thick clothing, and making a fire in the grate, whenever, even in the midst of summer, a change of temperature should occur, especially when it begins to rain. But few of those strictly following these rules, will ever be visited by the fever.

Mankind would undoubtedly be happy, were there no graver diseases than fever and ague, which, though disagreeable, are certainly not deleterious, much less dangerous. Deaths in consequence of fever and ague are nowhere reported, however closely the long lists and bills published by the newspapers, of the mortality prevailing in the various, most widely separated, cities may be examined. And where would the ague not be met with? the ague, which more or less occurs on newly-broken land, or meadows, or lands with a very rich humus, from which the golden fruits are gathered that fill the farmers' barns. The fever exists as well on the eastern seaboard, and in Europe, as in the Western States. Nobody will ever venture to call Hoboken, a pretty little city situated opposite New York, a place infected with fevers; though many cases of fever occur in those parts of it touching on meadowy ground, few of those residing in the vicinity of which, along the Hackensack River, having yet escaped being visited by this unwelcome guest, the ague. And on the other side of the ocean, in Europe, you will find the ague in the rich low lands of the Vistula, the great granary of Prussia, on the marshes of the Oder, and in the rich marshy lands of East Frieseland.

Should this book be doomed to reach the hands of none but those residing in Illinois, it would hardly be necessary to say anything concerning the sanitary condition of the State; every inhabitant being from his own experience sufficiently acquainted with it; but as it is designed to furnish information of a reliable character to such as intend to seek their homes in Illinois, the state of health of that country cannot be passed over in silence. The importance of the question as to the salubrity of a country, for those wishing to settle in it, being self-evident, we have felt it incumbent upon us to gather the opinions of men long resident in the State, and we now submit to the reader, the results arrived at by private gentlemen and doctors residing within its limits, from many years personal experience; to which is added the testimony of a gentleman from Massachusetts, who travelled through

Illinois in every direction, for the purpose of comparing the state of her affairs with those of the former. First, however, let us hear the doctors.

Daniel Stahl, M. D., of Quincy, Adams County, a resident of the United States for 22 years, and of Illinois for 14 years, a physician by profession, writes the following:

"We have here in autumn, bilious diseases, more or less; for instance, the ague, the intermitting, and the properly called bilious fever. In very rare cases, however, do these diseases prove dangerous or deleterious; every new resident of the West acquiring in a short time the knowledge of the very simple remedies by which their cure is effected. Fifteen or twenty years ago, these diseases, together with those always sure to accompany them, the hepatical diseases, hypochondriasis and jaundice, held such a formidable sway, that they spared but very few, especially of the immigrants. But as the land is becoming subjected to culture, as forests are cleared, and swamps and marshes dried up, these diseases more and more rarely occur, so that I now only render professional services to one-third of the number of fever-patients I formerly had in treatment, some ten or fifteen years ago. Diarrhœa prevails to some extent, but always in a mild form, being very rarely, if ever, dangerous. Infants suffer in great cities, from the "cholera infantum," which disease can nowhere be met with in the country; all those diseases, however, which are caused in all other countries by the rapid change of temperature, occur also here.

"Upon comparing the state of health of this country with that of Eastern Pennsylvania, of which I was a former resident, I must arrive at the conclusion, that we live in a comparatively very salubrious district."

The following is taken from a letter of Dr. J. G. Zeller, M. D., a physician of Springbay, Woodford County.

"In summer, miasmatical fevers prevail. Those residing along the ravines of rivers, or in their valleys, are usually visited by them; sometimes, also, particularly in a moist spring, the inhabitants of the prairies suffer from them. In fall and winter, the abdominal typhus fever sometimes occurs; but never the real typhus, properly speaking, as the miasma proceeding from morasses appears to be antagonistic to the typhus miasma. A regular habit of living can do much against these miasmatical diseases, and after a sojourn of two years in these regions, you may consider yourself acclimated."

T. A. Hoffman, M. D., a physician and resident since 1835, of Beardstown, Cass County, communicates the following:

"The tracts of uncultivated soil at that time, and the superabundance, especially in the rich bottom lands, of the exuberant vegetation which, if not used, was left to putrefy, caused, as in all western countries having a rich humus, intermitting fevers, particularly in fall, when the plants cease to perform their office of purifying the air. Ever since, however, the plains overgrown with tall grasses, were converted into fertile, arable land, and the morasses into meadows; whilst the stagnating waters were drained off by ditches dug for that purpose, the state of health has visibly improved."

Frederick Brendel, M. D., a physician of Peoria, communicates to us as follows:

"Intermitting fevers are the principal diseases of the country. As is the case in Peoria, the malady will remain confined to those portions of a city stretching along some river, whose opposite bank is marshy, while almost all those residing along rivers, both banks of which are dry, will be spared. Near houses on the more elevated prairies, whose inmates are down with the fever, you will almost always discover a pool of stagnating rain-water. Bilious fevers appear towards the end of summer, intermitting fevers in September and October, and in the latter part of autumn, typhus fevers, which, though lasting a long time, prove but very rarely dangerous. Diarrhœa also prevails. At the time of the raging of that great epidemic, cholera appeared here in a mild form; but in the last years it was chiefly confined to the immigrants, most of whom brought the disease with them. Pulmonary diseases seldom occur; those who came hither afflicted with them, manage to live longer than would have been elsewhere the case."

F. Wenzel, M. D., of Belleville, St. Clair County, communicates the following:

"The state of health is everywhere very satisfactory, save in marshy districts. The cases of fever, particularly of the intermitting and remitting bilious fevers decrease in number, from year to year. The time in which southern Illinois might with propriety be denounced as the fever country, has long passed by. The prairie is healthy. The last census of Belleville, and the whole county, exhibits so considerable a number of old people, that the state of health must be considered as in every respect very excellent."

In a letter of Dr. C. Hofman, a physician in Pekin, we notice the following:

"Patients down with intermitting fevers usually suffer but little; they get the fever once or twice, the disease disappearing each time before an adequate dietetical treatment, without any serious consequences; it will then reappear, after the lapse of some two, three, or four weeks, to be again expelled by the same treatment. Many experience but a single attack, after which they remain exempt for entire years.

"Very grave cases but seldom occur, perhaps only one among a hundred. Whenever they occur, they are chiefly the consequence of immoderate eating or drinking, incautious exposure during sleep or labor, the use, or rather the abuse, of dangerous remedies, and the neglect of the frequent use of pure cold water.

"The best preservative is cold water. Every morning, after rising, take a cold bath, or if this be inconvenient, wash your whole body with cold water; after which, while still jejune, drink a few cups of cold water, as also shortly before going to bed; select for your bedchamber a well ventilated room, in one of the upper stories; and be moderate in eating, especially in the use of fruit, bacon, fish, or eggs; all of which directions, if strictly followed, are well calculated to protect you from the fever.

"The best remedy is acid sulphuric Peruvian bark, in doses of from 2 to 4 grains, at intervals, till 10, 15, 20 grains are taken. There are many nostrums fabricated and sold at wholesale, whose chief substance, however, consists of Peruvian bark intermixed with arsenic.*

"So much in regard to the intermitting fevers.

"With respect to other diseases, Illinois is not worse off than other countries, nay, even decidedly far more healthy than many of those in which intermitting fevers are less frequently to be encountered.

---

* Persons should therefore be very cautious in using such remedies, whose substance has not been accurately ascertained.

Tuberculous consumption is extremely rare; people afflicted with it sometimes attain to a very considerable age, provided they came here at a not too far advanced stage of the disease, and did not indulge in any excesses. Illinois is the veritable paradise for those with tuberculous consumption, being in this respect to America, what Southern Italy is to Europe. I have seen men come thither in a very advanced stage of consumption, who by prudent habits of living soon stopped the further progress of the disease, and increasing in strength and corpulence, might deem themselves perfectly cured. A certain Mr. Robertson, from Pittsburg, Pa., was sent by his doctor to reside with his relatives in Illinois, in the vicinity of Pekin, in order to impede the farther advancement of a tubercular disease, with which he had already been afflicted for several years. He speedily improved, regaining his former strength, and becoming more corpulent than ever, and exposing himself to all those obnoxious influences, which in other constitutions superinduce the intermitting fever, without ever getting it. He then, contrary to the advice of his doctor, returned to Pittsburg. The climate of Pittsburg exercising anew its dangerous influence upon the disease, he had a relapse, of which he died. Had he remained in Illinois, he might have lived some twenty or thirty years longer.

"During the winter, acute inflammations of the lungs will sometimes occur, probably in consequence of the keen blasts, which rush wildly over the prairies, without encountering mountains or forests to break their fury; this malady, however, seldom presents a serious aspect, the patient easily recovering under an appropriate, careful treatment."

So far the statements by doctors, residing and practising physic for many years in the State, who must, therefore, have an exact knowledge of her sanitary condition; let us now listen to what other gentlemen, not physicians, but old inhabitants of Illinois, have to communicate on the subject.

Edward Bebb, Esq., of Fountaindale, Winnebago County, in his letter, dated January 23, 1856, writes as follows:

"The country is remarkably healthy; I cannot give you a better proof than that we have lived here—a family of seven—since the first of August, 1850, and have never had to call in a doctor on professional business."

John Williams, Esq., of New Albany, Coles County, says in a letter dated December 23, 1855:

"I have never been sick one whole day in thirty years; and there has been but one death in this neighborhood this season."

A. J. Galloway, Esq., of Ewington, Effingham County, says:

"There is little disease at any time in the State, which may not be traced directly or indirectly, to derangement in the biliary organs, and much of this should no doubt be attributed to the free use of heavy bread, strong coffee, a large amount of animal food, and the partial or total exclusion of vegetable diet. I think I am free from prejudice when I say that, except in the valleys of the larger streams, but more especially upon the high, rolling prairies of middle and Northern Illinois, a more healthy country is not to be found, even in the mountainous districts of the older States."

L. G. Chase, Esq., of Massachusetts, who travelled for several months through Illinois, writes, in a letter dated Pera, Dec. 22, 1855, as follows:

"So far as health is concerned, time will prove that the prairies of the West will compare well with any of the Eastern States. Eastern people have made a great bugbear of the miasma of the prairies; but if they will turn their attention to the thousands of alder swamps between their hills, where the sun and wind are almost strangers, they will discover more causes of ill-health concentrated there in a few acres, than is scattered over a whole prairie, where the purifying influences of the sun and wind have full scope. This season has been an unusual unhealthy one for this State, but during the most sickly time, I was wandering over the prairies, and saw but few instances where the ill-health could not be directly traced to infringements of physical laws, either through ignorance or necessity. In some cases of chills and fever that have come under my observation, a few outward applications of soap and water no doubt would have relieved the patient. Then again, if the pioneers would eat less pork, and more fruit and vegetables, it would be much better for them; and I only wonder, all things considered, that there is so much health here, where the people are such great sinners in a physical point of view. Pure water is an important item in the bill of health, though it is but little attended to. People all over the prairies drink surface-water, when by digging or boring, pure water can be had, or what might be still better for family use, cisterns can be sunk in the earth at a trifling expense, to save all of the rain-water from buildings. When the new settlers get the conveniences of life around them, the prairies will be regarded as more healthy than the Eastern States.

"The fevers of the West will never be a match for the consumption of the East."

In a letter written by Joseph C. Orth, Esq., of McCleary's Bluff, Wabash County, we find the following:

"As to health, I honestly believe Southern Illinois will compare favorably with any portion of the West. That scourge of the north, consumption, is almost unknown here. On the rich lowlands, bordering the streams, bilious disorders prevail to some extent, in the fall, but on the upland, good health may be enjoyed, with ordinary prudence. Diseases, the result of miasma, prevail in every new country south of the 44th parallel of latitude, when the virgin soil is first turned over and exposed to the atmosphere. It was so in the Genesee Valley, in New York, and in the Valley of the Miami, in Ohio; and it has been so in Illinois; but the country becomes more healthful as it grows older. A great deal of ague and fever is attributable to errors in diet, to imprudent exposures, to uncomfortable dwellings, and to the use of well-water where it leaks through the soil, instead of flowing through veins in the rock. By occupying comfortable tenements, avoiding needless exposure, eating suitable food, and using only sweet, pure, cistern water, for drinking and culinary purposes, as good health may be enjoyed in Southern Illinois as any where in the Union."

Lastly, Edward Harkness, Esq., of Southport, a resident in Peoria County, for twenty years, communicates the following:

"Those who have been induced to believe that Illinois is a very unhealthy country, would do well to examine the census-tables of 1850, and compare the bills of mortality with those in the States reputed to be healthy. I have not now those tables at hand, but well remember that the deaths for one year previous to June, 1850, was a less ratio in Illinois than in Massachusetts, and was considerably below the general average in the United States. The facts and figures of the census ought forever to stop the babblings of interested parties, who wish to divert western immigration to some other quarter. But they have repeated the falsehood so often, that many of them, no doubt, now believe it themselves. What, it may be asked, is there in the soil, climate, or habits of the people, to make Illinois an unhealthy country? The land is well drained—we have few pools of stagnant waters. The table lands, which comprise at least nine-tenths of the country, are high, dry, and fully exposed to the sweep of the wind. Our springs break out of the mountain limestone, and above the universal layer of stone there is no coal or other mineral deposit. The wells are sunk into clay, sand, or gravel, and very seldom reach down to the limestone. Hence the water from our wells and springs is very pure and good. With plenty of pure air, pure water, and wholesome food, is there any good reason why we may not live as long as other people? The only *native* of mature age, whom I know, is now 44 years old, 6 feet 1 inch high, and weighs 220 lbs.—is not overburdened with flesh, but is lithe, active, and strong. His oldest son is 15 years old, 5 feet 8 inches in height, weighs 140 lbs., and is a man at most kinds of business. Neither the father, the son, nor the still younger members of the family, have ever been seriously ill in their lives. The generation which has sprung up in the last twenty years, in this region, bears every mark of vigorous health.

"It is common among persons not very well informed, to think that where they happen to live, is a very healthy place, but off somewhere else, it is terribly sickly. And here I must be permitted to relate an anecdote, by way of illustration: While travelling along the national road in Indiana, many years ago, I met a moving family; an old man with his wife, two married daughters with their husbands, and some younger scions of the same stock, making twelve souls in all. They had a light wagon, which contained all their worldly goods—this had sunk into a deep mud-hole. Their two lean horses had been down in the mire, but had just been unharnessed and got out. One of the young men was absent in search of a team to haul out the wagon. The women had kindled a fire, were smoking their pipes, and at the same time bestowing upon their husbands all the terms of reproach they could muster, for bringing them 'from a nice, beautiful country, into such a horrible place.' During my stay to help them out of the difficulty, my conversation with the old woman was about as follows:

"'You speak of having come from a beautiful country. May I ask where you are from?'

Old woman. "''Way down below Norfolk, in old Virginny.'

"'Very fine country, that, I am told. Do you have the ague there?'

Old woman. "'Wall, we do have the ager proper bad sometimes, and the fever too.'

"'Are you ever troubled there with musquitoes?'

Old woman. "'O Yes! they are bad most all the year.'

"'It is a fine place to raise corn, is it not?'

Old woman. "'Wall, when I was young we used to raise pretty good corn, but the land is so worn out, we can't get much now.'

"'Have you and your family generally enjoyed good health?'

Old woman. "'La me, no! we've been sick most half our lives.'

"The appearance of the whole family testified to the truth of the old woman's remark; for they all looked more like shadowy ghosts, than veritable men and women with flesh upon their bones, and blood in their veins. Merely because they had encountered a slight difficulty in the way, these poor women were abusing their husbands for bringing them from the most miserable, forsaken spot on the American continent. I gave the poor woman and her family all the words of encouragement I could muster—the wagon was got out of the mud—they went on their way, and I have not since heard from them. But from what I know of the history of the class to which they belonged, it is fair to presume that these poor creatures have gained their health, have gradually surrounded themselves with the comforts of civilized life — that their frugal mode of living and habitual industry have enabled them, without the exercise of much intellect, gradually to accumulate property—that with this accumulation has come a greater self-respect, and a disposition to so educate their children as to fit them for a higher sphere of usefulness than their fathers were able to occupy. Thus it often happens that the grand-children of the poor, degraded sand-hillers, when subjected to the vivifying influence of the Free West, become *men*, high-minded, honorable, useful men!"

Mr. Harkness, in the above passage of his letter, refers, with regard to the respective mortality of Illinois and of other States, to the census of 1850. Page 105 of De Bow's Compendium of the seventh census, contains a review of the deaths which occurred in the single States, and of the ratio they bear to the entire population; according to which Compendium there died of the population

Of Illinois	1·36	per cent.
" Arkansas	1·44	"
" Mississippi	1·44	"
" Ohio	1·46	"
" Texas	1·46	"
" New York	1·47	"
" Rhode Island	1·52	"
" Kentucky	1·53	"
" Connecticut	1·56	"
" Dist. of Columbia	1·63	"
" Maryland	1·65	"
" Missouri	1·80	"
" Massachusetts	1·95	"
" Louisiana	2·31	"

Thus, of the above enumerated 12 States, in which many of those Eastern States are included that are habitually considered far more healthy than the West, as for instance, New York, Rhode Island, Connecticut, and Massachusetts, Illinois at once assumes the first rank in point of salubrity; for wherever fewest people die in proportion to the entire population, there human life must undoubtedly be considered safest from the insidious assaults of disease.

We cannot conclude this chapter without once more directing the attention of the settler to the fact, that pure wholesome water is a most important item in the bill of health. He who is no friend of disease, should particularly avoid drinking stagnant water. This can be easily done, for everywhere throughout the State, at a depth of from twelve to twenty-four feet, a large supply of excellent water can be had, and, moreover, the digging of a well is neither a very difficult nor expensive affair. Proper care should be taken to make the well deep enough, walling up its inner side with bricks, or blue clay, to the depth of several feet below the surface, lest the water on the surface of the ground might trickle down in the well, thus wholly frustrating your endeavor to obtain a supply of pure fresh water. Cisterns, if possible, should also be sunk to save all of the rain water from the roofs of the buildings; this, if properly filtered, is not noxious, and is readily drunk by those accustomed to it. The water of springs, which in many parts of the State are very numerous, is of course to be preferred to all others, provided, however, the springs, from which a supply of water is to be obtained, do not proceed from sloughs, since the water of such springs or rivulets is exceedingly unwholesome.

THE PRAIRIES.

THE most remarkable and striking feature, distinguishing the State of Illinois from the other States of the Union, consists in her extensive prairies, which, covered with a luxuriant growth of grass, and forming excellent natural meadows, by reason of which circumstance they received their present name from the earlier French settlers, commence on a comparatively small scale, near Lake Erie, and occupy the chief part of the land about Lake Michigan, the upper Wabash, and the Illinois, predominating in the vicinity of the Mississippi; so that this entire region is, properly speaking, nothing but a vast prairie, intersected by strips of woods, chiefly confined to the banks and the valleys of the rivers. The prairies are characterized by the absence of timber; they present, in other respects, the same varieties of soil and surface that are found elsewhere; some extend in immense level plains, others are rolling, others again broken by hills, while nearly all of them possess an inexhaustible fertility, and but few are sterile.

The prairies of Illinois may be divided into three classes: the alluvial, or wet, the dry, or undulating, and the bushy.

Those denominated alluvial, or wet prairies, are generally on the banks of the rivers, though sometimes at a distance from them; their soil, consisting of a deep stratum of alluvial land upon clayish ground, is black, friable, and of unsurpassed fertility, admirably adapted to the culture of Indian corn and wheat, and even of grapes, as may be judged from the specimens of wild grapes, which in these prairies exhibit a very luxuriant growth, and from the results hitherto known attending the attempts at vine culture, made in several parts of the State.

The dry or undulating prairies have but few springs. In general, the undulations are so slight, that if it were not for the ravines made by freshets, one might suppose that there was no inclination at all. Their fertility varies greatly, the prairie being in general considered the more productive, the more undulating its surface.

The bushy prairies have an abundant supply of wholesome water, and are covered with hazel and furze bushes, together with small sassafras shrubs, interspersed with grape-vines. Many species of garden-sage, mug-wort, dogwood, and an exhaustless variety and exuberance of gay, herbaceous plants, also grow on these prairies. Early in March the forests begin to blossom—the Loncera Flava, L., or yellow-flowered honeysuckle, and the Jasminum fructicans, or yellow jasmine, diffuse their delicious fragrance through the air, while the red-tufts of the Judas-tree (Cercis Canadensis), unfold their brilliant charms to the eye of the admiring lover of nature.

Of the prairies, the following lines by Captain Basil Hall, an intelligent English traveller, are highly descriptive:

"The charm of a prairie consists in its extension—its green, flowery carpet, its undulating surface, and the skirt of forest whereby it is surrounded; the latter feature being of all others the most significant and expressive, since it characterizes the landscape, and defines the form and boundary of the plain. If the prairie is little, its greatest beauty consists in the vicinity of the encompassing edge of forests, which may be compared to the shores of a lake, being intersected with many deep, inward bends, as so many inlets, and at intervals projecting very far, not unlike a promontory, or protruding arm of land. These projections sometimes so closely approach each other, that the traveller passing through between them, may be said to walk in the midst of an alley overshadowed by the forest, before he enters again upon another broad prairie. Where the plain is extensive, the delineations of the forest in the far background appear as would a misty coast at some distance upon the ocean. The eye sometimes surveys the green prairie without discovering on the illimitable plain a tree or bush, or any other object, save the wilderness of flowers and grass, while on other occasions the view is enlivened by the groves dispersed like islands over the plain, or by a solitary tree rising above the wilderness. The resemblance to the sea which some of these prairies exhibited, was really most striking. I had heard of this before, but always supposed the account exaggerated. There is one spot in particular, near the middle of the Grand Prairie, if I recollect rightly, where the ground happened to be of the rolling character above alluded to, and where, excepting in the article of color, and that was not widely different from the tinge of some seas, the similarity was so striking, that I almost forgot where I was. This deception was heightened by a circumstance which I had often heard mentioned, but the force of which perhaps none but a seaman could fully estimate; I mean the appearance of the distant insulated trees as they gradually rose above the horizon, or receded from our view. They were so exactly like strange sails bearing in sight, that I am sure, if two or three sailors had been present, they would almost have agreed as to what canvass those magical vessels were carrying. Of one they would all have said, "Oh! she is going nearly before the wind, with top-gallant studding-sails set." Of another, "she has got her canvass hauled up, and is going by the wind." And of a third they might say, "she is certainly standing toward us, but what sail she has set is not quite clear."

In spring, when the young grass has just clothed the soil with a soddy carpet of the most delicate green, but especially when the sun, rising behind a distant elevation of the ground, its rays are reflected by myriads of dew drops, a more pleasing and more eye-benefitting view cannot be imagined. You see the fallow deer quietly feeding on the herbage; the bee flies humming through the air; the wolf, with lowered tail, sneaks away to its distant lair, with the timorous pace of a creature only too well conscious of having disturbed the peace of nature; prairie-fowls, either in entire tribes, like our own domestic fowls, or in couples, cover the surface; the males rambling, and, like turkeys or peacocks, inflating their plumage, make the air resound with a drawled, loud, and melancholy cry, resembling the cooing of a wood-pigeon, or still more, the sound produced by rapidly rubbing a tambourine with the finger. The multitude of these birds is so surprisingly great, as to have occasioned the proverbial phrase, "that if a settler on the prairie expresses a desire for a dish of omelets, his wife will walk out at night and place her bonnet on the open ground, to find it full of eggs on her return next morning." The plain is literally covered with them in every direction, and if a heavy fall of snow had driven them from the ground, I could see myriads of them clus tered around the tops of the trees skirting the prairie. They do not migrate, even after the prairie is already settled, but remain in the high grass, near the newly-established farms; and I often saw them at no great distance from human habitations, familiarly mingle with the poultry of the settlers. They can be easily captured and fed, and I doubt not but they can be easily tamed.

On turning from the verdant plain to the forests or groups of high-grown timber, the eye, at the said season, will find them clad also in the most lively colors. The rich under- and brushwood stands out in full blossom. The andromedeas, the dogwood, the wood-apple, the wild plum and cherry, grow exuberantly on rich soil, and the invisible blossom of the wild vine impregnates the air with its delicious perfume. The variety of the wild fruit-trees, and of blooming bushes, is so great, and so immense the abundance of the blossoms they are covered with, that the branches seem to break down under their weight, and the eye of the spectator comes very near being over satiated.

The delightful aspect of the prairie, its amenities, and the absence of that sombre awe inspired by forests, contributes to forcing away that sentiment of loneliness, which usually steals upon the mind of the solitary wanderer in the wilderness, for although he espies no habitation, and sees no human being, and knows himself to be far off from every settlement of man, he can scarcely defend himself from believing, that he is travelling through a landscape embellished by human art. The flowers are so delicate and elegant as apparently to be distributed for mere ornament over the plain, the groves and groups of trees seem to be dispersed over the prairie to enliven the landscape, and we can scarcely get rid of the impression invading our imagination, of the whole scene being flung out and created for the satisfaction of the sentiment of beauty in refined men. The similarity of the whole frequently reminds the Englishman of the extensive parks of the great aristocratical palaces he used to admire in his country; the grass plots, the shaded walks, groves and bushes, produced there by a designing art, nature has spontaneously created here; and nothing but proud structures of lordly mansions, and the view of distant towns or villages are wanting, to make the resemblance complete."

In the summer the prairie is covered with tall grass, which is coarse in appearance, and soon assumes a yellow color, waving in the wind like a ripe crop of corn. In the early stages of its growth, it resembles young wheat; and in this state furnishes such rich and succulent food for cattle, that the latter choose it often in preference to wheat, it being, no doubt, a very congenial fodder to them, since it is impossible to conceive of better butter than is made while the grass is in this stage. On the lower, humid prairies, where the clayey stratum lies close to the surface, the middle or principal stalk of the grass, bearing the seed, grows very thick, having long and coarse leaves, and attaining a height of nine feet, so that the traveller on horseback will frequently find it higher than his head. Although the plants are very numerous, and stand alone by each other, they seem to grow up each one by itself, the whole effort of vegetation tending upward. On the undulating prairies the grass is finer, and exhibits more leaves, its roots are interlaced so as to form a compact mass, and its leaves spread in a dense sod, which rarely exceeds the height of 18 inches, until late in the season, when the seed-stalk shoots up.

In the earliest stages of its growth, the grass is interspersed with little flowers, the violet, the strawberry-blossom, and others of the most delicate structure. When the grass grows higher, these disappear, and taller flowers, displaying more lively colors, take their place; and still later a series of still higher but less delicately formed flowers appears on the surface. While the grass is green, these beautiful plains are adorned with every imaginable variety of color. It is impossible to conceive of a greater diversity, or discover a predominating color, save the green, which forms a beautiful dead color, relieving the splendor of the others. In the summer, the plants grow taller, and the colors more lively; in the autumn another generation of flowers arises, which possesses less clearness and variety of color, and less fragrancy. In the winter, the prairie presents a melancholy aspect. Often the fire, which the hunters annually send over the prairies, in order to dislodge the game, will destroy the entire vegetation, giving to the soil a uniform black appearance, like that of a vast plain of charcoal; then the wind sweeping over the prairie, will find nothing which it might put in motion, no leaves which it might disperse, no halms which it might shake. No sooner does the snow commence to fall, than the animals, unless already before frightened away by the fire, retire into the forests, when the most dreary, oppressive solitude, will reign on the burnt prairies, which often occupy many square miles of territory.

In the southern part of the State, the prairies are comparatively small, varying in size from those of several miles in width and length to those which contain only a few acres. Here many flowery prairies may be found, presenting a spectacle of unrivalled splendor. A rich soil is covered with innumerable turnsols (Helianthus tuberosus), great euphorbias, and purple lupines, intertwined with the rosy blossoms of the wild mallow, and the brilliant orange-tawny vermilion poppy, while the ground is literally crowded with beautiful violets. The traveller on horseback then looks down upon a sea of flowers, over which float thousands of the most sumptuously colored papilios and scarabees, with the many variegated buzzing insects, while he is nearly overpowered by the penetrating, delicious perfume, with which the immense multitude of blossoms impregnate the air.

In the north the prairies widen, and frequently extend from six to twelve miles in width, intersected in every direction by groups of forests and woods, alternately advancing into and receding from the prairie towards the water courses, the banks of which are usually to be found lined with timber, principally of magnificent growth. Between these rivers, in many instances, are groves of timber containing from 100 to 2000 acres, in the midst of the prairie, like islands in the sea, this being a common feature of the country between Lake Michigan and the Sangamon River, and the northern parts of the State.

As to the origin of the prairie-lands, various speculations have been indulged, giving rise to a diversity of opinions, the least tenable of which is that, according to which stately forests once covered these plains, afterwards being destroyed by fire; for nothing is better established than the fact, that the travellers who first entered upon these plains, 200 years ago, and gave them their present name, found them destitute of woods and forests; and, moreover, evidence may be adduced to the effect of showing, that wherever those dangerous enemies of the forests, the Indians and buffaloes, were expelled, and the settlers commenced planting trees, as well as in the vicinity of extensive inhabited tracts, the grass will at once recede, giving free scope for the forest to develope itself. In proof of our position, that these prairies were not formerly covered by forests, we may also refer to the immense savannahs and Llaños of South America and Middle Africa, where traces of former forests have yet to be discovered. Thus the late distinguished English traveller, Mungo Park, speaks of the plains of Mandingo, in Western Africa, as having probably existed there since the earliest times; he also describes their annual burning in the same manner in which that of the prairies in the Western States would be described now; the practice there, according to his account, being attended with the same results as here, the country there being also within a short time covered with a luxuriant growth of young and tender grass, on which the cattle feed with avidity.

According to another opinion, the truth of which is highly probable, the level surface of the State of Illinois was formed by inundations. The whole of the State, from a few miles north of the Ohio, where the prairies commence, affords tolerably conclusive evidence of having been once covered with water, which, having forced itself a passage, whereby it was drained off, the ground was left with a rich, soft, muddy, level surface, much of which was afterwards successively worn off by waters formed from the effect of rain; whence it will not be difficult to account for the greater dryness of the more elevated undulating prairie lands.

From whatever cause the prairies took their origin, they are no doubt perpetuated by the annual fires that have swept over them, from an era probably long anterior to the earliest records of history, and still often continue, lit by the hunters, in order to frighten and bewilder the game that bounds over these prairies, and thus render them an easy prey, or to replace the old grass by a luxuriant growth of tender herbage, which might serve as nourishment for the deer. Where the soil is too wet to produce a heavy annual growth of grass sufficient to sustain a strong fire, there is no prairie. Forests prevail along the streams, and in other places where vegetation does not suffer from the drought of the latter part of summer and early autumn, and, therefore, is less combustible than in the open plains. And the prairies themselves, wherever they do predominate, as will be found invariably the case on dry level regions, exposed to the heat of the sun, may be easily converted into wooded land, by destroying with the plough the tough sward which has formed itself on them. There are large tracts of country, where a number of years ago the farmers mowed their hay, that are now covered with a forest of young, rapidly-growing timber.

As soon as the prairies are ploughed, and the heavy grass kept under, timber or orchard trees, when planted in them, will grow with unexampled luxuriance. A resident of Adams County testifies to the effect, that locust trees planted, or rather sown, on prairie land near Quincy, attained in four years a height of twenty-five feet, and their trunk a diameter of from four to five inches; these grew in closely crowded rows, affording a dense shade. In a few instances, where the same kind of trees had been planted in a more open manner, they grew in the same period to a thickness of six inches, and in from seven to ten years from their planting, have been known to attain sufficient bulk to make posts and rails. In a like manner, the uplands of St. Louis, which were, in 1823, principally prairie lands, are now covered with a young growth of fine and thrifty timber, so that it would be difficult to find an acre of prairie in the county.

The first efforts to convert prairies into forest land, were usually made on the part of the prairie adjoining to the timber. A range of farms, which girded the entire prairie along its circumference, having been established, three furrows were ploughed all round the settlements, in order to stop the burning of the prairies, for the whole distance of the circuit in the neighborhood of these farms, and prevent injury to the fences and other improvements; whereupon the timber quickly grows up spontaneously on all the parts not burnt, the groves and forests commencing a gradual encroachment on the adjoining prairies, so that one after another concentric circle springs up inside of the preceding, and thus the entire prairie is steadily narrowed from all sides, until it is finally occupied, forming a vast region covered with timber and farms.

Such a prairie-farm is always conducted on a magnificent scale. The fences, if any there are, do not cut it up in little acre patches, but divide it into large squares. The sight of such a farm on a rolling prairie, partly in grass, partly in corn, partly in grain and garden vegetables, as the sun chases over it the cloudy shadows, and the light breeze waves the distant grove, to a lover of the beautiful is perfectly enchanting.

Early in the morning, when a mist is on the ground, the fog appears all around the edge of the timber in the prairies, rendering at times the residence on the circuit of the prairie less healthy than that on the middle or highest part, which latter is also connected with another advantage, to wit: the facility with which excellent water is procured, at a depth of 15 feet, whereas, along the borders of the timber, the common depth of the wells is 40 feet.

Let it not be supposed, that life on these boundless regions is monotonous and dreary, for nowhere does nature sit more majestically enthroned, overawing man by the terrible grandeur of her phenomena, than on these immense prairies. What can be more beautiful and charming than a summer's day—what more sublime and terrific than a thunder-storm, on these plains?—what language can convey the faintest idea of the splendor of their conflagration? And even when stern winter has thrown her snow-white mantle over the earth, and the silence of death seems to reign over the far-reaching waste, the apparent illimitation of which deeply impresses the mind of the spectator with the idea of the infinite Being ruling the universe, then the prairie presents a truly magnificent aspect, amply compensating for the hardships of an icy journey. Yielding to our entreaties, an experienced traveller, several spirited letters regarding his journey, written by whom, appeared under the title "A Rambler in the West," in the columns of the Pennsylvania Inquirer and Daily Courier, thus depicts in lively colors, the events of his seemingly rather dangerous journey:

"'Now sharp Boreas blows abroad, and brings
The dreary winter on his frozen wings;
Beneath the low-hung clouds, the sheets of snow
Descend, and whiten all the fields below.'

"Such was the burden of my song, when I awoke from a most refreshing slumber, and saw large white flakes descending, and the whole country covered with the snowy garb of winter. It is oft-times a very pleasant employment to watch the progress of a snow-storm, but then you must be sheltered from its violence; for I assure you you cannot at all sentimentalize when you are breasting its fury, and have a long and dreary journey before you. However, this morning I was in a peculiarly good humor, and disregarding the solicitations of my friends, who begged me to remain until the storm had abated, I determined to resume my journey. Soon the merry jingle of the sleigh-bells announced to me that my vehicle was at the door of my friend's hospitable mansion—into it I sprung with joyous gayety, and away we flew over the broad and boundless prairies. My noble steed seemed to feel a new excitement, as he inhaled the fresh morning breeze, which lent life and vigor to every nerve.

"A prairie is most beautiful in the spring time of year, for then it is a garden, formed and cultivated by nature's hand, where spring the clustering flowers which bloom in rich luxuriance, and shed their fragrance on the desert air. But when winter binds land and stream in icy fetters, then a prairie is a spectacle grand and sublime, and will well repay for the privations of western travelling. I was compelled, however, to ride against the wind, which whistled around and blew directly in my face. So violent was the storm, that I was almost blinded by the thick flakes that were dashed directly in my eyes. Had I acted with prudence, I should have discontinued my journey, and made myself comfortable for the remainder of the day, at the log hut where I dined — but I determined, in spite of wind and weather, to reach Peoria by night. Whilst progressing quietly on my way, gray twilight extended her evening shades on earth. Still I drove on, anxious to reach my point of destination. Not a single star peeped out from the heavens to shed its light on a benighted traveller. The storm increased in violence, and the cold winds whistled a wintry tune. I now found I had strayed from the road, and here was I on a broad prairie, without mark or mound, and had lost the track, which was, ere now, covered by the falling snow.

"Unfortunately, I had left my compass behind, and now I was on a broad sea without a chart or compass, and without one stray light in the heavens, whereby to direct my course. The mariner, when tossed upon the billows of the stormy ocean, has at least the satisfaction of knowing where he is, for the needle will always point to the pole, and his chart will tell him of the dangers in his path; but the weary traveller, who has lost his way on a prairie, is on a boundless sea, where he cannot even tell the direction he is pursuing; for oft times he will travel hour after hour and still remain at nearly the same point from which he started. Had even one accommodating star beamed in the heavens, I should not have been the least disconcerted, for then I could have some object whereby to guide my steps. But all the elements combined against me, and I assure you my feelings were by no means comfortable. Memory ran over the sad history of the numerous travellers who had been overtaken by night, and been buried in the falling snow: many who had started in the morning full of gay hopes and buoyant anticipations, who, ere another sun had risen, had found a cold and solitary grave—arrested in their course by the chill and icy hand of death. Alas, thought I, how true it is

> "For them no more the blazing hearth shall burn,
> Or busy housewife ply her evening care,
> No children run to lisp their sire's return,
> Or climb his knee, the envied kiss to share."

"Insensibly I felt a strong inclination to sleep. I had always heard that this was a dangerous symptom, and if I yielded to its influence, my life would certainly be lost. I endeavored to shake off the drowsy feeling. Never before did I exert myself more to keep awake. I halloed—I shouted—I beat my breast to preserve animation, and tried every method to prevent my yielding to the drowsy influence. My noble horse was almost exhausted, and I myself began to despair of reaching a place of shelter—when suddenly a ray of light beamed upon the snow, and cast a shadow around me. Encouraged by the favorable token, I urged on. My jaded steed also seemed to know that he was approaching a place of shelter, for he quickened his pace, and shortly afterwards I discovered at a distance, a small log-hut, from the window of which beamed a broad blaze of light. Soon was I at the door, and warmly welcomed by the kind owner, who shook the snow from my garments, and gave me a seat before a blazing fire.

"Oh how delightful was the sense of security from the wintry blast, as I listened to the tales of the inmates, many of whom had, like me, been overtaken by the storm, and now were relating the events of their journey. I have passed many delightful evenings, in the course of a short but eventful life—I have been at the festive board, where the wine-cup was pushed merrily around, and song and laughter, and merriment abounded—I have mingled in the society of the gay—I have been

> "Where youth and pleasure meet,
> To chase the glowing hours with flying feet,"

"But never have I passed a more happy evening, than in the small and narrow cabin of that Illinois farmer."

Thus narrates our traveller his somewhat perilous trip, and the wintry scene he witnessed. While we congratulate him upon his fortunate escape, and allow him to rest, our attention is next engaged on quite a different topic, by another traveller, Mr. Daniel S. Curtiss, who, after stating in his "Western Portraiture" that he never had seen the thunder-storm exhibit so much terrific grandeur—so much of the Mighty One's oratory—as while traversing one of the vast prairies of the West, proceeds to give the following glowing account of the one he beheld:

"Once in the summer of '48," relates he, "I had set out on foot to travel westward over one of those green, undulating prairies, between Rock River and the Mineral District, in the afternoon. I had been stepping on some hour or two, over the light swells and gentle slopes, when the storm came buzzing and bellowing portentously after me; directly I turned to look at the approaching storm, when soon an indescribably grand conflict or agitation of the elements was presented, where lightning, thunders, rain and wind, seemed to be contending for the mastery, in their startling displays. Thunder-bursts held you in awe—flashes of lightning would make you start and shrink—gusts of wind whirled you into the high grass—rain-torrents drenched you to the skin; yet, suffering and dreading all, you felt no power or will to escape—there was no retreat—no refuge—the jarring sounds vibrated on every hand—torrents and blaze poured around in every direction; the muscles, together with volition, seemed paralyzed—two sensations alone took possession of you—awe, and admiration—which, anon, as you looked aloft into the dread concave, were resolved into a feeling of heart-homage for Him who holdeth the storms in His hand. The herds which grazed upon these luxuriant meadows, ran in confused fright down the vales to the groves; the crane and wild bird flew screaming with fear to the forests for shelter. All was one boundless scene of rushing dread. The expanded prairie, carpeted in deep green, below; above, the dark blue clouds, with their pendant folds, were ranged along, one after another (like the lower edges of curtains in the theatre's dome), as you gazed towards the east, the nearest being darkest, then an interval of hesitating light falling between, then another cloud-sheet was swinging, and so on, in a series of some half-a-dozen, till at the farther end of the arched way greater light appeared, much as if you looked for miles through a vast tunnel, with occasional openings for light from above. While I was gazing, absorbed, upon this already gorgeous spectacle, the fury of the storm had abated, the black, upper clouds, were mostly dispersed, and as a brighter sky poured its flood of light into this magnificent, ample theatre, its splendor and beauty were heightened beyond all description, and presented a panorama to the rapt beholder, which unmistakeably proclaimed, that only by the Almighty could it have been thrown out before the world; and presently the Author's signature was dashed across it, in the bright bow which clasped the whole."

Thus far our traveller, who, one year afterwards, on an evening in the autumn of 1849, had the opportunity of witnessing, in almost a rapture of amaze and delight, the waving prairies on fire, for many miles around:

"I was driving," he relates, "in a buggy, from Platteville to Mineral Point, and reached Belmonte mound just at the coming in of twilight. The evening was one of those bland, mellow seasons, usual in the time of Indian summer; and on reaching the centre mound, which lay rolled up and shrouded in smoke, handsome as an apple-dumpling all steaming from the kettle, as I felt strongly tempted to know and see farther, I drove nearly to its summit, to take a leisure survey of the vast, flame-lighted, and enchanting panorama, flung out so profusely by artist nature; the moon and stars peered but dimly through the hazy air, adding mystic force to the scenes in the passing twilight.

"Soon the fires began to kindle wider and rise higher from the long grass; the gentle breeze increased to stronger currents, and soon fanned the small, flickering blaze, into fierce torrent-flames, which curled up and leaped along in resistless splendor; and like quickly raising the dark curtain from the luminous stage, the scenes before me were suddenly changed, as if by the magician's wand, into one boundless amphitheatre, blazing from earth to heaven, and sweeping the horizon round—columns of lurid flames sportively mounting up to the zenith, and dark clouds of crimson smoke curling away and aloft till they nearly obscured stars and moon, while the rushing, crashing sounds, like roaring cataracts mingled with distant thunders, were almost deafening; danger, death, glared all around; it screamed for victims, yet, notwithstanding the imminent peril of prairie-fires, one is loth, irresolute, almost unable to withdraw, or seek refuge.

"I now thought of the spot on the banks of the bright Kankakee, where some years ago two young persons—beautiful, betrothed lovers, perished in the prairie flames, their crisped forms being found near that of their horse, next day, by a hunter. It is a rich, beautiful prairie—the river murmured along to leeward of them, but the flames outstripped their fleet charger, upon which both were riding, before he could reach the stream. Why did they not have the presence of mind to set a 'back fire,' and take refuge on the burned space?

"But I am back to the mound: will the remorseless flames leap along the high grass that has grown luxuriantly upon the sides, to the very pinnacle of this cone? Surely the wind is this way, and my horse is already restive—aye, but I've a match in my pocket, and it is easily lighted. Persons travelling in prairie regions should bear this in mind. But see that ocean of flame, I must look still again, even my little match has sent a lively current dancing from the leeward slope, and I am admonished to follow it; but in presence of such scenes, at such an hour, the sensitive mind feels its frailty, and instinctively awards the homage due to the majesty of his Creator, from the creature.

"Next morning I again visited this mound, rode over the charred grass-stubble to its top, the scene of so much terrific brilliance but a few hours before! Now all that was changed, the green-brown carpet was displaced by the black spread—the ravaging flames had consumed everything, black destruction sickened the heart in sadness—the keenest, darkest emblem of desolation that can be imagined; even the livid, confused glimmer, still almost trembled around the eyes, from last night's flames—such as gleaming lights leave upon the optic nerve; now it was painful to contemplate for a moment, the same expanse which a few hours ago, it required an effort to withdraw from its enchanting, but fearful sublimity—like the giddy fascination of the serpent which holds its victim in thrall till destruction overwhelms be yond escape—is the charm of such spectacles. It was as if the destroying angel flew abroad, crying in terror-tones, breathing tempests of fire and smoke from his nostrils, that should awe and paralyze; I may not describe—my pen is tame and dark—but would you realize such emotions—experience its force—

> "O fly to the prairies and in wonder gaze,
> As o'er the grass sweeps the magnificent blaze,
> The earth cannot boast so magnificent a sight,
> A continent blazing with oceans of light."

So far Mr. Curtiss, to whose eloquent description of a prairie-fire we now subjoin several remarks, which, intended to form the conclusion of this brief sketch of the prairies of Illinois, we deem must be of essential service to those of our readers intending to settle on prairie-lands, by rendering them familiar with the measures of precaution they have to adopt, in order to secure themselves against loss of life and property, whenever such a conflagration occurs.

Conflagrations of prairies and woods are caused either accidentally or designedly, from wantonness, or with a view of bewildering the game; and often spread further than the incendiaries supposed or intended they should. Wherever extensive prairies are, one-half of them is burnt in spring, the other half in autumn, in order to produce a more rapid growth of exuberant grass, destroying at the same time the tall and thick weed-stalks, together with their seeds. The wind blowing to the side opposite the neighboring farms, the dry grass is frequently set on fire, it being supposed, (in fact it but rarely happens), that the flames would not spread beyond certain ways, ditches, or creeks; but a violent storm suddenly starting up from the opposite direction, drives the flames to the same, and, kindled to a tremendous heat, they spread with such rapidity, that riders on the fleetest steeds can seldom escape. The more violent the wind, and the greater the burning plain, from which the blaze spreads toward a neighboring farm, the greater also the necessity of burning back; that is, of igniting the grass or foliage of the woods close by the fences, in order to bring it to pass, that the larger devouring fire, upon arriving at the place already designedly ignited, becomes extinguished for want of aliment. In order to be able, however, to make proper use of this measure of safety, it is very essential, that every farmer should encompass with a ditch those of his fences adjoining the prairie, and clear a space at least twelve feet broad, of all trees along those situated in the forest

—thus preventing the withered leaves from accumulating. A much trodden road around the fences is of the highest importance, presenting, as it does, the best security against danger of fire; for the flames penetrating in even the smallest possible strip to the fence, the dry wood of the latter, kindled by the withered weeds, and the burning, whirling leaves, ignites with the most astonishing rapidity, firing, especially at night, the houses along the fields, ere their thoughtlessly slumbering inhabitants become aware of the extent of the danger, or even imagine it to be at hand.

The farmer, who, by the adoption of the above mentioned measures, has secured himself against ordinary fires, is also able to protect himself against very extensive conflagrations of the prairies or woods, by carefully sweeping away in the direction of the fire, all leaves that may happen to lie on the road, the grass and foliage on the other side of which he will ignite, fully convinced, that the blaze burning away from his hedges, will much less endanger them, than will that sea of flames waving from afar. Should the fences, nevertheless, be endangered, they must be torn down as quickly as possible, the fire being thus almost wholly prevented from spreading any farther. Should there be no road or ditch along the fence, and the soil be fit for the use of the plough, it would be advisable before firing, to plough several times along the enclosures, thus covering the dry grass with the largest possible clods of earth. When a large conflagration cannot be kept off by burning back, and there be no time to tear down all the fences exposed to the fire, acquiescing in what the hand of man proves too feeble to avoid, one should only break down that part of them nearest to the fire, in order to save the buildings, and stores of corn and provisions. Thus, a cautious, circumspect farmer, with the aid of his family, or men, can put a stop to a conflagration, that without much resolute action on their part, would have consumed and destroyed everything for an extent of several miles, as, we are sorry to say, happens here and there every year. Conflagrations of forests, during which the trees themselves stand in full blaze, only occur in forests of pine, fir, or other oily trees, and can only be stopped by large rivers, or heavy showers of rain, or be suppressed by the united exertions of the inhabitants of entire regions. Conflagrations of woods, during which the flames consume the dry foliage lying on the ground, may be more easily extinguished. It is, nevertheless, often quite a tedious, toilsome job, on account of the clouds of smoke and sparks, which roll far in advance of the fire. With shovels, spades, and brooms hastily made out of brushwood, the farmers, almost suffocated with the smoke, and singed by the flying sparks and blaze, exert themselves to approach the burning line, and by quickly beating out the fire, to conquer in the very line of operation of the enemy; a position whence, in all directions, the fire may be beaten out with the above instruments. When the wind is moderate, the fire is usually extinguished by the united efforts of the neighboring farmers. It occurring, however, not unfrequently, that flames apparently beaten out, are kindled anew by the wind, it is necessary to run several times in the most rapid course along the extinguished lines, promptly to despatch the fire which starts afresh.

Should the conflagration, however, in spite of all efforts, visibly gain ground, extending for so great a distance that there could be no reasonable hope of extinguishing it, in the manner above described, without wasting time or strength in fruitless efforts, one should rather resort to the safer method, used in protecting the fences, of burning back—even if a part of the best timber, which at any rate more or less suffers from such fires, should be exposed thereby. The "nil desperandum" applying to nothing better than danger by fire, the superhuman efforts which are frequently made to avert with little or no aid, the most imminent danger by fires, can scarcely be imagined. Language cannot convey, words cannot express, the faintest idea of the splendor and grandeur of such a conflagration of forest or prairie, during the night; one would think that the pale queen of night, disdaining to take her accustomed place in the heavens, had despatched a myriad of messengers to light their torches at the altar of the setting sun, and that now they were speeding on the wings of the wind to their appropriate stations. If you know that the conflagration can cause no damage, you do not cease to gaze with admiration upon the magnificent spectacle, but the news of its approach to the vicinity of a farm, rouses the gazers as would an electric shock, impelling those present who are able to work, instantaneously to rise and rush to the threatened places, indicated from afar by volumes of smoke and flame. Should the fire be seen in the day-time, or at an early hour in the evening, the neighbors residing so close together as to be able to succor each other, then it is advisable, that one or two persons should plough along the fences, however distant the danger may be, whilst the others should immediately commence extinguishing the flames, so that, should the danger be increased by a storm suddenly springing up, the expedient of burning back might yet safely and successfully be resorted to.

AGRICULTURE.

If any State of the Union is adapted for agriculture, and the other branches of rural economy relating thereto, such as the raising of cattle, and the culture of fruit trees, it is pre-eminently Illinois, whose extremely fertile prairies recompense the farmer at less trouble than he would be obliged to incur elsewhere, in order to attain the same results. Her virgin soil, adapted by nature for immediate culture, only awaits the plough and the seed, in order to mature within a few months golden ears of the most beautiful Indian corn, the heaviest wheat, and such other species of corn as are indigenous in the temperate zones. Here the husbandman is not obliged for whole years to squander his best strength in clearing the primitive forest, hewing down gigantic trees, and rooting out stumps and weeds, in order to gain after each and every year of toilsome labor, in the sweat of his brow, another patch of arable ground; but the soil only wants common tilling; here the farmer is not obliged to gather the stones from his acres, so that the halms may have a large scope for development, for the soil is so little encumbered with them, that, if you should require a proprietor of some twenty acres of prairie land to collect from them a cart-load of stones, in return for which he was to receive a cart-load of the purest gold, he would be compelled to decline accepting this handsome offer. Here no manure is wanted to fertilize the soil; it consists here of a rich black mould, several feet deep, that wants no dung, but is almost inexhaustibly fertile, and capable of producing the richest fruit, year after year, for entire generations. The Illinoisian farmer who cares not to improve the land, or enhance its fertility, as he should, has nothing to do but to plough, sow, and reap: less labor is here required than at other places where the usual demands of agriculture must first be satisfied. Hence a man of small means can more rapidly acquire wealth in this State, than at places where he must waste his best time and strength in occupations not required here.

The vegetable products of Illinois are especially — Indian corn, which is the staple commodity; wheat, which thrives well in all parts of the State; and also oats, barley, rye, buckwheat, potatoes, sweet potatoes, flax, hemp, peas, clover, cabbage, rapes, and the ordinary pot-herbs, tobacco, and the bean from which the castor-oil (ol. ricini) is obtained, are cultivated here; of the latter enough is raised for home use.

The culture of fruit-trees, though securing a handsome profit to the farmer, is chiefly confined to that of apples and peaches, most excellent varieties of which are grown here; besides these there are already several vineyards yielding a very good wine. The culture of fruit-trees and of the vine will be treated of in a special chapter, whilst in this present chapter we shall speak of agriculture particularly.

The amount of bushels raised per acre, first claims our attention, for the comparatively smaller or greater amount reaped by the farmer, in connection with the market prices of the produce, will naturally exercise a great influence in diminishing or increasing his revenue, and thus impair or enhance his prosperity.

As already mentioned in the preface of this book, we have received from a number of gentlemen, for many years resident in Illinois, among whom are also many practical farmers, information concerning all matters, so that the statements subjoined here may be relied upon as the results of a practical experience for many years. We quote here the testimony of several in regard to the amount of the various products per acre.

F. A. Arenz, Esq., of Beardstown, Cass Co., states the amount of produce, as follows: Indian corn, 50–70 bushels per acre; wheat, 18–25; rye, 35–40; oats, 40–45; potatoes, 150–200.

James G. Loulard, Esq., of Maple Lawn, Jo Daviess Co.; Indian corn, 30–100 bushels, per average 60; wheat, 15–40, per average, 22; oats, per average, 45; barley, 25–60, per average, 35; rye, 20–50, per average, 30; potatoes, 100–300, per average, 150.

Heinr. Funk, Esq., of Stout's Grove, McLean Co.; winter wheat, 20–30; spring wheat, 20–28; oats, 40–50; Indian corn, 45–70.

Stephen Feussner, Esq., of Marissa, St. Clair Co.; Indian corn, 30–50; wheat, 18–30; oats, 30; potatoes, 100–200.

Rev. F. Will. Holls, of Centreville, St. Clair Co.; barley, 40–45; wheat, 15–20; Indian corn, 50–55.

Michael Kleinhenz, Esq., of Henry, Marshall Co.; Indian corn, 50–70.

Wm. Ross, Esq., of Pittsfield, Pike Co.; Indian corn, 50–70; wheat, 20–40; oats, 40–50.

Dr. Danl. Stahl, of Quincy, Adams Co.; Indian corn, 60–70; wheat, 20–40.

Dr. Welsch, of Mascoutah, St. Clair Co.; Indian corn, 70–75; winter wheat, 22–25; barley, 40–45; castor beans, 30; oats, 40; potatoes, 50–80.

Geo. Bunsen, Esq., of Belleville, St. Clair Co.; Indian corn, 40–100; wheat, 16–25; barley, 40; rye, 16; oats, 40–60; potatoes, 100.

Isaac Underhill, Esq., of Peoria; Indian corn, 30–60; wheat, 15–25.

A. Collins, Esq., of Hadley, Will Co.; Indian corn, 50; oats, 40–60.

Thus, according to these observations, which were made in nine different counties of the State, throughout her longitudinal extension, from her northern boundary to St. Clair County, in her southern portion, we receive the following average numbers, per acre:—Indian corn, 56 bushels; wheat, 24; oats, 44; barley, 41; rye, 29; potatoes, 143.

Let us now listen to a well known authority, with respect to agriculture in Illinois. Mr. J. Ambrose Wight, of Chicago, who was for many years the accomplished editor of the "Prairie Farmer," an excellent journal, largely diffused, which, however, should not be wanting in the house of *any Illinoisian farmer*, and which should be studiously perused by every new settler,—in a letter dated Jan. 9, 1855, and addressed to John Wilson, makes the following statements:

"At your request, I would state, that, from an acquaintance with Illinois lands, and Illinois farmers, of eighteen years, during thirteen of which I have been engaged as editor of the 'Prairie Farmer,' I am prepared to give the following as the rates of produce which may be had per acre, with ordinary culture:

Winter wheat	15 to 25 bushels.
Spring wheat	10 to 20 "
Indian corn	40 to 70 "
Oats	40 to 80 "
Potatoes	100 to 200 "
Grass, (timothy and clover)	$1\frac{1}{2}$ to 3 tons.

"'Ordinary culture,' on prairie lands, is not what is meant by the term in the Eastern or Middle States. It means here, no manure; and commonly but once, or, at most, twice ploughing, on perfectly smooth land, with long furrows, and no stones or obstructions; when two acres per day is no hard job for one team. It is often but very poor culture, with shallow ploughing, and without attention to weeds.

I have known crops, not unfrequently, far greater than these, with but little variation in their treatment; say forty to fifty bushels of winter wheat; sixty to eighty of oats; three hundred of potatoes, and one hundred of Indian corn. 'Good culture,' which means rotation, deep ploughing, farms well stocked, and some manure applied, at intervals of from three to five years, would, in good seasons, *very often* approach these latter figures."

It will be seen that Mr. Wight's statements are in perfect harmony with the above observations, made for several years by practical Illinoisian farmers; hence these numbers may be considered the exact rates of average produce.

In another chapter we have noted the market-prices of corn, and other farm produce, as the newspapers stated them to rule during the first half of January, 1856, in 51 different places, scattered all over Illinois. According to this account the highest prices in the places mentioned before (with the sole exception of Chicago, which cannot be considered as a place of production), have been the following:

	$		
For Indian corn, in Joliet	$	54	cents.
" Wheat, in Aurora and Batavia	1	60	"
" Rye, in Freeport	1	00	
" Potatoes, in Springfield	1	00	
" Oats, in Cairo, Moline, and Ottawa		35	"
" Barley, in Quincy	1	50	"

While the average price

Of Indian corn, was		$33\frac{1}{3}$	"
" Wheat	1	27	"
" Rye		70	"
" Potatoes		42	"
" Oats		25	"
" Barley	1	03	

Let us now calculate in money, the probable produce of an acre.

Basing our calculation upon the average ruling prices of the various products, during the first half of January, 1856, and upon the above given average rates of bushels per acre, we should estimate every acre to be worth, if planted with

Indian corn	$18 67
Wheat	30 48
Rye	20 30
Potatoes	60 06
Oats	11 00
Barley	42 23

Basing our calculation, however, upon the above mentioned highest prices, we find every acre to be worth, if planted with

Indian corn	$30 24
Wheat	38 40
Rye	29 00
Potatoes	143 00
Oats	15 40
Barley	61 50

Having shown by the preceding, how much an acre of land at an average rate of produce, and at average prices, must yield, and how much at those highest prices, paid in the first half of January, 1856, (which latter calculation is also based on the average rate of produce), we now turn to the profitableness of farming itself.

Profits of farming.—Here, also, we cannot do better than to refer to the observations and statements made by practical men.

Edward Bebb, Esq., of Fountaindale, Winnebago Co., in a letter addressed to us, gives the following account of his first crop, on newly-broken land:

"In the summer of 1851, we had sixty-five acres of an eighty acre lot broken. In the spring of 1852, we fenced the whole eighty and sowed it with oats. The following is a statement of the crop:

80 acres of land, entered at $1 25 per acre	$100 00
Fencing 80 acres with post and board, (two boards only being put on)	320 00
Breaking 65 acres, at $2 00 per acre	130 00
Seed, 130 bushels, at 12 cents per bus., (oats being very cheap that spring)	15 65
Sowing and harrowing, at 37½ cents per acre	24 37
5 acres mown and fed before harvest, no account kept.	
Reaping 60 acres, at 50 cents per acre	30 00
Binding 60 acres, at 75 cents per acre	45 00
Threshing	120 00
Total cost	$785 02
3000 bushels of oats, sold in January, at 30 cents per bushel	900 00
Balance in favor of crop	114 98

In the foregoing statement I made no mention of the straw, which being cut before it was dead ripe, and gotten up without any rain, wintered, with scarcely any other feed, 25 head of cattle."

Wm. Waite, Esq., Rock Island Co., in the spring of 1853, purchased 80 acres of prairie land, at $4 50; his account of the first year is as follows:

80 acres of prairie, at $4 50 per acre		$360 00
Breaking 60 acres, at $2 50 per acre		150 00
Fencing 60 acres, at $1 00 per rod, 400 rods of board fence		400 00
Seed for 40 acres with winter wheat, 1½ bushels to the acre, at $1 00 per bushel		60 00
Sowing and harrowing, 75 cents per acre		30 00
Harvesting and marketing, $1 50 per acre		60 00
Threshing and cleaning, 1,100 bushels, at 10 cents per bush		110 00
Hauling 15 miles to rail-road, 6 cents per bushel		66 00
Ploughing 20 acres for corn in the spring, at 75 cents		$15 00
Marking off and planting		15 00
Cultivating, at $1 25 per acre		25 00
Harvesting, at $1 per acre		20 00
Threshing, and hauling 15 miles to rail-road, 1000 bushels, at 10 cents per bushel		100 00
Total cost of farm and crops		$1411 00
1100 bushels of wheat, at $1 15 per bushel	$1,265 00	
1000 bushels of corn, at 28 cents per bushel	280 00	
Total amount of crops		1545 00
Profits of 60 acres, after paying all expenses		$134 00

and 20 acres of land unbroken.—This farm is now worth $25 per acre.

Jos. Reinhardt, Esq., of Granville, Putnam Co., gives the following statement of the first year's crop of 80 acres, which he purchased at an original cost of $15 per acre:

80 acres prairie land, at $15	$1200 00
Breaking 70 at $2 50	175 00
320 rods fence, (480 rods would have been necessary, but for 160 adjoining rods of the neighbor's fence), at $1	320 00
Second ploughing and harrowing at $1 50	105 00
Sowing 105 bushels of wheat, at $1 25	131 25
Harvesting, at $1 per acre	70 00
Threshing and transporting, at $1 80 per acre	126 00
Total cost	$2127 25
Assuming, at a moderate calculation, every acre to yield 20 bushels, we have 1400 bushels, at $1 25	1750 00
Hence, the 80 acres, after the first harvest, will cost only	$377 25

Relying on my own experience, I have based the above calculation upon the highest cost, an average price of wheat, and the low produce of 20 bushels per acre, although I myself have reaped 25 bushels, and many others from 30 to 35 bushels. I also assumed only 70 acres fit to be broken, as, among 80 acres of prairie lands, there are in most cases 10 acres of lowland, best fit for meadows. Every such acre may be safely supposed to yield 2 tons of hay, worth from $2 to $4 per ton, which amount does not form one of the items of my calculation.

Jno. S. Peironnel, Esq., of Peru, gives the following statement of a crop from 10 acres, purchased by him April, 1855, at $30 per acre:

J. S. Peironnel,		Dr.
To 10 acres of land at $30 per acre		$300 00
" 6 months' interest		9 00
" 3½ days' ploughing		8 75
" 1 do harrowing		2 50
" 1¼ do drilling		2 75
" 5 days with cultivator and shovel plough		8 75
" paying for husking		28 90
" shelling and taking to market		24 00
		$384 65
J. S. Peironnel,		Cr.
By 723 bushels of corn, at 53 cents	$383 19	
" corn cobs from same	8 00	$391 19
Due J. S. Peironnel, above every cost		$6 54

Ralph Anderson, Esq., of Silver Creek, Stephenson Co., estimates the costs and receipts of 34 acres, as follows:

34 acres purchased last winter, at $5	$170 00
Fencing	100 00
Breaking	87 00
Sowing and tilling	400 00
68 bushels of seed wheat	68 00
Harvesting	71 00
Threshing and taking to market	100 00
Total cost	$996 00

RECEIPTS.

950 bushels, sold at $1 05	$997 50
200 " on hand, "	210 00
Total receipts	$1,207 50
Deducting costs	996 00
Net proceeds of the first year	$211 50

A correspondent of the Alton Courier, writes the following from Shipman:

"I saw a communication in the 'Courier,' over the signature of 'Amand,' in which it is stated that Col. Wm. B. Warren, of Jacksonville, had a crop of wheat which netted him $20 per acre, clear of all expenses, at present prices, and that the wheat crop of Mr. Constant, of Sangamon County, netted him $17 per acre.

"They were certainly profitable crops. I threshed my crop of Maryland white wheat, a few days ago, a small one it is true. The thresher measured 317 bushels, the most of which was measured by him into the sacks of farmers, for seed, at $1 25 per bushel. I have been asked a great many times how many acres of ground that crop of wheat grew on (with numberless other questions), and my answer invariably was, 'about eight.' I have since measured the ground, and there was a little less than 7¾ acres. I submit the following items, which were set down as they occurred:

EXPENSES.

To 10 bushels of wheat for seed, at $1 25	$13 50
Two days with cultivators, one horse, and one hand, at $1 50	3 00
Cutting off cornstalks in spring	1 00
Cutting 7¾ acres, at 75 cents	5 81
Nine hands for binding and shocking, at $1 25	11 25
Three days stacking, with 2 hands	9 00
Threshing 317 bushels, at 5 cents	15 85
Hands and team for same with same	15 00
	$74 41

CREDIT.

By 317 bushels of wheat at $1 25	$396 25
Net profit	$320 84

Which would be a little more than $41 49 per acre.

W. R. Harris, Esq., of Palmyra, Lee Co., makes the following communication concerning the management of his farm:

"I commenced here in the spring of 1847, with a capital of $700, with which I purchased twenty acres of timber, and one hundred and sixty acres of prairie land. The first season I broke up fifty-five acres, with a pair of horses and one yoke of oxen, breaking two acres per day. The third year, I added eighty acres to my farm, and hired fifty acres broke at $2 per acre. The fourth year, I hired ten acres more broke, at $2 25 per acre, which gave me one hundred and fifteen acres under cultivation. This is all that I have had under cultivation, and I have sold the product this year for over $2000. I have now been engaged here for about eight years, and my capital of $700 has increased to between $8000 and $10,000."

Charles W. Murtfeldt, Esq., of Oregon, Ogle Co., gives the following account of the management of 80 acres, purchased by him at $20 per acre, and planted, 53 of them with wheat, and the remaining 27 with Indian corn:

10 per cent interest on $1600, being the purchase money of the 80 acres, at $20 per acre	$160 00
Taxes	7 00
Ploughing, at $1 per acre	80 00
Sowing and harrowing 53 acres at 75 cents	39 75
Cutting and binding 53 acres, at $1	53 00
Stacking of the wheat	39 00
Seed of wheat	88 00
Seed of Indian corn	1 75
Planting and cultivating Indian corn	50 00
Harvesting Indian corn	30 00
Threshing 1100 bushels of wheat, at 5 cents	55 00
Other work and labor	30 00
	$633 50
The receipts were, for 1100 bus. of wheat, at $1 ....$1100	
For 750 bushels of Indian corn, at 50 cents 375	1475 00
Gain	$841 00

Rev. Jno. S. Barger, of Clinton, De Witt Co., in a letter dated 22d Jan., 1855, states the following facts in relation to the management of his farm:

"From 1848 to 1850, I purchased in De Witt County, and nearly adjoining Clinton, 400 acres of fine farming land, through which the Illinois Central Railway passes; and in the vicinity three timbered lots, containing 140 acres, making in all 540 acres, at a cost of $1513 19. In the spring of 1853 I determined to make my farm, and accordingly contracted for the breaking of 300 acres, at $600; also for making 400 rods of fence, at $4 75 per 100 rails in the fence, equal $494 19; making altogether, $1094 19. Having obtained the privilege of joining to 720 rods of fence on adjoining farms, I thus enclosed 360 acres, and had 280 prepared for seeding.

"The breaking was done from the 27th of May to the 9th of July. The greater portion of this ploughed land might therefore have been planted in corn, and harvested in time for seeding with wheat; and thus I might have added considerably to the avails of the first year, had I not been 80 miles distant, engaged in the labors of the Jacksonville district.

I paid for seeding 300 acres		$230 00
To 325 bushels seed wheat		243 75
Add the cost of making the farm		1094 19
		$1567 94
I paid for harvesting, threshing, packing, and delivering at the Clinton depôt, distant from the farm from ¼ to 1¼ miles		1650 00
		$3217 94
Sold at the Clinton depôt, 4378¾ bus. of wheat, for	$4378 82	
I kept for bread	50 00	
Making the gross income of the first year		4,428 82
From which take the entire expenditure		3,217 94
And you have the net proceeds of the first year		1,210 88
To which add the cost of making the farm		1,094 19
Making the entire avails of the first year		2,305 07

"Furthermore, to do justice to the productiveness of the soil, and to show what the well directed efforts and judicious management of a well-trained and practical Illinois farmer would have done, it should be stated that, at least in my judgment, some 1500 bushels of wheat were wasted, by untimely and careless harvesting and threshing, equal to $1500 net proceeds. Then add $55 33, excess of payments for ploughing and seeding only 280 acres, which a skilful farmer would have known before making his contracts, and you have a loss which ought to have been a gain of $1,555 33. This amount saved, would have shown the avails of the first year's operations, on 280 acres of the farm, to have been $3,860 40.

"Now, sir, if one under such circumstances, with but little more than a theoretical knowledge of farming, has succeeded even *so* well, having hired all the labor, and mostly at very high prices, how much larger profits might have been realized by a skilful and practical farmer, devoting his whole time and attention to his appropriate occupation. How much more successful thousands of farmers and farmers' sons, on our eastern seaboard, and in the Eastern States, might be, were they, or could they be induced to move on and apply their skill, industry, and economy, in the cultivation of the rich and productive prairies of Illinois."

The "Prairie Farmer," of January 24, 1856, contains the following letter of a farmer residing in Warsaw, Hancock Co.:

"I purchased these acres of woodland, three-fourths of a mile from town, for the purpose of making a fruit orchard. By the time I could get it cleared and enclosed, the season had so far advanced that I could not plant trees—so I contented myself with putting in such a crop as the advanced season would justify. About the 20th of June, I finished planting three acres of white beans, two of corn, pumpkins and garden vegetables, and half an acre of potatoes; and later, say about the 1st of July, I sowed about two and a half acres of buckwheat.

"In the autumn I harvested the following crops, worth, in the market at home, the prices annexed:

35 bushels of beans, at $2	$70 00
50 " buckwheat, at 70 cents	35 00
40 " potatoes, at 40 cents	16 00
Corn with the fodder	15 00
Pumpkins, cabbages, tomatoes, melons, sweet potatoes, &c.	14 00
Total	$150 00

"This, it strikes me, was a tolerably fair result. I did not expect to do much, as the season was so far advanced when I commenced; yet I have demonstrated to my own satisfaction, that with a good season next year, and fair prices in the fall, I can make my little farm of ten acres bring me $300—besides growing an indefinite number of young fruit trees; and that too without going beyond mere ordinary farm crops.

H. H. Hendrick, Esq., of Batavia, Kane Co., calculates the value of a farm of 160 acres, as follows:

"A small farm would be worth more per acre, with the same improvements, than a very large one. For example, take 160 acres, purchased at $10 per acre:

First cost of 160 acres, at $10 per acre	$1600 00
Breaking one hundred acres, at $2 25	225 00
160 rods fence on front side, or road, $1 per rod	160 00
Half of the other three sides	240 00
Building house, &c	500 00
Fruit trees, &c.	25 00
Amounting to	$2750 00
It is probably now worth $25 per acre, which will be	4000 00
Leaving a profit for owner of	1,250 00
Or, at $20 per acre, still leaves a balance of	450 00

"It is probable that the fence may be built for a little less than $1 per rod; but as I have made no allowance for cross fences, yards, &c., and calculated only half of three sides, and one whole side for the road, I think the excess of price will not more than pay the expense of building the necessary fences inside. I have also left sixty acres for meadow and pasture. If the purchaser have means to make the necessary improvements, or most of them, I think he would do well to settle on such lands."

The "Prairie Farmer," of February 14th, 1856, contains a very detailed account of the management of a farm, by Mr. Wm. P. West, of Blackberry, Kane Co. This account, which has but this present moment been published, was originally intended for the Agricultural Society, of Kane Co. The farm of Mr. West containing 240 acres, this account deserves particular notice, because of its comprising all the branches of rural economy. The account is herewith subjoined:

1852.	23 ACRES,		DR.
June.—To breaking 23 acres, 3 inches deep, at $1 50 per acre			$34 50
Aug.—To 8 days cross ploughing, 4 inches deep, at $2			16 00
Sept. 1st.—To 46 bu. Soule's seed wheat, at 75c. per bu			34 50
" " 2 days' work sowing the same, at $1			2 00
" " 6 days' work harrowing, at $2 per day			12 00
" " cost harvesting 23 acres, at $1 50 per acre			34 50
" " threshing 690 bu. at 8c. per bu			55 20
" " hauling the same to market, at 2c			13 80
			$202 50
1853.			CR.
By 30 bu. per acre, 690 bu., at 95c			$655 50
Cost			202 50
Net profit			$453 00
Cost per acre		$8 80	
Net profit per acre		19 70	

1852.	17½ ACRES WHEAT ON CORN GROUND.		DR.
Aug. 20.—To sowing 1½ days, at $1 per day			$1 50
" " 35 bu. Soule's seed wheat, at 75c			26 25
Aug. 20.—To 4 days' work, man, horse and shovel plough, at $1 50 per day			6 00
" " 2 days' work, man, horse, and small harrow, at $1 50 per day			3 00
" " 6 days' work, hoeing in wheat around hills			6 00
" " cost harvesting 17½ acres, at $1 50 per acre			26 25
" " threshing 394 bu., at 8c. per bu			31 52
" " carting 214 bu. to market, at 2c. per bush			4 28
Total cost			$104 80
1852.			CR.
By 22½ bu. per acre, 394 bushels.			
" 214 bu. sold at 95c. per bu			$203 30
" 180 bu. sold at farm, at $1 per bush			180 00
			$383 30
Cost			104 80
Net profit, 17½ acres			$278 50
Cost per acre		$5 93	
Net profit per acre		15 91	

1853.	12 ACRES OF OATS.		Dr.
April 15.—To 5 days' ploughing, at $2			$10 00
" " 4 days' harrowing, at $2			8 00
" " 36 bu. oats for seed, and 1 day's work at $1			10 00
" " threshing, $42—harvesting, $18			60 00
Total			$88 00
1853.			Cr.
By 87½ bu. per acre, making 1050 bu., at 25c			$262 50
Cost			88 00
Net profit			$174 50
Cost per acre		$7 33	
Net profit per acre		14 54	

1852.	9½ ACRES SPRING WHEAT.		Dr.
Sept.—To 5 days' ploughing, 8 inches deep, at $2			$10 00
" " 19 bu. Rio seed wheat, at 75c			14 25
1853.			
March 25.—1 day sowing the same			1 00
3 days' work harrowing, at $2			6 00
Cost harvesting 9½ acres, at $1 50 per acre			14 25
Cost threshing 228 bu. 8c			18 24
To carting the same to market at 2c			4 56
Total cost			$68 30
1853.			Cr.
By 9½ acres, 24 bu. per acre, 228 bu., at $1			$228 00
Cost			68 30
Net profit			$159 70
Cost per acre		$7 20	
Net profit per acre		16 81	

1852.	2¼ ACRES WINTER RYE.		Dr.
Sept.—To ploughing 1 day			$2 00
To 4 bu. seed, 50c			2 00
To sowing and harrowing, 1 day			2 00
To harvesting the same			3 75
To threshing 50 bu. rye, 8c			4 00
To carting the same to market, 2c			1 00
Total cost			$14 75
1852.			Cr.
By 2¼ acres, 22 bu. and 7 qts. per acre, 50 bu. at 50 c			$25 00
Cost			14 75
Net profit			10 25
Cost per acre		$6 50	
Net profit per acre		4 55	

1853.	5½ ACRES BARLEY.		DR.
April.—	To 2½ days' ploughing, at $2		$5 00
	To 12 bu. seed at 40c		4 80
	To 1 day's work sowing same		1 00
	To 1½ day's work harrowing, at 2$		3 00
	To harvesting 5½ acres, at $1 50		8 25
	To carting 182 bu. to market, 2c		3 64
	Threshing the same, 8c		25 69
Total cost			$40 25
1853.			CR.
By 5½ acres, 33 bu. 3 qts. per acre, 180 bu., 40c			$72 90
Cost			40 25
Net profit			32 55
	Cost per acre	$7 32	
	Net profit per acre	5 92	

28½ ACRES CORN GROUND.

One half of this was fall ploughed, the balance timothy sod, broke May 1st, 1852, 7 inches deep. Cost of tending about the same as fall ploughing.

To 28½ acres ploughing, at $1 per acre		$28 50
To 5 days' harrowing, at $2		10 00
To 4 bu. seed corn, 75c		3 00
To 9½ days' planting, 7s		8 31
To 26 days' cultivating corn, $1 25		30 50
To 12 days' hoeing, 88c		10 56
To 57 days' husking, $1		57 00
Shelling and marketing 1710 bu. at 4c		68 40
Total cost		$216 27
		CR.
By 28½ acres, 60 bu. per acre, 1710 bu. at 50c		$855 00
Cost		216 27
Net profit		$638 73
Cost per acre	$7 59	
Net profit per acre	22 41	

1853.	ONE ACRE POTATOES.	DR.
To cost of raising		$10 00
		CR.
By 150 bu. potatoes, 25c		$37 50
Net profit		$27 50

ONE HUNDRED AND THREE SHEEP.	Dr.
To cutting and stacking 25 tons hay, at $1	$25 00
To feeding 30 bu. corn, 50c	15 00
To feeding and salt	10 00
To washing and shearing sheep, and marketing wool	10 00
Total cost	$60 00
	Cr.
By 103 fleeces, average 3 lbs. 10 oz. 373 lbs., at 46c	$171 58
By 53 lambs at $1 25	66 25
	$237 83
Cost	60 00
Net profit	$177 83

FIFTEEN HEAD OF CATTLE AND ONE COLT.	Dr.
To cost keeping to hay	$25 00
To 25 bu. corn feed, 50c	12 50
To labor and salt	10 50
Total cost	$47 00
	Cr.
By growth on cattle and colt	$150 00
Cost	47 00
Net profit	$103 00
Dr. To fatting one sow and four pigs, 80 bu. corn at 50c	40 00
Cr. By 1500 lbs. pork, at 5c. per lb	75 00
Net profit	$35 00
25 bu. apples, $1	25 00
8 bu. peaches, $1	8 00
5 swarms bees, $5	25 00
50 lbs. honey, 12½c	6 25
24 turkeys, 50c	12 00
60 chickens, 12½ c	7 50
	$83 75
Cost of keeping the above	10 00
Net profit	$73 75

TWENTY-ONE ACRES TIMOTHY SEED.	
Dr. To harvesting, threshing, and cleaning	$45 00
Cr. By 84 bu., at $2 per bu	168 00
Net profit	$123 00

RECAPITULATION.

	Cost of growing.	Net profits.
23 acres of wheat	$202 50	$453 00
17½ acres wheat	104 90	278 50
9½ acres spring wheat	68 30	159 7C
2½ acres rye	14 75	10 25
5½ acres barley	40 25	32 55
12 acres oats	88 00	174 50
28½ acres corn	216 27	638 73
1 acre potatoes	10 00	27 50
103 sheep	60 00	177 83
Cattle and colt	47 00	103 00
Pork	40 00	35 00
Apples, peaches, bees, turkeys, &c	10 00	73 75
21 acres timothy seed	45 00	123 00
Total	$946 87	$2287 31

The preceding twelve accounts kept of farms in the most widely separated parts of the State, will be sufficient to give the reader an idea of the comparative profitableness of husbandry in Illinois. To these accounts we now add several other communications, which, though not calculations themselves, serve nevertheless very well to show that the Illinoisian farmer has all reason to be satisfied with his lot.

John Williams, Esq., of New Albany, Coles Co., says, in a letter dated Dec. 23, 1855:

"I can raise on my farm, and have done it, 60 to 100 bushels of corn to the acre; 30 to 40 bushels of wheat per acre, and every kind of vegetables in the greatest abundance. I harvested off my farm this season 15,000 bushels of corn; two men raised for me with but little more than their own labor, about 7,000 bushels of corn and oats; this corn is now worth in the crib over 25 cents per bushel. My neighbors raised from 25 to 38 bushels of wheat per acre, and sold it on the spot at from $1 25 to $1 30 per bushel. Early in the season, Mr. Cuthbertson, a neighbor of mine, sold the crop of wheat off of 50 acres of land, as it stood, for $1500, cash."

"The "Chicago Democratic Press," dated Dec. 23, 1855, states that, in that year, Mr. Lewis Prettyman derived from his farm of 80 acres, the sum of $3965, receiving, among others, $230 for cider, $460 for apples, $10 for pears, $20 for asparagus, and other pot-herbs, $375 for wheat, $168 for oats, $1320 for Indian corn, $20 for potatoes, $200 for hay, $400 for horned cattle, $450 for horses, &c., &c

Peter Unzieker, Esq., of Groveland, Tazewell Co., in a letter dated Nov. 20, 1855, says the following:

"In 1848, I purchased a farm of 182 acres, together with a dwelling house and a good well, for $1,250; in 1853, a man from Pennsylvania offered me $4000 cash for it, and if I would sell it now, I would receive much more for it; but I do not think of it. I have now been fourteen years in America, and came soon after my arrival in this country to Illinois, when my resolution of settling here became irrevocably fixed, and I am now very glad to have executed it. I am of opinion that any man, especially however, the farmer, can acquire and obtain in Illinois, as contented and independent a living as he could anywhere else. I have travelled through many States, but was never pleased better than when settling on the exuberant soil of Illinois."

A short time since there appeared in the "Hunterton Gazette," New Jersey, a letter written by a well known citizen of that State, who, having travelled through Illinois to see whether it would be advisable for him to settle there, takes occasion to drop the following remarks concerning the state of affairs there. We quote from his letter the following passage:

"Let me cite a few facts which I know to be true, however large they may seem to be. Mr. Peter C. Rea, who resided twelve years in Raritan, near Clover Hill, and emigrated to Fulton County, Illinois, in the early part of this year, told me he had raised and sold more wheat since he had been there, than he had done in twelve years he had resided in Raritan. He simply raked and burned the cornstalks in the spring, and without ploughing the ground, sowed it with spring wheat, and harrowed it in; and in a few months he reaped a fine crop of spring wheat. He has, besides, on his farm, a good prospect for a crop of winter wheat. I ate at his house some bread made of the flour from his spring wheat, and it was as white and as good as any I ever ate in New Jersey. He also told me he should probably make as much money this year in Illinois, as he did in twelve years in New Jersey.

"I saw a farmer in Peoria County, who lived on a rented farm of eighty acres, for which he paid $200 rent for the land, and $26 for the house; he did all his work himself, except some help in planting corn; had one team of horses, and after paying his rent and supporting his family, would clear one thousand dollars this year.

"My friend, Mr. D. H. L. Sutphen, of Pike County, formerly of this county, had a field sown with wheat, and harvested therefrom upwards of 3000 bushels. He hired everything done, and if I remember correctly, had cleared over and above all expenses, about $2000 by the operation. He introduced me to a gentleman by the name of Simpkins, in that county, who came there a few years ago with nothing save his health and his hands. He was now farming, and he told us that he would sell this year, produce from his farm amounting to between $17,000 and $18,000. I saw his hog-pen, containing 481 fat hogs, which would average 350 pounds each."

D. L. Phillippi, Esq., of Anna, Union Co., in a letter dated 22d Jan., 1856, recites as proof of the facility with which a man may acquire an easy, independent competence, in Illinois, the following facts:

"Winstead Davis, Esq, a native of Tennessee, came to Jonesboro thirty years ago, without means of any kind. He has been for many years both merchant and farmer. Owns now many thousand acres of land, and has succeeded well as a merchant. Has under cultivation between 2500 and 3000 acres of land. Rent corn this year, at 10 bushels per acre, 12,000 bushels; he is supposed to be worth $300,000.

"Willis Willard, Esq., a native of Vermont, farmer and merchant, commenced in the world penniless, and was left an orphan when very young. Owns, say 10,000 acres of land—possibly much more. Has, perhaps, 2000 acres in cultivation. Is one of the heaviest dry goods dealers in the southern half of the State, and is estimated to be worth $250,000 or $300,000. Mr. Willard came to Jonesboro when a small lad.

"Jacob Randleman, farmer and tanner, a native of North Carolina, came to Union County when quite young; commenced poor; has now some 500 acres of land in cultivation; sold during the past year his crop of wheat to Messrs. Bennett & Scott, the amount was 3000 bushels, for which he received nearly $4000. Has on hand now, for sale, 4000 bushels of corn. Has always been healthy, and has raised a large family of healthy children."

To this he adds:

"Hundreds of other men might be named, who have succeeded well on a smaller scale, who commenced here without a dollar."

Jas. Philipps, Esq., of Nashville, Washington Co., in a letter dated Dec. 26, 1855, states the following instances, in which men acquired wealth by agricultural pursuits, in Illinois:

"There is Mr. K——, who came here a poor adventurer, with nothing of this world's goods; he went to farming, continued it assiduously, turning his farm produce into stock, his stock into cash, and his cash into lands. He is now worth about fifty thousand dollars.

"A son of the preceding commenced about ten years ago, doing business for himself. He had about one thousand dollars to start with, and has gone on increasing his wealth at the rate of a thousand a year. This was done exclusively by farming.

Colonel P—— came here as one of the early pioneers of this country, went to tilling the land, and followed it up to the present time, engaging in nothing else; he is now worth about twenty thousand, having begun with less than one hundred dollars." He adds: "These are a few of many that might be cited. One remark about this country; one fair crop of any of the usual grains grown here, is worth, when harvested, what the land will cost; so that an emigrant can easily calculate what he can do on an average. Thus, if he can plant and till one hundred acres of land by putting in corn or wheat, he can pretty safely estimate that when he threshes his wheat, or cribs his corn, it will be worth the prime cost of his one hundred acres of land. This is not all; for when his land is ploughed and fenced, it is worth double what it was before subjugation."

The "Prairie Farmer," of May 6th, 1856, says: "A farmer in Morgan County, sold last year, $60,000 worth of cattle, at a very handsome profit."

Jno. S. Barger, Esq., in his above mentioned letter, states as proof how easily fortunes are made here, the following facts:

"I will now give you a concise history of the operations of Mr. Funk. Both before and since his marriage he had made rails for his neighbors, at twenty-five cents per hundred. But when the lands where he lived came into market, 25 years ago, he had saved of his five years' earnings $1400, and says if he had invested it all in lands, he would now have been rich. With $200 he bought his first quarter-section, and loaned to his neighbors $800 to buy their homes; and with the remaining $400 he purchased a lot of cattle. With this beginning, Mr. Funk now owns 7000 acres of land, has near 2700 in cultivation, and his last year's sale of cattle and hogs, at the Chicago market, amounted to a little over $44,000.

"Mr. Isaac Funk, of Funk's Grove, nine miles distant from his brother Jesse, and ten miles northwest from Bloomington, on the Mississippi and Chicago Railroad, began the world in Illinois, at the same time, having a little the advantage of Jesse, so far as having a little borrowed capital. He now owns about 27,000 acres of land, has about 4000 acres in cultivation, and his last sales of cattle amounted to $65,000."

We do not consider it a matter of any importance, that there exist such rich men in Illinois as the Funks: for wealth may be inherited, and fast by the most magnificent wealth the most squalid poverty may drop her bitter tears; but we consider it a matter of no small moment, that the Funks have risen to their present condition from that of humble day-laborers; that they acquired this enormous amount of property in Illinois, and that all those willing to devote themselves to agriculture, can easily acquire wealth and independence in Illinois. Illinois is the paradise of the farmer; we have above stated several instances, in which the purchase-money was either wholly, or almost wholly, repaid by the produce of the first harvest. These are not such rare occurrences as will only happen under the most favorable circumstances, but it is the usual course of development, as it is conditioned by the state of affairs in the country; whoever would take the trouble of travelling through Illinois, in order to collect such instances, would have to register thousands of such cases.

After having thus presented to the eyes of our readers various calculations of the average yield of an Illinoisian farm, we cannot conclude this present chapter without having submitted to him also a very interesting parallel between the profitableness of rural economy in Illinois on the one hand, and that of husbandry in other Western States, on the other. This parallel is thus drawn up in a little interesting pamphlet just published by A. Campbell, Esq., of La Salle, entitled "A Glance at Illinois."

"Now if the following plan were adopted, it would probably be as profitable a division as could be made for farming purposes, and would suit the means and views of a majority of farmers, as well as any other which could be made:—Say with a farm of 160 acres, you appropriate 40 acres to buildings, orchards, and pasture grounds; upon which also may be raised the vegetables for the family, and a portion of the provender for the stock; 20 acres for mowing; 30 acres for wheat, and 70 acres for corn.

"We will assume that the wheat and corn crops are the only ones of which the farmer will have any surplus. This may of course be varied to suit the views and circumstances of the cultivator, but will not materially affect the general result. With fair farming, 20 bushels of wheat to the acre is not too large an estimate, nor are 50 bushels of corn by any means a large average yield upon our rich prairie lands. Therefore, assuming the above to be a fair estimate of the yield, we have

30 acres of wheat, at 20 bushels per acre = 600 bushels.

70 acres of corn, at 50 bushels per acre = 3500 bushels.

"Now if you retain 200 bushels of wheat, for seed and family use, and 900 bushels of corn, for working stock, and fattening animals for family use, both of which allowances are, undoubtedly, sufficiently large—you will have left for market, 400 bushels of wheat, and 2600 bushels of corn,—in all 3000 bushels of grain.

"And as this is a strictly agricultural country, it must depend upon an eastern or foreign market for the sale of its surplus produce. And with the present and prospective railroad facilities, communicating with Lake Michigan, we are safe in assuming that, as a general thing, all surplus north of the 40th parallel of latitude, not only in this State, but from the country west, must inevitably, by the laws of trade, find its outlet to the eastern market by what is termed the Northern or Lake route.

"Although there is a considerable consumption of meat and grain upon the sugar and cotton plantations of the south, and in the West Indies, the country south of the line we have named, is at all times fully adequate to the supply, except in case of a short crop.

"A bushel of grain is worth upon the farm as much less as the cost of carrying it to market. And the cost of transporting wheat or corn by railroad, is about eight cents per bushel per hundred miles, and for meats about fifteen cents per hundred pounds, per hundred miles. The average cost per bushel for transporting wheat or corn from Chicago to Buffalo, by way of the lakes, will not exceed seven cents, during the season of navigation; while from Cleveland to Buffalo, it is about four cents per bushel.

"Now as the comparative advantage of different points in the west, for farming purposes, is the object we wish to arrive at, suppose, in making a comparison, we take for one locality, the vicinity of Columbus, Ohio:—another, 80 miles west or southwest of Chicago, in Illinois, on the line of any of the numerous railroads diverging westerly or southwesterly from that point. For a third, Iowa City, the capital of Iowa, which is 242 miles west of Chicago; and Fort Des Moines, in Iowa, for a fourth; this is 367 miles west of Chicago, by way of the Rock Island Railroad, which is now completed to Iowa City, and in process of construction to Fort Des Moines.

"From Columbus, Ohio, to Cleveland, 125 miles, at eight cents per hundred miles, by railroad, the cost would be ten cents; from thence to Buffalo by the way of Lake Erie, four cents; from thence to New York, twelve cents; total, twenty-six cents. From the points 80 miles west or south-west of Chicago, by railroad, it would be seven cents to Chicago; from thence to Buffalo, seven cents; from thence to New York, twelve cents; total, twenty-six cents. From Iowa City to Chicago, 242 miles, the cost would be nineteen cents per bushel; thence to Buffalo, seven cents; thence to New York, twelve cents, would give a total of thirty-eight cents, from Iowa City to New York. From Fort Des Moines to Chicago, 367 miles, the cost would be twenty-nine cents; from thence to Buffalo, seven cents; thence to New York twelve cents; total cost, from Fort Des Moines to New York, forty-eight cents. And in like ratio for any distance greater or less.

"The value of the crop upon a farm of 160 acres, at Columbus, Ohio, and upon one of the same size 80 miles from Chicago, are equal; whilst there is a difference in favor of the latter over the one at Iowa City, of 360 dollars; and over the one at Fort Des Moines, in Iowa, of 660 dollars. Three hundred and sixty dollars will pay an interest of six per cent upon a valuation of $6000; and $600 is the interest at the same rate upon $10,000. This shows that a farm of 160 acres within 80 miles of Chicago, is worth $6000 more than one of the same size in the vicinity of Iowa City; which is equal to $37 50 per acre, and $1100 more than one at Fort Des Moines; which is equal to $68 75 per acre, when appropriated to raising grain."

SOIL.

In regard to agriculture, the soil of Illinois is divided into three classes. On the prairies it is a vegetable mould of different depth, on a substratum from 3 to 4 feet thick, of rich mulatto loam or clay, being in most cases entirely free from stones, and requiring only a single tilling in order to produce all the various species of corn and fruits peculiar to these latitudes. The wild grass growing on the prairies furnishes a very nutritious article of food, which will at once account for the universal renown of the beef of Illinois.

The bottom lands skirted by the rivers are of extraordinary fertility, but exposed to frequent inundations, and covered with tall forest trees. Here the vegetable mould attains a depth of from three to twelve feet; its inexhaustibility is easily accounted for by the consideration that the rivers impregnated with the humus of the prairies through which they flow, deposit it in the bottom lands, whenever a rise of the water causes the latter to be inundated.

The soil of the openings covered with scattered trees of the forest, and these mostly oak, though not as good as that of the prairies, will yet yield as fine a crop without any manure, as can be obtained in the Eastern States with the aid of manure.

But it should be added that the character of the soil differs in the different sections of the State. The substratum is clay, (this is invariably the case in Central Illinois), which precludes the idea that the fertility of the soil ever could be lost. By injudicious tillage the lands may, after years, tire, but can never be worn out. Upon the large water-courses, and in the extreme north and south, the soil is sandy, and the substratum sand and gravel, with some clay. In Central Illinois the soil is without sand; on the undulating, or rolling prairies, the soil is of a mulatto, or yellow cast; on the level lands it is black; but no difference can be discovered in the fertility of these two-thirds of soil, both producing equally well all kinds of grain and grasses. The depth of the black soil is from twenty to thirty inches; the yellow from fifteen to twenty-four inches. It is the prevailing opinion that the level or table-lands stand a drought better than the rolling. The soil in Central Illinois partakes largely of limestone, without the appearance of the stone itself, therefore rendering it the more valuable, and easy of cultivation, and causing it to stand a long and continued drought, with less injury to growing crops than those portions of the country where rock is interspersed through the cultivated lands.

BREAKING THE SOIL.

It is difficult to place a man in any situation where he feels more like an honest conqueror than he does when turning over the verdant turf of the prairies. His plough must have a keen edge, and cut from twenty-two to thirty-six inches wide. A thin sod of two or three inches thick is cut smooth and turned completely upside down. The bottom of the furrow and top of the reversed sod are as smooth as if sliced with a keen knife. Every green thing is turned out of sight, and nothing is visible but the fresh soil. When the prairie is broken, and the sod has time to decompose, the land is thoroughly subdued, and in a good condition for any crop—not a stump or a stone in the way, over a whole quarter section; free from weeds, rich, fresh, and mellow; it is the fault of the farmer if it is not kept so.

Some farmers are accustomed to cross-plough the land, about two months after it has been broken, but others say cross-ploughing is not necessary; however, it will do no harm to the land if cross-ploughed, but increase its fertility.

The cost of breaking prairie is from two to three dollars per acre; and it is principally done by men who keep teams for the purpose, and do their work by the job. A three-horse team will break two acres per day, and a heavy ox-team with a 36 inch plough, will break three acres per day.

The breaking of prairie is done in the different sections of the country at different times; say from the 1st of May till the 20th of July, monthly from the 10th of May till the 20th of June.

FENCING.

After the farmer has broken his land, his next care must be to enclose it with a fence in order to secure his crops against the cattle. You may find in Illinois all sorts of fences, from the clumsy zig-zag fence, to the hardly visible, cheap, and wood-saving wire fence; that fence, however, which is the most conformable to the purpose, the cheapest, and at the same time the most embellishing, is the living, to wit: the Maclura hedge, which, with every new year, may be seen planted and growing more and more.

Referring to the special chapter, wherein the culture of the Maclura hedge is more particularly described, we shall here call the attention of our readers to the fact, that every farmer commencing his business here, should at once proceed to plant this hedge, which affords most ample security against all kinds of animals, provided his means permit him to do so. Although it is true, that such a hedge will first afford security four years after its being finished, so that during that time another fence must be erected outside of the Maclura hedge, the money expended on it is not lost, but amply compensated for, since the live hedge affording perfect protection at the end of this time, the other fence may either be sold, or its wood used for some other purpose.

The two best kinds of wood fences are the zig-zag, and the board fence. He who is about erecting the first, and owns no wooded tract of land, should purchase a couple of acres, and have the rails split under his immediate supervision. The hewing and splitting is usually paid for at the rate of one dollar for every hundred, the wood costing about as much, so that the expenses of fencing must be computed not higher than three dollars for every hundred rails. To diminish the cost, it would be advisable for friends to purchase contiguous lots, so that for the tracts owned by them, only one external fence would be required at first. Twenty acres will require 4704; forty acres, 6720; one hundred and sixty acres, 13,440; and a full section, or six hundred and forty acres, 28,880 cross-beams.

In building board fences, iron posts and pine boards are made use of, and constructed in such a manner that two posts and three boards constitute a panel. The cost would be for boards and hauling $1 15 per rod; the boards for 320 rods of fencing, the amount for 40 acres, would cost $368. About 700 posts, at eleven cents each, would cost $77; for putting up the fence the cost would be—for digging post holes and setting posts, $28; for nails, $19; for nailing, $14; making the whole cost of fencing 40 acres, $506. For enclosing 640 acres in one field, the cost is four times as much, viz., $2,024.

DIVISION OF FARMS, ROTATION OF CROPS, AND MANURING.

The division of a farm after the various species of corn and other products, of course depends on the northern or southern exposure of the farm. We may, however, regard it as a division conformable to the purpose, if one-half of the entire tract of land destined for the culture of grains and vegetables is planted with Indian corn, while three-fourths of the residue are sown, equally with wheat and oats. The culture of barley, rye, and potatoes, depends upon the character of the respective farms, and their comparative distance from the markets.

Heretofore but little has been said concerning the rotation of crops in Illinois; the exuberant soil yields whatever is required from it, and most farmers deeming it unnecessary to pay any regard to the land, are under the impression of best guarding their interests by exclusively cultivating that which commands the highest price at the time. While one cultivates Indian corn and wheat for a succession of ten or fifteen years, or more, another will plant Indian corn for a few years, next oats, and then wheat in the stubble of the oats, repeating this for several times, after which he plants again Indian corn. A third will first plant Indian corn for a couple of years, then winter-barley, after which oats. Thus, without caring much about a fixed order of crops, a majority of the farmers will husband and grow rich within a short time, without considering, however, that a proper succession of crops would considerably increase and enhance their wealth.

Little as on most farms a fixed succession of crops, that would necessitate a division of the entire farming lands into certain fields, is observed, a manuring of the soil is *never* thought of. It is true, as we have already mentioned, that the rich soil of Illinois produces without any manure at all; yet how much larger would its produce be, were that which by annual cultivation is withdrawn from the soil, restored to it by manuring the same.

The average produce of an acre of Indian corn has been stated by us at 56 bushels; we now cite an instance to show how enormously this amount may be swelled by cultivation and by manure.

Two years ago, three men in Ogle County vied with each other to see who would raise the best acre of corn, and obtain the premium to be awarded at the County Fair. Each manured his land slightly, and cultivated it well with the hoe; and the result was that they obtained respectively 127, 131, and 134 bushels from the acre.

But if such results can be attained, would it not amply compensate a farmer for his trouble in directing his undivided attention to this subject, the more since, by being manured, the land would not become exhausted, but on the contrary be rendered more valuable and productive?

We cannot abstain from quoting, what in regard of the succession of crops, and general cultivation of farms, is said in his letter to Browman Murray, by Mr. Jas. N. Brown, of Island Grove, the former President of the Illinois State Agricultural Society; in which letter, after stating the productiveness of an acre at from 20 to 25 bushels of wheat, 60 to 80 of oats, and 40 to 50 of Indian corn, he proceeds as follows:

"Such poor results should not be, except from an imperfect system of tillage. When the farmer breaks his land from three to four or five inches deep, the plough cutting ten or twelve inches, and covering five or six more, (thus leaving one-third of the ground untouched), covers the corn with a horse, ploughs the crop three times, and twice out of the three times ploughs with two furrows in the row, and this completes the tillage: it is surprising that he raises any crop at all. And yet the fertility of our soil is such that it yields abundance to such poor cultivation as this, whilst in other parts of our country such results are not obtained except by judicious culture and rotation of crops. Such culture and rotation I warmly recommend. After turning over the prairie sod, cultivate three or four years in corn, then oats or rye, which should be pastured and turned under, then corn again; and then clover and timothy for four or five years. Be careful not to burn any manure that may be on the land, such as corn stalks for stubble, as is the custom of many of our best farmers, who seem to forget that it is as important to feed their land as to feed their stock, and that no labor pays so great a return as the labor expended in manuring their lands intended for the plow. Haul your manure, and feed stock on lands intended for corn, during the autumn and winter; being careful to keep the stock from stubble land, when soft and rainy; the treading of sod in soft weather in winter will not injure the land intended for corn or grass the next year. Our yield by adopting this or a similar system, (with four workings, the first with a two-horse harrow, and thinning and suckering the corn when about knee high), would be from eighty to one hundred bushels per acre.

"In confirmation of the foregoing views I give the following experiment:—Last April I broke thirty-five acres of old pasture land; the first portion has been in grass eighteen years, the second portion fourteen, the third part ten or twelve years. The portion that had been in grass eighteen years I partially manured with dung from the horse and cow yards, and turned under immediately after spreading it. The whole field was prepared in the same manner with the exception of the manure. It was all planted the same week in May, and received the same tillage, to wit: one harrowing and three ploughings, with suckering and thinning out to three and four stalks in a hill. The distance of the rows apart was four feet by three, and the yield was as follows: —That portion that had been in grass eighteen years, and was partially manured, contained nine and a half acres, yielded a hundred bushels to the acre; the second piece, fourteen years in grass, and manured six or seven years since, produced one hundred and twenty-three bushels per acre—number of acres, five and two-thirds; the third lot, ten years in grass, twenty acres, yielded eighty bushels per acre. It will be seen from the above experiment, that by an imperfect system of rotation in crops, and rather poor farming, I have increased my yield of corn over the common yield of our virgin soil, from twenty to one hundred per cent. My land, after nineteen years' cultivation, affords a larger yield of corn and grass than it did when fresh, and is consequently more valuable."

From the preceding it will appear, that by manuring, a proper cultivation, and succession of crops, a much higher product will be attained, than the soil by itself is able to bring forth. On the other hand we shall not omit to point out the fact, that the very largely prevalent opinion that the soil of Illinois is totally inexhaustible, and of indestructible fertility, rests on a slight error. Even the deepest well can at last be emptied, and the most fertile soil, whose productive powers are used without being restored again, must, at last, either partially or wholly lose its fertility. No doubt much time will be required to exhaust the soil of Illinois so far, that even very deep ploughing should be found insufficient to insure good harvests; yet, unless the farmers can be persuaded, that the preservation of the fertility of the soil requires those productive powers, which it has expended in bringing forth a crop, to be restored to it, that time must speedily arrive. And further, but few farmers perceive that by wasting the straw of their wheat, they inflict as great an injury upon themselves, as they would by destroying the very wheat, since the production of wheat depends upon the production of straw; a feeble halm will but rarely bear a stout ear; and if you insist upon being wasteful, you might as well feed the cattle with the wheat, as with the straw upon which it grew. A good field of wheat yields about 2000 pounds of straw per acre, which entire weight, save only the carbonate which it contains, is withdrawn from the soil, thus diminishing its productiveness for the following harvest, by just the same amount; therefore we are right in saying that if the straw is cut close to the ground, by the reaper, as is usually the case, this would be no less a prodigality than to feed the cattle on the wheat altogether. So much of the straw taken from the acre as would be restored to it, would increase the faculty of producing new straw on the part of the soil; on the straw the wheat thrives well, and luxuriant halms bear stout ears.

The soil of the prairies has been stated above to consist generally of clay, which much impedes the further descent of the water trickling down to it from the surface—thus protecting and securing the natural fertility of the soil, and preventing the escape of the powers derived by the soil from being manured; on the other hand, it must be admitted, that this property of the soil is the reason why many level sections of the prairies are frequently wet, and thus unfit for advantageous and immediate cultivation of corn. Such humidity on the part of the soil will in most cases admit of being obviated by deep ploughing and manuring; often deep ploughing will be found sufficient to obviate the difficulty; where, however, deep ploughing or manuring should not prove adequate to accomplishing this object, a few ditches properly dug will not fail to dry the land.

LABOR, WAGES, AND FARM IMPLEMENTS.

What Illinois requires is a further increase of her laboring population, the farmers in every section of the State loudly complaining of the want of hands, adding that much more land might be tilled, if a sufficient number of hands could be found for the purpose. We subjoin a review of the wages, which, during 1855, were paid in the various sections of the State:

County.	Monthly wages, (with board.)	Daily wages.
Cass	$12 00 to $20 00	$1 00 to $2 00
De Kalb	12 00 " 20 00	
Du Page	10 00 " 12 00	
Jo Daviess	10 00 " 15 00	
Macoupin	14 00 " 15 00	1 00 " 1 75
Marshall	15 00 " 18 00	1 00 " 1 50
McLean	12 00 " 20 00	1 00 " 1 50
Peoria	12 00 " 16 00	
Rock Island		1 00 " 1 00
Sangamon	12 00 " 16 00	
St. Clair	10 00 " 14 00	75 " 1 50
Tazewell		1 25 " 1 50
Woodford	12 00 " 16 00	1 00 " 1 50
Will	15 00	1 00 " 1 75
Winnebago	15 00 " 20 00	

The higher rates are, of course, only paid during the harvest, but these, in many counties, exceed the above amounts; the remuneration in winter is less than that in summer. Much new land having been broken during 1855, many farmers express their fears that wages will be still higher in 1856.

The many difficulties which a single farmer has to surmount, in the pursuit of his business, render it difficult to determine how much work a man with two horses is able to perform; from thirty to forty acres, it is usually reckoned, can be easily tilled by a single man, provided he procures himself some hand to assist him during harvest time. Two men with four horses can easily till one hundred acres, and three men with five horses one hundred and sixty acres. We know of a man who, together with a boy of some twelve years, and now and then with an assistant (who, however, did not cause him more than fifteen dollars annual expense), and five horses, tilled a farm of forty acres of Indian corn, ten acres of wheat, ten acres of oats, six acres of flax, ten acres of prairie, besides breaking some twenty acres of new prairie, and sowing it with sod corn.

Two acres are estimated a good day's work for a single team of horses, and one and a half for oxen; on many places, however, more is done. Many farmers prefer horses to oxen, horses always having this advantage, that they go faster; and many farmers also contend that they turn up the land better than oxen. A man walks about twenty-five miles while ploughing a day.

What facilitates the labor of a farmer in the west, and especially in Illinois, is the use of mechanical power, as the same is employed in the Eastern States—excellent agricultural machines being, in fact, turned out in the west. Most of the ploughs are made of steel plates, and are polished on wheels, so as to shine like mirrors, furrowing the soil to a great depth. There are ploughs which furrow the ground for the breadth of forty inches. That such large, smooth, and sharp ploughs, will do their work much faster than others, is self-evident. Very good ploughs are turned out by the manufactory of J. Drew, Moline, Rock Island County.

Wheat and other grain is usually sown with the rotation-sowing machine, by the use of which seed and time are saved, and a successful crop ensured. The machines most frequently used were invented by Piersons and Garling.

The grains are in most cases gathered by harvesting machines, the most excellent of which are those of McCormick and Henry, to which were awarded the highest premiums at the "World's Fair."

For the cutting of hay on the prairies, reapers are used, and especially those of Scoville, Danforth and McCormick.

Lastly, the threshing is done by threshing machines, either at once, on the fields, or in the barns.

While speaking of agricultural implements, we shall here particularly mention two machines, which, though not yet introduced into Illinois, seem so well adapted and calculated for that State, that it cannot be long ere they are introduced: we refer to the steam plough, and the wind-mills.

With the first, whose inventor, Mr. Obed Hassey, also probably constructed the first reaping machine, experiments were not long ago made at the exhibition of the Maryland Agricultural Society, that proved completely satisfactory. The machine steamed alone to the field, distant two and a half miles, where the experiment was to be made; there four great turf ploughs being attached to it, it entered upon its task, furrowing the earth fourteen inches deep. The ploughing was exceedingly well done, many of the farmers present expressing their opinions to the effect, that the machine was particularly adapted for breaking the soil of the prairie. We trust it will not be long ere we shall see the steam plough furrowing the fertile soil of the Illinoisian prairies, and thus annually and more rapidly than ever before, subjugating to culture many thousands of new acres.

Of wind-mills there are but few, as yet, in Illinois, though the large prairies are admirably adapted for the use of the wind, as mechanical power. Perceiving this, several gentlemen of Rochester, N. Y., have formed themselves into a company, to erect, during 1856, fifty windmills on the western prairies; and in Peoria a company has been organized for a like purpose. The mill to be constructed by the last will contain two different milling apparatus, the grinding stones used in which are four feet in diameter; the whole, including the building and the right of using the patent, to cost $4000. A mill thus constructed in Rochester, will grind thirty bushels of grain per hour, and it being estimated, that these mills can be in active operation for full ten months in a year, they ought to be preferred on this account, if on no other, to water-mills, since but few of the latter might be found in constant operation for such a length of time.

Five bushels of prime wheat will make one barrel of superfine flour, leaving a handsome pay to the miller.

Another project for the purpose of rendering available the power of wind, has been started by Mr. M. D. Codding, of Lockport, Will Co., who has, three miles from that place, established a machine-factory, and, for the above purpose, has constructed a machine which, simple, substantial, and low-priced, can be used for a number of purposes; for instance—for sawing wood, whetting stones, pumping water, etc. Mr. Codding turns out these machines of any power desired, from that of one man to twenty horse power. A machine of one horse power, inclusive of gearing, can be had for $25 to $30; the expense of larger machines of this kind not exceeding a just proportion to this.

INDIAN CORN.

There are a great number of varieties of corn in cultivation, and these varieties have become considerably intermingled. The principal varieties, which may be distinguished by the number of rows or grains, on the cob, and the color, shape or size of the kernels, may be classified and described as follows:

1. Yellow Corn, Golden Sioux, or Northern Flint Corn; having a large cob, with twelve rows of moderate sized grains, very oily, and is regarded as one of the best varieties for fattening animals, or for human food. By skilful tillage, 130 bushels have been raised to the acre, weighing 9,216 lbs. in the ear, when dry: 75 lbs. of ears gave a bushel when shelled.

2. King Philip, or the Eight-Rowed Yellow Corn. Its ears, which contain only eight rows, are longer than those of the Golden Sioux, and it will yield about the same quality of oil. It is a hardy plant, which belongs to a high latitude; grows to about nine feet in height; stalks small, ears from ten to fourteen inches in length.

3. Canada Corn, or Eighteen-Rowed Yellow. This corn, which is smaller, earlier, and more solid than any of the preceding, contains more oil than any other variety, except the Rice Corn, and the Pop Corn. It is exceedingly valuable for fattening poultry, swine, &c., and is grown by many in gardens, for early boiling.

4. Dutton Corn. The cob sometimes grows to the length of fourteen or fifteen inches, but the grain is so compact upon it that two bushels of small ears have yielded five pecks of shelled corn, weighing 62 lbs. to the bushel. With proper management, an acre of ground will yield one hundred to one hundred and twenty bushels to the acre. As it is very oily, gives a good yield, and ripens early, it has always been a favorite variety for culture in the north.

5. Southern Big Yellow Corn. The cob of this corn is thick and long, the grain much wider than it is deep, and the rows unite with each other. The grain contains less oil and more starch than the Northern Flint kinds; yet its outward texture is somewhat flinty, solid and firm. It comes to maturity rather later, affords an abundant yield, and is much used for fattening animals.

6. Southern Small Yellow Corn. The ears of this variety are more

slender, as well as shorter than the last named; the grains are smaller though of the same form, of a deep yellow, more firm and flinty, and contain an abundance of oil, which renders it more valuable for the purpose of shipping, or for feeding poultry or swine.

1. Rhode Island White Flint Corn. The grains of this variety are about the size and shape of those of the Tuscarora Corn, but differ from them in containing an abundance of a transparent and colorless oil, which may be easily seen through their clear, pellucid hulls. The farinaceous parts of the grains are white, and as the quantity of oil which they contain is large, the flour or meal is more substantial as an article of food, and less liable to ferment and become sour.

2. Southern Little White Flint Corn. The kernels of this variety are considerably smaller than those of the preceding, and much resemble them in shape, but they are more firm and solid, contain more oil, and consequently are of more value for feeding poultry and swine, and for human food.

3. Dutton White Flint Corn. A variety not differing materially from the Yellow Dutton Corn, except in the color of the oil.

4. Early Canadian White Flint Corn. Cultivated principally for early boiling or roasting, while green.

5. Tuscarora Corn. The ears contain from twelve to sixteen rows of grains, which are nearly as deep as they are broad, of a dead whitish color on the extreme end, are entirely composed within of pure, white dextrine, and starch, except the germs. As it contains neither gluten nor oil, it may be profitably employed in the manufacture of starch. It is much softer and better food for horses than the flinty kind, and if used before it becomes sour, it may be converted into excellent bread. It is also an excellent variety for boiling, when green, or in the milky state.

6. White Flint Corn. The ears of this variety contain twelve rows of rather white, roundish, thick grains, which are filled with a snowy white flour, composed principally of starch, but does not contain either gluten or oil. It is much used. As it possesses similar properties with the preceding variety, it may be profitably employed for the same purpose. It is also an excellent variety for boiling, when green.

7. Virginia White Seed Corn. The ears of this corn, which are

not very long, (nor is the cob so long as those of the Big White, or Yellow Flint), contain from twenty-four to thirty-six rows of very long, narrow grains. These grains, at their extreme ends, are almost flat, and grow so closely together from the cob to the surface, that they produce a greater yield than any other variety, in proportion to the size of the ears. They contain more starch, and less gluten and oil, than those of the Flint kinds, and from their softness they serve as better food for horses, but are less nourishing to poultry and swine. This variety ripens later, though it is more productive than any other kind.

8. Early Sweet Corn. There are two kinds of this corn; one with the cob red, and the other white. The ears are short, and usually contain eight rows, the grains of which, when mature, are of a lighter color, and become shrivelled, appearing as if they were unripe. It contains a very large proportion of the phosphates, and a considerable quantity of sugar and gum, though but little starch. It is extensively cultivated for culinary purposes, and is delicious food when boiled green.

9. Rice Corn. A small variety, with small conical ears, the kernels terminating in sharp points, which give them the appearance of burrs; the kernels in size and shape something like rice. It contains more oil and less starch than any other kind, and when ground, its meal cannot be made into bread alone, but is dry like sand. From its oily nature and peculiar size, this corn is well adapted for feeding poultry.

10. Pearl Corn. Commonly called pop-corn, from the fact of its being used for popping, or parboiling. The ears of this variety are small, the grains are round, of various shades of color, the white of a pearly appearance; and contain, with the rice corn, more oil and less starch than any other variety.

11. Chinese Tree Corn. It is a pure white variety, a very handsome ear, about ten inches long, has ten rows, grain very closely set, long and wedge-shaped, well filled out, to the end of the cob; some of the grains slightly indented. One peculiarity of this corn is, the ears grow on the ends of the branches, hence its name "Tree Corn." It is said to yield from one-fourth to one-third more than the common varieties. When ground into meal it is handsomer and better flavored

than the common varieties of white corn. There are generally two ears on a stalk, and often three.

There are many other species of corn, but the foregoing embrace pretty much all those worthy of cultivation.

To raise a good crop of corn, a man must of course have all the implements required for it. If the planting is to be done on old ground, the old stalks should be cut and broken down first. This is usually done with a roller or a cylinder of wood, which is within a square frame, and about four feet long, and nineteen inches in diameter, and has four blades placed at equal distances around it, and running its entire length; drawn along by the horses, this instrument breaks down the stalks and cuts them up in fine style, leaving the stalks so cut about a foot long, and finishing about from six to eight acres per day in this manner. After this, the farmer should plough in the direction in which the stalks were broken down, so as to bring them under the earth turned up, which is easily accomplished; and never forget to harrow on rough or heavy land. If he then proposes making a marker, he should construct four wedge-shaped forms, 2½ feet long, 5 inches thick, 10 inches wide at one end, and running to an edge at the other. These forms may be made of two inch plank; and two floor joists, one close to the points, and the other close to the heads, may be laid between them. A pole being then procured for a tongue, the back end should be run over the front joist, and under the back one, and bolted at the two places where it touches them, in such a manner that when the end rests in the neck-yoke, the points of the wedges are lifted a little. A marker thus constructed, makes a broad mark, proof against a fortnight's rain, and destroys young weeds at the same time, to a great extent. The land being thus marked both ways, get Randall & Jones' Double Hand Planter, which is light, substantial, and rapid, sowing two rows at once, of any number of kernels required, on pressed earth, from which the germ will sprout rapidly, the covering being as certain as if done with the hoe. Ten or twelve acres can thus be planted in a single day.

Corn-land should always be rolled after planting, since this, in dry weather, will prevent evaporation and diminish the surface exposed to the rays of the sun. Rolling should be repeated if the land continues dry, in order to bring up by capillary attraction, the moisture from the subsoil. In tending corn, the earth should not be turned away from the hill in the day-time, since this would increase the chance of its drying through; and in throwing the earth up to the hill, the part of the stalk above the bulb, from which the supporters put out, should be prevented from being covered.

One of the best cultivators known to us is that one which has the general form of the common dray-shaped cultivator, except that it is just as long and wide again as that, and the two iron bars are made like the beam and knees of a sleigh. Its steel teeth run very flat in the ground—it runs with the broad end forward, straddles a row, and requires two horses to draw it, but will perform twice as much work as can be done by any of the common methods.

Indian corn is frequently sown as the first grain on newly-broken land; but as there is no reliance to be placed upon sod corn, many farmers prefer to leave the broken land lying fallow, until September, when it is sown with wheat. The planting of sod corn is done by sticking an axe or a spade between the layers of sod, and after dropping the corn apply the heel of the boot freely. Some farmers prefer to drop the seed into every third furrow, and turn a furrow on it. If the latter plan is adopted, the ground must be well rolled to ensure a good crop. To corn put in on the sod, usually no further attention is paid till harvest. The times of planting and harvesting depend upon the northern or southern exposure, and the harvest will often last until the end of November.

In 1835, Mr. Jno. Schoonhover raised an ear which gave one quart and one gill of the shelled corn.

We have just enumerated the different varieties of maize, which are cultivated, and before concluding this chapter we cannot forbear to point out a new variety, the cultivation of which has but just begun, viz., the Wyandott Corn. The seeds of this were obtained three years ago, from the Wyandott Indians, and first cultivated by a farmer in Waverly, Morgan County, who produced a crop of 150 bushels per acre, and who, at the Agricultural State Fair, at Chicago, in the fall of 1855, sold the single ears of this variety at twenty-five cents each. The ears are from five to nine inches long. It is a fine, pearly white, has but little chit, and grinds nearly all into meal. A chemical analysis of its properties proves it to contain a large portion of glutinous, starchy qualities, and less of spirit and strength than the Great Yellow Dog Tooth Corn, for which Suckerdom is famous. This corn is planted one kernel to the hill, and sometimes in drills. The one kernel forms a mass of rooty fibres, often as large as a man's hat, and from these start up from four to nine shoots or stalks, and each of these stalks will bear from one to five ears. A hill of this corn was grown in Upper Alton, from one kernel, which multiplied to the extent of over eight thousand kernels.

WHEAT.

The kinds of wheat mostly cultivated in the State of Illinois, are the Canada Club, Italian, Hedgerow, White Flint, and the Rio Grande. Spring Wheat succeeds well, but has been blighted for a few years past. One ploughing is deemed sufficient, and better than two, even on a summer fallow. No manures are used on this or any other crop, except that from the barn-yard, which is usually spread on the corn-field. With special regard to *Spring Wheat*, it may be of importance to say, that for preparing the ground, fall ploughing is best, since the land is in better order, and can be sown one or two weeks earlier, which is a great advantage. The earlier it is sown the better, if the ground is in order for the harrow, no matter how cold, the frost will not hurt young wheat. The land should by all means be ploughed, although some may be for ploughing in the cornstalks, and harrowing in. Experience has taught, that in this latter case, the crops at harvest have been so full of weeds, that the usual average proceeds were considerably diminished. Plow your lands not over two rods wide, and in a direction to lead off the water best; cut cross furrows in every slough or sag, so as to let no water stand on the wheat. Old land ought to be ploughed in the fall, but if ploughed in the spring, should be ploughed deeper.

Corn stubble is preferable to wheat or oat stubble.

The Canada Club is as good a kind as can be found. It is a good plan to change seeds frequently, as it has appeared that by continuing the same seed on the same land, it becomes diseased and sickly. To prevent smut wet your wheat and mingle slaked lime with it, at the rate of one bushel to twenty of wheat. If there are oats in the seed, the whole may be put in strong brine, and the oats skimmed off. It is in fact necessary to examine the seed well, for it will not grow if it has heated, or become musty; but this cannot always be detected by the eye, and it will therefore be better to try a sample, and see what portion will germinate; this will give you the quantity needed per acre. Of good seed, one bushel and a third to one and a half is about the right quantity. The "disease" it takes on, comes from sowing much imperfect seed, which never can produce vigorous, healthy plants. Let only the best seed be used, that which is free from all light, imperfect grains, and there will be found little "disease" or degeneracy. Spring Wheat is liable to grow too rank; it should be sown as soon as the frost is out of the ground, that the straw may have a stunted growth. The winter crop may be got in at a time when other labor does not press, and the whole preparation for it may be so managed as to interfere with no other work. It is easier sown therefore than Spring Wheat, and moreover it is easier harvested; from the fact that it ripens from two to four weeks earlier, the harvest season is prolonged to that extent. It will undoubtedly be both of great use and unparalleled interest to wheat growers and others who are engaged in farming, to listen to the advice and hints on the subject of the culture of wheat of an Illinoisian farmer, who has been engaged in the business in the fertile prairie sections for many years. He says that manures for the preparation of the soil are no more necessary than the application of any other substance. The land is turned over in June, and ploughed deeply and thoroughly. Immediately after ploughing, the whole springs up into a dense and vigorous growth of "Pigeon Grass." The land may be left in that condition until the middle of July, when you give it a single harrowing, letting all the stock you can command, run and tread upon it till a week before sowing. Then harrow it till the surface is sufficiently mellowed to cover the grain; this is best done with a drill. One-fourth or half an inch is enough to cover the grain. This should be done in the middle of September, and a plough should not be allowed to touch the land afterwards. The very best mode would be, to put it in with a cultivator, and then run a roller over it. The treading with the feet of cattle on the loose prairie soil, before getting in the seed, is something very necessary, and should therefore not be looked upon with indifference and carelessness. The soil in those regions is loose, and therefore must be packed together, to hold the roots of the wheat plants; and for the same reason it would not be a good practice to give the land more than one good ploughing. As confirmatory of this, at least as far as the packing of the soil is concerned, the same farmer adds, that every farmer must notice places about his fields, where there is a road, or the land has been tramped hard from some cause, where there is no killing of his wheat, even though all the rest of the field may be killed. He happened to put in part of a crop on some summer-fallowed land, without the usual ploughing before sowing, and his surprise was great, when harvest came, to find that here was a splendid crop, while all the rest of his wheat had either failed, or turned out badly.

It is supposed, that the common fault must be to put in the wheat too deep, and as usually cultivated, it is very likely the fact, that the depth is too great if the ground can be made to stay where it is put. A half inch, if the kernel is made to stay, and also the ground above it, is about the right depth.

In the north of the State wheat should be sown broad-cast, and harrowed both ways, or drilled in by a proper machine about the beginning of September. Wheat sown upon such land, in this manner, rarely fails to produce an excellent crop. The best way I think, to raise Winter Wheat on new prairie, is to break it in June very shallow, and cross-plough it a little deeper than it was broken, about the end of August, then sow and harrow it well, and leave it as rough as you can. If among corn, sow about the last of August, or first of September, and put in with a double shovel-plough, by going twice in a row. Cattle must not be allowed to run on it and tramp it, unless the ground is covered with snow. The stalks must be broken down or cut, in spring. To break them, one takes a pole, ten or twelve feet in length, and hitches a team to it, so as to draw it sideways, when the snow is off, and the ground and stalks frozen, and break three rows at once. One man with a team will break thirty acres in a day. I roll all my small grain in spring, thinking that it grows more evenly, and knowing that it is better harvesting.

A surprising fact, which deserves to be mentioned is, that many good farmers in the State of Illinois have often looked upon growing Winter Wheat as an enterprise which is not always attended with the best success, or which comparatively affords but little profits; while it may be derived from very reliable sources, that at the time when the country was first settled, some farmers in the neighborhood of Rock River did not seldom produce over forty bushels of wheat to the acre. For fear of ill success in growing Winter Wheat, they mostly depend upon Spring Wheat, and there can certainly no failures of the crops occur, if the soil is but properly tilled, that is to say, if you plough deep enough, not only three inches, but from three to six inches deep, which practice, though requiring more labor and expense, will amply recompense, and be of incalculable advantage to those who do not object to it. The result of the first crop is of greater importance to the new settler or beginner, than any of the subsequent ones, because at the beginning such heavy expenses will arise, that no one should neglect the somewhat exhausting labor of tearing open the sod turned round. Winter Wheat will then yield a splendid crop. On older land the culture of Winter Wheat deserves a particular attention, where the seed cast between the corn rows still on the field, is ploughed in with a three-shovel cultivator. Seldom as this last method is adopted, several years' practice have shown, that such winter seed is least exposed to freezing, because the dropping corn-leaves screen it exceedingly well, and the wheat soon overtops the stubble, so that at harvest-time, it forms no obstruction. One could certainly put in a great deal more wheat in this manner, if there would not usually be too much weed amongst the corn-rows, or if as it frequently happens, the wind had not broken or bent so many corn-stalks. Another fact which should not be left unobserved, is, that seed wheat should never be threshed with a machine, but should be carefully shelled to prevent its cracking; from a continued use of threshed wheat for seed, it becomes more and more degenerated every year, and the blasting or sickening in general, of the wheat designated for seed, may really be derived from the wrong method of threshing the same, it becoming spoiled by the thresher. Many kernels are broken or partially mashed, and can never produce a perfect crop, but on the contrary, render poorer and poorer every succeeding harvest.

OATS.

Oats are extensively grown in almost every part of the State, and never fail to produce a remunerating crop. In order to prevent their lodging or falling out, which they are apt to do soon after heading out, the farmer sows on corn land, and harrows in the crop, without using the plough, putting from two to three bushels on the acre. Mr. Jas. N. Brown, former Secretary of the State Agricultural Society, in a letter to the above named institution, says, that in his judgment, farmers are in the habit of putting too little seed of oats or other grain upon the acre; he thinks that if the land is too thinly sown, the deficiency resulting will be supplied by noxious weeds. The accounts of persons for many years engaged in farming, show that in some locations, only from 40 to 50 bushels of oats per acre have been obtained, while in other parts of the State, for example, in the vicinity of Springfield, from 60 to 80 bushels per acre, are obtained. It may not be a wrong suggestion that much depends on the quantity of seed oats planted in an acre; three bushels of seed will undoubtedly yield a more plentiful crop, than one and a half or two bushels, provided that the soil is well tilled.

BARLEY.

Barley is commonly sown after Indian Corn. It seldom thrives on newly-broken soil. A gravelly soil, which is light, warm, and sandy, is best fitted for it. It should be prepared as early as possible in the season.

The ground for barley, more than for any other grain, must be deeply ploughed and finely pulverized. Twice ploughing is necessary, and unless the soil is very light, it would be an advantage to have one ploughing done in the fall. Barley may be sown after corn, potatoes, or beans; it is sometimes sown after wheat or oats, but though the grain in this case is always finely colored, it is bad farming, and, except under peculiar circumstances, should never be done. The earlier it is done the better, but it is sometimes sown as late as the last of May.

No crop, perhaps, is benefitted so much by rolling as barley. Wood ashes are an excellent manure for barley. Fresh barn-yard manure should not be used. Well rotted manure from the yard, thoroughly mixed with the soil, will give the tender grain a quick and vigorous start, and add greatly to the yield. Dry weather, after sowing, is highly favorable to this crop, but wet weather is injurious.

On new prairie-land barley is not a profitable crop, unless the soil be deeply broken up in the fall, and then thoroughly worked in the spring, with a cultivator, or by light ploughing, so as not to disturb the sod. Barley is one of the best crops to sow grass-seeds with, and ranks among those species of grain which are much cultivated, and very successfully, in a portion of the State.

RYE.

Although rye is not extensively raised in Illinois, it cannot be denied that if the culture of it is properly managed, pretty good crops may here and there be obtained. Some farmers in St. Clair County and neighborhood, have, for some years past, been pretty successful with it. The farmers who live in the neighborhood of towns in this State, generally devote part of their land to the cultivation of it, in order to meet the demands of bakers.

BUCKWHEAT

Is an excellent crop, as far as it goes, and for the uses required. It is easily raised, requiring neither an over rich soil, nor a culture more particular than good management would demand for any crop. The best time for sowing it is the advanced part of the summer, when it will also work the destruction of the weeds; so that the culture of this crop is favorable for cleaning the fields.

It may be sown in the course of the month of June, and it has even been put in as late as the 4th of July, and good crops have been obtained. It is usual to sow about one bushel per acre, or a little less, broadcast, and cover with the harrow. It is better to roll the ground after sowing. By so doing the crop grows slow; but without careful management, will be liable to become foul with sand or earth, and thus injure the flour made from the grain. The ground should be well tilled; there is no other difficulty in the culture. The crop is cut with the cradle before frost, and should be raked very carefully on a dry day, to avoid dirt. It is advisable to set up the gavels on the beds for drying, and to carry them to the floor and thresh immediately. The crop is liable to heat if staked or packed closely in a mow, and the grain must be thoroughly cleaned, if it is desired to serve as food for human beings.

A correspondent of the Ohio Cultivator says, that he "has made experiments to render land designed for wheat-culture more fertile, breaking up and ploughing under buckwheat plantations." This seems to be a method which meets the general approbation of those who have ever made the same experiment, with care and attention.

HOPS.

This branch of agriculture comes more and more into use, and is very lucrative to the farmer, if he understands the proper and judicious management. Considering the great increase of the production of beer, it is not to be expected that the prices will ever be lower than twenty cents. The middle and southern parts of Illinois seem to be particularly favorable for the growing of hops. In the neighborhood of Belleville, and in Missouri, the most promising beginnings have been made in the culture of hops.

Deep, loamy soil, is best for hops, and good corn land is good hop land also. To prepare land for hops, plough nine or ten inches deep, the land to be furrowed the same as for corn. Hops have running roots, from one foot to three feet long, with joints or eyes to them. These roots are cut from the old hill, every spring, after they have been planted two years. The joints or eyes are two or three inches apart. These are the roots to be planted; they must be cut so as to have three joints to a piece, and put three pieces to a hill. They are covered three inches deep. The second year, the quantity and quality are likely to be as good as ever from the field. Hops are generally planted at a distance which gives eight hundred hills to the acre They twine around poles from thirteen to twenty feet long.

POTATOES.

In order to obtain good potatoes for seed, make choice of a small spot of arable, well-drained land—an eastern slope, and new land, are the best—ploughed early in the spring, and furrowed four or five inches deep, 2½ feet apart. Select middling-sized potatoes, which have touched the ground during the winter previous; but do not cut them. Drop one every eight inches along the furrows, and cover them by filling the furrows with earth. Then cover them with a top dressing of forest-leaves and straw, two inches deep. As soon as the tops of the young plants are two or three inches high, pass between them with a shovel plough, followed by a hoe, destroying the weeds and levelling the ground; do not hill. This is all you have to do until fall; when the ground begins to freeze, cover over with straw, chaff, or forest-leaves, six inches deep, to keep them from frost. Your potatoes will now have a chance to rest and ripen during the winter. In this way you will have the greatest yield and best quality. Continue this course from year to year, and the rot will not only disappear, but your crop will increase from 25 to 100 per cent.

The third year you may increase your field crop, by ploughing in fine manure.

In some parts of the State we learn that the rank growth of the crop has chiefly developed itself in the vines, which are luxuriant beyond precedent, while the essential root itself, the potatoe, is found, upon being pulled, to amount to almost nothing, being very small and poor. This, however, may be no sign of a bad crop, for strong vines are considered a proof of good potatoes. There is time enough yet for the roots to grow to their full size, and they probably will, if the vines continue in good health. The crop is a very large one, and if the yield proves to be abundant, the price will fall much below its present cost.

Mr. Albert Weinberger, a farmer of thorough experience, in Whitefield township, Marshall County, Illinois, gives good encouragement in speaking of his own potatoe growths; he says, that the average crops in his neighborhood may be laid down at about 100 bushels per acre, although he himself raised 150 bushels per acre last year, and so did several of the neighboring farmers, in spite of the more or less injurious influences of the weather during the summer; this is a very good crop. The average price of potatoes last year, in some markets of Illinois, was about fifty cents per bushel, and it is not an uncommon occurrence, that speculators make engagements for potatoes, even as early as the time of their planting.

In opposition to the system of planting potatoes late in the season, a communication was made to us by a farmer, that he raised no less than two hundred bushels of potatoes per acre, having planted them about the middle of May, that they should be well advanced by the time the hot weather comes on; or, according to his opinion, they may not be planted till after the middle of June, that they may have the benefit of the September rains. He says that last season, late planted potatoes in his neighborhood were almost an entire failure.

SWEET POTATOES.—*Convolvulus Batatas.*

These are now existing in a number of varieties. The roots are usually spindle-shaped and farinaceous; the vines are herbaceous, taking roots at intervals; the leaves are hastate, (cross-bow shaped), and consequently three-lobed. The flowers, which are few, are white externally, and purplish within. In Northern Illinois, only one variety succeeds perfectly, viz: the Nansemond, brownish-yellow, short variety, which can be grown as far north as the varieties of Indian corn.

The ground should be trench-ploughed, at least one foot deep, and the soil thoroughly pulverized; this should be done at the time of setting the plants, and is a principle to be observed in all hoed crops—to plant in newly-ploughed land. No manure should be used, as this gives an excess of vine at the expense of tuber, nor will the potatoes be so rich, for with high manuring, they incline to be watery.

The best seed-time is about the first of April, and as the season is usually pretty rough then, it is necessary to put the seed-potatoes in hot-beds, for sprouting, and then cover them with hay or straw, to shelter them from rain or snow, still much prevailing at that early season. About the first or middle of May, the plants will be several inches high, and should be transplanted as soon as no more danger of frost is to be feared. The ground into which they are then planted, and which has been prepared as above described, is laid off with a two-horse plough, in ridges about four feet wide.

These ridges are then divided with a hoe into hills the same distance apart, making four feet each way, so as to allow of culture with a shovel-plough both ways. The hills should be made large, like a two-bushel basket, though a little broader at the base; a small excavation is made with the hand in the top of the hill; at the bottom of which a plant is set in the usual way, and a little water is then poured in, to settle the earth about the plants; if ordinary care has been bestowed on them, very few will fail. In the after culture a shovel-plough is run through in both directions, which, with the aid of the trowel about the top of the hills, will keep the crop free from weeds. The shovel-plough not only kills the weeds, but by breaking the crust, admits the air to permeate the soil, which is of high importance to the fair growth of all tuberous-rooted plants. The crop should be worked in this way several times, until the vines too much obstruct the way, when little farther attention is required, except to raise the vines with a stick, or by the hand; since they then have a disposition to send down roots at the joints, which should not be permitted.

Being in possession of various accounts from persons in this State, who have been growing the sweet potatoe for several years, we are led to the conclusion, that even the rich, loamy, prairie soil, with its abundance of vegetable mould, yields pretty good average crops of this favorite variety of tuberous plants; while on the other hand it may be considered as a long established fact, that sandy loam answers the purpose still better.

No rotation with other crops is required in growing the sweet potatoe; it succeeds well year after year in the same place. The great advantage to be derived from this is, that a suitable place can be selected, in which every excellence is united. The principal objects are to have a place where the plants may enjoy much heat and sunshine, and where they are at the same time protected from cold winds and blasts.

It were to be wished that farmers and gardeners, even in the northern counties of this State, would give this vegetable the attention it deserves.

FLAX

Is grown to a certain extent in several parts of the State, as well as in most of the Western States of this country. It is not only the seed, but the fibre also, which makes this a plant of high value.

No country in the world presents so many and so great advantages for the production of flax, as our own. In any of the Western States, the seed will always pay the expenses of growing, and give to the grower the average profit of 50 to 75 per cent. The production of flax has sometimes been encouraged by manufacturers of woven goods in the Eastern States, for they have always been obliged to import their supplies of flax from Europe; and the prices paid for it, including the cost of transportation, duties, etc., makes the material pretty expensive before it reaches their hands; the question, therefore, arises, whether flax would not be much less expensive as a home product. There can be no doubt that it would—and great sums would be added to the present profits of flax-growing, which are only based upon the yields of flax-seed.

It is thought by some, that the growth of flax is injurious to the soil; but the experience of those who have paid complete and long attention to it, entirely contradicts this.

The soil best adapted to flax, is a rich, alluvial, or sandy loam, or a loose marl, neither too wet nor too dry. Upon poor, wet, or gravelly soils, it will not succeed, and manure should be applied on land of an inferior kind. Good wheat land will also be good for flax; soils of medium quality are best suited to its growth.

The ploughing should be done in fall, and the land be well drained, and repeatedly and carefully cleansed from weeds. In the spring the cultivator may be passed over the land to the depth of four or five inches; a light harrow may then be run over it. Then the land should be rolled and harrowed, to make a fine surface for the reception of the seed, and a firm and compact bottom.

The expense of preparing grass land directly for flax, may sometimes be too great, and it is therefore desirable that some other crop should intervene, of plants such as do not occupy the land long, and which during their growth want frequent stirring; such plants as beans, peas, &c., because the repeated stirring renders the mould soft and loose, and at the same time destroys the weeds which would otherwise do much damage to the flax.

The seed may be sown any time between the middle of April, and the middle of June; later sowing is not to be recommended, as the crop always blossoms in the month of July, and if sown later, the plant is short, and the fibre soft and brittle. The seed should be spread evenly, and, if possible, in moist weather.

The roots penetrate downward about half the length of the stem; and a soil of the above description, loose and loamy, should therefore be chosen for the cultivation of flax; a soil which is not liable, either to contain too much moisture, or to be too dry, but is capable of being well tilled, answers the purpose best. With regard to the choice of seed, it should be of a bright, brownish color, oily to the feel, and at the same time heavy. The seed from Holland not only ripens sooner, but it also yields more fibre than most others. American seed produces a common fine flax.

The quantity of seed required per acre is from two, to two and a half bushels, when sown broadcast. It may, however, be added, that with regard to the quantity of seed, much depends upon the quality of the soil, and also on the weather; for if too much seed is sown on rich and fertile land, the crop is in danger of lodging.

If the cultivation is performed in a proper manner, an acre of good soil will readily produce 20 bushels of this seed, which is worth from $1 50 to $2 per bushel, according to the quality.

In regard to the preparation of the flax, the following is to be observed: If we take straw, break it, and carefully examine it, it will be found to consist of three distinct parts; the centre is occupied by a sort of cellular tissue, having the appearance of wood; this is usually called the "shave," or "bean;" it is composed of bundles of long and tough fibres, the whole enveloped by a thin and delicate bark or skin.

The first process is called the "steeping," or "dew-rotting;" in this, the straw is spread on the grass, and carefully watered, sufficient moisture being supplied to support the action of fermentation in the tissues of the plant. This method, however, is very tedious, and requires several weeks for completion. The usual method is to immerse the straw, either in tanks or pits, constructed for the purpose, or in slowly-running streams. In a few days, a scum appears on the surface of the water, and is succeeded by the evolution of gaseous bubbles, arising from the decomposition, which is now actively at work.

Great care must then be taken to prevent this from proceeding too far, and effecting injury to the quality of the fibrous portion; it must be constantly watched, and removed as soon as the desired end has been attained. This is known immediately by a person of experience, from the manner in which the fibre separates from the straw, in breaking a portion of the stalk. Great judgment is required in determining the proper time for drawing the flax from the steep;—if the process has not been carried far enough, the fibre is coarse, and can only be used for the manufacture of the common goods.

The temperature of the steep is kept between 80 and 90 degrees.

BROOM CORN.

This corn is not very extensively cultivated, as yet, in the State, but the usefulness of it makes it a subject worth mentioning, as it may be cultivated in localities adapted for it. Mr. Beebe, a farmer near Platteville, Illinois, is known to have cultivated this corn for about three years, raising, however, but a small quantity, until last year, when he planted about 12 acres, and obtained an excellent crop. The soil best adapted for it seems to be the broken sod of an old prairie or pasture. Any soil which will serve for the cultivation of Indian corn, is equally adapted for Broom corn. It is not necessary to apply manure if the soil is but of a middling quality. Broom corn is considered to be a crop which will hardly fail, if it is not sown too late. The soil is prepared almost in the same manner as for Indian corn, but should be tilled a little more with the roller and cultivator, because the seed is smaller, requiring a more loosened soil for sprouting. The ridges are laid about three and a half feet distant from each other, so that the sun's rays may penetrate to the roots; the hills 18 inches apart; and from 10 to 12 kernels are taken for each hill. It is best to plant as early as the season will permit. As soon as the corn is grown high enough to distinguish the rows, it is worked with the cultivator and the hoe, not leaving more than four or five stalks to a hill; the hoeing is usually performed twice.

There are two methods of harvesting,—the one is, to cut the stalks as soon as they are ripe, to bring them to the barn, remove the seed, and place the stalks on planks for drying. In this manner the stalks preserve their original bright color, and the brooms bring a higher price. The other method is to let the crop stand until the seed is perfectly ripened, then to cut it and spread it on the field for two or three days, to get dry; it is then taken to the barn and put on scaffoldings, for thorough drying, in such a manner as to allow the air to pass freely over it, and to prevent its rotting. By following this latter method, from 30 to 50 bushels of good seed per acre are obtained, which are equal in value to the same quantity of oats, for feeding poultry, cows, sheep, etc. The average yield is about 400 brooms per acre—100 pounds of good brush make about 70 medium sized brooms.

The brush of Mr. Beebe's Broom corn crop, of last year, was of the finest order; and he was engaged during the fall in manufacturing brooms. He intends to build larger shops, and carry on the business on a more extensive scale. He is ready to furnish seed, and will purchase, next fall, all good Broom corn which may be offered him. It is beyond any doubt, that the raising of this corn, will soon prove very profitable for the farmers in this State, as well as for those who are engaged in the manufacture of brooms made of this domestic material About one peck of seed is required per acre.

CHOCOLATE CORN.

This seems to be a variety of the so-called "millet corn," and as it may, perhaps, be little known as yet, I take this opportunity of presenting to the reader the information that was given to me with regard to this corn, by Mr. Feussner, in St. Clair County, Illinois; he says:—"I raise a plant for my household use, which seems to be a variety of millet, having a black seed. The right name of it I have not been able to find—we call it "chocolate corn," a name which may be derived partly from the way in which it is used, and partly from the manner of its cultivation. We use it as a very delicious substitute for coffee; and it sometimes also serves us as a savory dish at our meals. It is easy of digestion, and tastes precisely like weak chocolate, and even resembles it in color. It is sown in the beginning of May; it ripens about the beginning of September, and is not affected by light night-frosts. This plant is cultivated like Indian corn or potatoes; the seed, if sown, is covered but one inch high. The hills are to be kept apart a distance of three or four feet, and from five to seven plants are left to each hill.

"The preparation of a beverage from this corn, is accomplished in the following manner:—

"We want for our table four pints of chocolate; we take one and a half ears, nearly filling the funnel of our coffee-mill, which is about 4¼ inches wide, and 1¾ inches high, and grind the kernels a little fine; having proceeded thus far, we mix the ground substance with two pints of water, and boil it until the starch contained in it forms into a lump, the liquid is then passed, to separate it from the grains, through a fine wire sieve, or tin colander; two pints of sweet milk, from which the cream has been skimmed, and a good tablespoonful of common powdered sugar, and a little cinnamon are then added to the decoction; it is now boiled once more, and a most delicious beverage, which is scarcely distinguishable from light chocolate, is ready for use. If you wish to improve it still further, you may add an egg, and a little nutmeg."

If this corn could gradually be brought to serve as a substitute for coffee, considerable sums which are every year paid for this latter article would be saved.

CHINESE YAM. (*Dioscorea Batatas.*)

This tuber has not been cultivated, as yet, in the State; but as it can be raised in Illinois, we think it a duty to call the attention of the farmers and settlers to it.

From a report made by the agricultural division of the Patent Office, it appears that this variety of tuber has lately been introduced into the United States, for experiment.

The method of cultivation as adopted by the Chinese, appears to be easy and simple.

"In the autumn, they select the smallest tubers, preserving them from injury by frost, by covering them in a pit with earth and straw. The spring succeeding they plant them near each other, in a trench, in well prepared soil. When they have put forth shoots, one or two yards in length, the joints and leaves, containing the buds, are cut off and planted for reproduction. For this purpose, they form the ground into ridges, on the top of which a shallow trench is made with the hand, or some suitable implement, in which these joints are planted, covered slightly with finely pulverized earth, with the leaves rising just to the surface. Should it rain the same day, they shoot immediately; if not, they must be gently watered, until they do so. In fifteen or twenty days, they give birth to new tubers and stalks, the latter of which it is necessary to remove from time to time, to prevent them from taking root on the sides, and thus injuring the development of the tubers already formed."

By the report of the gentleman to whom the yam was sent for experiment, we learn that it is growing finely, promises an abundant yield, and appears to be well adapted to the soil and climate.

Another communication, received from a gentleman in the State of

Illinois, with regard to the "Yam," treats this interesting subject as follows:

"I cannot forbear to make mention of a plant, which may probably soon take its way to our Western States, and to which the general attention may already be directed, since it promises to bring greater benefits to the Eastern as well as to the Western Hemisphere, than perhaps any other plant heretofore known. A 'Yam' tuber of the variety above mentioned, was sent some six years ago by the French Consul, M. de Montigny, at Shanghai, to Paris, where it was planted and cultivated with much care. From thence plants were sent to America."

Mr. Prince, on Long Island, has already obtained a full crop of yams. The accounts of Professor Decaines, at Paris, the Chinese and Japanese news, and the opinions of Mr. Prince, and others, establish this point, that the plant may be grown in all countries where potatoes succeed well. It does not suffer from frost, when kept in the ground, and may be preserved in cellars, in good and sound condition, for ten months. It is easy to transplant and increase it, and it is sure to give abundant yields, even on a small, but well cultivated piece of land. It is not liable at all to disease or rot, and is more nutritive, healthy, and palatable, than our common potatoe, and seems to be designed to become the nourishment of many people.

Small, sound tubers of the "Chinese Yam," are sold at $6 per dozen, sent by mail, if ordered soon, at Ellwanger & Barry's, Mount Hope Nurseries, Rochester, New York.

GRASSES.

This State, especially in the central part, may properly be considered a good grass-growing region. The cultivation of *tame grass*, was, in former years, when farmers were yet scarce, and the surrounding prairies still afforded a sufficiency of grass for hay-making, not deemed to be necessary, and was entered on by but few, till it was found that in the course of time, the natural prairie-grass in the neighborhood of farms, remarkably diminished by the pasturing of cattle. Farmers then came to the conclusion that the raising of grass crops would be highly important and even very necessary for them. The varieties generally grown are clover and timothy.

In order to get a permanently good pasture, it is necessary to cultivate the old land for some time in corn, wheat, and other grain, as by this method, the wild properties of the soil, the weeds, and the wild grass, will be effectually destroyed. For this, six or seven years' good tillage of the land that is to be prepared for grass, is required; and such land, if after this time sown with clover, may serve exceedingly well as pasture for 5 or 6 years. The sod may then be broken again, and the same rotation, commencing with the cultivation of grain, be repeated. In some parts of the State, timothy is better adapted for permanent pastures than clover. If timothy is on rich and good soil, two crops may be obtained; one mowing is then performed in the earlier part of the summer, and another, in the latter part of it.

The best time for sowing grass is considered to be in the month of March; at least this may be the case in Central Illinois, while in more northern regions it may perhaps be more advisable to sow a little later. Some farmers in Central Illinois mix their grass-seeds together, and sow at the rate of one-third clover, and two-thirds timothy, using one bushel of clover, and two bushels of timothy, on twelve or thirteen acres. Stock should not be suffered to run on grass during March and April. If the seeds are not mixed, the average quantities required for sowing are about as follows: clover, one bushel to ten acres; timothy, one bushel to five acres.

Blue grass is also cultivated, but not so extensively as clover and timothy.

Mr. Weinberger, a farmer in Marshall County, directs our attention to a variety which is known by the name of Millet grass. This variety would deserve greater attention if it were perennial, but it is only a one year's plant, and therefore must be sown every year. The variety was made known and cultivated some years since in that county, and is very valuable, not only for the excellence of the blade, but also for its seeds, which are in fair demand. Dry land is best adapted for its growth; it grows to the height of seven or eight feet. If much attention is to be bestowed on the *seed*-crop of millet, it is better to sow the seed broad-cast, since this will promote a fuller development of the seeds. But if a good *hay*-crop is expected, one may sow thicker; the stalks will thus be prevented from growing too hard and coarse. The average yields of this variety may be about four tons of hay per acre, and twenty bushels of seed.

FRUIT CULTURE.

THE culture of fruit has for many years been carried .on more or less extensively, in those parts of this State in which the localities appeared to be adapted. In Middle and Southern Illinois, orchards have existed for a long while, and even in the north of this State, near the Lake Michigan, the culture of some kinds, especially the apple, has been attended with pretty good success. The principal varieties of fruit grown in Illinois, are, the apple, peach, pear, quince, plum, &c.

The State Fair held at Springfield, last year, offers great inducements to *pomologists* and fruit-growers in general. The most beautiful specimens of apples and other fruit were there to be seen, and several premiums were awarded.

THE APPLE.

The apple, as a tree, as well as a fruit, is said to have reached a high degree of perfection in some parts of Central and Southern Illinois. The crops raised in a year of abundance are often superior to the best crops obtained in the States of New York, Pennsylvania, and Ohio, both in quality and in quantity.. It is an established fact, that each desirable variety of the apple has its own latitude, in which it attains its highest perfection, and that every departure from this particular latitude depreciates, in a greater or less degree, the value of the fruit. The orchards in the State contain, for the most part, grafted fruit alone. The soil best adapted for planting apple-trees is a mixture of loam, mould, and lime; a sloping hill is preferable to a level place. Among the numerous varieties, may be mentioned as the most approved: *Red June, Early Harvest, Tops of Wine, Sine qua non, Rambo, Newark, Pippin, Alexander, Fameuse, Golden Pippin, Æsopus Spitzenberg, Yellow Bellflower, Priestley, Long Green, Nonpareil, Red Baldwin, Newton Pippin, Lansinburg, Michael Henry,* and *Pippin.* The best cider is obtained from the Virginia, and Siberia Crab.

Sweet apples are more nourishing and healthy than acid ones. For feeding stock of all kinds, an orchard of sweet apples is as profitable as anything which the land will produce.

The following are good kinds for planting: *Early Golden Sweet, Hog Island Sweet, Ramsdell Sweet, Pound* or *Pumpkin Sweet, Tolman's Sweet, Peach Pond Sweet,* &c. With regard to the crops, it may be said that they are sometimes very remunerating. Examples may be given, where single trees have yielded from five to ten dollars a year in fruit. Apple trees are generally transplanted from the nurseries after one year's growth, at which time they will be from three to four feet high.

Apple trees, to any amount, and of all varieties, can be had in our nurseries from 12½ to 15 cents a-piece.

THE PEACH.

With regard to the peach tree, it may be said that, in some portions of this State, it may be cultivated with considerable success, while here and there, in the northern regions, it is liable to be killed by the winter. The reason for this may be attributed to the tenderness of the tree, which is of eastern origin. Some peach-growers are of opinion that seedling peach trees are more successful in their growth than those raised from buds, and that it is the better plan to continue them through seeds.

The peach is considered rather an uncertain crop in North Illinois. The failures of crops usually arise from the winter killing of the fruit-buds.

A dry soil, containing but few organic substances, seems to be best adapted for peach trees. Mr. Harkness, a farmer in Peoria County, who, from his personal experience, knows the results of the fruit-crops in that portion, during more than twenty years, thinks that the peach tree, when cultivated, is not sufficiently cared for, and that it is not always planted in a sufficiently sheltered situation; therefore its blossoms will sometimes freeze in early spring. It is, however, not only the spring frost, but also a certain degree of severe frost during the winter, which is injurious to the peach tree, but if no damage of such kind has been done to the trees, they are sure to yield very full and abundant crops; and this will be still more the case if there be some little cultivation on such peach lands, in a bearing year; the cultivation needed, is a loosening and stirring up of the ground a little in the early part of the summer. Young trees often commence to bear in their third year. The peach, more than any other kind of tree, can stand great drought.

There are but few farmers who are entirely without peach trees, and they are found both wild and grafted. The principal varieties known in Illinois, are: 1. The *Clingstone*, or *Plum Peach*, which is juicy, aromatic, and hard. 2. The *Freestone Peach*, white, with a loose stone; and 3, the *Nectarine*, plum-like, with a smooth skin; very delicious, but a little difficult to raise.

THE PEAR.

Although the pear is not frequently seen in this State, it may, in some districts, be found as large, as fine flavored, and as perfect in every respect, as anywhere in the United States. The pear, we know from good authority, to have certainly been reared in western nurseries, some fifty years ago, and even for a longer time. Some men are not in favor of growing pears, from the mere prejudiced opinion that they do not promise a crop sufficiently profitable to make it worth while to cultivate this fruit. There is certainly much truth in the assertion, that the trunks and larger branches of the pear tree are frequently affected by the blight, and that then a large portion of the standard pear trees, which have come into bearing, are swept away. Those which have been but partly destroyed, will sometimes revive and begin to bear again. For planting, one should be careful to select a place where the soil is not too dry, and heavy rather than too light and too mellow; the trunks and roots should then be well screened from the influence of the heat, at noon. As manure, urine, soap-water, bones, ashes, etc., may be used. As a reason for the dying of the trees, carelessness in the treatment has been alleged, and a farmer whom we met, said that the destruction is caused by a neglect in the proper setting and trimming, and insufficient protection from insects. Good varieties of pears are not much found in our markets, and comparatively high prices are paid for them, on account of their scarcity;

yet it should be remembered that it does not cost much more to grow a good quality of pears, than of apples. A sound, bearing tree, will produce almost as much fruit as an apple tree, and it will live many years. There are now more than eighty distinct varieties cultivated in this country, many of which may be had at every nursery.

The principal varieties known in this State, are: the *Bartlett*, the *Bergamotte*, the *Beurre*, the *Basse*, the *Napoleon*, the *Virguleuse*, the *St. Germain*, the *Pound Pear*, the *Dix*, the *Seckel*, etc.

THE QUINCE.

As far as it has hitherto been cultivated, the quince seems to be hardy and productive. It is a small tree, or large shrub, is very slow in coming to a bearing condition, but is one among the oldest fruit-trees known in the country. Some very good and plentiful crops have already been produced, in cases where proper management has been bestowed.

THE PLUM.

The cultivation of the plum, as a grafted fruit-tree, has not as yet become so extensive as to give much for experience to say on the subject. A fruit-grower in Peoria County says, that in that region, wild plums were, for eight or ten years after the settlement of the country, found in great abundance. During the progress of civilization, he says, came the plum *Curcusio*, and now one will not meet with a sound wild plum in a whole season. Our cultivated plum trees grow well and blossom abundantly; the young fruit is often very promising, but the insect above named is so universal, that very little of it ever comes to maturity. North of latitude 41° the *Curcusio* is not so troublesome, and, in those parts, plums have therefore been cultivated in many places with success.

The climate best adapted to the plum, seems to be nearly distinct from that suited to the peach. North of latitude 41° is the proper region of the plum.

THE PRUNE.

This variety of fruit is of German origin, and among fruit-growers the opinion has been prevalent, that it degenerates in this country, and that a fruit would be produced which in shape and quality would perfectly resemble our common plum, but this has been fairly refuted by an experienced fruit-grower, who goes as far as to protest that within his own knowledge and experience, prune crops have even surpassed apple crops, and that splendid results have been attained with imported young trees. This must necessarily lead to the conclusion that both soil and climate, in this country, are exceedingly good for the culture of this fruit. It may also be observed that the prune tree is one of the fruit-trees which do not suffer from frost, and that its fine appearance makes it desirable as an ornament, in gardens.

THE CHERRY.

Most of the large wood cherries grow so fast as to be liable to winter kill, and can only be grown with success on thin, poor soil, or in a grass plat. The Morilles, and May Cherries, are hardy and productive. It is a great drawback, that a large portion of the crop is consumed by the birds.

The principal varieties of cherries are, the *Mayduke*, the *Early Whiteheart*, the *Late Duke*, &c.

The Blackberry is abundant and fine in all the groves where the timber has been partly cut away.

The Raspberry. The black variety is common in the open woods, but the red is not found here, except as a cultivated plant; where planted, it thrives and grows luxuriantly. There are several varieties, foreign as well as domestic, well known in this State.

The Strawberry. The prairie soil is well adapted for the cultivation of this delicious berry, which may at the same time be found in very great abundance, growing in the woods, in a wild state. Several experiments which were made with the cultivation of the strawberry, have proved, that apple orchards are very proper places for planting them, especially for those northern varieties, the leaves of which are much affected by very hot sunshine. If strawberry plants of almost any variety are planted upon orchard land, (no matter how close the trees stand, for the shade is not at all injurious, but on the contrary, quite beneficial to strawberry growth,) a crop of about 25 or 30 bushels may be obtained upon an acre. The varieties most admired are the *Hovey's Seedling*, *Mammoth Alpine*, *Burr's*, *New Pine*, *Black Prince*, and *Hudson*.

The Currant. This bush grows exceedingly well and vigorously, and should be shaded a little from the intense heat of the sun, that it may mature well. The common red currant gives the highest yield, but requires a cool situation, and a moistened, loose soil.

The Gooseberry. It is not much found in the southern part of this State, and requires almost the same properties of soil as the currant bush. The berry, as it grows hereabouts, is smooth and of medium size. It is found in abundance in the groves, but is much improved by cultivation. Some of the large foreign sorts are subject to mildew, but the natives and smaller class of imported sorts, flourish and bear well.

The Cranberry will succeed very well in the most northern parts of Illinois, on a swampy soil.

Nurseries. The number of nurseries in this State is truly a matter of astonishment. In Northern Illinois, nurseries are found capable of supplying the surrounding country with apple, as well as other fruit, and ornamental trees, and flowering plants. And yet, more trees are planted from Eastern nurseries, than from home establishments. It is a fact, however, that as far as our principal variety—the apple—is concerned, the eastern trees are worth less, and cost much more than those of the same size or age at home. They are worth less, because usually more attenuated in form, and unacclimated here, and when badly handled—which is often the case with those peddled about the country—they have less vitality, and are more apt to die, or become diseased; and they cost more, because heavy charges and large commissions have to be added to the nursery price. It is known that eastern apple trees, which are "peddled" through the West, at from 20 to 30 cents per tree, are bought East at from $80 to $100 per thousand.

The principal nurseries in the State of Illinois, are:

The *Grove Nursery*, of J. & O. Kennikott, at West Northfield, Cook County, office No. 47 Clarkson Street, Chicago.

The *Lake Nursery*, at Waukegan, Robert Douglas, proprietor; this nursery is thirty-five miles north of Chicago, on the Chicago and Milwaukie Railroad.

The *Franklin Grove Nursery*, A. R. Whitney, proprietor. Franklin Grove, Lee County, is located but one mile south of Franklin Station, on the Chicago and Dixon Air Line Railroad.

The *Pleasant Ridge Nursery*, Perry Aldrich, proprietor, five miles east of Hennepin, one mile east of Swaney, on the Hennepin and Indiantown road, town of Aripze, Bureau County.

The *Bloomington Nursery*, F. K. Phœnix, proprietor, at Bloomington, Ill.

The *Kankakee Nursery*, at Kankakee, Ill. McGrew, Leas & Co., proprietors, where first-rate Osage plants for hedging may be had at reasonable prices.

The *Dupage Nurseries*, Lewis Ellsworth & Co. proprietors, at Naperville, Dupage County, Ill.

The *Persimmon Grove Nursery*, at Princeton, Bureau County, Ill., Arthur Bryant, proprietor.

In any of the above-mentioned establishments, fruit trees of good parentage and germ, as well as shrubs, and various plants for hedging and ornamental purposes, may be had; and all those that are engaged in the cultivation of choice trees or plants, will do well to get their supplies as little away from these places as possible.

GRAPE CULTURE.

AFTER many tiresome attempts that have been made in the west and southwest of the United States, to promote this important branch of culture, it may now be considered as a department of national agriculture, whose progress cannot be checked.

Experiments in the cultivation of the grape were made many years ago in this State; it appears that the first trials to introduce it were made in the years 1830 to 1836, in the neighborhood of Belleville, by Germans, who had emigrated to this country from the banks of the Rhine. They at first only planted such varieties as may be found on the banks of the Rhine. These grape vines grew but poorly, for some years bore very little fruit, and gradually died away. This want of success created discouragement. It was generally believed that the climate of that part of the country was altogether unfavorable to the grape, and hence no farther attention was bestowed on that branch of agriculture, until a few years since, when it became known that the grape culture, near Cincinnati, made rapid and encouraging progress. Therefore in the years 1845 to 1847, this culture was resumed by the grape-growers near Belleville, and for that purpose they had some cuttings of the American *Catawba* sent to them from Cincinnati. The Catawba derives its name from a variety growing wild near the Catawba River. The soil near Belleville, and that in St. Clair County, seems to be particularly adapted for the grape, since it is a sandy loam, containing neither too little nor too much moisture. The open prairie-land seems to be less adapted for grape culture, and this may frequently prove so, on account of the too great fertility and richness of the soil. With regard to the best mode of cultivation, it should be remembered that it is not necessary to lay out the land in ridges, by trench ploughing. It will be sufficient to dig holes two feet square, or to make them three feet long, and two feet deep.

In a vineyard newly laid out, the principal object is to keep the ground cleansed of weeds; but as soon as the vines have attained their full size, it is sufficient to plough and hoe the land twice a year; the first time in spring, and again soon after the vintage. If, in the meantime, the weeds should grow too high, they should be cut off with the sickle. The tillage of the soil should be deferred until after the middle of May, when no more injurious night-frosts are to be dreaded. These are the most important suggestions concerning the tillage; as to the treatment of the vines themselves, let it not be forgotten that the stocks should be planted from six to eight feet apart; this open space, as may be easily conjectured, will cause them to grow strong, vigorous, and productive of good and plentiful crops.

The two principal home varieties, are the *Isabella* and the *Catawba*. The former is more adapted to northern latitudes, from 42° upwards, while the latter grows better in a southern region, perhaps not much above 37°.

Of distinguished foreign varieties, the *Rhenish Grape*, originating on the banks of the Rhine, and first grown in this country in the State of Ohio, near Cincinnati, deserves to be mentioned. A farmer in Peoria County obtained a few samples of this kind, and says that they have produced a fair crop of grapes, fifteen seasons in seventeen. It has a considerable resemblance to the Isabella, in appearance and flavor, but the vine is of much slower growth, and very hardy. The destruction to which grapes are more or less exposed, is caused by the rot, produced by excessive rains, followed by very sultry weather. If the winter lasts very long, the frost will sometimes affect, and even kill the buds, without, however, injuring the vines. The best quality of wine, which may be had at Belleville, is the Catawba wine, which is far superior to any other kind grown in the United States. That the grape culture is quite remunerating near Belleville, and even a little farther north, is confirmed by the statements of most of the growers there. One of these informs us that from two acres of land, which have been in a bearing condition since 1850, he obtained 640 gallons in the first year, and 652 gallons in 1853; this, however, shows only the richest crops he obtained in the course of six years; but though the vines may have yielded but half as much at other times, it will still leave a handsome average yield—about 160 gallons per acre.

The market price of the Catawba is from two to three dollars a gallon.

The rot, and the mildew, to which the grapes are more or less subject, may be diminished by very careful treatment in the cultivation, as well as a judicious selection of the locality. If we consider the difficulties and risks attending the cultivation of foreign grapes, which may either degenerate or prove to be failures, it will doubtless appear a better plan to bestow a little more attention on the grafting of those wild varieties of grapes, which nature allows to grow and thrive freely in the Mississippi valley. This enterprise has already been started by a few people, who commenced their researches last year, going to the Ozark Mountains, as far as Springfield. They gathered whatever they thought valuable of the kind, and returned with five new varieties of grape vines, and a quantity of seed. Not a little work and labor were expended in rendering useful these wild children of nature.

The most valuable varieties thus discovered are:

1. The *Halifax* vine, a native of the east; the grapes are pretty large, of good, rather peculiar flavor.

2. The *Wine Home* vine, was found growing wild in a rocky place; the dark grapes are of medium size, and the juice nearly colorless.

3. The *Waterloo*, or *Rockhouse Indian* vine, growing wild in the neighborhood of Waterloo, Ill. This vine grows very luxuriantly, and has a rough appearance. The little grapes are close together, and contain a very dark colored juice. This grape ripens about the middle of October. The wine has a fine, bright, reddish-blue color, and strongly resembles the best Burgundy.

4. The *Ozark Muscat* wine, from the Ozark Mountains; in appearance it is similar to No. 2. The grape tastes like nutmeg, a peculiarity which is not shared by the wine.

5. The *Little Ozark* vine. The whole plant has a bright and fresh appearance; the dark and long clusters nestle close under the shining, green leaves, and not a rotten berry is to be seen on the whole stock. They ripen about the beginning of October.

6. The *Ozark Seedling*. Most of the seedlings reared from the seeds gathered in the Ozark Mountains, after some years proved to be

unpromising varieties. The grapes are a little larger than those of the varieties above named.

It is to be hoped that the cultivation of the grape, certainly the most valuable of all fruits, will be extended more and more throughout the west and southwest of the United States; and it is beyond all doubt, that those who engage in this business will be amply rewarded.

GROWING OF TIMBER.

THERE is not so much wood in this State as there is in the Eastern States, and in some districts a scarcity of fuel, of fencing and building material, may be noticed. The prairies do not exhibit impenetrable forests, but are only interspersed with groves of limited extension. Upon first viewing the vast prairie-lands, it would seem that there must be something in the soil of the prairies which is hostile to the growth of trees, and yet a careful comparison would detect no difference in the qualities of the soil where timber grows, and where it grows not. The small groves at the head of streams, and along the river banks, were sufficient for the wants of the first settlers, but these were far from sufficient for fencing the vast prairies; and it was plain, that whatever should be used as a fencing material, must be grown upon the soil. The prairie is well supplied with all the elements necessary to the growth of the most gigantic trees.

The following varieties have been cultivated with success:

American White Pine,	Yellow, or Pitch Pine,	Hemlock,
Balsam Fir,	Silver Spruce,	White Cedar,
European Larch,	Austrian Pine,	Pinus Maritima
Norway Spruce,	Black Locust,	Yellow Poplar, (Tulip Tree.)
American Chestnut,	American Birch,	Yellow Birch,
Weeping Willow,	Alanthus,	Osier Willow,
Black Spruce,	American Larch,	Black Birch.

All these trees have done well upon the prairie soil, and most of them grow with a vigor astounding to those who have only seen them upon the barren lands of their native localities. The prairie farmer, if he be a lover of beautiful trees, need not long be without them. He can surround his farm with a belt of evergreens, at a trifling expense; this will add greatly to its beauty and value. The nurseries in the West as well as in the East, can supply him with almost every variety of trees for his lawn, or his timber plantation.

While some counties of this State possess but few attractions for settlers, being destitute of timber, other districts, Marshall County, for example, afford a sufficiency of timber to meet the wants of new settled farmers, whom they therefore attract.

As a building material, the Locust deserves to be recommended for its durability; used for posts it will last from fifty to a hundred years.

The cultivation of timber on the prairies as a shelter, is highly important.

As very rapid growers, and of an immediate effect, the following varieties are recommended; they have been successfully cultivated:—the *Soft Maple*, the *Golden Willow*, the *Butternut*, and the *Black Walnut*.

Such as wish to have the very best kinds, should take Evergreens, of which the *Norway Spruce*, the *Hemlock*, and *American Arbor*, are the most desirable for screens.

The cultivation of the *Locust*, of which we spoke before, is performed as follows:—The seeds, if new, may be made to vegetate readily, by being placed in a vessel in which some hot water has been poured; the water is then turned off, and the seeds are mixed with a little sand, and placed in a box, in which condition they are to be exposed to the rains and frosts of the winter and spring. About the middle of April, sift the sand, and plant the seeds in a well-prepared soil, about one inch deep, in rows three or four feet apart, so as to admit the passage of the cultivator between them. By fall, if the trees are properly cultivated, they will be from three to five feet high. The following spring, prepare by ploughing and harrowing the ground well; lay off the ground with a plough in rows, six or eight feet apart. Dig the brier carefully, cut off at one-third or one-half their height from their tops, and lay them into the furrows, putting the roots of one close to the top of another, covering the roots eight inches deep, letting the tops gradually rise to within one inch of the surface. The first and second years the ground should be ploughed and kept clean from weeds, after which the ploughing may be discontinued.

The Willow Tree. Some people think, and they may perhaps not be wrong, that these trees are as profitable as plums, peaches, &c

Willow wands have for some time been in fair demand, and our markets can by no means be sufficiently supplied from our home produce. The amount of wands annually imported from Germany and France, is variously stated to be from five to six millions of dollars worth.

It will be seen with regard to willow trees, that they readily grow in the vicinity of swamps or pools, or properly speaking, in places that can hardly be used for anything else.

The prairie soil must, to a certain extent, be very well adapted for willows, as there are many marshes or "sloughs" within the prairie region.

There is a variety called the "*Osier Willow*," which is used in the manufacturing of baskets, chairs, cradles, &c. The raw material for all this work is imported from Europe. The manufacture is mostly confined to foreigners. If our enterprising farmers would commence its culture they would find it very useful for many purposes. As the material for a hedge or fence, it could be used with advantage, by weaving together the stalks and branches.

Before concluding this chapter, it will not be amiss to make a few remarks about the right season for cutting timber. The method frequently pursued in woodlands, is to girdle or deaden the trees, in July or August, when the sap is up, and after a few years the decay in their limbs and body will be so great, that the trees can be cleared up, and the land put in corn. When girdled during the winter months, when the sap is down, the decay will not be half so rapid. Hickory and ash timber for wagon-work is generally cut in July, and left on the ground for use until winter. The peeling of timber designed for rails has sometimes been advocated, as improving the durability, but the durability may perhaps depend on the period at which the timber is cut; for it has been ascertained that timber cut towards the end of May, or at the beginning of June, is exempt from the worms, whether it be peeled or left with the bark on.

THE MACLURA HEDGE.

THE first settlers of the country, who took good care to locate as near the groves as practicable, had no difficulty in enclosing their farms with the heavy worm-fence. But when the prairies became settled, rail-timber soon began to grow scarce and dear, and in many places it was plain there was not timber to be had for reconstructing the fences already built. The great and only remedy for this want of timber is now seen to be the formation of live hedges, in the place of rails or boards. And after a fair trial of various shrubs and trees, foreign and native, it is now universally conceded that the Maclura, or Osage Orange, is the best known plant for a living hedge on the prairies. This opinion is not founded upon mere theory, or partial experiments. Hedge planting has already become a regular branch of business.* The Maclura hedges which have been planted four years or more, have become a fixed, tangible, and well established reality. There is no mistake about their being respectable barriers against the intrusion of domestic animals of every kind. This wild orange, of which the hedges are made, is very similar in appearance to the orange of the tropics.

* Among the gentlemen whose business is Osage Orange planting, we note Messrs. McGrew, Leas & Co., of Kankakee City, and Messrs. W. A. Allender & Co., of Lawrence Co. The first named firm charges for plants of one and two years growth, from $2 to $3 per thousand, according to quality and amount. 100,000 plants to one order, boxed and delivered at railroad depot, for $2 per thousand, for those of one year; $2 50 per thousand, for two years old. The latter firm charges for setting, resetting, (if necessary) pruning, cultivating, and completing a perfect hedge, 60 cents per rod, payable in rates of 20 cents at the time of setting, and yearly 10 cents, the balance when completed. The farmer has to prepare the ground, to board hands while setting and attending the hedge, and to protect it from all damage by stock, or other injury.

The leaves are a little more pointed, but have the rich gloss, and deep green peculiar to the cultivated plant. They are, in truth, very beautiful. The fruit is not edible, but is large, showy, and very full of seeds. The oldest plants in Illinois are now in full bearing. Branches full of fruit were exhibited at the recent State Fair, so that the necessity of importing seeds from Arkansas and Texas, will soon be abolished.

The merits of the Osage Orange as a hedge-plant, may be briefly summed up as follows:

1st. The seeds may be obtained in any desirable quantity, at a cost of ten to twenty dollars per bushel, and a bushel of seeds will produce from 80,000 to 120,000 plants.

2d. The seeds, when properly treated, are as certain to germinate as seed-corn.

3d. The young plants are rarely, if ever, attacked by insects, and will grow large enough in one season to plant out in hedge-rows.

4th. No plant bears removal better than the Osage Orange. Hence an even and uniform start in the hedge-row is attained without difficulty.

5th. The growth of the hedge where the land has been properly prepared and cultivated, is very rapid. A good fence, fit to line the public highway, is often obtained in two years and a half after planting.

6th. The wood is durable, as much so as cedar, and both the leaves and the wood are as yet free from the depredations of insects.

7th. When pruned, it will always throw out sprouts from the extreme points of the living wood.

8th. It never throws up any suckers from the roots, but always sprouts at or above the collar—of course it will never spread off on each side of the hedge-row, as many varieties of hedge-plants will do.

9th. The spines are strong, durable, and very offensive to all domestic animals. Hence no animal familiar with its appearance will touch it.

10th. It will grow on any soil, where any description of timber will grow.

Regarding the culture of the plant itself for the purpose of hedging, the following rules and directions, laid down by practical farmers, and evidently the fruit of much observation and experiment, should be adhered to.

Seed should only be procured from a responsible source, and great care should be taken in its selection. The most certain way of testing it is to take a tumbler and fill it two-thirds full of warm water, then put cotton enough into it to keep whatever seed you put on it just above the surface of the water; the cotton in this way will remain wet, and keep the seed moist, and yet the seed will get air, and if kept in a warm room it will soon vegetate. The water may have to be renewed several times during the process.

The best method of sprouting seed is as follows: Soak the seed in warm water at least for forty hours; (an entire week, if possible,) then put it in shallow boxes, not more than four or five inches deep. To every bushel of seed put one half bushel of sand, (smaller quantities in proportion), then mix it thoroughly, keep it in a warm place, and wet it as often as twice per day with warm water, and stir it thoroughly, as often as three times a day. A more frequent stirring would be better. The seed should be put to soak about the fifteenth or twentieth of April, at a temperature of from sixty-five to seventy degrees. Seed attended to as above described, and kept in a warm place, at a proper temperature, would sprout sufficiently in ten days to be put into the ground. It is necessary, however, to have the seed well separated before planting. Much care should be taken in the selection of a good piece of ground for the nursery, or place of planting the seed. The ground should be fresh, fertile, and free from the seed of weeds and grass. It should be mellow, not subject to bake, and rather inclined to be wet than otherwise. Good prairie, that has been broken the year previous, is undoubtedly preferable to any other ground. The ground should be well ploughed, harrowed, and rolled, if necessary. When the ground has been thus prepared and well pulverized, the most expeditious way of making the drills is to obtain a common wheat drill, and take out one-half of the planters. Have large points put upon those that are used in making the drills; the points or shovels upon the planters, about five inches in width, of the same shape as the common points. The drills made in this way will be sixteen inches apart, and by putting weights upon the drag bars, the drills can be made of sufficient size and depth. They will be regular, and it is a very expeditious manner of making the drills. The seed must then be drilled in the above described drills or furrows, by hand, putting one quart to three or four square rods, which would amount to from one and a quarter to one and a half bushels per acre. The covering can best be done with light steel rakes. The hands engaged in covering should walk upon the side where the seed is covered; by so doing, they would draw all the earth one way, in filling up the drills and covering the seed. When the planting, as above described, has been finished, nothing more is necessary to be done until the plants begin to come up in sufficient numbers to indicate the situation of the drills. The space between the drills should then be hoed, and the weeds and grass in the rows, among the plants, pulled out by hand. This process of hoeing the spaces between the rows, and weeding the rows, should be repeated as often as necessary to keep the weeds down, and the ground loose, and in good condition. If the soil is good, the season favorable, and the proper cultivation given them, they will be sufficiently large for transplanting the following spring.

The process of taking them up is as follows: A subsoil plough should be used to cut them off; the share of the plough should be steel, quite large, and as flat as possible; the depth of its running can be regulated by a wheel in front, at the end of the beam. Cutting them off in this way, the larger portion of them will remain standing in their place until they are gathered by hand. They should be cut off about eight or ten inches below the surface of the ground. They can then be gathered into bundles, and the roots covered to keep them moist, after which they can be taken out, assorted, tied up in bundles of fifty or a hundred, and the tops cut off upon a block with an axe, or hatchet. They are then ready for boxing and shipping. In boxing them, the boxes should not be too tight, for some air is necessary to prevent them from moulding. Small boxes, and those of moderate size, are best—say about eighteen or twenty inches wide, about the same depth, and three or three and a half feet long. The plants may be packed in the most convenient way.

We now come to the setting of the hedge. The ground should be thoroughly broken up, to the depth of twelve or fourteen inches; the space broken at least ten feet wide, and the hedge set in the centre, would leave five feet to be cultivated upon each side. When a hedge is to be set along an old fence-row, the fence ought to be moved the year previous, and the ground broken up and cultivated. It would then be in a better condition to receive the hedge. After the ground has been fully prepared, it is necessary to stake off the row, and draw a line to work by. The hole for inserting the plants should be made with a dibble, twelve inches in length, and three and a half inches in diameter at the top, having a wicket into which to insert a handle, with a pin at the top of the socket to bear the foot upon, in pressing it into the ground to make the holes; these holes should be about eight inches apart; the plants then to be put into the holes about an inch deeper than they were in the ground when in the nursery—the earth to be then well packed about the roots. Proper transplanting is one of the most important matters in getting the hedge properly started. Too much care cannot be taken in this particular. Afterwards comes the cultivating, hoeing, ploughing, &c. The soil on both sides of the hedge needs thorough cultivation, and the hedge row must be kept clean during the whole of the summer season. No stock should be allowed in the enclosure where the hedge is set until after harvest; and it is better to have none until fall. The summer's growth will by that time become hard, and will thenceforward protect itself.

The next spring, a year from the time the hedge was set out, it must be cut off at the surface of the ground, below all the buds, just at the top of the yellow root. The root will then swell up, and put out a number of strong shoots, just at the surface of the ground. It then needs to be thoroughly cultivated until about the middle of June, when it should have another cutting within two inches of the former one, and then cultivate as usual. By this process of cutting, is formed at once a strong and firm base; and if this process of cultivating thoroughly, and cutting down completely, is carried out systematically, success is certain. It is thought by some that it is necessary to cut down more than twice a year, but it is a mistake, for any one who has had any experience in matters of this kind, as one practical farmer assures us, will know that it is necessary to let a tree form a top to a certain extent, in order to obtain roots and trunk; and by keeping it trimmed too closely it will paralyze its growth. The following spring cut within three or four inches of the former cutting, and again in June four or five inches above that, continuing the cultivation until it is four years old, and even after it has attained the size necessary to answer the purpose of a good fence, the ground alongside of it should be kept in good condition.

Many persons have supposed that the plant will not endure severe cold. It certainly has endured cold 35° below zero, and will undoubtedly meet the contingencies of hard winters; but like every thing else upon a farm, it ought never to be treated with neglect. The only difficulty is the first winter, on ground that cracks badly with frost. A sure remedy for this is to cover the ground close up on both sides with straw, in the fall. The straw need never be removed, as it keeps the ground moist, and the weeds from growing in the summer.

The fourth spring it may be cut six or seven inches above the former cutting. The following June eight inches higher, after which the latter part of the summer's growth will make it sufficient to answer the purpose of a good fence. After this, trimming once a year will be sufficient; this should be done in the latter part of the summer or fall, before the wood hardens. It will be found that much less trimming is necessary after the hedge is formed. The reason is very obvious, to wit: its manner of growing will cause each plant to spread and throw out a great number of branches, to be supplied with sap, and cause the former vigorous growth to be exhausted, so that it will then grow more slowly.

The first cutting, that of one year after the hedge has been set, can be best done with a pair of shears made for the purpose, and to be had at most hardware stores. The second cutting can be done with a short, heavy, briar scythe, hung upon a strong, stiff snathe. The second year's cutting can also be done with a scythe. The best way is to walk along the right side of the row, and cut half way, or to the centre of the row. When you get to the end of the row, turn around to the right, and come back upon the other side, cutting the other half in a similar manner. In so doing it can be cut of an oval shape. Then by taking a large cutter, such as are used for cutting up cornstalks—it should be kept very sharp—using the knife and cutter to trim the sides, and keep them in proper shape, at all times letting the lower branches extend out, in order that they may become strong, that the base may be wide. It should be at least four or five feet wide at four years old. If the lateral shoots are trimmed as frequently, and with as much thoroughness as the upright shoots, they will soon lose their vigor and strength, as the natural tendency of the growth is upward—hence the necessity of skill and judgment to properly form the hedge. Great care should be taken to secure a close, strong, and firm base, since a large portion of the hedges that have been set have failed, for want of the use of a proper method in forming the base. The trimming of the third year can be done in the same manner as that of the second year. The fourth year's trimming will have to be done mostly with the knife, at all times keeping the hedge in the shape of the one above represented.

Concerning the amount of time and labor expended in planting and cultivating this plant for hedge purposes, another practical farmer assures us, that it takes four or five years to make a fence, costing one day's work for forty rods in planting, as much for cultivating and hoeing as it would cost to hoe a row of corn, and no more; say half a day for cutting and hoeing forty rods yearly, which for five years would be

two and a half days for forty rods; in all, at $1 per day, the cost would be $3 50. He speaks of companies who set out thousands of rods of Osage hedge yearly; they charge sixty cents a rod, but get but little pay down; they guarantee a good fence, and wait for most of the pay until the fence is perfected. It is true, says our farmer, that the ground should be well prepared, and all the work well done, and in season, to make a good hedge row; so it must be to make a good row of corn, and there is no more difficulty, and but little more labor in cultivating the Osage Orange row, than the row of corn.

Such are the merits and excellencies of this plant, that in the opinion of the most experienced hedge-growers, the Osage Orange will rapidly take the place of all other fences on the prairies, inasmuch as it is more protective, easier to be kept in repair, and the cost is but trifling.

The preceding cut represents a full grown and completed hedge fence: nothing would add more to the beauty and protection of a farm, than being surrounded and divided by well trimmed and thrifty hedges.

MAPLE SUGAR.

THE preparation of maple sugar is considered one of the most agreeable of their occupations, by farmers residing in districts where many sugar maple trees grow wild. A great part of the forests of Northern Illinois consists of these valuable trees. Towards the latter part of March, when the buds begin to swell, and the nocturnal frosts are followed by warm days, these trees are tapped with augers, about two feet above the earth, and hollow elder tubes being inserted in the bores, the sap is made to trickle through them into troughs placed below. Every morning the contents of the troughs are emptied into kettles, and the sap, at first but slightly sweet, is boiled the whole day until it assumes the thickness of syrup; from the moment it commences to thicken, it is continually stirred. This maple syrup has a very agreeable and aromatic taste, as if it had been mixed with vanilla, or the extract of orange blossoms, and hardens within a few hours after being poured out of the kettle into flat vessels. If it is previously clarified with milk, or the white of eggs, the sugar receives a light brown color; without such previous purification, however, it has a dark brown appearance, having, nevertheless, a sweet and pleasant taste. From one bore of a tree a gallon of sap runs out, within about twenty-four hours, three or four gallons yielding a pound of sugar. At spring time, a family can prepare from one hundred and fifty to two hundred pounds of sugar within eight days. Tapping the trees does not damage them, if, after the sap has ceased to flow, the holes are stopped with clay.

In districts where no sugar maples grow wild, every farmer should plant a half or a quarter of an acre with these trees, which may be easily raised from the seed. In the short space of eight or ten years, he might raise a sufficient supply for himself, and in a longer period, even much for sale. Whilst the trunks are still young, the land may be turned to account as a meadow; and lastly, the wood itself is far more valuable than common timber, being admirably suited for purposes of joinery and turning, and therefore commands a higher price than any other species of American wood.

BREEDING CATTLE.

THIS State is well adapted for the raising of stock, of almost every variety, on account of the rich grass-land, and the prairies, which yield an abundance of excellent fodder.

The value of cattle consists chiefly in the quantity and quality of milk and beef they will produce at maturity.

The Durham breed seems to thrive very well in Illinois; they are the kind called also short horns. A few of the most prominent and never-failing characteristics, are: color, which is always red or white, or a mixture of the two—no other colors are ever found upon them—and a bright, full eye, encircled with a skin of rich cream color; the nose also of the same color. Any variations from these—any black in the skin of the nose, is an indication of an impure breed. The horns are small and tapering, generally bent, and of a yellow or light waxy color; small, but lengthy, tapering head; fine, tapering tail; rather short legs; fine, and bony body.

James N. Brown, the first President of the State Agricultural Society, is one of the best stock farmers of the State—his herd of "short horns" standing almost unrivalled, and his other stock being the best of their kind. If any one desires to see a fine sample of a Central Illinois stock-farm, and some of the best Durhams in the State, he need only go to Mr. Brown's farm, at Island Grove, Sangamon County, Illinois.

Another gentleman, B. F. Harris, Esq., residing in the edge of the Sangamon timber, ten miles west of Urbana, is also a very successful and enterprising stock-farmer. A herd of one hundred cattle, averaging 1965 pounds, fed by him, took the premium at the World's Fair, in New York.

For stock-raising, Central and Southern Illinois offer great advantages, as the winters are comparatively mild and short, and domestic animals consequently require less feeding, and can be raised with less expense than in a higher latitude.

Last year, cattle did well upon the prairies until late in December. It is expedient to feed from the middle of November until the latter part of March. A pasture of blue grass will keep cattle and other live stock in good condition for ten months.

The different kinds of cattle reared and bred in this State, are, besides the Durham, or "short horn," of which we have spoken before, the *Devons*, the *Herefords*, the *Ayrshires*, the *Holsteins*, and the *Alderney*, or *Guernsey* cattle. Although it must be admitted that the Durhams grow to a larger size, and come to maturity younger, it should not be asserted that they are, for these reasons, superior to all other breeds. The Devons are notable, and perhaps even superior to any other kind, for the creamy properties of their milk, for being first-rate working cattle, and for the quality of their beef. They are of two kinds—the North, and the South Devons. The North Devons are of a deep red color, with long, well turned, and beautifully tapering horns; stand low, on small bony legs; compact, symmetrical forms, so much so as to deceive the eye with regard to their weight; hair soft and silky, and generally in curled and wavy lines; eyes bright and prominent, encircled with a golden-colored skin; small, well-formed heads, shorter and broader than the Durhams; muzzle fine, the skin of the nose like that around the eyes, of a rich, golden color; tail set on high, even with the back, and rather long, terminating in a tuft of silvery white hair. These are never failing marks of the breed.

Price of Cattle and Beef.—Working oxen are sold from $80 to $125 per yoke. Young cattle cost from $2 50 to $3 per hundred weight, or about $25 per head. Cows sell in the fall at from $20 to $25—in the spring, together with the young calf, at $30. Some five years ago, the price for cow and calf was not over $15. The prices rise more and more every year, and it is seldom now that a weaned calf can be bought in autumn as low as $6.

Good beef sells at present at from $4 to $5 per hundred weight. Of all markets in the State, the most extensive business in cattle and beef is done at Chicago, which from its location offers such facilities for eastern transportation.

The dairying interest of Illinois must doubtless be very great. The value of the butter and cheese of Illinois, for 1850, was $1,668,076. Each cow in the great State of Illinois, produced on an average for her owner, in 1850, 42 pounds of butter, and from 4 to 5 pounds of cheese, which brought him about $5 50. Butter in the Chicago market usually averages about 22 cents per pound. Cheese usually sells for from 8 to 12½ cents.

Horses.—Illinois is well adapted for the rearing of horses.

Till within a few years, little attention has been paid to the improvement of horses. Hay is abundant, and oats can always be raised at a trifling cost, so that there is no reason for this want of attention to the breeding of horses, the more since the climate in general is so well suited to the most perfect development of the carriage, the draught, and the dray-horse.

Horses are rather high in price—a good working horse sells now at from $125 to $150, while some four or five years ago, they were worth from $75 to $100. A weaned foal is worth in his first fall, from $30 to $40.

As the buying of horses entails a considerable expense on farmers, they would do much better to raise them themselves, and to keep for the purpose at least one good mare. There is no scarcity of stallions. The mare should be spared a couple of weeks before and after the foaling, leaving her in the prairie for grazing. The young foals are left with the mare for about four or five months, after which time they are to be accustomed to the collar with care, and kept in the stable for a short time. The foals are usually broken for work after they are three years old, and one should not commence with them sooner.

Mules are also raised pretty extensively in this State, and high prices are paid for them; they may feed upon coarser food than horses, and are often fed with corn-stalks, straw, &c.

Sheep do very well in Illinois, and are found to be a profitable stock, since wool-growing is becoming quite a business in some portions of the State. There are a number of flocks in Sangamon, Morgan, and adjacent counties. Prairie-wolves in the early history of this State, made great havoc among the flocks, but they make their appearance very seldom now, and in some sections they have been en tirely exterminated. A herd of sheep will do very well on a farm for trimming the pastures; and some farmers say the average yield of fleece from large flocks is about three pounds. The flocks in some parts of Central Illinois are not sheltered in winter. It may be said that sheep consume food in proportion to their weight, that is to say, two sheep weighing 150 pounds each, require as much food as three sheep weighing 100 pounds each. A good fattening food for sheep is cake or corn, with chaff and roots.

Shorn sheep, sufficiently fat for the market, will contain about fifty pounds of carcass in every hundred pounds of the unfatted live weight.

Hogs.—This State is considered to be very suitable for raising swine. The favorite food of this animal, consisting in corn, is, we have seen, abundantly produced here. It is true that on prairie farms they are not found in large numbers, owing to the law which prohibits the running about of hogs, on account of the danger to the newly-erected fences; prairie farmers are therefore compelled to keep their hogs shut up in a comparatively small place, where the feeding of them during the whole year costs a great deal more than it would if they could freely run about, in search of their food.

One may therefore find larger herds in the neighborhood of woods, where the hogs are allowed to go to the bottoms after acorns, nuts, &c. Such food is very good for fattening them, and making them fit for market.

The hog may be reared and fatted at much less expense than any other domestic animal.

The breeds of swine that are most valued in North Illinois, are the Middlesex and the Suffolk; these two varieties are very like in most respects; they are famous for their early maturity, as well as for their small consumption of food, and great proclivity to fatness. They do not grow to a large size, but their rapid development, in addition to their above mentioned qualities, renders them marketable much sooner than other varieties. This more than recompenses the farmer for their want of size. Suffolk pigs have been slaughtered when they were not over six months old, and their weight was then between three and four hundred pounds; they will easily bring from 1½ to 2 cents per pound more than other varieties of hogs, on account of their fine quality of meat and little loss in offal.

Many experiments have already been made by farmers in this State, with regard to hog-breeding; more than twenty different kinds exist here, and yet experience has led most farmers to the conviction, that the "Suffolk breed" is the best and most profitable of all varieties that are known throughout the State. The Suffolk may be continued either pure or crossed with the Mackay or different other varieties; by this means an increase in the size of the breed will be created.

The Suffolk pig was brought to this country by a gentleman of Boston, who, amongst other importations, obtained this breed from Suffolk County, England, whence the London markets have received most of their supplies of pork during the last eight or ten years.

The inclination to fatness in hogs may be distinguished by the following points: head small; short snout; a dished face; neck thick and short; the ear thin and small; the breast broad; the ribs round; the back straight; the loin broad; the rump long, from the hips backward; legs pretty small, and straight; the skin soft and smooth, with fine, thin bristles.

The principal varieties of "swine," besides those already mentioned, are: the Mackay breed; the Neapolitan; the Essex; and the Middlesex breed.

It would make this treatise too lengthy, should a full description, with all the particulars of these varieties be given; it may therefore suffice to say, that no practical farmer will fall short of his expectations, if he breeds the "Suffolk;" and if he should wish to have larger hogs than are usually found in this race, he may try to make a breed, by using a full blood Suffolk or Middlesex, and an Essex boar. The breed thus raised will probably grow to a pretty large size, and weigh from 600 to 800 pounds, at the age of 15 or 18 months.

The average price for pork during the last four or five years, was from 3½ to 4 cents a pound, while formerly it was still cheaper. At the beginning of last winter, (1855–6) an advance in pork took place, and from 7 to 7½ cents per pound were paid; but these high rates gradually declined, so that soon after New Year's day the market prices were as follows:

Pigs from 150 to 200 pounds, at		....	4 cents.
"	200 to 300 "	....	$4\frac{1}{2}$ "
"	over 300 "	....	5 "

The Charleston (Ill.,) Courier, says that, for the year 1855, the hogs sent from Coles County, will not return less than $500,000.

The traffic in pork, is, in the Western States, one of the most extensive branches of business. The principal markets, Cincinnati, (Ohio,) and Chicago, (Ill.,) make very considerable exports in this article. They have, in both places, large packing establishments for pork, and smoke-houses for smoking hams, shoulders, and bacon. Even our Eastern markets are indebted to the West, for a large portion of their supplies in the above produce.

The following table shows that in most towns of Illinois the pork traffic has diminished, while in Peoria it has considerably increased:

	1854–5.		1855–6.
Farmington,	sold 8,000 hogs.		
Beardstown,	" 22,400 "	....	27,400 hogs.
Quincy,	" 32,443 "	....	43,600 "
Naples,	" 16,327 "	....	7,426 "
Alton,	" 23,000 "	....	28,000 "
Pekin,	" 18,000 "	....	3,000 "
Canton,	" 28,000 "	....	19,000 "
Lacon,	" 9,400 "	....	9,700 "
Peoria,	" 30,000 "	....	55,000 "
Springfield,	" 24,000 "	....	21,000 "
Springberg,	" 1,300 "	....	200 "
Chicago,	" 73,000 "	....	70,000 "

Stock of Cattle in Illinois.—According to the official reports of the State Auditor, the present stock of the entire State, with the exception of the counties of Alexander, Bond, Carroll, Fulton, Moultrie, Pope, and St. Clair, exhibits the following result:

Horses	395,692 head.
Cattle	1,175,838 "
Mules and Asses	19,528 "
Sheep	811,827 "
Hogs	1,689,537 "

The total value as obtained from the estimates, amounts, for

Horses	$20,364,812
Cattle	14,619,529
Mules aud Asses	1,106,094
Sheep	1,044,181
Hogs	1,689,537
Total,	$38,824,153

MARKET-PRICES,

In several places of Illinois, during the first half of January, 1856.*

Indian Corn, per bushel: In Alton, shell, 35 cents; in ears, 30 cents. Aurora, shell, 34–35; in ears, 35 per 75 lbs. Batavia, shell, 42–44; in ears, 35 per 75 lbs. Beardstown, shell, 33–35; in ears, 30. Belvidere, shell, 40; in ears, 35 per 70 lbs. Cairo, 25–30. Canton, 30–35. Central City, 25–30. Chicago, 55–60. Clinton, shell, 22–28; in ears, 18–25. Dixon, shell, 40; in ears, 30. Decatur, shell, 25. Freeport, 33–36. Galena, in ears, 30–35. Galesburg, shell, 30 per 60 lbs. Geneseo, shell, 30; in ears, 28. Jerseyville, in ears, 25. Joliet, shell, 40–54; in ears, 35–50. Kankakee, shell, 35; in ears, 25. Knoxville, 30. La Salle, shell, 40; in ears, 30. Marshall, 20–25. Mendota, 37. Moline, shell, 40. Monmouth, 25. Morris. 35. Oquawka, shell, 30; in ears, 28. Ottawa, shell, 38 per 60 lbs; in ears, 38 per 80 lbs. Paris, shell, 25; in ears, 20–25. Peoria, shell, 40; in ears, 35. Pontiac, 30–33 per 60 lbs. Quincy, 33. Rockford, shell, 45 per 60 lbs; in ears, 35 per 70 lbs. Rock Island, shell, 40; in ears, 25–35. Shawneetown, shell, 35–40; in ears, 33–35. Shelbyville, 20. Springfield, shell, 30; in ears, 25. Sterling, shell, 40 per 60 lbs; in ears, 30 per 60 lbs. Walnut Grove, shell, 35; in ears, 25–30. Waukegan, shell, 50 per 74 lbs; in ears, 37 per 74 lbs.

Wheat, per bushel: In Alton, 120 cents. Aurora, winter, 150–160; spring, 125–130. Batavia, winter, 150–160; spring, 135–140. Beardstown, 100–150. Belvidere, winter, 125; spring, 112. Cairo, 135–155. Canton, 110–140. Central City, 120–140. Chicago, winter, 150–170; spring, 125–150. Clinton, winter, 110–125; spring, 100–110. Dixon, winter, 145–150; spring, 120. Decatur, winter, 130–140; spring, 115. Freeport, winter, 135–140; spring, 115–125. Galena, winter, 110–135; spring, 100–115. Galesburg, 100. Geneseo, winter, 125–130; spring, 110–112½. Jacksonville, winter, 120–125; spring, 90–100. Jerseyville, 120–125. Joliet, winter, 145–155; spring, 135–145. Kankakee, winter, 135–140; spring, 112. Knoxville, winter, 115–125; spring, 107. La Salle, winter, 135–140; spring, 120–125. Marshal, 125. Mendota, winter, 125; spring, 120. Moline, spring, 125. Monmouth, win-

* According to the newspapers of said places.

ter, 120–125; spring, 110–115. Morris, winter, 130–135; spring, 110–120. Oquawka, winter, 120–135; spring, 115-120. Ottawa, winter, 140; spring, 125–130. Paris, 120–125. Peoria, winter, 125–135; spring, 110–115. Pontiac, winter, 125; spring, 100. Quincy, 100–150. Rockford, winter, 130–135; spring, 120–125. Rock Island, winter, 100–125; spring, 100–110. Shawneetown, 110–120. Shelbyville, 110. Springfield, winter, 116–130. Sterling, winter, 125; spring, 115–118. Walnut Grove, winter, 110–125; spring, 105–115. Waukegan, winter, 150; spring, 140–150.

Rye, per bushel: In Aurora, 85 cents. Batavia, 85–90. Belvidere, 85. Central City, 50–65. Chicago, 95–100. Freeport, 90–100. Galena, 60–65. Geneseo, 75–80. Jacksonville, 50. Kankakee, 70. Oquawka, 60. Paris, 50. Peoria, 80. Quincy, 75. Shelbyville, 50. Springfield, 65. Walnut Grove, 75. Waukegan, 85–90.

Oats, per bushel: In Alton, 27–30 cents. Aurora, 23–24. Batavia, 24–25. Beardstown, 25. Belvidere, 22. Cairo, 30–35. Canton, 25. Central City, 20–25. Chicago, 29–30. Clinton, 30. Dixon, 30. Decatur, 25. Freeport, 28–30. Galena, 30. Galesburg, 28 per 35 lbs. Geneseo, 25–27. Jacksonville, 15–20. Jerseyville, 20–21. Joliet, 25–26. Kankakee, 22. Knoxville, 30. La Salle, 27. Marshall, 20. Mendota, 22. Moline, 30–35. Monmouth, 25. Morris. 22. Oquawka, 22. Ottawa, 27–35. Paris, 18. Peoria, 25. Pontiac, 25. Quincy, 22–23. Rockford, 30 per 32 lbs. Rock Island, 25–30. Shawneetown, 25. Shelbyville, 25. Springfield, 22–25. Sterling, 28 per 32 lbs. Walnut Grove, 20. Waukegan, 25–28.

Barley, per bushel: In Aurora, 95-100 cents. Batavia, 95–100. Belvidere, 100. Canton, 110-125. Chicago, 100–115. Dixon, 80–100. Freeport, 100–110. Galena, 75-100. Geneseo, 95-100. Jacksonville, 125. Kankakee, 100. La Salle, 100–112½. Mendota, 100 Paris, 100. Peoria, 60–62. Quincy, 150. Rock Island, 100. Springfield, 115-125. Sterling, 95. Walnut Grove, 100. Waukegan, 100.

Buckwheat, per bushel: In Aurora, 55 cents. Batavia, 62. Springfield, 100.

Wheat Flour, per barrel: In Alton, 850–950 cents. Aurora, 700–900. Batavia, 900. Beardstown, 850–900. Cairo, 750–850. Central City, 700–800. Chicago, 525–950. Clinton, 900. Dixon, 800. Decatur, 700–800. Galena, 650–850. Galesburg, 700–800. Geneseo, 875. Jacksonville, 650–850. Jerseyville, 800–900. Joliet, 950. Kankakee, 800–900. Knoxville, 800–900. La Salle, 850–900. Marshall, 825. Mendota, 900. Moline, 800–850. Monmouth, 900. Morris, 500–900. Oquawka, 850. Ottawa, 875. Paris, 700–800. Peoria, 800–900. Pontiac, 900–1000. Quincy, 750–900. Rockford, 650–700. Rock Island, 800. Shawneetown, 750–850. Shelbyville, 800. Springfield, 850–925. Sterling, 750–825. Waukegan, 800–900.

Corn Meal, per bushel: In Beardstown, 60 cents. Cairo, 75–80. Chicago, 150-175 per 100 lbs. Decatur, 40. Jacksonville, 50. Jerseyville, 50. Kankakee, 90. La Salle, 65–75. Marshall, 35. Moline, 60. Paris, 40. Pontiac, 50–60. Quincy, 70. Shelbyville, 40. Springfield, 50.

Potatoes, per bushel: In Alton, 50 cents. Aurora, 37½. Batavia, 37. Beardstown, 40–50. Belvidere, 30. Cairo, 40–50. Central City, 50. Chicago, 55–60. Clinton, 25. Dixon, 50. Freeport, 35–40. Galena, 50–75. Galesburg, 35. Geneseo, 35. Jacksonville, 30–40. Jerseyville, 80–100. Joliet, 34–40. Kankakee, 20–25. Knoxville, 25. La Salle, 50. Marshall, 40. Moline, 45–50. Monmouth, 25. Morris, 50. Oquawka, 20–25. Ottawa, 35. Paris, 30. Peoria, 50–60. Pontiac. 25–30. Quincy, 50–60. Rockford, 37½. Rock Island, 25–30. Shelbyville, 50. Springfield, 75–100. Sterling, 40. Walnut Grove, 25–30. Waukegan, 40–50.

Hay, per ton: In Alton, 1000–1200 cents. Cairo, 2000. Chicago, 700–1200. Decatur, 800–900. Jacksonville, 800. Peoria, 800–1200. Pontiac, 500. Quincy, 1200. Rock Island, 1000–1100. Shelbyville, 700. Sterling, 550–600.

Hams, per pound: In Cairo, 14–15 cents. Central City, 9–12. Chicago, 11–12½. Clinton, 10–15. Jacksonville, 12½–14. Jerseyville, 12½–15. Moline, 10½–12½. Paris, 12½. Quincy, 11–12. Rockford, 7–8. Shawneetown, 12½–15. Sterling, 7–8. Waukegan, 12.

Shoulders, per pound: In Cairo, 11½–12½ cents. Chicago, 8–10. Clinton, 6–8. Jacksonville, 8–10. Jerseyville, 10–12½. Moline, 7–8. Paris, 9. Quincy, 6–8. Rockford, 6–7. Rock Island, 8–9. Shawneetown, 10–12½. Sterling, 8–9. Waukegan, 9.

Pork, per 100 pounds: In Alton, 400–450 cents. Aurora, 475–525. Batavia, 550–600. Belvidere, 425. Central City, 450–500. Chicago, 500–550. Dixon, 400–500. Freeport, 400–565. Galena, 300–425. Galesburg, 400–475. Geneseo, 450–475. Jacksonville, 375–450. Joliet, 550–600. Kankakee, 400. La Salle, 550–600. Mendota, 500. Monmouth, 450–500. Oquawka, 450–500. Ottawa, 500. Pontiac, 450–500. Rock Island, 450–500. Shelbyville, 500. Springfield, 400. Sterling, 700–800. Walnut Grove, 450–500. Waukegan, 600–650.

Beef, per pound: In Chicago, 4–5 cents. Clinton, 5–7. Dixon, 5–6. Joliet, 5–6½. Knoxville, 6. Marshall, 5. Monmouth, 6–8. Paris, 5–7. Pontiac, 6–7. Shelbyville, 5–8. Sterling, 7–8. Walnut Grove, 5–6. Waukegan, 4–5.

Mutton, per pound: In Chicago, 3–4 cents. Springfield, 4. Waukegan, 4–5.

Lard, per pound: In Aurora, 12½ cents. Batavia, 10–12. Beardstown, 10. Cairo, 14. Central City, 9–10. Chicago, 11–13. Clinton, 10–12. Dixon, 11. Freeport, 8–10. Galena, 9. Galesburg, 10–11. Geneseo, 8–10. Jacksonville, 10–12½. Kankakee, 8. Knoxville, 8. Marshall, 10. Moline, 10–12½. Monmouth, 10. Morris, 12. Paris, 10. Pontiac, 8–10. Quincy, 9–10. Rockford, 10. Rock Island, 9–10. Shelbyville, 10. Springfield, 10–12½. Sterling, 10. Waukegan, 10–12.

Butter, per pound: In Alton, 15–25 cents. Aurora, 20. Beardstown, 15–20. Belvidere, 20. Cairo, 25. Central City, 20. Chicago, 18–25. Clinton, 20–25. Dixon, 20–23. Decatur, 20–25. Freeport, 16–18. Galena, 16–20. Galesburg, 22–25. Geneseo, 20–25. Jacksonville, 15–20. Jerseyville, 20–25. Joliet, 18–20. Kankakee, 18. Knoxville, 15–20. La Salle, 20–25. Marshall, 16. Moline, 25–30. Monmouth, 20. Morris, 18–20. Oquawka, 20. Ottawa, 20. Paris, 20. Peoria, 25–30. Pontiac, 20. Quincy, 20–25. Rockford, 16–18. Rock Island, 15–30. Shelbyville, 15. Springfield, 20–25. Sterling, 17–20. Walnut Grove, 25. Waukegan, 20–22.

Cheese, per pound: In Aurora, 9½ cents. Batavia, 10–12. Cairo, 10–11. Chicago, 8–12. Clinton, 15–16. Freeport, 11–15. Geneseo, 10–12½. Jerseyville, 12½–15. Joliet, 12–15. Kankakee, 10. Knoxville, 10–12½. La Salle, 11½–12½. Moline, 11–15. Monmouth, 12. Morris, 9–10. Quincy, 10–12. Rockford, 8–10. Springfield, 12½–15. Sterling, 10–13. Waukegan, 12.

Turkeys, each: In Alton, 50–75 cents. Batavia, 8–10 per lb. Beardstown, 60. Belvidere, 7 per lb. Chicago, 9–10 per lb. Clinton, 50–60. Decatur, 50–60. Galena, 75. Monmouth, 50–60. Peoria, 75–100. Springfield, 50–75. Waukegan, 75–100.

Geese, each: In Alton, 30–40 cents. Chicago, 50–60. Galena, 50. Waukegan, 37½.

Ducks, per dozen: In Alton, 250 cents. Chicago, 125–150.

Chickens, per dozen: In Alton, 200–225. Aurora, 7 per lb. Batavia, 6–8 per lb. Beardstown, 150. Belvidere, 10 each. Central City, 140–200. Chicago, 18–20 each. Clinton, 150. Dixon, 20 each. Decatur, 175. Galena, 15 each. Geneseo, 8 per lb. Jacksonville, 150. Jerseyville, 150. Marshall, 125–150. Monmouth, 150. Paris, 150. Peoria, 20 each. Quincy, 150–200. Rockford, 7 per lb. Rock Island, 165–200. Shawneetown, 100–125. Springfield, 155–175. Waukegan, 150–175.

Eggs, per dozen: In Alton, 16–18 cents. Aurora, 20–22. Batavia, 20–22. Beardstown, 12½. Belvidere, 20. Cairo, 15–20. Central City, 15. Chicago, 25–27. Clinton, 10–15. Dixon, 20. Decatur, 20. Freeport, 18–20. Galena, 20–25. Galesburg, 18–20. Geneseo, 18–20. Jacksonville, 15–20. Jerseyville, 20. Joliet, 18–25. Kankakee, 18. Knoxville, 8. La Salle, 20–25. Marshall, 10. Moline, 25. Monmouth, 20. Morris, 20. Oquawka, 20. Ottawa, 18. Paris, 8. Peoria, 25. Pontiac, 15–20. Quincy, 15–20. Rockford, 20. Rock Island, 35. Shawneetown, 8–10. Shelbyville, 10. Springfield, 20–25. Sterling, 20–23. Walnut Grove, 18. Waukegan, 25.

Prairie Chickens, per dozen: In Alton, 225 cents. Central City, 175–200. Waukegan, 200.

Wood, per cord: In Alton, 450–500 cents. Central City, 200. Chicago, 600–1000. Clinton, 250. Dixon, 400–500. Decatur, 250–300. Galesburg, 350–500. Geneseo, 300. Jerseyville, 250–300. Joliet, 400–500. Rockford, 200–500. Rock Island, 400–500. Springfield, 500. Sterling, 600.

GEOLOGY AND MINING.

THE entire area of Illinois seems at one period to have been a level plain, or ocean bed, which has not since been disturbed by any considerable upheaval. The present irregularities of the surface are clearly traceable to the *washing out* and carrying away of the earth which once filled the spaces occupied by our valley. The Illinois River has washed out a valley about 250 feet deep, and from 1½ to 6 miles wide. The perfect regularity of the beds of mountain limestone, sandstone, and coal, as they are found protruding out of the bluffs on each side of this valley, on the same levels, is pretty conclusive evidence, that the valley itself owes its existence to the long-continued action of the water. The lower bed of the coal as at present worked, which is 30 feet above the river, is found along the banks of Kickapoo Creek for 15 miles from its mouth at nearly the same elevation from the water. The upper bed of coal is 65 feet above the lower, and 95 feet above the bed of the river. The mountain limestone is 65 feet above the upper bed of coal, and 160 feet above the river. It is supposed that there is another, or third workable bed of coal, below the bed of the river. The limestone and the three uppermost beds of coal are identical in character at La Salle and in Peoria County. This lowermost bed of coal, as found at La Salle, is quite different in its quality from the other two, and is quite free from sulphur.

Among the valuable natural products noted up to this time, may be mentioned the ores of iron, lead, and zinc; coal, porcelain earth, fire-clay, potter's clay, fuller's earth, marble, oolitic marble, limestone, grit-stones, flags, &c. The value of the salt-springs in the southern portion of the State, cannot yet be estimated. Notwithstanding they have been worked from the earliest settlement of the country, nothing sufficient seems to have been developed, upon which an estimate of their true value could be based. The investigations made in the southern coal region, have led to some conclusions, which will, ultimately, be of great service to the public in preventing the loss of capital by vain explorations for that mineral in sections where it does not exist, and also by pointing out the special conditions under which labor and capital may be employed with a prospect of success.

Marble, lime, and sandstone are found, either the one or the other, in each county; secondary sandstone forms the basis of the rocks in the whole northern part of the State. Near Athens, in Du Page County, fine, milk-white limestone quarries have been found; the stone is of a marble-like appearance, and susceptible of receiving an excellent polish. Near Chicago is found quite a peculiar variety of stone, of a dark grey color, a variety of marble, of a granulous cleavage, from which a bituminous matter constantly oozes.

If lime should ever be largely used in farming concerns in Illinois, or if it should be deemed worth while to export it, many of the counties would be able to supply large quantities of it.

Sandstone, which when dug out, hardens through the influence of the air, is preferred to lime. In Randolph County are the finest marble quarries. Quartz crystals are found in Gallatin, and the adjacent counties; gypsum in St. Clair County. In general, however, metallic ores are considered to be of a higher value; and though in this branch Illinois cannot boast of gold and silver mines, it is in possession of other ores which are of a far greater importance. There are in the State two hilly districts, one in the north-east of the State, north of Galena, which derived its name from *galena* (lead ore), and one in the south of Illinois, in the counties of Union, Johnson, Pope, Hardin, Gallatin, and Williamson, which latter seems to be a continuation of the hilly regions which are encompassed by the Cumberland and Tennessee Rivers. These two districts form the metallic region. The southern metallic districts have only been worked for a few years.

In prospecting and sinking shafts for the lead mineral, or *galena*, after penetrating the earth from 40 to 70, and even 100 feet, the miner sometimes finds himself in caverns of different dimensions, varying in size from about three to six rods. It will sometimes happen that he hits on a crevice, which hardly affords space enough to crowd the body through. A great many of these subterranean apartments present scenes of grand and brilliant splendor, from the various crys-

32 *

tallizations found in them. Calcareous spar, in great diversity and beauty of shape, is often found in considerable quantities, in some of the richest of these mineral-bearing grottoes.

In some of the caves, more particularly in the vicinity of the copper mines, the sulphates of lime are to be found in different forms, such as opaque plaster and gypsum; and sometimes in beautiful crystallized forms, as *selenites* and *alabastrites*, which are generally of a pure, sparkling white. The richest and most abundant lead ore is generally found in caves, beneath an earth whose drippings are fruitful with these beautiful specimens of spar; it is in most cases a clay or marl soil, in which *aluminum* constitutes a large ingredient, and where soap-clay is found in abundance. It can be easily cut or modelled into various forms and images, and hardens when dried—but shakes into fragments when exposed to the air.

Iron is one of the most considerable productions of the State.

In the year 1850, the pig iron produced in this State amounted in value to $65,000, for which iron 5500 tons of ore were required. Of cast iron, 4477 tons were manufactured of pig iron, and 50 tons of old iron. The entire capital invested in the iron manufacture, amounted to $325,400; the cost of the ore, expenses, &c., to $197,830; wages, $153,264; and the total value of the manufactured article, to $511,385.

Copper has been found in large quantities, in the northern counties of the State, especially at the mouth of Plum Creek, and other little creeks. It is also found in small quantities in Jackson County, on Muddy River, and back of Harrisonville, in the bluffs of rivers in Munroe County, to some small extent.

Zinc exists in considerable quantities in several districts of the State.

Silver has been found in rather small quantities in St. Clair County, two miles from Rock Spring; whence Silver Creek has derived its name. It is said that in early times, the French sunk a shaft here, and tradition tells us that considerable quantities of the metal were then obtained; and it is even asserted that in the southern part of the State, several sections of land were reserved from sale, owing to the silver ore which they were supposed to contain.

Before commencing to speak of coal mines in this State, it will not be improper to give a few more hints with regard to the geological formation of this vast State, which may serve as an addition to what was already mentioned, concerning geology, at the beginning of this chapter.

The profile of the country, in fact, does not present one uniform, dead level, but a succession of gentle undulations, which have very forcibly been compared to the swells of the ocean. The highest, or culminating points, attain an elevation of not more than 800 feet above the Ohio River, and about 300 feet above the level of Lake Michigan. The valleys cut through the superfical deposits, and occasionally expose the rocky strata beneath; while from the main channels start numerous ravines.

The Illinois Central Railroad passes over all those systems of rocks which are included between the Upper Carboniferous, and the Lower Silurian. The greater portion of the underlying rocks consists of sandstone, shale, and limestone. The question has, as yet, not been solved, whether they form an uninterrupted assemblage of strata, dipping towards a common centre, or are arranged like the Appalachian coal-field, in a series of undulations.

The continuity of the coal-bed has been found in one or two instances, to be interrupted by older rocks, interfering between them; but if the supposition be made that the coal-bearing strata had once been arranged in a series of waves, or corrugations, and that in the progress of time their crests had been abraded, so as to expose the subjacent rocks, all those phenomena would be exhibited which one attempts to explain by a resort to limited basins.

Geological Structure of the Southern Division.—The strata contiguous to the above mentioned railroad, may best be divided into three groups, which are in the ascending order, thus:—

Group I.—Alternation of blue compact limestone, black slate, and fine-grained sandstone, with traces of hydrated brown iron ores.

Group II.—Small pebbles, mill-stone and grindstone grit, and sandstone of various colors, or variegated sandstone.

Group III.—Alternations of shale with vegetable impressions, fire-clays, impure limestone, and sandstone, with seams of coal, and traces of iron carbonate.

Geological Structure of the Northern Division.—In the northern, or north-eastern part of the State, adjacent to the Central Railroad, is found the La Salle coal-field, the northern margin of which extends but a few miles north of the Chicago and Rock Island Road. The intermediate space between its outcrop and *galena*, is occupied by groups of strata below the Carboniferous.

The buff-colored magnesian-limestone also belongs to this series; in its texture it is compact, and close-grained, and may be worked easily by the chisel, into any form, and is from that reason very well adapted for building, the more so, since it is but little more expensive than brick. It is found in layers, the under surfaces of which are covered with water-marks. Such rocks as contain a large number of ingredients, not chemically combined, are apt to crumble; but this objection does not apply in this case.

Near La Salle, Dr. Norwood, the State Geologist, discovered one of the most interesting facts in the history of the Carboniferous period of America, viz: *the existence of the coal seams upon the upturned strata* of the Lower Silurian series.

Visiting the "Split Rock," about three miles east of La Salle, he observed a coal-seam with a thin intervention of shale, occasionally wanting this, reposing, though only at intervals, upon strata which contain fossils belonging to some of the earliest forms of organic life.

The vast series of rocks that are so conspicuously displayed in the slate of New York and Pennsylvania, interposed between the Lower Silurian, and the productive coal strata, as well as the carboniferous limestones and sandstones, which form so prominent a feature in the geology of Southern Illinois, are here entirely wanting. Examining further, it will be perceived that the sandstone here comes out in bold scarps, and is surmounted by limestone containing fossils, and reposes upon a magnesian limestone which contains traces of early animal life. This sandstone stratum is about 100 feet in thickness.

The limestone reposing upon it, according to Dr. Norwood's measurement, is about 250 feet thick.

The coal-field at La Salle occupies the trough-like depression thus created. Its lowest seam sometimes reposes upon the older rocks. Its thickness is from three to four feet. Between the lower seam and the middle one, there is an interval of 176 feet, consisting of alternations of shale and limestone, with thin bands of sandstone.

The middle seam is about six feet in thickness; the upper part, for the distance of a foot, or fifteen inches, consists of an impure, slaty cannel. The upper seam, appearing 53 feet above, is nearly four feet thick. The interval between consists of alternations of shale and limestone, with a belt of sandstone twenty feet in thickness. The coal seams dip towards the south-west. The mines are on the right bank of the canal, and adjacent to the Chicago and Rock Island Railroad.

Illinois has as much and perhaps more coal than any other State in the Union. Till within the last few years her mines have been very imperfectly worked, but it is found, that as the deposits are worked at a greater depth, the quality becomes much better, and there is no doubt that after a few years, the people of Illinois will be able to supply their own markets, with fuel equal to the best Pennsylvania or Ohio coal.

Nature, in fact, seems to have anticipated the inconvenience to which the inhabitants of the prairies would be subjected by the scarcity of timber for fuel, and long ago provided for it a compensation, by carefully storing beneath their surface, an almost unlimited supply of excellent mineral, or stone coal. Nearly the entire State is underlaid with it, south of a line running west, from the southern extremity of Lake Michigan. It is found at a little depth below the surface, and crops out upon the banks of most of the streams in that part of the State.

There is no doubt that this article must ultimately become a great source of wealth to this region of the country, and it already attracts the attention of capitalists.

Mining is largely practised on the line of the Chicago, Burlington, and Quincy Railroads, in the counties of Stark and Knox, by means of shafts sunk in the prairie, immediately on the line of the road. Also on the line of the Chicago, and Rock Island Railroad, in Grundy, La Salle, Bureau, and Rock Island Counties. Extensive works are in operation at the city of Rock Island, where a large amount is mined from the outcrop of the veins in that vicinity.

The mines at Sheffield are owned and worked by a wealthy company, and are yielding a large amount of good coal, which is chiefly shipped to Chicago. The coal is raised from these mines by a stationary engine.

The La Salle coal basin, in La Salle County, contains the most extensive and valuable deposits of coal on the northern outcrop.

The lower seam of coal crops out in the bluffs of the Illinois, from the eastern boundary of the county, to near La Salle, where a sand-ridge occurs, running in a north-west and south-east direction, thus dividing the Ottawa and La Salle coal-fields.

The La Salle coal basin contains three workable beds of coal, which are of about the following average thicknesses :—The lower bed, two and a half to three feet; the middle bed, five and a half to six feet; the upper bed about four and a half feet. These beds "crop out" in the bluffs of the Little Vermillion River, and adjacent ravines; and all reappear in the bluffs of the Big Vermillion, on the south side of the Illinois River; the lower bed being here four feet thick; some fifteen to eighteen miles up this stream, the middle vein is found eight feet thick, and of good quality. The coal is found all along the Big Vermillion, from its mouth, near La Salle, to the southern boundary of the county. It also extends into the northern part of Livingston County.

The La Salle coal basin embraces an area of country about eighteen miles in length, by ten miles in breadth, being 180 miles square, or, 114,000 acres. A coal bed, one foot thick, contains 1400 tons per acre, and estimating the workable coal to be twelve feet in thickness, the average yield would be 16,800 tons per acre, or to the whole coal basin the quantity of 1,931,920,000 tons.

Although the usual method for working consists in sinking shafts, to reach the coal beds, at various depths, another system of mining has lately been carried on, which is called *drifting*.

A vertical shaft is run into the coal bed, entering at the "out crop," and this method has been found a very successful one.

At La Salle, all three of the beds are worked by "drifts." There are some twelve to fifteen openings on the bank of the canal, and in the valley of the Little Vermillion, and contiguous ravines. The lower bed of coal is now being worked to some extent, at Marseilles, near the eastern boundary of the county. The bed is largely worked at Buffalo Rock, and near Ottawa, for the supply of that city, the surrounding country, and the shipping. The variety of coal principally found here, as well as in the whole State, is the bituminous; but an excellent article of cannel coal has lately become known. It was taken from a shaft opened a few miles above La Salle, near the Rock Island Road, where a vein about eighteen inches thick has lately been struck, and is likely to increase in thickness as far as progress is made. The coal is of a quality equal to the best Liverpool Cannel Coal that was ever seen; it is equally frangible, susceptible of as fine polish, does not soil the fingers, and leaves but four or five per cent. of ashes.

The following companies, whose shafts are located for the greater part in the neighborhood of the Little Vermillion River, and Swanson Ravine, from one to four miles distant from La Salle, all carry on their coal-mining by "drifting:"

Field & Rounds; Egletson & Parsons; A. J. Hartshorne; La Salle Coal Mining Co.; James Forsyth; Munsell & Heath; J. Robsan & Co.; William Ireland; Sanderson & Co.; Thomas Evans; William Reevely.

It will not be uninteresting to give some information here, in relation to the operations of some of these companies. The first named, Field & Rounds' coal bank, is situated immediately west of the tunnel on the Chicago and Rock Island Railroad, about two miles east of La Salle. They are working the lower bed of coal by three different drifts, the entrances to which are but a few rods from the Illinois and Michigan Canal, and the Rock Island Road. They employ at present about sixty-five miners, with eight laborers, a carpenter, blacksmith, teamsters, &c., and are mining about sixty tons per day. The bed of coal which they are working, averages about three feet in thickness. The quality of coal now being taken out from their drifts, which have been carried in to the extent of about 150 yards—is said to be the best ever taken from the lowest bed. With but little addition to their present working force, they can very easily mine 100 tons per day. At most of their banks coal is worth two dollars and a half per ton.

The La Salle Coal Mining Co., generally known by the name of the "Kentucky Co.," have been for several months past engaged in sinking a shaft on the west side of Little Vermillion River, near the line of the Illinois Central Railroad, about one mile north of La Salle. This is the first shaft that has yet been sunk in the La Salle coal basin, west of the Little Vermillion. The first, or upper workable bed of coal was reached at the depth of 198 feet. The company is expecting to be able to mine and hoist not less than 100 tons per day, or 30,000 tons a year. There are at present in the La Salle coal basin, about twenty, or even more, shafts open and being opened. The number of men employed in and about these works, is about 300. The amount of coal taken out is about 600 tons per week, of which about 450 tons are sent off by the Illinois Central Railroad, while the remainder is sold at the banks for home consumption. The price for which the coal is delivered at La Salle is four dollars per ton. The price paid for mining is five cents per bushel, and about 27 bushels make up a ton. Where mining is carried on upon leased land, one cent per bushel, or twenty-five cents per ton, is paid to the land owner, as a bank-rent, or "royalty."

The price of transportation on the railroad, from La Salle to Mendota, is 75 cents per ton; to Amboy, $1; to Dixon, $1 35; to Polo, $1 65; to Forreston, $1 75; to Freeport, $2; to Eleroy, $2 25; to Lena, $2 25; to Warren, $2 75; to Apple River, $3; to Galena, $3; to Dunleith, $3 50.

As the land owners, who lease lands to practical miners, receive a "royalty" of twenty-five cents per ton, for the coal taken out, the revenues thus obtained, alone yield $4,200 to the acre.

The La Salle Basin, being the northern limit of the coal in this State, the market to be supplied must, for centuries to come, continue as great as the supply which can be furnished. Chicago will also afford a constant demand. Erie coal sells in that city at $8 per ton; while La Salle coal, adding the cost of transportation, which by canal would not exceed one dollar per ton, can be sold at $5, and even less.

The Peru Coal Mining Company has been organized for some time, and intend to commence the work of sinking their shaft immediately.

The Chicago and Danville Coal Mining Company. The deposit of the said company is at Danville, in Vermillion County. The Great Western Railroad, which passes through Danville, crosses this field from east to west. They have made arrangements for working these mines extensively, with a view to supply the country along the line

of the Chicago branch of the Illinois Central Railroad, as well as the Chicago market.

The Northern Coal Mining and Transportation Company, is the name of a new association, lately formed at La Salle; their coal beds are adjacent to the lands of the La Salle Coal Mining Company; they are about to commence operations by sinking a shaft on the line of the Central Railroad, about half a mile further north.

The mines in the vicinity of Morris, in Grundy County, are yielding a large amount of coal.

The Kingston Coal Mines are situated in Peoria County, and the lands of that region consist of about 1180 acres. The depth at which the coal lies varies, the surface being very uneven. Its greatest depth is seventy-five feet, while in other places, even where it has been worked, it is no more than ten. It lies 108 feet above the river level. It is divided into two unequal parts by the intervention of a thin stratum of plastic clay.

There are also extensive and valuable mines on the line of the Illinois Central Railroad, in the southern part of the State. Those at Du Quoine, and De Soto, are yielding abundance of a good quality.

The valleys of the Sangamon and Spoon Rivers also contain beds of coal, and it is also found in Schuyler, and several other counties lying between the Illinois and Mississippi Rivers—that district usually called the "Military Tract."

Salt Springs are found in the southern counties. Several years since they were worked quite extensively, and as some of them yielded largely, they will doubtless again come into use, as soon as it shall be deemed practicable to invest more capital in the enterprise, and when labor becomes less expensive, so as to enable the owners to work them with profit.

With regard to this branch of industry, the reader may direct his attention to the Saline, Coal, and Manufacturing Company. This company has bought a portion of land, commencing at a point about two miles below the mouth of the Saline, on the Ohio River, (106 miles above the mouth of the latter,) in Gallatin County, Illinois, and extending two miles along the banks of the Ohio, from the mouth of the Saline.

The fact of the existence of salt here, was well known, even whilst this spot was yet Indian territory, when millions of bushels were manufactured. When it was ceded to the United States, by a treaty made with the Indians, such portions of the tract as were known to contain a salt deposit, or other minerals, were reserved from sale by the government. However, it was subsequently donated to the State of Illinois. It is supposed that some 15,000 bushels of salt can be obtained, per annum, from these Salines. The company, however, have made the production of iron their principal business. The difficulties in carrying on the salt manufacture are by no means as great here, as in Missouri, on the iron mountains, or on Lake Superior—as in those places the facilities for conveyance are not fully established.

The company, with their capital of three millions, have on hand a sufficiency of fuel, and have very excellent landing and shipping places, and considering the continued and constantly increasing demand for iron, they cannot be in want of custom. The annual call for bar iron amounts to 350,000 tons, of which 250,000 are imported. The land in this section is well timbered, and furnishes a first class building material; numerous salt springs water the land. The coal veins crossing the land at this place are of an average thickness of 32 feet, and the coal contained in these beds is estimated at about 180 millions of tons, while the quality of coal is said to be as good as any in the whole State of Illinois.

In the southern part of Illinois deposits of marble of different colors have been found. They will compare favorably with most of the imported marbles, used for ornamental purposes, and it closely resembles some varieties of Egyptian marble. Several pieces of black marble, remarkable for depth of color, and high polish, have lately come from that region. A light-colored, nearly white marble, from the vicinity of Thebes, appears to be among the best that has been met, for almost every purpose of in and out-door work.

A specimen of marble conglomerate from Pike County, is one of the most beautiful ornamental rocks that has ever been met with in the West. It much resembles the "Potomac marble," used in the pillars of the capital at Washington, and seems to be quite durable.

Argentiferous Lead Ore.—There is a quantity of lead now worked by the *Linden Mining Company*, near Chicago, which is highly argentiferous. Three specimens of the ore, assayed by a competent assayer, of Philadelphia, Pennsylvania, have yielded: 1840 ounces of silver to the ton of ore; another, 1200, and the third, 1600 ounces. The agent of the company, not satisfied with this test, has sent an average sample of the ore to Dr. Hays, of Boston, the State Assayer of Massachusetts. Should he pronounce it argentiferous, containing only the lowest estimate of the Philadelphia assayer, then there can be no doubt, judging from the quantity of ore already raised, the known extent of the mine, and the ease and cheapness with which it is worked, that it is far the most valuable mine of any description in the United States.

The two north-western counties of the State of Illinois, form a part of the richest and most extensive lead region known in the scientific world.

During the year 1854, there were received in Chicago, by the Galena Railroad, 4,051,346 pounds of lead; and it further appears, from authentic statements, that the products of these lead mines shipped during the last five years, from Galena, were as follows:

1851.—474,115 pigs,	equal to	33,188,050 lbs.,	of the value of	$1,534,062	44.
1852.—408,628 "	"	28,603,960 "	"	1,178,483	95.
1853.—425,814 "	"	29,806,980 "	"	1,639,383	90.
1854.—423,617 "	"	29,653,190 "	"	1,630,925	45.
1855.—430,365 "	"	30,125,550 "	"	1,732,219	02.

Nothing can better show the wealth and importance of the mining region of the Upper Mississippi, than the above statement. The consequence is, that the city of Galena and surrounding country have increased in wealth and population very rapidly, of late years.

Arrangements are now being made for the construction of white-lead works, at Galena, and there is no other spot in the United States, where a manufactory of this kind would be as profitable.

A short time ago, a discovery of a rich layer of iron ore was made, about two miles distant from the little town of Moline, in Rock Island County. This layer is supposed to extend over a space of 75 acres. The veins of ore appear two or three inches below the surface of the earth, and they are eight or ten inches thick.

The annexed geological map will explain to the reader the great geological riches of the State, more fully than it can be done by words.

COMMERCE AND MANUFACTURES OF CHICAGO.

In comparing Chicago, as it was a few years since, with Chicago of to-day, we behold a change whose veritable existence we would be inclined to doubt, were it not a stern, indisputable fact. Rapid as is the customary development of places and things, in the United States, one will yet be forced to admit, that the growth of Chicago and her trade, stands without a parallel. Chicago, now hardly twenty years old, whose port in 1831 was frequented by four small vessels, two brigs, and two schooners, then fully adequate to satisfy the commercial wants of Northeastern Illinois and Northwestern Indiana, together, in 1855 witnessed, beating in her harbor, 6610 vessels, of 1,608,845 tons burden, and in the same year exported more grain than any other commercial emporium throughout the world; Chicago, which in 1823 was but a wretched village of ten frame huts, and sixty inhabitants, in 1855 numbered 83,509 inhabitants, and in the same year dealt more largely in timber than the markets hitherto the most considerable in the world can boast of.

Thus, as far as regards the grain and lumber trade, Chicago has surpassed all rivals, and as far as regards the money market, has also already evinced that independence, which alone can form the safe and substantial basis of a far-reaching commerce. In spite of an obstinate bank dispute, and the diminution by several millions, of the bank capital of Chicago, in consequence of the redemption, in part, of the Georgia bank notes, till then circulating in Chicago, the capital concentrated in that city proved, nevertheless, fully adequate to all wants created by the increase of business, and the immense importation of grain.

There are many reasons why the position Chicago will assume a few years hence, will be even much more important than that which she now occupies; one of the most essential of which is the opening of the direct line of water communication, between the city and Lake Superior. By the St. Mary River Canal, easy access is possible from Chicago to the inexhaustible iron and copper mines of Michigan; and by the Illinois Central Railroad, the illimitable coal beds of Southern Illinois are placed within her reach; and by these means she has secured for herself that degree of industrial development, which gives a firm support and lasting warranty to trade. Already the surveyor's chain has designated the places in Chicago where the manufacture of iron wares will be carried on to such an extent, as continually to keep pace with the incessantly increasing demands of the immense north and south-west.

No sooner were the great copper mines at Lake Superior opened, than the steamers of the ship-owners of Chicago hastened closely to attach the interests of that important region to their city; only a short time has passed since, and already the wholesale dealers of Chicago count the people of those mining districts among their regular customers. The fruits of the bold, but sure policy of Chicago, are already visible to a larger degree on another field.

The immense tracts of land of Middle and Southern Illinois, then without any, either natural or artificial, means of communication, for years awaited purchasers in vain, notwithstanding the low price ($1 25) at which Congress sold each acre of the richest land, whose cultivation did not present the slightest difficulty. No sooner were the rails of the Illinois Central Railroad laid through the entire length of the State, from Galena to Cairo, than towns and villages sprung into existence along the track, as if by magic, and the granaries of Chicago were filled with the produce of thousands of fertile acres, then for the first time subjected to culture. At the same time that the quantity of the yield increased, its quality was improved. The general use of machine power, nowhere proved of greater advantage than on the vast plains of Illinois; the rapidly progressing intelligence of the Illinoisian farmers, which, far from being contented with having created agricultural societies in every county of the State, now already calls for the erection of an agricultural university, will account for the fact, that a great part of the grain sold as "Extra Genesee," may be safely considered "Extra Illinois," disguised in some shape or another.

In consequence of these, and many other improvements, among which we may notice the continuation of the Galena Railroad to Dubuque, of the Fox River Valley Railroad to Richmond, and of the Illinois and Wisconsin Railroad, to Woodstock, the Indian corn crop reaches the enormous yield of 130,000,000 bushels, which must be chiefly attributed to the advent of Southern Illinois on the commercial stage. The wheat crop of Illinois, amounting, as it does, to 20,000,000 bushels, has secured to Chicago its prominent position among the grain-exporting commercial cities. In 1855, Chicago exported twice as much grain as Galatz and Braila, the great wheat emporiums of the Lower Danube, and four times as much as Dantzic, the place of export of the Polonian wheat.

The following comparison of those cities in Europe which possess the largest corn-trade, with Chicago, will place the great importance of the former in this respect beyond a doubt:

1854.	Wheat. Bushels.	Indian Corn. Bushels.	Oats, Rye, & Barley. Bushels.	Total. Bushels.
Odessa	5,600,000		1,440,000	7,040,000
Galatz, and Braila	2,400,000	5,600,000	320,000	8,320,000
Dantzic	3,080,000		1,328,000	4,408,000
St. Petersburg				7,200,000
Archangel				9,528,000
Riga				4,000,000
Chicago	3,644,860	6,837,899	3,419,551	12,902,310
Chicago (1855)	7,115,250	7,517,625	2,000,938	16,633,813

And yet the present position of Chicago is only the beginning of the beginning. The area of the State is upwards of 55,000 square miles, 80 per cent. of which are corn lands of the first quality. These 44,000 square miles, or 28,160,000 acres, planted with Indian corn, at an average yield of 50 bushels per acre, would fix the productiveness of the entire State, at the enormous rate of 1,408,000,000 bushels. Adding to this the facility of cultivation, the reader will have an idea of the almost fabulous wealth, that, accumulating in Illinois, in its reaction upon Chicago, the great commissioned agent of these treasures, must incessantly propel her onward in her career of progress.

The eyes of the world are already fixed upon the high, commanding position, which Chicago assumes on the globe; this will appear from the fact that in 1855, agents of the French and English Governments attended the meetings in the Chicago Corn Exchange. Chicago, indeed, is the only place in the world, where orders of many millions of bushels can be promptly attended to and executed.

If thus the productiveness of the State has surpassed even the most sanguine expectations, the increase of so powerful an instrument for the acquisition of wealth, on the other hand, has also not been slow. Large sums of money, following the law by which they are inevitably attracted to the place where they bring the highest profit, concentrated at Chicago, whose numerous sumptuous stores and bazaars, fitted up in the most elegant, fashionable style, and enormous granaries, with their steam-cranes lifting on one side of the building the grain from the railroad trains, and lowering it at the other side into the vessels, together with great numbers of new buildings, (2700 of which were erected in a single year), as also the fact, that in every branch of business within her limits, the demand far exceeds the supply, are characteristic of her prodigiously increasing prosperity. Everything doubled or quadrupled! And upon reviewing the shipping interest of Chicago, we find the same surprising increase. The tonnage of all vessels owned by Chicago, and registered in that city until the end of 1855, amounts to 56,670 tons. So considerable, indeed, is the commercial navy of Chicago, that in a single season, that of 1855, not less than 120 large vessels put into that port on one day. The enormous stores of grain accumulated within Chicago, keep busy an entire flotilla, in proof whereof, we might refer to the fact, that in 1855, a single firm contracted for the transportation from Chicago to Buffalo, of 500,000 bushels, kept in store within that city. As already mentioned, during the season of 1855, not fewer than 6610 vessels, of 1,608,845 tons burden, entered the port of Chicago. Dividing them into classes, according to their respective tonnage, we subjoin a list of the vessels registered in the Chicago custom-house, as having entered that port:

Steamers of less than 500 tons	141
" from 500 to 1000 "	237
" more than 1000 "	59

Screw steamers, of less than 400 tons	193
" more "	287
Sailing vessels of less than 150 tons	2,131
" from 150 to 350 "	2,546
" from 350 to 500 "	865
" of over 500 "	100

With respect to her commerce and navigation, Chicago has already projected a new enterprise, which, if executed, as no doubt it will be, taking into consideration the indomitable energy of the west, must astonish the world; nothing less being intended than to place Chicago, an inland city, situated in the far west, 1500 miles from the seaboard —in possession of direct communication by sea with all the sea-port towns of the world, by shortening the eastern water-passage from Chicago some 500 miles, and avoiding the dangerous St. Clair Flats. Using Georgia Bay and several small Canadian lakes, it is contemplated to connect Lake Huron with Lake Ontario, thus opening for the commerce of Chicago a free access to the Atlantic.

The commerce of Chicago was also favorably affected by the Canadian reciprocal treaty, her lumber trade receiving a considerable impulse from the Canadian imports, in consequence of that treaty. While pushing her railroads far into the interior of the pine forests of Wisconsin, Chicago at the same time sends her fleet to the Canadian hickory forests, paying with the luxuriant grain of the fertile Illinoisian prairies, for the timber which the people of Illinois require for building their houses, or fencing their lands.

We will now review the state of the Chicago market, as far as regards the various staple articles:

Flour.—While in 1853 not more than 18,247, and in 1854, 158,575 barrels of flour were imported, the quantity of flour imported in 1855 reached the colossal amount of 240,662 barrels. Besides these, three mills of Chicago turned out 79,650 barrels, thus making an aggregate of 320,312 barrels for the year 1855.

Owing to the increased European demand, prices ranged higher in 1855 than in 1854, as may be seen from the following table:

		1854.	1855.
January	per barrel	$5 50	$7 50
February	"	6 75	7 50

		1854.		1855.
March	"	7 25		7 50
April	"	7 25		7 50
May	"	7 25		7 50
June	"	7 75		9 75
July	"	8 25		9 75
August	"	7 75		8 75
September	"	8 25		8 25
October	"	8 25		7 25
November	"	7 75		9 00
December	"	7 50		8 00

Wheat.—The wheat import reached the already very considerable total of 3,038,955 bushels in 1854, while in 1855, more than double this quantity was exported, viz., 7,535,097 bushels. No other market on earth can boast of such a traffic; and the facts, that the harvest of 1855 was by no means one of the best, and that, in every new year, many additional thousands of acres are subjected to culture, cause us to conjecture such a development and progress in this branch of business, in Chicago, as would startle even the boldest calculation.

The following table shows the prices as they ranged in 1854 and 1855:

		1854.		1855.	
		Summer.	Winter.	Summer.	Winter.
January	cts. per bushel	95	115	120	140
February	"	120	140	118	150
March	"	106	130	122	155
April	"	100	120	145	160
May	"	130	150	160	200
June	"	130	150	170	200
July	"	100	120	155	185
August	"	110	150	110	150
September	"	120	140	110	145
October	"	105	140	135	165
November	"	125	145	146	175
December	"	110	125	135	165

Indian Corn almost everywhere failed in 1854, in consequence of the wet season, so that the importation of 1855, it was supposed, would scarcely equal that of the preceding year; and yet, while the maize import of 1854 amounted to 7,490,753 bushels, that of 1855 amounted to 8,532,377 bushels, being an increase of 1,031,624 bushels. The prices in 1854 and 1855 were as follows:

	Per bushel of 60 lbs. 1854.	1855.
January	55	40
February	46	51
March	50	51
April	44	55
May	45	69
June	46	76
July	51	73
August	55	72
September	61	69
October	55	64
November	52	72
December	47	50

Oats.—In 1855, the importation of oats had diminished by 1,247,197 bushels, in comparison with the preceding year; this may be ascribed to the fact, that the cultivation of this species of corn proves least profitable to the farmer. The imports in 1854, amounted to 4,194,385 bushels, and in 1855, to 2,947,188 bushels, and the prices were as follows:

	1854.	1855.
January	26@26½	26@27
February	30 31	30
March	27 28½	29 30
April	26½ 27	34
May	30 31	44 46
June	30 31½	48
July	31 33	45 46
August	29 30	44 45
September	32 33	25 26
October	33 34	25 26
November	32 33	28 30
December	28 28	28 30

Rye.—The rye imports had also diminished, partly owing to the indifferent demand, it being less cultivated than other species of corn, and partly because considerable quantities of it were used for distillery purposes. The imports of 1854 amounted to 85,691 bushels—those of 1855, to 68,086. The prices in 1854 and 1855, were as follows:

	1854.	1855.
January	55@60	70@75
February	70 75	70 75
March	75 78	75 85
April	65 70	88 90
May	70 75	95 100
June	70 75	110 120
July	80 85	100
August	55 60	70 80
September	65 70	70 75
October	80 85	83 85
November	80 81	90 93
December	65 70	95 100

Barley.—The imports of 1854 amounted to 201,764 bushels, and in 1855 to 201,895 bushels, or about the same. The price of barley ranged considerably higher in 1855 than in 1854, as will appear from the following:

	1854.	1855.
January	43@47	90 100
February	45 50	110 120
March	56 58	100 112
April	50 56	115 125
May	65 70	115 125
June	50 60	75 100
July	50 55	100
August	45 50	80 85
September	50 60	80 90
October	85 90	100 110
November	90 100	115 130
December	75 85	130 135

The imports in 1854 and 1855, of the various species of grain, amounted in the aggregate to the following totals, respectively:

	1854. Bushels.	1855. Bushels.
Wheat	3,038,955	7,535,097
Indian Corn	7,490,753	8,532,377
Oats	4,194,385	2,947,188
Rye	85,691	68,086
Barley	201,764	201,895
	15,011,548	19,284,643
Flour (set down as wheat)	792,875	1,203,310
Total	15,804,423	20,487,953

The total export of grain was as follows:

	1854. Bushels.	1855. Bushels.
Wheat	2,106,725	6,298,155
Indian Corn	6,837,899	7,517,625
Oats	3,229,987	1,889,538
Rye	41,153	19,318
Barley	148,421	92,082
	12,364,185	15,816,718
Flour (set down as wheat)	538,135	817,095
Total	12,902,320	16,633,813

Grass-seeds; chiefly timothy-grass, less of clover, or flax. The imports of 1854 amounted to 3,047,945, and of 1855, to 3,024,238 pounds. The price of timothy-seed varied between $2 and $2 37½ per bushel.

Butter.—Imports in 1854 amounted to 2,143,569 pounds; in 1855, to 2,473,982 pounds. Although the excellent pasturage grounds, of which the prairies of Illinois consist, offer great advantages for the preparation of cheese and butter, but little attention is directed to it. The market prices of butter, in 1854 and 1855, were as follows:

	1854.	1855.
January		13@16
February	11@15	12 13
March	10 15	12 14
April	9 14	12 14

	1854.	1855.
May	9@16	12@13
June	9 14	12 13
July	11 13	12 13
August	12 14	12 14
September	12½ 15	14 19
October	17 25	14 15
November	12 15	15 19
December	13 20	18 20

Lard.—Imports in 1854 amounted to 4,380,978 pounds; those of 1855 cannot be exactly stated, (lard being chiefly mentioned under the head of pork and provisions,) however, they are estimated at from 5 to 6,000,000 pounds. Prices can be seen from the following table:

	1854.	1855.
January	8½@9	8½@9
February	8½ 9	8 8½
March	9 10	8 8½
April	8½ 9	8 8½
May	8½ 9	9 9½
June	8½ 9	9 9¼
July	8½ 9	10
August	8½ 9	10 10¼
September	9½ 10	10½ 11
October	10 10	11 12
November	9½ 10	11 12½
December	9 10	11 12

Hogs and Pork.—The trade of Chicago has of late so considerably increased in this respect, that, unless indeed all tokens should prove fallacious, Chicago, also, in this branch of commerce, will soon have rendered all rivalry with her hopeless. Imports of the season 1853–4 amounted to 115,680 head, or, 20,834,062 lbs., and in the season of 1854–5, to 136,515 head, or, 25,778,879 lbs. The prices in 1854 and 1855, were as follows:

	1854.	1855.
January (per 100 lbs)	$3 25@4 00	$3 00@3 75
February	4 25 4 50	3 50 3 88
March	4 50 4 75	4 25 4 50
November	3 00 3 50	6 75 7 00
December	3 25 3 75	5 50 6 00

Beef.—Chicago mess beef is being already preferred to all other beef, both in Europe and America. The condition of the cattle driven

34

to Chicago, in 1855, was very excellent, so that that season has substantiated the fame of Chicago in this respect also. In 1854 there were slaughtered 23,691 oxen, weighing 13,402,223 lbs, and in 1855, 28,972 oxen, weighing 16,032,138 lbs. We note the prices of 1854 and 1855:

	1854.		1855.
September	$6 00@6 50		$6 50@7 50
October	5 50 6 25		5 50 6 25
November	5 50 6 50		6 00 6 50
December	4 50 6 00		6 50 7 00

The *lumber trade* of Chicago ranks next in importance to her corn trade, being unsurpassed by that of any other market. In 1847, the importation of boards amounted to but 32,000,000 feet; in 1853, however, already over 300,000,000 feet. In 1854, the imports amounted to 228,326,783 feet of boards; 32,431,550 laths, and 82,061,250 shingles; in 1855, to 306,553,467 feet of boards; 46,487,550 laths, and 158,770,860 shingles.

Wool.—Imports in 1854, 951,838 lbs.; in 1855, 1,369,039 lbs. Prices in 1854 and 1855, as follows:

	1854.		1855.
June.........(per lb.)	20–30		20–34
July	23–31		25–36
August	20–30		25–38

Lead.—Owing to the completion of the Galena and Illinois Central Railroads, imports had more than doubled in 1855; in 1854, they amounted to but 4,247,126, in 1855, however, to 9,965,950 lbs.

Fire-wood and coal are among the dearest articles in Chicago. Owing, however, to the great wealth of the Illinoisian coal beds, this condition of things cannot last long; especially since several new coal mines will probably soon be opened, so that the prices of coal will quickly fall, which will again exercise an influence upon the price of fire-wood, to the same effect. Imports in 1854; 50,650 cords of wood, and 56,768 tons of coal; in 1855, 74,810 cords of wood, and 110,075 tons of coal.

Duties.—Duties paid at the custom-house for imported merchandise, amounted, in 1854, to $575,802 85; in 1855, to but $278,978; which fact points out the great developments which must have taken place in the industrial activity, and in the *manufactures* of Chicago.

These are also fully brought to light by the following statements, published by the "Democratic Press," and chiefly based upon figures given by the parties interested. Where these were wanting, reliable, competent judges were consulted, so that the estimate must be considered as rather too low than too exaggerated.

	Capital.	Hands.	Value of Manufactures.
Iron Works, Machinery, &c	1,102,000	1,395	1,926,500
Agricultural Implements	454,000	480	649,790
Railroad Cars, &c	750,000	550	950,000
Brass, Tin, Copper Ware, &c	142,000	188	377,200
Type, Printers' Furnishing, &c.,	15,000	12	
Carriages, Wagons, &c	417,000	792	702,104
Lead Pipe, &c., (estimated)	20,000	75	50,000
Planing Mills, Sash Factories, Shingle Mills, &c	374,000	396	749,684
Cabinet Furniture, &c	300,000	530	455,500
Marble and Stone	578,000	676	588,900
Whiskey, Ale, Porter, Beer, &c.	397,500	180	826,645
Oils, Soap, Candles, &c	361,000	104	464,130
Gas, Coke, &c			126,442
Leather	150,000	130	290,000
Brick	56,000	220	260,000
Saddlery	52,000	120	142,000
Musical Instruments	16,000	38	45,000
Daguerreotypes, Photographs, &c	43,500	47	70,000
Jewelry, Silver Plating, &c	77,000	37	80,100
Quick Lime	80,000	110	96,000
Confections	24,000	60	80,000
Stoves	80,000	92	195,000
Wooden Ware, Brooms, &c	90,000	48	120,000
Blank Books, Book Binding, &c	26,500	66	124,000
Barrels	30,000	100	105,000
Glue	10,000	15	4,072
Ship Building	50,000	250	300,000
Hats, Caps, &c	17,000	30	40,000
Mill Stones,	5,000	14	23,418
Trunks	50,000	80	180,000
Lithography, Engraving, &c	10,000	15	20,000
Salæratus	6,000	8	18,000
Matches	5,000	21	18,000

Boots and Shoes, Clothing, Millinery, Tobacco, Crackers, Bread, Coffee and Spices, Surgical Instruments, etc.	506,500	1,866	1,954,006
	$6,295,000	8,740	11,031,491
For the year	4,220,000	5,000	7,870,000
Consequently—increase during 1855	$2,075,000	3,740	$3,161,491

With this we conclude our chapter on the commerce and manufactures of Chicago. When to her present age of twenty years, Chicago shall have added four new lustres, our readers, on reviewing the statistics grow before them, will smile at the insignificance of the numbers, however far beyond belief they may appear to them now. Chicago, indeed, has a splendid and magnificent future.

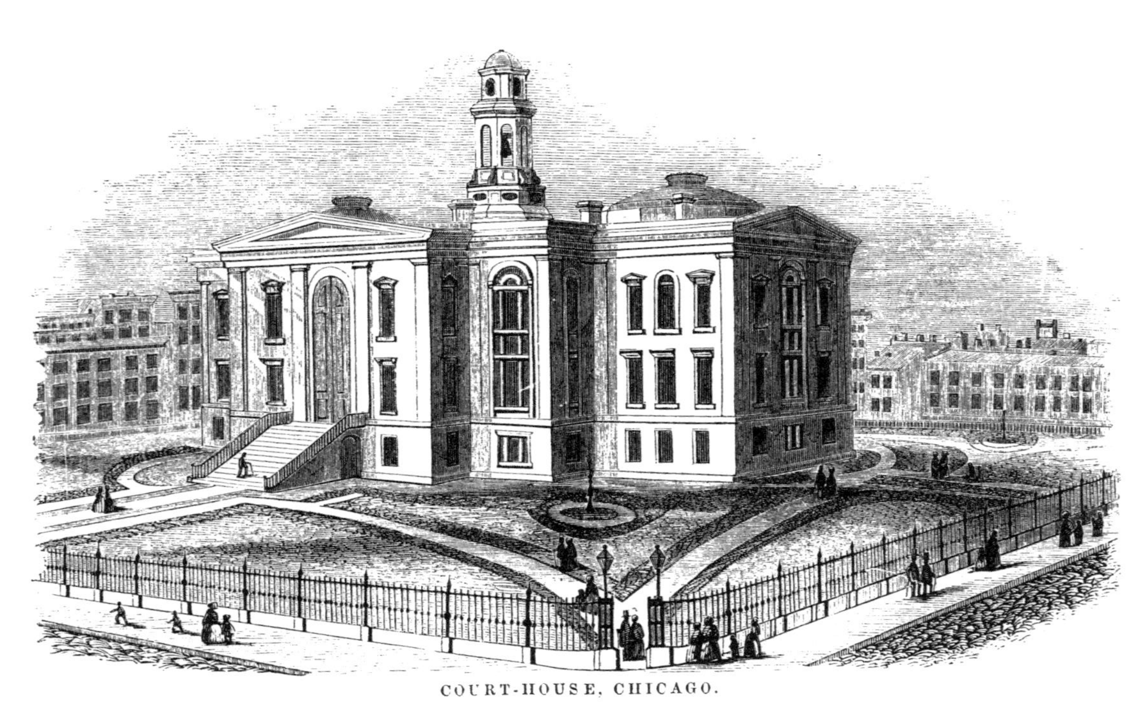

COURT-HOUSE, CHICAGO.

LANDS AND THEIR PRICES.

DURING the last few years there has been a steady advance in the price of lands in Illinois, as well as throughout the United States generally; in the former, they are, however, still offered at very different prices, and, with proper judgment and care, advantageous purchases may readily be made.

Lands may be purchased, — 1. of the Federal Government; 2. of the Illinois Central Railroad; and, 3. of private proprietors.

The quantity of public lands has been considerably diminished. According to the State Auditor's report there are only about 100,000 acres in the market, and the greater part of these is situated in the eastern and southern part of the State. Their price is from 12½ cts. to $2.50 per acre, and purchasers must apply to the Land Office at Springfield, the only one still existing — those at Chicago, Dixon, Quincy, Palestine, Edwardsville, Shawneetown, and Kaskaskia, having been closed some time ago.

The lands which were granted to the Illinois Central Railroad amount to about two millions and a half of acres, over 800,000 acres of which were sold in the course of the last two years, thus leaving about 1,700,000 acres unsold; these are situated in a strip, thirty miles in breadth, lying along the said railroad, and afford a rich choice. In the next chapter, we will give fuller details concerning these lands, by the cultivation of which the population of the State is being greatly promoted.

Private lands and farms are also to be had in almost every part or county of the State, and deserve to be recommended to purchasers who wish to buy farms already under cultivation and well organized. The prices vary, according to the quality of the soil and the greater or less distance from the towns, rivers, and railroads. It being our object to give authentic accounts on this subject, we have classified the information obtained by us, as to the prices of private lands in different districts of the State, in the order of the respective counties, viz.: —

In Cass county, land may be bought at from $1 to $40 per acre. Land bought, some seven years ago, for from $6 to $10 per acre, is now worth from $25 to $30. Wild land costs from $5 to $15, and farms from $15 to $40 per acre. This county contains about 2000 acres of swamp-land, which sells at from 50 cts to $2.25 per acre.

In Du Page county there is but little wild-prairie land to be had. Farm-land is worth from $8 to $30 or $40 per acre; wood-land from $15 to $90 and $100.

In La Salle county the prices are about the same as those mentioned in the preceding county; and well-arranged farms can be bought at proportionate prices.

In Lee county, land, which only four years ago was sold at from $5 to $10, now sells at from $50 to $100 per acre. Mr. J. H. Cropsey of Dixon, three years ago, bought a large tract of land at $8 per acre, and, in December, 1855, sold it again for $25 per acre.

In Livingston county, Mr. J. L. Miller, in February, 1855, bought 212 acres, partly prairie-land and partly wood-land, at $12½ per acre, which, ten months afterwards, he sold for $25 per acre. In December, 1855, Judge Babcock sold a farm of 1436 acres, on which there were two groves, containing together 130 acres, with a dwelling-house and barn, for $30,000. He had bought these lands, successively, in smaller tracts, paying $10, $6 per acre, and for some not more than the government price.

In Macoupin county farms are sold at from $10 to $30 per acre.

In Marshall county, an acre of wild prairie-land, two or three miles distant from Henry or Bacon, sells at from $18 to $20, six miles distant at $10, and fifteen miles distant at $5 per acre. Good wood-land on the bluff is worth from $15 to $25. The price of cultivated and improved farms, in the vicinity of the towns or at a distance of from three to four miles, is from $30 to $35, and six miles distant, from $20 to $25 per acre. In 1850, prairie-land two or three miles distant from Henry was sold at $6, that situated five or six miles off at $2½, and Congress-land nine or ten miles from Henry could be bought at $1¼ per acre.

In MacLean county, land costs from $5 to $30 per acre. Land

for which $4 an acre was paid four years ago, now brings three times as much; and for cultivated farms, which were then worth from $10 to $15 per acre, from $25 to $35 are now paid.

In Menard county, a farm, situated a few miles from Petersburg, and containing 250 acres, was sold, in December, 1855, for $7500.

In Morgan county, a farm of 640 acres, near Jacksonville, was also sold for $32,000.

In Peoria county, wild land is now worth from $15 to $20 per acre.

In Putnam county, cultivated farms, for which from $12 to $20 per acre were paid six years ago, are now sold at from $25 to $35. Wild prairie-land, formerly worth from $4 to $6, now brings from $10 to $15, and wood-land from $15 to $30 per acre.

In Rock Island county, near the town of the same name, an acre fetches from $30 to $100; farther off, from $5 to $30.

In St. Clair county, three or four miles from Belleville, cultivated land costs from $40 to $50 an acre, and at a distance of from ten to fifteen miles from the town, from $20 to $25. In the year 1855, a tract of land, situated two miles from Belleville, which, twelve years ago, had been bought at $15 an acre, was sold for $120 per acre. Wild prairie-land has here reached the following prices: in 1840, $3; in 1845, $5; in 1850, $10; and in 1855, $20 to $25.

In Sangamon county, land has doubled its price within the last three years. Wild land costs from $10 to $20 per acre; cultivated land, from $20 to $40.

In Tazewell county, farms are sold at from $35 to $40 per acre. Land for which, five or six years ago, from $4 to $5 was paid, cannot be bought at present below $20 or $30 per acre.

In Will county, wild prairie-land, which, four years ago, could be bought at Congress price, is now as high as $10; and farms worth $6 per acre four years ago, now sell at from $20 to $25.

In Winnebago county, as late as the year 1852, wild prairie-land could still be bought at the Congress price of $1.25, but from $12 to $25 per acre is now paid for it.

In Woodford county, pretty good land cannot be bought below $10 an acre; farms bring from $30 to $40, and wood-land from $15 to $20.

In the eastern part of the county, wild prairie-land can yet be bought at from $3 to $4 per acre.

The above instances, taken from nineteen different counties of the State, will be sufficient to enable the reader to form a tolerably correct idea of the price of land in general, while, at the same time, they show the relative rise in prices during the last few years, and with what reasonable prospects of gain capital may at present still be invested in the purchase of Illinois lands. The supposition, that prices have reached their culminating point, cannot be admitted; for, setting aside every other consideration, Illinois has, by the construction of the Central railroad, made these immense uncultivated tracts in the heart of the State easily accessible to the cultivator; and along the whole extent of country intersected by the road, numerous towns have sprung into existence, where, but a short time ago, nothing except the flower-covered carpet of the prairie and the blue canopy of heaven was to be seen.

We do not take too sanguine a view, in asserting that, in the year 1860, we shall look back upon just such a period of great advance in the price of lands, as we now do when looking back to the year 1850. At that time, who would have ventured to anticipate the enormous rise in real estate that is now actually exhibited?

Any one who may prefer to hire land or a farm, rather than to acquire the ownership of it, will find good chances to do so in almost all the counties. The rents, with some few exceptions, are nearly as follows: —

1. For the use of cultivated land, from $1½ to $2 per acre.

3. If the tenant, besides the land, also receives from his landlord a house, &c., the rent amounts to $3 per acre; or,

3. The tenant gives all the work, seeds, &c., and furnishes the working-cattle, and then gives one-third of the returns or crops to the owner of the land; or, finally,

4. The tenant furnishes the work, and in return obtains a dwelling-place, working-cattle, agricultural implements, seed, &c., and then the owner is entitled to one-half of the crops.

We cannot conclude this chapter without mentioning an extraordinary instance of the rapid increase in the value of real estate.

In the year 1848, Mr. William Green, of Chicago, bought a tract of land containing 200 acres, for which he paid $100 per acre, making a sum total of $20,000. Of this tract he has already sold, as follows: —

In 1855, a plot, for	$40,000
" " " "	10,000
" " " "	50,000
" 1856, 150 acres, for . . .	600,000
and he has lots left, with a front of 1700 feet, worth $100 per foot, amounting to	170,000
Total,	$870,000

Thus, within eight years, he made, with a capital of $20,000, a profit of $860,000! Where else, in another country, can such a result be even approximated to?

THE LANDS OF THE ILLINOIS CENTRAL RAILROAD COMPANY.

ON the 20th of September, 1850, the Congress of the United States passed a law by which two millions five hundred and ninety-five thousand acres of the public lands were granted to the State of Illinois for railroad purposes; and on the 10th of February, 1851, the Illinois Central Railroad Company was incorporated by an act of the Legislature of the State of Illinois, and the whole of the immense tract of land before-mentioned was granted to the company, to aid in the construction of the railroad projected by it.

By this grant of lands, and the consequent construction of the railroad, that new era has been opened for Illinois, which manifests itself in the unparalleled growth of its population and in its great wealth. This road intersects the entire State from north to south: running, first in two branches, viz., from Chicago to Centralia, and from Dunleith to Centralia; and then, in but one branch from Centralia to Cairo. The great prairies of Central Illinois, so particularly distinguished for the rich fertility of their soil, but hitherto lying entirely uncultivated and almost wholly excluded from the markets by the want of means of communication, have thus been rendered accessible to cultivation.

However speculative the construction of a railroad seven hundred and four miles in length, and through a territory almost entirely uncultivated, may at first have appeared, the excellence of the great undertaking is fully demonstrated by the immense advantages already derived from it. Not only is it true that the Central Railroad Company is doing a splendid business, and that the bonds issued by it are commanding pretty high rates, as compared with other railroad bonds, but it is also a fact, that by the construction of this road, those vast and desert prairie-lands have been transformed into well-cultivated farms, which are now annually contributing many millions of bushels of excellent grain to the general produce of the State, and still present the prospect of much larger crops in future; and, moreover, the population of the State has been increased by the addition of thousands of industrious and enterprising citizens, who are mostly farmers. The State of Illinois has thus came to be ranked among the most important States of the Union.

The lands of the company extend themselves on both sides of the road, in a breadth of thirty miles, so that it mostly runs through the middle of them. The greater part of these lands are well-watered and intersected by creeks, and where such are wanting, good water may be obtained by digging to the depth of a few feet below the surface.

A kind of loam, well suited for the manufacture of bricks, is frequently found near the surface; and bituminous coal, which, as has been already mentioned, underlies almost the entire State of Illinois, is found at several points of the railroad, furnishing a very excellent and cheap fuel. The soil, to a depth of about five feet, is of a rich black substance, with a surface partly undulating or rolling, and partly level, and well adapted to all the various branches of agriculture and cattle-breeding. In some parts, there is a fine growth of oak and other trees.

Besides all the above advantages, the farmers who settle on these lands have still another great benefit, in their immediate, or at least very near, connexion with the State's mighty artery of intercommunication, by which they are enabled, without the slightest difficulty, to forward their products to the markets, and there to realize good prices for them.

Of the 2,595,000 acres which were granted to the Illinois Central Railroad Company, 528,863.11 acres were sold, in the short space of seventeen months, namely, from August, 1854, up to the 31st day of December, 1855, and brought the sum of $5,598,577.83.

Since the 1st of January, 1856, there have been sold, in each month respectively, as follows: —

In January	11,481.36	acres, for		$175,057.46
February	4,959.04	"		75,509.09
March	26,880.14	"		327,331.54
April	12,853.22	"		211,442.17
May	18,328.45	"		293,360.96
June	15,529.56	"		241,291.96
July	19,509.97	"		301,066.16
August	27,288.88	"		381,744.09
September	43,018.35	"		662,014.23
October	56,421.76	"		906,800.58
November	54,004.76	"		859,290.47

So that on the 1st of December, 1856, 819,138.60 acres were already sold for $10,033,486.54; leaving only 1,775,861.40 for future purchasers.

These extraordinarily rapid sales, — this unexampled sudden transformation of such a large territory, hitherto lying in a wild and uncultivated state, into luxuriant cornfields, inviting farms and fruitful orchards, must not be attributed solely to the location and fertility of the land, but also, in as great a measure, to the unequalled and ready facilities that are afforded to the owner and cultivator by the Illinois Central Railroad Company. The same advantages are still offered, and persons, even with limited means, may yet acquire valuable property, and thus come to enjoy wealth and independence within a comparatively short time.

Influenced by these reasons, hundreds of people are weekly coming from the Eastern States to Chicago, because they have become discouraged with the hard and unenriching labour bestowed on eastern land, and now choose rather to apply their energies and industry to the productive virgin soil of Illinois. In the morning, long before the hour of opening, the doors of the Illinois Central Railroad Company's Land Office, at Chicago, are thronged with people; and when opened, the office is soon densely filled with eager purchasers. It is not a trifling business of everyday life, such as a stranger to these scenes might suppose, that is here daily transacted, but lands to the value of hundreds of thousands of dollars in their monthly aggregate are disposed of.

The settlement of these lands, which has been accelerated as if by a stroke of magic, is made on the following conditions: — The Company requires no payment of purchase-money during the first two years from the day of purchase; and further, a long credit is given to the purchaser, while the interest on the purchase-money does not exceed three per cent. per annum.

The prices vary from $5 to $25 per acre, according to the quality and location of the lands, — whether they lie next to, or more distant from, the railroad, towns, or town-sites.

The first instalment of the purchase-money, being one-fifth, becomes due at the expiration of two years from the time when the contract was made; another fifth at the close of each subsequent year, with three per cent. interest: so that the last instalment will become due at the end of six years.

The interest for each ensuing year is paid in advance, upon making the first, second, third, and fourth payments. The interest for the first two years is to be paid upon making the contract.

The purchaser is obligated to cultivate at least one-tenth of his land every year; and upon making the last payment of instalments he will be entitled to a deed in fee simple.

Purchasers who are willing to pay six per cent. interest may enjoy a longer credit. An allowance or deduction of twenty per cent will be made on cash-payments; and the construction-bonds of the company will be taken, and considered as equivalent to cash.

Now, let us suppose a purchase of 80 acres, at $10 per acre, to be made on the 1st of May, 1857, the payments on the same would then run as follows: —

May 1, 1857.	Received contract for a deed for 80 acres of land, at $10 per acre ($800), and paid two year's interest, at 3 per cent. per annum, in advance,		$48 00
" 1859.	Paid first instalment of principal, being one-fifth of $800,	$160 00	
	One year's interest, in advance, on balance due ($640), at 3 per cent.	19 20	
			179 20
" 1860.	Paid second instalment, being one-fifth, as above,	160 00	
	One year's interest, in advance, on balance due ($480), as above,	14 40	
			174 40
	Carried over,		$401 60

	Brought over,		$401 60
May 1, 1861.	Paid third instalment, being one-fifth, as above,	$160 00	
	One year's interest, in advance, on balance due ($20), as above,	9 60	
			169 60
" 1862.	Paid fourth instalment, being one-fifth, as above,	160 00	
	One year's interest, in advance, on balance due ($160), as above,	4 80	
			164 80
" 1863.	Paid fifth instalment, being one-fifth, as above, and received deed,		160 00
Making the full payment, principal and interest,			$896 00

If the purchaser of these 80 acres brings only 20 of them into cultivation each year, by raising Indian corn on the one half and wheat on the other, according to the average yield, as stated on page 291, viz., 56 bushels of Indian corn, and 24 bushels of wheat, per acre, the average price of the former, as mentioned on page 292, being 33 cents per bushel, and that of the latter $1.27 per bushel, his yearly returns will be as follows :—

In the first year —		
560 bushels of Indian corn,	$184 80	
240 " wheat,	304 80	
		$489 60
In the second year —		
1120 bushels of Indian corn,	369 60	
480 " wheat,	609 60	
		979 20
In the third year —		
1680 bushels of Indian corn,	554 40	
720 " wheat,	914 40	
		1468 80
In the fourth year —		
2240 bushels of Indian corn,	739 20	
960 " wheat,	1219 20	
		1958 40
Hence, in the first four years..............................		$4896 00

From the sum thus obtained, deduct the entire purchase-money, amounting to $896, with interest included, and there will remain an average annual income of $1000 to be used for *alimony* and the defraying of farming expenditures, which will be found more than sufficient to cover such expenses. The farmer will, then, not only be free from debts, and possess an unencumbered farm of 80 acres, but the value of his farm will in the mean time have increased to two or threefold its original cost.

Considering the ease with which prairie-soil can be put under cultivation, it is hardly probable that an enterprising farmer will be satisfied with making only 20 acres arable in each year. As stated on page 317, one man, with a team of horses, can farm about 40 acres, needing hired help only in harvest time; and hence we may suppose that the owner of 80 acres will make them all arable within two years, or 40 acres in each year, and in this case his returns will be as follows: —

In the first year —		
1120 bushels of Indian corn,	$369 60	
480 " wheat,	609 60	
		$979 20
In the second year —		
2240 bushels of Indian corn,	739 20	
960 " wheat,	1219 20	
		1958 40
Hence, in the first two years,		$2937 60

And he will thus, at the expiration of such a very short term, be enabled to hold his property entirely free from debt.

These figures, although they are merely assumed as an approximation to what may be realized, nevertheless furnish an irrefutable proof that the credit system, as established by the Illinois Central Railroad Company, affords the greatest and most favourable facilities to persons, even of very limited means, to become possessed of valuable real estate, independence, and wealth.

While on this subject, let us regard the testimony of one who, in the year 1853, himself purchased, from the Illinois Central Railroad Company, forty acres of land, situate in the neighborhood of Bloomington, and who therefore speaks from his own experience. In a letter to Mr. Chas. M. Du Puy, Mr. John Lindley says: —

DEAR SIR: —

Having seen a publication, made by you, in relation to the value and productiveness of the lands belonging to the Illinois Central Railroad Company, I take the liberty to make the following statement of my own experience in the premises.

In August, 1853, I purchased of said company the N. W. quarter of the S. W. quarter of section 32, township 23, north of range 2, east, containing 40 acres of prairie-land, six miles from Bloomington, in the county of McLean, and State of Illinois.

I broke up the 40 acres of land, and put it all in fall wheat; and from my first crop, which I harvested in July, 1854, I raised, on the 40 acres, eleven hundred and ten bushels of first quality white Genesee wheat, which I disposed of as follows: —

1st. I sold, to different individuals, 100 bushels, at $1.25	$125 00
2d. I sold Brown & Mayers 300 bushels, at $1.25	375 00
3d. I sold to Brown & Mayers 600 bushels, delivered at Bloomington, at $1.50	900 00
110 bushels I kept for my own use, say	165 00

Showing the aggregate value and receipts to be .... $1565 00 as the production of 40 acres of land for one season, and that being the first crop raised on said land, — being what is known as fall wheat — crop sown upon the sod, after the first breaking up and turning over of the prairie.

My whole expense of producing the same was: —

Fencing, say	$200 00
Breaking 40 acres of land	100 00
Wheat for seeding $50, sowing the same $15	65 00
Harvesting, say	75 00
Threshing, say	60 00
	$500 00

Leaving a net profit, on 40 acres, of $1065.

And now, as the 40 acres of land are fenced and broke up, and in fine condition for cultivation, I can readily sell the land at $25 per acre, cash; but I should decline selling if offered thirty dollars per acre.

I make the aforesaid statement for the information of all persons who contemplate coming to this State, that they may know the agricultural advantages of Illinois.

No one having an intention to settle in Illinois, and whose means are not very great, should neglect to examine the lands of the Illinois Central Railroad Company, before making a purchase in any other quarter. There is much advantage in the method of paying the purchase-money by instalments, bearing an interest of only three per cent. per annum. On this account, not only settlers from the Eastern States, but even Illinois farmers, heretofore living in other parts of this State, are settling on the lands of the Company, and here providing new homes for themselves.

These lands become liable to taxation only at the time when the last instalment is paid, and after the purchaser has received his deed.

A service may be rendered to those who intend to settle on these lands, by giving a description of them, in their whole extent along the line of the railroad, with particular regard to the qualities of the soil. We will, therefore, commence by following the route of the Chicago Branch-road to Centralia, and thence along the main line from Cairo up to Dunleith.

Calumet, Thornton, Richton. — Land level and rich. By ditching, it may be made well adapted to grazing, and supply Chicago with milk, vegetables, and hogs.

Monee, Manteno. — Splendid rolling-prairie; rich, deep, black soil. Extremely valuable, owing to its vicinity to the Chicago market. A sulphur spring in township 32, range 10, east.

Bourbonnais, Kankakee, Chebanse.—Beautiful prairie-country; well watered and timbered.

Ashkum, Onarga. — Rich, gently rolling prairie; well adapted to grazing. Streams fringed with ash, oak, elm, &c. Fine living springs pouring into the Iroquois river.

Loda. — Beautiful rolling-prairie, thinly interspersed with timber. Well adapted to grazing and tillage. Watered by a number of streams.

Pera. — Land high and rolling; watered by the Big Vermillion and Sangamon rivers.

Rantoul. — Vast prairie; highly adapted to grazing and raising stock.

Urbana, Pesotum. — Fertile in the highest degree, and well wooded. The Great Western Railroad crosses south of Urbana, and brings coal from the Danville coal-fields.

Okaw. — Rich rolling-prairie. The Indiana and Illinois Railroad passes north of Okaw. Country well watered by the Kankaskia and its branches. Streams fringed with timber.

Arno. — Prairie and wood-land; rich, fertile, and well watered. The Terrehaute and Alton Railroad intersects south of Arno.

Nioga, Effingham. — Rolling, rich prairie; well supplied with streams and fine groves of timber. Excellent farming country. The National road passes through Effingham.

Edgewood. — Timbered with oak, hickory, &c.; interspersed with almost the same quantity of prairie.

Farina, Tonti. — Fine, open prairie, and interspersed with groves of timber.

Cairo, Villa Ridge. — Cairo is the southern terminus of the road, and is situated at the confluence of the Ohio and Mississippi rivers. Country back heavily timbered with poplar, oak, cotton-wood, gum, elm, cypress, &c.

Ullin, Jonesboro'. — High, rolling land, heavily timbered with beach and cotton-wood. Wheat, of a very superior quality, ripens in May. Iron ore is found near Jonesboro'.

Macanda, Carbondale. — A fine, timbered country, covered with gum, poplar, sugar-tree, mulberry, oak, and ash; watered by the Big Muddy river, &c. Coal is found in this region. Tobacco is also cultivated here.

De Soto, Du Quoin.— The centre of the coal region. At Du Quoin it is mined thirty feet from the surface. Fine, open prairie, interspersed with walnut, oak, sugar-tree, &c. Excellent farming lands.

Tamaroa. — Northern limit of the coal-field. About an equal quantity of timber and prairie; watered by the Big Muddy river, &c.

Ashley, Richview, Centralia. — Gently-rolling prairie, well watered. Proceeding north, prairie more rolling, and interspersed with groves of oak, ash, &c.

Sandoval, Patoka. — Country well watered, and interspersed with timber. The Ohio and Mississippi Railroad crosses at Sandoval.

Vandalia. — Well watered. Climate mild; winters short. Cattle thrive on the prairie for nine or ten months in the year.

Ramsey, Oconee. — Level and rolling prairie, interspersed with timber, and well watered. The Terrehaute and Alton Railroad passes through this section.

Pana, Tacusah. — Fine prairie; streams fringed with timber. The Terrehaute and Alton Railroad intersects at Pana.

Moawequa, Macon, Decatur. — Rich prairie, well timbered, and watered by the Sangamon river, &c. The Great Western and the Indiana Central Railroad intersect at Decatur.

Maroa. — Gently-rolling, rich prairie, well watered. Streams fringed with hickory, elm, walnut, and pawpaw.

Clinton, Wapellah, Elmwood. — Rolling, rich prairie, with groves of timber, watered by Sugar creek and the Kickapoo.

Bloomington, Hudson. — A beautiful, fertile, and rolling farming-country, well watered, and supplied with timber. Highly adapted for settlement.

Kappa, Panola, Minonk. — Rich, rolling prairie. Timber in groves and on creeks. Watered by Panther creek, &c. The Peoria and Oquawka Railroad passes south of Panola.

Wenona. — Level and rolling prairie, interspersed with timber, and well watered. Deep and rich soil. The Fort Wayne and Lacon Railroad intersects at Wenona.

Tonica, La Salle, Homer. — The great belt of coal, passing through the centre of the State, is found extensively at La Salle, and ranges a long distance east and west. Junction of the Illinois Central and Rock Island railroads; also, intersection of the Illinois and Michigan canal.

Mendota, Soublette, Amboy. — In Mendota, the junction of the Illinois Central, Military Tract and Aurora Branch railroads. High, rolling land, occasionally interspersed with timber. Good water-power.

Dixon. — Country well settled throughout. Excellent agricultural land, well watered by Rock river, &c. The Galena and Chicago Air Line Railroad intersects at Dixon.

Foreston. — High, dry, and upland prairie, well timbered and well watered.

Freeport, Elleroy, Lena, Nora. — Magnificent farming-country, well watered. The Galena and Chicago Union Railroad intersects at Freeport.

Warren, Scales Mound, Council Hill, Galena, Dunleith. — A rapidly growing country. Fine agricultural soil throughout the section. Galena is the centre of the lead region. Dunleith is the northern terminus of the road.

Through the above brief description, the reader may become somewhat acquainted with the general character of the country traversed by the Illinois Central Railroad, as well as with the peculiar qualities of the various sections of land brought into market by the Company. It remains still to be mentioned, as a striking proof of the extraordinary progress already made in the development and cultivation of these lands, that, in the year 1856, in the neighbourhood of Urbana alone, within a circuit of fifteen miles, about 20,000 acres were tilled and sown with wheat; which more than doubles the quantity of all the land together that had been previously broken up and cultivated in this region. It is further supposed, that, from the crop of 1856 alone, between 300,000 and 400,000 bushels of wheat will be sent only to the market at Urbana. From this we can form some idea of the rapid increase in the quantity of tilled lands throughout the whole of this rich and fertile country.

Lastly, the following table, which is constructed from data collected in January, 1856, shows the rapid growth and great strides towards municipal importance of the numerous towns and villages already founded in this bountiful territory, and which lie dotted along the line of the railroad and its branches, in the whole of the long distance between the beginning and the end. In fact, many of these places have during the last year doubled the number of their inhabitants; and, therefore, although these data have been so lately and carefully collected, they will enable the close examiner to form merely a reasonable conjecture of what is the present state of things.

Table showing the number of inhabitants, houses, churches, &c., of the towns on the route of the Illinois Central Railroad, in 1850 *and January,* 1856.

NAME.	When started.	INHABITANTS		HOUSES		Churches.	Schools & Academies.	Stores.	Hotels.	Saw & Flour Mills.	Factories.
		in 1850.	in Jan'ry 1856.	in 1850.	in Jan'ry 1856.						
Amboy	1850	16	1329	3	300	2	1	30	3	1	8
Apple River	1854	......	140	......	30	...	1	6	1	...	...
Ashley	1854	......	150	......	60	2	1	8	2	1	3
Bloomington	1832	2200	5500	400	1540	10	17	26	8	7	8
Cairo	1836	300	1300	15	150	4	1	25	3	3	...
Calumet Settlement	1838	50	150	12	40	2	2	2	2	2	...
Carbondale	1853	......	350	......	90	2	1	6	2	2	5
Centralia	1854	......	600	......	60	1	1	11	4	1	1
Chebanse	1854	......	25	......	5	...	...	2	...	...	...
Clinton	1845	760	1500	300	500	2	3	20	3	1	8
Council Hill	1828	300	400	75	100	1	2	3	3	1	4
Decatur	1829	600	2200	175	600	6	4	30	4	4	19
De Soto	1854	......	500	......	70	...	1	4	2	3	...
Dixon	1839	540	3200	not k.	not k.	6	3	43	6	2	3
Dunleith	1853	5	700	1	175	1	2	6	4	3	1
Du Quoin	1853	......	125	......	20	...	1	6	1	1	...
Elleroy	1850	18	225	8	42	...	1	5	1	...	...
Foreston	1855	......	90	......	13	...	...	2	1	...	...
Freeport	1838	1400	5000	200	1000	9	5	85	10	5	6
Hudson	1836	25	103	6	21	1	1	1	...	...	...
Jonesboro'	1818	584	803	113	162	2	2	13	3	3	3
Kankakee	1852	......	2400	......	400	4	4	45	3	3	3
Kappa	1853	......	150	......	35	...	1	2	2	2	...
La Salle	1839	200	3500	25	800	4	8	60	4	2	5
Lena	1853	5	350	1	65	2	1	5	1	1	16
Loda	1855	......	100	......	10	...	...	3	2	...	...
Macon	1854	......	28	......	3	...	...	...	...	...	...
Makanda	1854	......	14	......	1	...	...	...	...	1	...
Manteno	1854	......	175	......	22	...	1	3	1	...	...
Mattoon	1855	......	150	......	40	...	1	9	2	...	...
Mendota	1853	......	1800	......	200	2	3	25	7	1	...
Minonk	1854	......	70	......	15	...	1	1	1	...	...
Moawequa	1853	......	300	......	40	1	1	7	2	1	2
Monee	1850	145	800	26	200	1	3	3	1	1	...
Nora	1852	......	300	......	60	1	1	7	3	1	5
Oconee	1854	......	70	......	10	...	...	4	...	...	...
Onarga	1854	......	100	......	26	1	1	3	2	...	...
Pana	1855	......	250	......	32	...	...	7	3	1	1
Panola	1853	......	150	......	15	...	...	2	1	1	1
Polo	1854	......	550	......	130	1	1	18	2	...	...
Pulaski	1854	......	100	......	13	...	1	1	2	2	...
Richview	1840	65	525	13	120	1	1	9	1	3	14

Table showing the number of inhabitants, houses, churches, &c., of the towns on the route of the Illinois Central Railroad, in 1850 *and Jan.*, 1856. — Continued.

Name.	When started.	Inhabitants in 1850.	Inhabitants in Jan'ry 1856.	Houses in 1850.	Houses in Jan'ry 1856.	Churches.	Schools & Academies.	Stores.	Hotels.	Saw & Flour Mills.	Factories.
Sandoval	1854	......	120	......	20	...	...	3	2	...	...
Scales Mound	1850	14	256	2	35	2	2	4	1	...	...
Soublette	1855	......	185	......	38	2	2	3	1	...	...
Tacusa	1855	......	40	......	5	...	...	...	...	...	...
Tamaroa	1854	......	48	......	14	...	...	3	1	...	...
Thornton	1853	......	120	......	21	...	...	3	1	1	...
Tonica	1850	3	180	1	41	1	1	3	1	1	3
Ullin	1854	......	110	......	10	...	...	...	1	5	...
Urbana	1835	500	1145	not k.	not k.	2	2	22	4	2	3
Urbana (West)	1854	......	416	not k.	not k.	2	1	10	2	1	...
Vandalia	1820	360	1000	60	125	4	1	9	4	...	1
Wapella	1853	......	275	......	35	...	...	5	1	...	...
Warren	1850	25	350	4	155	2	2	10	2	3	...
Wenona	1853	......	80	......	15	1	...	3	1	...	...
Woosung	1855	......	54	......	12	...	1	1	...	1	...

BANKS.

THE banking system of Illinois is regulated by two acts of the Legislature, passed respectively on the 15th of February, 1851, and on the 10th of February, 1853.

The following are the principal enactments and provisions of these several laws: —

No bank shall be organized with a less capital than $50,000; and stocks to be deposited to secure the circulation, &c. The amount of circulation shall in no case exceed the capital stock set forth in the certificate of incorporation; but the deposit of stock securities and the circulation may be increased from time to time, until they equal the maximum of the certified capital stock.

Bank charters shall not be granted for a longer period than twenty-five years.

All notes issued by the banks must be payable on demand, at the respective places where the banks are located, and be countersigned, numbered, and recorded by the register.

No bank shall be authorized to put into circulation a larger amount of notes than the amount of stocks deposited as security with the State auditor.

The stock thus deposited is intended, in the first place, for the redemption of the notes in circulation, provided the bank itself should fail to redeem them; and in the next place, they are made to subserve the purpose of liquidating all the liabilities of any bank thus failing. Each stockholder is also made individually liable in proportion to the full amount of capital stock owned by him.

If any bank shall refuse or neglect to redeem any one of its notes, and such fact be properly certified by an ordinary protest, drawn up and acknowleged by any notary public, it shall be the duty of the auditor of the State, as soon as he shall be informed of the fact, to take immediate measures against such bank.

It is the duty of the commissioners of banks to examine into their condition once in every year.

Every bank shall, at the end of each quarter, make a full statement of its funds and business transactions to the State auditor.

In writing this book, we have been guided, as far as possible, by the principle of pointing out facts merely, and hence we have generally refrained from expressing our own bare opinions. However, although we do not now intend to go into a particular criticism of the banking laws of Illinois, we cannot forbear from remarking, that, in our opinion, a general alteration and amendment of them is necessary to preserve the people of the State from the great inconveniences which otherwise must sooner or later arise under the present law.

According to a statement published by the State auditor, on the 10th of January, 1856, (Congressional Documents, on Banks in 1855, pages 176 and 177,) there were, at that time, forty-five banks in the State of Illinois, having, altogether, stock securities deposited to the amount of $4,134,879.62, while their note circulation reached only $3.514,911 — showing an excess of $619,968.62, in deposits, over the amount of notes in circulation.

At the present time, (December, 1856,) there are fifty-two banks in the State, — nine of which, however, are about to wind up their business.

We here give the names, location, &c., of those fifty-two banks, together with their respective capitals, as shown in the statement above mentioned, the amount of capital stock actually paid in, and the amount of stock securities deposited, with the circulation based thereon; and, also, the maximum capital authorized by their several charters, as it is set down in the Banker's Almanac for the year 1856: —

Alton Bank — Alton.

E. Marsh, President; Chas. A. Caldwell, Cashier.

Charter,	$100,000	Stocks deposited,	$61,581.32
Capital Stock paid in,	59,845.21	Circulation,	51,819

Agricultural Bank — Marion.

S. B. Wheelock, President; R. M. Herndly, Cashier.

American Exchange Bank — Raleigh.

W. H. Parish, President; C. H. Miner, Cashier.

Bank of America — Chicago.

G. Smith President; E. W. Willard, Cashier.

*Charter,	$1,000,000	Stocks deposited,	$89,000
Capital Stock paid in,	50,000	Circulation,	50 000

Bank of Aurora. — Aurora.

M. V. Hall, President; B. F. Hall, Cashier.

Bank of Belleville. — Belleville.

E. Miltenberger, President; S. E. Mandelbaum, Cashier.

Charter,	$100,000	Stocks deposited,	$65,000
Capital Stock, paid in,	56,990	Circulation,	56,990

Bank of the Commonwealth. — Robinson.

I. N. Whipply, President; I. H. Low, Cashier.

Bank of Elgin. — Elgin.

A. J. Waldron, President; J. J. Town, Cashier.

		Stocks deposited,	$200,000
Capital Stock paid in,	$100,000	Circulation,	94,380

Bank of Galena. — Galena.

Henry Corwith, President; C. C. P. Hunt, Cashier.

Charter,	$100,000	Stocks deposited,	$104,814.75
Capital Stock paid in,	57,000	Circulation,	73,668

Bank of Hutsonville. — Hutsonville.

		Stocks deposited,	$100,000
Capital Stock paid in,	$90,950	Circulation,	90,950

Bank of Illinois. — New Haven.

G. C. Smith, President; P. C. Briggs, Cashier.

Bank of Naperville. — Naperville.

W. Scott, President; A. Keith, Cashier.

Charter,	$100,000	Stocks deposited,	$55,000
Capital Stock paid in,	50,000	Circulation,	52,780

Bank of Northern Illinois. — Waukegan.

C. D. Bickford, President; Chas. R. Steele, Cashier.

Charter,	$100,000	Stocks deposited,	$53,000
Capital Stock paid in,	50,000	Circulation,	50,000

* According to Monroe's Bank Note List, $200,000.

Bank of Ottawa. — Ottawa. (*Closing.*)
B. C. Cook, President; G. S. Fisher, Cashier.

Charter,	$150,000	Stocks deposited,	$25,000
Capital Stock paid in,	20,654.70	Circulation,	20,500

Bank of Peru. — Peru.

Charter,	$100,000	Stocks deposited,	$55,000
Capital Stock paid in,	88,500	Circulation,	50,002

Bank of Pike County. — Griggsville.
Thos. I. Ludus, President; R. M. K. Ludlow, Cashier.

Bank of Quincy. — Quincy.
Jno. McGinnes, President; M. Boon, Cashier.

Bank of Raleigh. — Raleigh.
Wm. Stadden, President; R. C. Spain, Cashier.

Bank of the Republic. — McLeansboro.
J. Rockwell, President; C. H. Rockwell, Cashier.

Bank of Southern Illinois. — Bolton.
E. K. Willard, President; W. L. Joiner, Cashier.

		Stocks deposited,	$75,000
Capital Stock paid in,	$75,000	Circulation,	68,550

Belvidere Bank. — Belvidere. (*Closing.*)
A. Neely, President; Chas. Neely, Cashier.

*Charter,	$100,000	Stocks deposited,	$31,000
Capital Stock paid in,	80,000	Circulation,	29,397

Central Bank. — Peoria.
E. B. Elwood, President; S. Matteson, Cashier.

Charter,	$200,000	Stocks deposited,	$50,500
Capital Stock paid in,	50,500	Circulation,	47,975

Chicago Bank. — Chicago.
Thos. Burch, President; I. H. Burch, Cashier.

Charter,	$100,000	Stocks deposited,	$119,328.25
Capital Stock paid in,	59,501.29	Circulation,	50,014

Clark's Exchange Bank. — Springfield. (*Closing.*)
N. H. Ridgely, President; Chas. Ridgely, Cashier.

*Charter,	$200,000	Stocks deposited,	$21,056.41
Capital Stock paid in,	10,107.07	Circulation,	10,000

* According to Monroe.

Commercial Bank. — Chicago. (*Closing.*)
I. Cook. President; A. Gilbert, Cashier.

		Stocks deposited,	$27,000
Capital Stock paid in,	$52,000	Circulation,	25,005

Corn Exchange Bank. — Fairfield.

		Stocks deposited,	$60,000
Capital Stock paid in,	$50,000	Circulation,	52,300

Du Page County Bank. — Naperville. (*Closing.*)
W. Scott, President; A. Keith, Cashier.

Stocks deposited,	$5000
Circulation,	4470

Edgar County Bank. — Paris.
H. Sanford, President; G. E. Loving, Cashier.

Exchange Bank of H. A. Tucker & Co. — Chicago. (*Closing.*)
H. A. Tucker, President; H. B. Dox, Cashier.

Circulation, $1186

(Has returned, as required by law, the amount of notes in circulation, and withdrawn its stocks.)

Farmers and Traders Bank. — Charleston.
W. H. Murstin, President; Thos. A. Marshall, Cashier.

		Stocks deposited,	$157,500
Capital Stock paid in,	$150,000	Circulation,	149,735

Grand Prairie Bank. — Urbana.
W. N. Coler, President; T. S. Hubbard, Cashier.

Charter, $100,000

Grayville Bank. — Grayville.
E. Chasy, President; L. B. Clark, Cashier.

		Stocks deposited,	$458,297.86
Capital Stock paid in,	$331,698.91	Circulation,	331,696

Hamilton County Bank. — McLeansboro.

		Stocks deposited,	$110,000
Capital Stock paid in,	$110,000	Circulation,	101,870

Lafayette Bank. — Bloomington.
W. H. Cord, President; J. L. Stockton, Cashier.

Marine Bank of Chicago. — Chicago.
J. Y. Scammon, President; B. T. Carver, Cashier.

Charter,	$550,000	Stocks deposited,	$198,767.15
Capital Stock paid in,	150,000	Circulation,	100,705

McLean County Bank. — Bloomington.

C. A. Gridley, President; T. Pardee, Cashier.

Charter,	$100,000	Stocks deposited,	$68,000
Capital Stock paid in,	65,000	Circulation,	64,998

Merchants and Drovers Bank. — Joliet.

Wm. Smith, President; R. E. Goodell, Cashier.

Charter,	$250,000	Stocks deposited,	$191,346.92
Capital Stock paid in,	189,638	Circulation,	178,331

Merchants and Mechanics Bank. — Chicago. (*Closing.*)

James H. Woodworth, President.

*Charter,	$100,000	Stocks deposited,	$6000
Capital Stock paid in,	85,500	Circulation,	5561

Mississippi River Bank. — Oxford,

C. C. Merriam, President; W. H. Merriam, Cashier.

Morgan County Bank. — Jacksonville.

H. R. Reed, President; W. W. Wright, Cashier.

*Charter, $50,000

National Bank. — Equality.

E. J. Humphrey, President; W. H. Crawford, Cashier.

		Stocks deposited,	$80,000
Capital Stock paid in,	$80,000	Circulation,	74,376

Peoples Bank. — Carmi.

S. Vorhies, President; E. Dodge, Cashier.

		Stocks deposited,	$500,000
Capital Stock paid in,	$464,516	Circulation,	464,515

Prairie State Bank. — Washington.

J. L. Marsh, President; H. Lee, Cashier.

		Stocks deposited,	$115,000
Capital Stock paid in,	$104,160	Circulation,	104,160

Railroad Bank. — Decatur.

P. D. Kline, President; C. H. Fuller, Cashier.

Charter,	$50,000	Stocks deposited,	$50,000
Capital Stock paid in,	$56,000	Circulation,	48,050

Rock Island Bank. — Rock Island. (*Closing.*)

M. B. Osborn, President; S. H. Mann, Cashier.

*Charter,	$100,000	Stocks deposited,	$18,000
Capital Stock paid in,	50,000	Circulation,	16,007

---

* According to Monroe.

Rushville Bank. — Rushville.

		Stocks deposited,	$81,500
Capital Stock paid in,	$73,300	Circulation,	73,300

Southern Bank of Illinois. — Belleville. (*Closing.*)

R. Hinckley, President; F. Hinckley, Cashier.

*Charter	$300,000	Stocks deposited,	$7000
Capital Stock paid in,	7000	Circulation,	6000

Southern Bank of Illinois. — Grayville.

L. Hinckley, President; C. D. Affleck, Cashier.

		Stocks deposited,	$60,000
Capital Stock paid in,	$53,380	Circulation,	53,380

State Bank of Illinois. — Shawneetown.

J. Bowles, President; A. B. Safford, Cashier.

		Stocks deposited,	$471,186.96
Capital Stock paid in,	$431,305.03	Circulation,	425,389

Stock Security Bank. — Danville.

D. Clapp, President; W. W. Fellows, Cashier.

		Stocks deposited,	$200,000
Capital Stock paid in,	$183.400	Circulation,	183,470

E. I. Tinkham and Co.'s Bank. — McLeansboro.

S. Tinkham, President; W. Rickords, Cashier.

		Stocks deposited,	$265,000
Capital Stock paid in,	$255,000	Circulation,	233,385

Warren County Bank. — Monmouth.

T. L. Mackey, President; J. Quimby, Cashier.

The following banks have been closed during the latter part of the period above stated. Those marked with a † have returned, as required by law, the amount of notes put in circulation, and withdrawn their stocks; the notes of the others are at present redeemed at the auditor's office.

†*Bank of Lucas and Simonds* — Springfield.
Bank of Rockford — Rockford.
City Bank — Chicago.
Farmers' Bank — Chicago.
Mechanics' and Farmers' Bank — Springfield.
Phœnix Bank — Chicago.
†*Quincy City Bank* — Quincy.
Union Bank — Chicago.

* According to Monroe.

According to the Congressional Documents, the amount of capital employed by bankers, banking without charters, and by money and exchange brokers, was, in

Galena	Dec.	22,	1855	$550,000
Peoria	"	18,	"	550,000
Elgin	"	22,	"	10,000
Aurora	"	20,	"	50,000
La Salle	"	20,	"	20,000
Henry	"	19,	"	15,000
Peru	"	20,	"	48,000
Springfield	"	19,	"	300,000
Chicago	"	17,	"	273,100
Waukegan	"	24,	"	10,000
Quincy	"	22,	"	130,000
Decatur	Feb.	—,	1856	45,000
Ottawa	"	15,	"	200,000
Bloomington	"	11,	"	50,000
Freeport	Dec.	31,	1855	70,000
Princeton	Feb.	22,	1856	10,000
Belvidere	Jan.	—,	"	110,000
Jacksonville	Mar.	7,	"	5,000

RAILROADS.

THE present position of Illinois as regards the natural and artificial elements that make a great and prosperous State, is mainly attributable to the construction of her railroads, by which the State, in all its length and breadth, is traversed, and every possible facility afforded for an unlimited domestic and foreign trade and intercourse; and this, considering her immense territory and the enterprising character of her population, must, for all future time, necessarily secure to her an equal position with the highest in this great confederation of sister States.

Up to the year 1850, Illinois had only one railroad, running a distance of fifty-five miles. At the beginning of the year 1855, there were already 1892 miles; at the beginning of 1856, 2215 miles, and at its close, there were over 2600 miles, nearly all completed, while several new roads were either being projected, or even already in progress of construction.

Among the States of the Union, New York and Ohio have the greatest share of railroads: the former having 2795, and the latter 2725 miles. Illinois, indeed, is now but little behind them, and no doubt in a very brief time will surpass both, and possess more miles of railroad than any other State.

By means of the railroads, Illinois is in immediate communication with the East and the West, with the South and the North. The State itself is traversed by railroads in all directions — within one year's time, there will hardly be a single spot in it, from which one of the railroads cannot be reached within one day's travel.

The number of railroads that either pass entirely through the State, or, coming from adjacent States, merely traverse it in some parts, is no less than forty-eight, which are nearly all completed and in successful operation. They are all enumerated in the subjoined alphabetical list, in which are also stated, the points of commencement and termination of each road, the points at which it is crossed or intersected by other roads, together with the number of miles, &c., as far as we were able to ascertain.

The Alton and Illinoistown Railroad —
Connects Alton and Illinoistown, and is 25 miles long.

The Atlantic and Mississippi Railroad —
Will run from Illinoistown, northeasterly, to Terre Haute, Indiana, and cross the main line of the Illinois Central Railroad at Vandalia, the Chicago branch of the same at Effingham, and the Wabash Valley Railroad about ten miles from the frontier of Indiana.

The Belleville and Illinoistown Railroad —
Connects Belleville and Illinoistown, and is 15 miles long.

The Belleville and Mount Vernon Railroad —
Will, in coming from Belleville, cross the main line of the Illinois Central Railroad south of Richview, and terminate at Mount Vernon, Jefferson county, by an intersection with the Massac and Sangamon Railroad.

The Belleville and Murphysboro Railroad —
Will run southeast of Belleville, cross the Kaskaskia river near Athens, then cross the main line of the Illinois Central Railroad at Carbondale, and touch the Ohio river at Brooklyn, Massac county.

The Beloit Branch of the Galena Railroad —
Runs, in a northwestern direction, from Belvidere, Boone county, to Beloit, Wisconsin. Length, 20 miles.

The Bureau Valley Railroad —
Joins the Rock Island Railroad at Bureau Junction, Bureau county, and follows, in a southern direction, the Illinois river; at Lacon, crossing the Fort Wayne, Lacon, and Platte Valley Railroad, and terminating at Peoria. Length, 47 miles.

The Cairo and Vincennes Railroad —
Is intended to run south, from Vincennes, and, crossing the Massac and Sangamon and the Belleville and Murphysboro railroads, to have its ter minus at Cairo.

The Central Military Tract Railroad —
Forms a portion of the Burlington and Quincy Railroad, from Mendota, La Salle county, up to Galesburg, Knox county; in Bureau county, it crosses the Rock Island Railroad, and at Galvy, Knox county, the Fort Wayne, Lacon, and Platte Valley Railroad. Length, 80 miles.

The Chicago, Alton, and St. Louis Railroad —

Connects Chicago and Alton, in a distance of 260 miles. It runs from Chicago, in a southwestern direction, via Joliet, at which latter place several railroads cross each other. Between Dwight and Odell, it crosses the Fort Wayne, Lacon, and Platte Valley Railroad; at Peoria Junction, the Logansport and Pacific Railroad; at Bloomington, the Illinois Central Railroad, and at Springfield, the Great Western Railroad.

On the last of November, 1856, the privilege was granted to this company to extend the road through Alton, so that there is now an uninterrupted railway communication between Chicago and Illinoistown.

The Chicago, Burlington and Quincy Railroad —

Connects Chicago and Burlington, in a distance of 210 miles. It runs, westerly, to the Junction, where the Fox Valley, the Chicago, St. Charles, and Mississippi, and the Chicago, Fulton, and Iowa Central railroads terminate; and, proceeding thence in a southwestern direction, via Mendota and Galesburg, it reaches its terminus at Burlington. (See Central Military Tract Railroad.)

The Chicago and Cincinnati Railroad —

Will use the track of the Chicago and Alton Railroad from Chicago to Junction; thence run towards the southeast, and, north of Calumet, cross the Chicago branch of the Illinois Central Railroad; and, passing Roselle and Logansport, finally reach the Indiana line.

The Chicago and Fort Wayne Railroad —

Uses the track of the Chicago branch of the Illinois Central Railroad as far as Calumet, and from thence, as far as Lake, the Michigan Central Railroad; from the latter point, it will be continued, via Roselle, to Fort Wayne.

The Chicago, Fulton, and Iowa Central Railroad —

Also called *the Dixon Air Line*, or *the Galena Air Line*, forms the shortest route (only 135 miles) from Chicago to the Mississippi. It crosses the Rockford and Central Railroad west of Lane, and the main line of the Illinois Central Railroad at Dixon.

The Chicago and Milwaukie Railroad —

Along the shore of Lake Michigan, forms a connection between Chicago and Milwaukie. Its whole length is 85 miles, of which 40 miles are within the State.

The Chicago and Oswego Railroad —

Will run from Chicago, in a southwestern direction, to Athens, and from thence, after crossing the Lockport and Junction Railroad, will reach its terminus, near Oswego, by intersecting the Chicago and Burlington Railroad.

The Chicago and Rock Island Railroad —
Runs via Joliet, at which place it crosses the Illinois river. At La Salle it crosses the main line of the Illinois Central Railroad, and the Burlington and Quincy Railroad between Wyanet and Princeton, and then goes westward to Rock Island. Length, 182 miles.

The Chicago, St. Charles, and Mississippi Railroad —
Will run, via Junction and St. Charles, as far as Savannah, Carroll county, on the Mississippi river. On its way, it will cross the Rockford and Central Railroad, the main line of the Illinois Central Railroad, and the Dixon and Galena Railroad. It is now completed as far as St. Charles.

The Chicago, St. Paul, and Fond du Lac Railroad —
Formerly called *the Illinois and Wisconsin Railroad*, runs from Chicago, via Janesville, Wisconsin, through Wisconsin, crossing the Fox River Valley Railroad at Crystal Lake. Its whole length will be about 360 miles, of which about 60 miles are within the limits of Illinois. It is finished as far as Janesville.

The Dixon and Galena Air Line Railroad —
Will run, in a straight line, from Dixon, in a northwestern direction, and, after crossing the Chicago, St. Charles, and Mississippi Railroad, lead directly on to Galena.

The Fort Wayne, Lacon, and Platte Valley Railroad —
Is intended to form a connection, in a straight line, between Fort Wayne, Indiana, and the Mississippi river; south of Bourbonnais, it will cross the Chicago branch of the Illinois Central Railroad; the Alton and Chicago Railroad south of Dwight; the main line of the Illinois Central Railroad north of Wenona; the Bureau Valley Railroad near Lacon; the Chicago and Burlington Railroad near Galvy, and terminate about ten miles below Muscatine, near the Mississippi.

The Fox River Valley Railroad —
Commences at Elgin, and runs through the Valley of the Fox river up into Wisconsin. Near Crystal Lake, it crosses the Chicago, St. Paul, and Fond du Lac Railroad. It is finished to the State boundary line Length, 34 miles.

The Galena and Chicago Union Railroad —
Runs from Chicago, via Junction and Elgin, as far as Freeport. Near Belvidere, terminates, north, the Beloit Branch Railroad, and at Rockford, south of it, will terminate the Rockford and Central Railroad. Length, 121 miles.

The Great Western Railroad —

Runs from Lafayette, Indiana, via Danville, Vermillion county, as far as Naples, on the Illinois river; it touches the Chicago branch of the Illinois Central Railroad between Urbana and Tolono; crosses the main line of the last-mentioned railroad near Decatur, and the Alton and Chicago Railroad near Springfield. Its length, from Naples to the Indiana State-line, is 174½ miles.

That portion of this railroad which connects Springfield with Naples, was the first railway constructed within the State of Illinois (in the year 1837), but it soon fell into dilapidation, and continued so up to the year 1847, when it was purchased from the State by several capitalists, under whose direction it was reëstablished, and the construction of it gradually continued, until it was ready as far as the Indiana State-line.

The Jacksonville and Alton Railroad —

Will form a connection between Jacksonville and Alton. The subscriptions for it were started in October, 1856.

The Illinois Central Railroad —

Being 704 miles long, is the longest railroad in the State — one of the longest in the Union. To its construction and use, the State of Illionois is unquestionably indebted for the great progress that has been made during the last few years.

This railroad may be subdivided into three sections, viz.:

1. *The Main Line*, from Cairo to La Salle — 308 miles.
2. *The Galena Branch*, from La Salle to Dunleith — 146 miles.
3. *The Chicago Branch*, from Chicago to Centralia — 250 miles.

The Main Line will be crossed at Carbondale by the Belleville and Murphysboro Railroad. It crosses the Ohio and Mississippi Railroad at Sandoval. At Vandalia it will be crossed by the Atlantic and Mississippi, and by the Massac and Sangamon railroads. At Panola it will be crossed by the Terrehaute and Alton Railroad; at Decatur, by the Great Western Railroad, also touching, at the latter place, the Indiana and Illinois Central Railroad. At Bloomington it crosses the Alton and Chicago Railroad, and it will also be crossed, at the same place, by the railroad which it is in contemplation to construct from Peoria to Danville. South of Panola it will be crossed by the Logansport and Pacific Railroad; and, north of Wenona, by the Fort Wayne, Lacon, and Platte Valley Railroad; while at La Salle it is crossed by the Rock Island and Chicago Railroad.

The Galena Branch crosses the Burlington and Quincy Railroad at Mendota; at Dixon, the Chicago, Fulton, and Iowa Central Railroad; and it will be crossed, south of Foreston, by the Chicago, St. Charles, and Mississippi Railroad, while it joins the Galena and Chicago Union Railroad at Freeport, and thence runs as far as Dunleith.

The Chicago Branch crosses the Michigan Southern and Northern Indiana Railroad east of Junction; and north of Richton, the Joliet and Northern Indiana Railroad. South of Manteno, it will be crossed by the Wabash Valley Railroad; south of Bourbonnais, by the Fort Wayne, Lacon, and Platte Valley Railroad; north of Onarga, by the Logansport and Pacific Railroad. At Tolono, it crosses the Great Western Railroad, and south of Pesotum, it will be crossed by the Indiana and Illinois Central Railroad. At Mattoon, it crosses the Terrehaute and Alton Railroad; at Effingham, it will be crossed by the Atlantic and Mississippi Railroad, and at Tonti, by the Massac and Sangamon Railroad; at Odin, it crosses the Ohio and Mississippi Railroad, and then terminates in the main line at Centralia.

By means of its great number of junctions and crossings, the Illinois Central Railroad has the advantage of being in the closest connection with all parts of the State, and while it traverses the same from Chicago to Cairo, and from Cairo to Dunleith, it connects the South with the Northeast and Northwest.

The construction of this railroad was rendered possible by a grant of two and a half millions of acres of land. It was commenced on Christmas, in the year 1851, and on the 27th of September, 1856, the last rail was laid; so that, through excellent management, this great work was accomplished in the comparatively short space of four years and nine months. While we look upon the marvellous manner in which this road has been constructed as something unique and unsurpassed in the history of railroad building, and consider of what inestimable value it is to the State of Illinois, we must likewise, looking upon it as a mere individual speculation, undoubtedly, give it the highest rank among similar enterprises. The receipts of the Company from passengers and for the transportation of goods increase from month to month; its stocks always command a high price; and there is no doubt but that the sales of the land belonging to the Company will soon enable it to liquidate its entire debt, after which there will still be enough land left to enable the Company to make a dividend of fifty per cent. on the capital stock. Hence, in every respect, the Illinois Central Railroad maintains a position which makes it worthy to be ranked among the greatest enterprises of the present century.

The Illinois Coal Company Railroad—

Connects Caseyville with Brooklyn. It is, as indicated by its name, only a coal road, but it also does a passenger and freight business.

The Illinois River Railroad—

Is expected to run from Naples to Pekin, or to some other spot on the eastern shore of the Illinois river, opposite Peoria. The counties which this road will traverse, have already made large subscriptions for the construction of it.

The Indiana and Illinois Central Railroad —

Will be constructed from Indianapolis, Indiana, to Decatur. It will cross the Wabash Valley Railroad north of Bloomfield, and the main line of the Illinois Central Railroad between Pesotum and Okaw, and then join the Great Western Railroad at Decatur. Length, 149½ miles.

The Joliet and Athens Railroad —

Runs from Joliet, in a northerly direction, to Athens.

The Joliet and Northern Indiana Railroad —

Runs from Joliet to Lake, where it meets the Michigan Central Railroad. It crosses the Chicago branch of the Illinois Central Railroad north of Richton. Length, 45 miles.

The Logansport and Pacific Railroad —

Running in a straight line from Logansport, Indiana, towards the West, will cross the Wabash Valley Railroad at Middleport, the Chicago branch of the Illinois Central Railroad north of Onarga, the Alton and Chicago Railroad at Peoria Junction, and the main line of the Illinois Central Railroad south of Panola; then, pursuing a southwestern direction, terminate on the Illinois river, opposite Peoria.

The Lockport Junction Railroad —

Is intended to run from Lockport, in a northwestern direction, to Junction, via Naperville, after previously crossing the Chicago and Oswego Railroad, and at Junction joining the several roads which terminate there.

The Massac and Sangamon Railroad —

Is intended to run from Massac, on the Ohio river, via Marion, Frankfort, and Mt. Vernon, crossing the Ohio and Mississippi Railroad at Salem, the Chicago branch of the Illinois Central Railroad at Tonti, the main line of the latter at Vandalia, and the Terrehaute and Alton Railroad at Hillsboro, to Springfield.

The Michigan Central Railroad —

Runs from Calumet, on the Chicago branch of the Illinois Central Railroad, in a southwestern direction, through the northern part of the State of Indiana, and into the State of Michigan, to Detroit. The whole length of this road is 282 miles, of which, however, only a few miles are within the State of Illinois.

The Michigan Southern and Northern Indiana Railroad —

Runs from Chicago to Monroe, Michigan. It commences at Junction, on the Rock Island and Chicago Railroad, crosses the Chicago branch of the Illinois Central Railroad, and turns to the southeast, traversing Northern Indiana, and penetrating into Michigan. Its whole length is 245 miles, of which but a few miles are within the State of Illinois.

The Naples Hannibal Railroad—
Is intended to form a continuation of the Great Western Railroad, and to traverse the region between the Illinois and Mississippi rivers, so as to connect Naples and Hannibal.

The Northern Cross Railroad—
Runs from Galesburg to Quincy. Length, 100 miles.

The Northern Cross Branch Railroad—
Will run from Morgan City, on the Great Western Railroad, to Camp Point, on the Northern Cross Railroad, and traverse, near Mount Sterling, the Peoria and Hannibal Railroad.

The Ohio and Mississippi Railroad—
Runs from Vincennes, Indiana, to Illinoistown, thus traversing the southern part of the State in its entire bread h. It will be crossed, near Salem, by the Massac and Sangamon Railroad. At Odin, it crosses the Chicago branch of the Illinois Central Railroad, and at Sandoval, the main line of said road. Length, 145 miles.

The Peoria and Hannibal Railroad—
(Also called *the Bureau Valley Extension Railroad*) will be opened at Peoria, and run in a southwestern direction, crossing the Northern Cross Branch Railroad near Mt. Sterling, and terminate at Hannibal. Its length will be about 120 miles.

The Peoria and Oquawka Railroad—
Runs, in a northwestern direction, from Peoria to Galesburg, where it joins the Chicago and Burlington Railroad. Also the eastern branch of this road is already under construction; at Bloomington it will cross the Alton and Chicago Railroad, and the main line of the Illinois Central Railroad; at Urbana, the Chicago branch of the latter road, and join the Indiana roads at Danville.

The Peoria and Rock Island Railroad
Will bring Peoria and Rock Island into immediate connection. It will cross the Chicago and Burlington, and the Fort Wayne, Lacon, and Platte Valley railroads. Length, 82 miles.

The Rockford Central Railroad—
Will run from Rockford, in a southern direction, crossing the Chicago, St. Charles, and Mississippi Railroad, and the Chicago, Fulton, and Iowa Central Railroad, and join the Illinois Central Railroad at Mendota.

The Terrehaute, Alton, and St. Louis Railroad—

Soon after passing the Indiana frontier, will be crossed, near Paris, by the Lake Erie, Wabash, and St. Louis Railroad. It crosses the Chicago branch of the Illinois Central Railroad at Mattoon, the main line of said road at Pana, and then runs, in a southwestern direction, to Alton. At Hillsboro, it will be crossed by the Massac and Sangamon Railroad. Length, 173 miles.

The Vincennes and Paducah Railroad—

Will run, almost in a southern direction, from Vincennes, to Brooklyn, Massac county, opposite Paducah, in Kentucky.

The Wabash Valley Railroad—

Will run from Joliet, in a southern direction, to Vincennes; it will cross, south of Manteno, the Chicago branch of the Illinois Central Railroad, then the Fort Wayne, Lacon, and Platte Valley Railroad; then the Logansport and Pacific Railroad at Middleport; the Great Western Railroad at Danville; then the Indiana and Illinois Central Railroad; the Terrehaute and Alton Railroad at Paris; and, finally, the Atlantic and Mississippi Railroad.

The Warsaw and Rockford Railroad—

Will run from Warsaw, Hancock county, to Port Byron, Rock Island county, and have a length of 62 miles.

PUBLIC INSTITUTIONS.

The Illinois University, at Springfield, was established by an act of the Legislature, in the year 1855. Although the main object of its establishment was to diffuse useful knowledge, science, and art, in general, yet there have been established principally —

1. A department for the education of teachers of the common schools.
2. An agricultural department, for the education and accomplishment of farmers; and
3. A mechanical department, for instruction in the mechanical sciences.

The management of the University is entrusted to the care and supervision of a president and twelve trustees, while a number of professors impart instruction in the various branches.

The number of students is about 130.

The Northern Illinois University, at Henry, Marshall county, was likewise established in the year 1855, and is placed under the patronage of four Methodist conferences.

The Illinois College, at Jacksonville, was established in the year 1829. It has from seven to eight professors, and about 140 alumni and students.

The Shurtleff College, at Upper Alton, under the superintendency of the Baptists, and in connection with a theological seminary, was established in the year 1835. It has seven professors, and about 70 alumni and students.

The McKendree College, at Lebanon, under the superintendency of the Methodists, and likewise established in the year 1835, has six professors, and about 150 alumni and students.

The Knox College, at Galesburg, was established in the year 1837. It has seven professors, and the number of its students and alumni is from 90 to 100.

The Rush Medical College, at Chicago, established in the year 1842, has nine professors, and counts about 130 students and graduates.

The Illinois Hospital for the Insane is at Jacksonville. In the years 1851 to 1854, there were 404 persons admitted into it, of which number 148 were cured, and 27 died. Of the 404 patients admitted, 46 were born in Illinois, and the rest partly in other States of the Union, and partly in Europe. The majority of these patients were males.

In 197 of the patients, causes of their insanity were unknown. Of the other cases, among the known causes, the following deserve to be mentioned: — 37 in consequence of other diseases and defects of the constitution; 33 from child-bearing and certain female diseases; 12 through hereditary imperfections; 13 of injuries to the head; 2 by sun-stroke (coup de soleil); 4 from intemperance; 35 through grief; 22 from pietism; 8 by "spirit rappings," or spiritualism; 17 from unhappy love; 6 from excessive study; 2 of home-sickness; 4 from distress for money; 1 through jealousy; 1 by seduction, and 1 through ambition.

Of the 22 patients whose insanity was caused by pietism, 17 were males and 5 females; of those from unhappy love, 11 were males and 6 females; and of those who suffered through the influence of spiritual manifestations, 7 were males, and 1 a female.

Since the 16th of June, 1854, the institution has been under the superintendency of Dr. McFarland, late superintendent of the New Hampshire Asylum for the Insane. During the two years, from the 1st of December, 1852, to the 1st of December, 1854, the receipts of the institution amounted to $104,696.59, and the expenditures to $100,680.93.

The Institution for the Education of the Blind is at Jacksonville, and stands under the superintendency of Joshua Rhoads, Esq. According to the Report of the first of January, 1855, there were at that time 35 pupils in it.

The Institution for the Education of the Deaf and Dumb is likewise at Jacksonville. At the beginning of the year 1855, there were 99 pupils in it, of whom 59 were males, and 40 females. Ninety-five were of Illinois, and four from Missouri.

The State Penitentiary is at Alton, and the usual number of its inmates is from 450 to 500.

NEWSPAPERS.

It is a well-known observation, that the superiority or inferiority of a people with respect to intelligence may be fairly estimated by the greater or lesser activity of the newspaper press in their midst. We therefore record it, as a very satisfactory fact, that Illinois, although but a virgin State, and just entering the period of her real development, already possesses a large amount of daily literature. According to the information we have obtained, there are not less than 161 newspapers published within the State: of these, 147 are printed in the English, 13 in the German, and 1 in the French language. The subjoined is an alphabetical list of them, according to their respective places of publication: —

ALTON. — *The Courier*, by G. T. Brown. Daily, weekly, and tri-weekly.
The Democrat, by J. Fitch. Daily and weekly.
Illinois Beobachter. Weekly. (German.)
The Telegraph, by J. L. Baker & Co. Weekly.

AURORA. — *The Beacon*, by D. & J. W. Randall. Weekly.
The Guardian, by S. Whiteley. Weekly.

BATAVIA. — *The Fox River Expositor*, by Risk & Co. Weekly.

BEARDSTOWN. — *The Central Illinoisian*, by Shaw & Reavis. Weekly.
The Gazette. Weekly.

BELLEVILLE. — *The Advocate*, by J. S. Coulter. Daily and weekly.
Der Deutsche Democrat. Weekly. (German.)
Belleviller Volksblatt, by Dr. Wenzel. Weekly. (German.)
Belleviller Zeitung, by I. Grimm. Daily. (German.)

BELVIDERE. — *The Standard*, by R. Roberts Weekly.

BLOOMINGTON. — *The Flag*. Weekly.
The Pantagraph, by W. E. Foote. Weekly.
The Times. Weekly.
The Central Illinois Times, by J. W. Underwood & Co. Weekly.

CAIRO. — *Times and Delta*, by E. Willet & L. G. Faxon. Tri-weekly and weekly.

CALEDONIA. — *Pulaski Democrat*, by Miller. Weekly.

CARLINVILLE. — *Macoupin Statesman*, by J. L. Dagger. Weekly.

CARLYLE. — *The Age of Progress*, by I. W. Snow. Weekly.

CARROLTON. — *The Gazette*, by G. B. Price. Weekly.

CENTRAL CITY. — *The Gazette*, by E. Schiller. Weekly.

CHARLESTON. — *The Courier.* Weekly.

CHESTER. — *The Herald*, by Hanna and Phillips. Weekly.

CHICAGO. — *Bank Note List*, by F. G. Adams. Semi-monthly.
Chicago Abendzeitung, by Committi & Beckert. Daily. (German.)
Christian Times, by Church & Smith. Weekly.
Commercial Advertiser, by A. Dutch. Daily, tri-weekly, and weekly.
Congregational Herald, by I. C. Halbrook. Weekly.
The Democrat, by John Wentworth. Daily and weekly.
The Democratic Press, by Scripps, Bross & Spears. Daily, tri-weekly, and weekly.
The Evangelist, by Patterson & Curtis.
The Garden City, by Sloan & Co. Weekly.
The Journal, by Wilson & Co. Daily, tri-weekly, and weekly.
Illinois Staatszeitung, by Höffgen & Schneider. Daily and weekly. (Germ.)
National Demokrat, by Diverzy & Schade. Daily. (German.)
New Covenant, by Skinner & Day. Weekly.
Northwestern Christian Advocate, by J. V. Watson. Weekly.
The Prairie Farmer, by A. F. Kennicott & Co. Weekly.
Prairie Herald, by J. A. Wright. Weekly.
The Times, by Cook & Co. Daily and weekly.
The Tribune, by Fowler & Co. Daily and weekly.
Western Crusader, by J. Dow & Co. Weekly.
Western Enterprise, by E. P. Little. Weekly.
Western Pathfinder, by W. B. Hanner. Weekly.
Western Tablet. Weekly.

DANVILLE. — *The Illinois Citizen.* Weekly.

DECATUR. — *Gazette*, by G. Shoaff. Weekly.

DE WITT. — *The Courier*, by Jones & Watkins. Weekly.

DIXON. — *The Telegraph*, by B. F. Shaw. Weekly.
The Transcript, by Stevens and Johnson. Weekly.

DU PAGE. — *The Journal*, by Keith, Edson & Co. Weekly.

ELGIN. — *Kane County Journal*, by Lyman & Smith. Weekly.
The Palladium, by Rowe & Joslyn. Weekly.

FAIRFIELD. — *Independent Press*, by F. C. Mawley. Weekly.

FREEPORT. — *The Bulletin.* Weekly.
Deutscher Anzeiger, by W. Wagner. Weekly. (German.)
The Journal, by H. M. Scheetz. Weekly.

FULTON City. — *The Advertiser*, by McFaddon & Laighton. Weekly.
Whiteside's Investigator. Weekly.

GALENA. — *The Advertiser*, by H. H. Houghton. Daily, tri-weekly, and weekly.
The Courier, by Leae, Crouch & Co. Daily.
The Jeffersonian, by Ray and Sanford. Weekly.
North Western Gazette, by Houghton & Co. Weekly.

GALESBURG. — *Free Democrat*, by W. J. Woods. Weekly.

GENESEO. — *The Standard.* Weekly.

GENEVA. — *Kane County Democrat*, by Herrington & McQuillen. Weekly.

GRAYVILLE. — *The News*, by J. Prather. Weekly.

HAVANA. — *Mason County Herald.* Weekly.

HILLSBORO. — *Montgomery County Herald*, by C. D. Dickerson. Weekly.
Prairie Mirror, by G. H. Gilmore. Weekly.

HUTSONVILLE. — *Wabash Sentinel*, by E. Callahan. Weekly.

JACKSONVILLE. — *The Constitutionist.* Weekly.
The Morgan Journal, by Selby and Clayton. Weekly.

JERSEYVILLE. — *The Prairie State*, by A. Smith. Weekly.

JOLIET. — *The True Democrat*, by A. McIntosh. Weekly.
The Signal, by C. & C. Zarley. Weekly.

KANKAKEE CITY. — *Gazette*, by Leonard & Grooms. Weekly.
Journal de l'Illinois. Weekly. (French.)

KNOXVILLE. — *The Journal*, by J. Regan. Weekly.

LACON. — *The Herald*, by S. Ramsey. Weekly.
Illinois Gazette, by A. N. Ford. Weekly.

LAKE ZURICH. — *The Banker*, by S. Paine. Weekly.

LA SALLE. — *The Press*, by Boynton & Co. Weekly.

LEWISTOWN. — *The Fulton Democrat*, by J. M. Davidson. Weekly.
Fulton Ledger. Weekly.
Fulton Republican. Weekly.

LINCOLN. — *The Illinois Citizen*, by Moody Fuller. Weekly.

LOCKPORT. — *The Telegraph*, by Dagett & Holcomb. Weekly.

MACOMB. — *McDonough Democrat*, by Smith & Royalty. Weekly.
McDonough Independent, by G. W. Smith. Weekly.

MARSHALL. — *The Eastern Illinoisan*, by Robinson & Zimmerman. Weekly.
The Telegraph, by S. P. Andrews. Weekly.

MENDOTA. — *The Press*, by C. R. Fisk. Weekly.

METAMORA. — *Woodford County Visitor*, by S. P. Shope. Weekly.

MIDDLEPORT. — *Iroquois County Press*, by Keady & Scott. Weekly.

MOLINE. — *The Workman*. Weekly.

MONMOUTH. — *The Atlas*, by C. K. Smith. Weekly.
The Review, by A. H. Swain. Weekly.

MORRIS. — *The Gazette*, by A. J. Ashton. Weekly.
Grundy County Herald, by Buffington & Soutard. Weekly.
The Grundy Yeoman, by I. C. Watkins. Weekly.

MOUNT CARMEL. — *The Register*, by T. S. Bowers. Weekly.

MOUNT STERLING. — *The Chronotype*, by J. R. Bailey. Weekly.
The Western Spy. Weekly.

MOUNT VERNON. — *The Jeffersonian*, by J. S. Bogan. Weekly.

NAPERVILLE. — *Du Page County Observer*, by G. Martin. Weekly.

NASHVILLE. — *The Monitor*, by H. Johnson. Weekly.

OREGON. — *The Ogle County Reporter*, by M. W. Smith. Weekly.

OQUAWKA. — *The Plaindealer*, by Dallam & Bigelow. Weekly.
The Spectator. Weekly.

OSWEGO. — *Kendall County Courier*, by H. S. Humphrey. Weekly.

OTTAWA. — *The Freetrader*, by W. Osman. Weekly.
The Republican, by T. Hampton. Weekly.

PARIS. — *The Prairie Beacon*. Weekly.
The Valley Blade, by Pratt & Brendt. Weekly.
The Wabash Valley Republican. Weekly.

PEORIA. — *Illinois Banner*, by A. Zotz. Weekly. (German.)
Illinois Republikaner, by I. P. Stibolt. Weekly. (German.)
Morning News, by G. W. Raney. Daily.
The Press. Daily and weekly.
The Evening Republican, by S. L. Coulter. Daily, tri-weekly, and weekly.
The Transcript, by N. G. Nason. Daily and weekly.

PERU. — *Der Anzeiger*, by Heinrichs. Weekly. (German.)
The Chronicle, by J. F. Linton. Weekly.

PITTSFIELD. — *Pike County Free Press*, by J. G. Nicolay. Weekly.

PONTIAC. — *Livingston County News*, by Cook & Renoe. Weekly.

PRINCETON. — *The Post*, by Ch. Faxon. Weekly.

QUINCY. — *Illinois Courier*. Weekly. (German.)
The Herald, by A. Brooks. Daily and weekly.
Quincy Journal. Weekly. (German.)

QUINCY. — *The Republican*, by D. S. Morrison & Co. Daily.
The Western Patriot, by Warren & Gibson. Weekly.
The Whig, by Norton & Ralston. Daily, tri-weekly & weekly.

ROCKFORD. — *Rock River Democrat*, by Dickson & Bird. Weekly.
The Register, by E. C. Dougherty. Weekly.
The Republican, by Blaisdell, jr., & Co. Weekly.

ROCK ISLAND. — *The Advertiser*, by O. P. Wharton. Daily.
The Morning Argus, by Danforth & Shurly. Daily.
The Republican, by J. B. Danforth. Weekly.
Rock Island Beobachter. Weekly. (German.)

RUSHVILLE. — *Prairie Telegraph*, by J. Scripps & Son. Weekly.

ST. CHARLES. — *Kane County Democrat*, by J. S. Jones. Weekly.

SHAWNEETOWN. — *The Southern Illinoisan*, by Edwards & Son. Weekly.

SHELBYVILLE. — *The Shelby Banner*, by P. L. Schutt. Weekly.

SPRINGFIELD. — *The Illinois Farmer*, by S. Francis. Weekly.
The Illinois State Journal, by Bailhache & Baker. Daily, tri weekly, and weekly.
The Illinois State Register, by Lanphier & Walker. Daily.

STERLING. — *The Times*, by Narwood & Goodrich. Weekly.

SYCAMORE. — *The Republican Sentinel*, by H. A. Hough. Weekly

TOULON. — *The Prairie Advocate*. Weekly.

URBANA. — *The Union*. Weekly.

WARSAW. — *The Express*, by Thos. C. Sharp. Weekly.

WATERLOO. — *Monroe Advertiser*, by H. C. Talbott. Weekly
Monroe Demokrat. Weekly. (German.)
The Patriot, by G. Abbott. Weekly.

WAUKEGAN. — *The Gazette*, by N. C. Geer. Weekly.

WILMINGTON. — *The Herald*, by W. H. Clark. Weekly.

WOODSTOCK. — *The Republican Free Press*, by C. C. McClure & Co Weekly

WEIGHTS AND MEASURES.

BY an act of the last Legislature of Illinois, it was ordained, that whenever any of the articles specified below shall be contracted for, or sold and delivered, the weight of each shall be the number of pounds per bushel set opposite to it, unless there shall be a special contract or agreement to the contrary.

	Pounds.		Pounds.
Wheat	60	Blue Grass Seed	14
Shelled Corn	56	Buckwheat	52
Corn in the ear	70	Dried Peaches	33
Rye	56	Dried Apples	24
Oats	38	Onions	57
Barley	47	Salt	50
Irish Potatoes	60	Coal	80
Sweet Potatoes	55	Malt	38
White Beans	60	Bran	20
Castor Beans	46	Turnips	55
Clover Seed	60	Plastering Hair	8
Timothy Seed	45	Unslacked Lime	80
Hemp Seed	44	Corn Meal	48
Flax Seed	56	Fine Salt	55

HINTS TO IMMIGRANTS.

As this book is designed to be read and used, not only by those who already enjoy the happiness of being citizens of the Prairie State, but also by those who may hereafter seek to establish homes for themselves within its borders, it will doubtless be quite acceptable to the latter class, to receive, in addition to the information contained in the preceding chapters, a few hints, dictated by experience, in respect to what is in the first place most expedient and necessary to be done by them, and next as to what they may expect, in their efforts to secure a fortunate settlement.

In the first place, then, no immigrant should neglect to make a tour of the State, and carefully examine for himself into the diversified nature and quality of its soil, as found in the various districts; and until he has done so, he should not purchase any land. Time and means, it is true, are both required for this purpose, but certainly, neither will be lost or spent in vain. The advantages that may thus be gained, will amply repay the investment; and it will be found far better, than to purchase in haste, and repent at leisure, as is too often the case with inconsiderate settlers. Besides, since the opening of the railroads, travelling in Illinois is so much facilitated, that one may visit almost every place at a trifling cost.

Persons who have large means at command, will undoubtedly do well to purchase their land in the immediate vicinity of some railroad or large town; while those whose means are limited, will find it more advantageous to make their choice of land in districts lying farther removed from such centres, but where the soil is equally notable for its excellent qualities, and the price a great deal lower.

A person with small means, having found from forty to eighty acres, situated in a neighborhood which he likes, and but five or six miles from a place where building and fencing materials, as well as fuel, can be bought at reasonable prices, should endeavor to effect a purchase, under an arrangement for a credit on three-fourths of the purchase-money for a sufficiently long term; and, after succeeding in this, he should then immediately set to work and lay the foundation of his new family hearth.

A pair of good horses, a wagon, one cow, a couple of pigs, several domestic fowls, two ploughs (one for breaking up the prairie, and the other for tillage), together with a few other tools and implements, are all that is necessary for a beginning. A log house can soon be erected. Thus provided for in the outset, and working with a joyful heart and honest perseverance, the confiding farmer will, surely, under the blessing of heaven, soon be enabled to replace his log hut with a cheerful dwelling-house, and to meet the payments of purchase-money as they become due, and still have a handsome surplus. In the course of a few years, therefore, one whose means in the start are rather stinted, may become an independent farmer, and enjoy his own farm and homstead free of debts. Of such success, innumerable instances may be found in the State of Illinois.

In the chapter on "Agriculture," we have shown, by several accounts of the yield of crops, how easy it is for a farmer to rise in this State. We will here cite but one instance, to show that a mechanic may also, with equal ease, secure wealth and independence. It is found in an extract from a letter of Mr. J. H. Atkinson, of Pekin, dated December the 5th, 1855. This gentleman, speaking of Pekin, writes thus: —

This town has about two thousand inhabitants, and contains two houses engaged in the manufacture of wagons; four, of ploughs; two, of carriages and buggies; two places for horse-shoeing, exclusively; two gunsmiths; two cabinet-makers; one chair-maker; three coopers' shops; one foundry and machine shop; one large manufactory of reaping and mowing machines, and one pottery; — all of which may be said to be doing a first rate business, in proportion to the amount of capital invested, which is, in some instances, very small, and in others proportionately large.

All composing said manufacturing firms (making no exceptions) came here, or were raised here (poor men), mechanics or artisans, and have pretty much the same circumstances marking the history of their rise. All, by steady industry, have commenced small shops on their own hook, and work on repairs or job work, filling in their spare time on new work, which gradually grew into a business, only varied in the amount of its prosperity by the difference in energy of its proprietors, or its own susceptibilities of extension or enlargement. In a few instances, this rapidity of growth is truly astonishing. I will give you one instance: — The firm of T. and H. Smith & Co. now works on a capital of probably fifty thousand dollars, and employs, regularly, from fifty-five to sixty men, mechanics and artisans of all descriptions, at prices varying from $1.50 to $3 per day; turn out one wagon per day, at a price varying from $90 to $130, according to quality; a great many buggies and carriages, at prices from $115 to $700 each; together with a plough business, amounting to near one thousand ploughs a year of all descriptions. Said firm, five years ago, consisted of T. and Henry Smith, two poor Hanoverians, the one a wagon-maker, the other a blacksmith, who rented a small shop, and went to work on repairing wagons, shoeing horses, &c., and were soon enabled to buy the old shop and lot on which it stood; after which, they began by filling in spare time on new work, to be able to make a business of it, which has gradually increased up to its present limits, and instead of the old shop first rented, only large enough to contain one work-bench and one smith's fire, the lot first mentioned and five adjacent ones are occupied by large and commodious workshops, each branch of the business being headed by one of the firm, all of whom are mechanics (brothers), and all work.

This is the history of every shop in town and the adjacent country. All were, only a few years ago, poor men, and now many of them are wealthy; and we have no instances of men who have commenced, even in the smallest way at first, who have attended to their business, and lived within their means, not meeting with the same success. Our business men, merchants and storekeepers, millers, pork packers, bankers—in fact, every man who now figures in this town, as being above the condition of laboring men, are men who came here poor — most of them very poor.

Let the immigrant consider this. Such advantages as those here stated are still everywhere open to the honest, industrious, and economical settler. What is said of Pekin is but the oft-repeated story of many other places, and will be as frequently verified in the future history of the State.

In the preparation of this work, whenever it became necessary to state our opinions on any particular subject, we have always fortified them by the authority of reliable persons who have for many years resided in Illinois — we have frequently even made use of their own words; and now, in giving these hints to new settlers, we will again avail ourselves of the information communicated to us by practical men, whose actual observations for many years past enable them to speak familiarly and authoritatively "on matters and things in general," as they exist in the State of which they are citizens. We will, therefore, here introduce to our readers an old settler, Mr. John Williams, of Albany, Coles county, who, in a letter dated December the 23d, 1855, says: —

I have lived in Illinois about thirty years, and have seen some ups and downs in that time. I moved from Kentucky, and settled first in Vermillion county; after living there thirteen years, I moved into Champaign county, lived there three years, and then went over into Platt county, Missouri; but not having seen the land there before moving out, and finding it did not equal my expectations, I returned to Illinois, and settled in Coles county, where I have remained ever since. You can, therefore, see that I have been over some of the West, in search of the best place to make the "almighty dollar;" and, as I think I have found it, I will here say, that, after a man has lived in the State of Illinois, and farmed its rich soil for a few years, he will find it hard work to hunt up a better country.

When I first settled in Vermillion county, the representation of our district comprised all the State lying up along the Lake, including Chicago, which then consisted only of the old block fort on the lake shore. At that time, we, in the centre of the State, had no market for any of our produce; we had no railroads, and were forced to kill our hogs at home, team them to Terre Haute, sixty miles, and then get $1.50 to $2 per hundred weight, taking half the amount in store goods at a very high figure.

So farmers had to work along, in those days. I have known corn to sell for five to eight cents per bushel; and yet, even then, they did well, from the fact that they could raise everything they wanted to eat, and in abundance too.

My advice to farmers in the East is, to leave their rocks and hills, where they are just grubbing out a living, and come on to these splendid prairies, as they lie all ready for the plough, and where everything which the farmer plants yields such an abundant return.

Mr. James N. Brown, of Island Grove, formerly President of the State Agricultural Society, in a letter dated November the 28th, 1855, says: —

Let the industrious poor man know, that all he has to do, is, to become the holder of forty or eighty acres of land, build his cabin, and go to work with his team, and turn over the sod, and commence tilling the soil, — and that the laws of the land protect him against the depredations of stock —

and, my word for it, we shall see, in a very short time, all our prairies brought into cultivation, and teeming with an industrious and happy population, adding millions to the wealth of the State.

Rev. J. S. Barger, of Clinton, De Witt county, in his letter of the 22d of January, 1855, says: —

Let them come by thousands and tens of thousands — there is room enough — and examine the country. They will find rich lands, and good water, and general health, almost everywhere. This is not a wilderness. They will find schools and churches springing up in almost every settlement made, and now being made, throughout the State. Illinois is not a moral desolation. It literally and spiritually "blossoms as the rose." Let them come to Chicago, and go to Galena, and visit Cairo. But let them not remain at either place, unless they choose. The Illinois Central Railroad and its branches traverse the finest portion of the globe. Let them glide through our State, on these and other roads, now checkering the entire of this "Garden of the Lord," and stop where they will, to "examine the land, of what sort it is," and they will no longer consent to dig among the rocks, and plough the sterile land of their forefathers. But they will long bless the day, when they found, for themselves and their children, such comfortable homes, as they still may obtain in this rich and beautiful Prairie State, destined soon to compare with — nay, to surpass, in all the most desirable respects — the most prosperous State in the Union.

We think we cannot conclude this last chapter of our book in a better manner than with the words of one of the worthiest citizens of Illinois, and who, having been one of its earliest settlers, now looks back through a long life of toil and experience. This gentleman is Mr. Edson Harkness, of Southport, Peoria county, to whom we are also indebted for valuable contributions to this work, as well as for the kindness through which we are privileged to place before our readers the following extract from his excellent "Volunteer Advice to Immigrants": —

A few suggestions, to those who are desirous of building up a home in the rich and rapidly improving West, may not be out of place, from an old man, who has seen much of pioneer life. It can hardly be expected, that you will be entirely free from those amiable prejudices, which spread a sort of sanctity over the manners, customs, language, and habits of the home you have left. You will find yourself constantly instituting comparisons between the old state of things to which you have been accustomed, and the changed condition of affairs which you find in the West. If the old and the new are alike, you will conclude that all is well. But the old will be very apt to be set up as a *standard of right.* This state of mind you must endeavor to change, as soon as possible, and to decide every question upon its intrinsic merits.

You will come in daily contact with people from all the other States and from all the nations of Western Europe. There will be many of them speaking strange dialects of the English language — that is, strange to you. But you must not forget that yours is also strange to them. Be therefore very cautious how you criticise the bad English of others — for they can, perhaps, point out as many defects in your pronunciation, as you can in theirs. The best way is, to look over your dictionary occasionally, correct your own errors, and let other people, if they will, do the same.

Again, be very careful not to underrate the intelligence or the capacity of those with whom you may come in contact. Many of our people are very plain in their manners; but they are, like yourself, all immigrants — have seen a great deal of the world, and have become shrewd observers of character. With such men, you will soon find your level, wherever that level may be. — It is not uncommon for young men, who have received the best educational advantages, to come out to the West with high expectations of honor and distinction among a people not peculiarly blessed with the means of intelligence. Such expectations are pretty sure to end in disappointment. Our people are eminently practical, but too stupid or too gain-loving to appreciate very highly the refinements of the mere scholar, whose claim to distinction is based upon a knowledge of books alone.

If the scholar will in any way bring his knowledge to bear upon the practical interests of society, he may do well enough. If he will teach a country school for from twenty to thirty dollars per month, and "board round," he may soon get the good will and esteem of the community. He must be careful not to use a language which is "all Greek" to his hearers — must treat every one with respect and kindness — must take an interest in the welfare of every family, and, at the same time, turn a deaf ear to the small scandal and small gossip of the neighborhood.

A young man may learn more that is really useful by teaching a country school for one winter, than in twice that time spent in college — that is, if he thoroughly studies the living "subjects" around him. If he has tact and good sense enough to keep on the right side of his pupils and their parents he is then fairly started on the highway to honor and distinction. He can then go and make his "claim," or his purchase of wild land, and prepare to set up as a farmer. If he had not a cent in his pocket when he came to the "settlement," if he is orderly, prudent, and industrious for a year, his credit will be established.

He can then purchase what may be indispensable, in the way of a team and implements, for starting business on a small scale. After toiling on a year or two more, some one of the bright-eyed maidens who attended his school, will begin to pity his lonely condition, and consent to share the joys and the sorrows of life with him.

A small house is then built, and is enlarged as the inmates multiply. The farm is also enlarged as the wealth of the owner is increased. Orchards are planted — ornamental trees, shrubs and vines start up, and grow luxuriantly about the house. The house itself, having been built a piece at a time, from the necessities of the hour, begins to look shabby, and yet below the condition of the owner, — a new and splendid one is accordingly built, near the site of the old one, so as to save the shrubs and trees for the new lawn. The old house is sold to some new settler, and taken away.

The poor schoolmaster has become a man of affluence, and has filled various public offices with advantage to the State, and with credit and honor to himself.

This is no dream, — no fancy sketch — but the literal history, so far as it goes, of thousands of our western farmers.

But, perhaps, there may be too much *hard work* implied, in the foregoing sketch, to suit the refined tastes of a portion of those who, in imagination, are rearing their future castles on the broad western prairies. Let me say to you, young man, if you come to a new country to avoid hard work, you will commit a great error. If you are a preacher, lawyer, physician, farmer, or mechanic, you must *work* — *work*.

We have, out here, got rid of the old feudal prejudices of caste. Work is not only honorable, but the only means of distinction. We have, it is true, a large and flourishing establishment, provided by the State, as a home for those who endeavor to get their living without honest work: but it is not popular to go there — in fact, none go, unless compelled to do so by positive law, and under the escort of — a sheriff.

If you are willing to work at any honest business, for which your previous training has fitted you — if willing to join the great army, which, with the axe, the plough, and the steam-engine, is striking out into the desert, and conquering an empire greater than was ever ruled by a Tamerlane or a Bonaparte — COME ON! we will give you a place in our ranks, and if you act the part of a good, brave soldier, in the struggle for personal independence, you shall be promoted. It is the object of every true soldier in this great army, to "conquer a piece" of rich and bountiful land, for himself and his posterity. Our ranks are not full. We have room enough to take in half a million of recruits annually for the next century, and still there will be room for more! Come on, then, and work out life's problem, as best you can, in the free and boundless West.

THE END

KEEN & LEE

Offer to the Trade of the North-West the following CATALOGUE OF GOODS connected with the Book and Stationery Business.

Their connections with large Importing and Manufacturing Establishments, both at the East and in Europe, as well as frequent visits thereto, enable them to have constantly on hand a complete assortment of Goods, which they can supply to the Trade at the very lowest prices, and on the best terms.

Merchants from the Country visiting Chicago, are requested to call and examine their stock.

CATALOGUE.

SCHOOL BOOKS.

Readers.

McGUFFY'S FIRST READER.
" SECOND, THIRD, FOURTH, and FIFTH do
SAUNDERS' FIRST READER, (Old Series.)
" SECOND " "
" THIRD " "
" FOURTH " "
TOWN'S FIRST READER.
" SECOND, THIRD, and FOURTH do.
DENMAN'S STUDENT'S FIRST READER.
" " SECOND "
" " THIRD and FOURTH do.
PARKER'S FIRST READER.
" SECOND, THIRD, FOURTH, and FIFTH do.
SANDERS' NEW FIRST READER.
" " SECOND, THIRD, FOURTH, and FIFTH do.
WEBB'S READER, Nos. 1, 2, and 3.
" NORMAL READER.
" FIFTH "

SARGENT'S STANDARD FIRST READER.
" " SECOND and THIRD do.
" " FOURTH and FIFTH do.
INDIANA FIRST READER.
" SECOND, THIRD, and FOURTH do.
GOODRICH'S FIRST READER.
" SECOND, THIRD, FOURTH, and FIFTH do.

Spelling Books.

WEBSTER'S ELEMENTARY SPELLER.
SANDERS' OLD and NEW SPELLER; McGUFFY'S do.
TOWN'S OLD and NEW SPELLER.
DENMAN'S STUDENT'S SPELLER.
PRICE'S SPELLER; WEBSTER'S PICTORIAL do.

Arithmetics.

THOMPSON'S MENTAL ARITHMETIC.
" PRACTICAL "
" HIGHER "
" TABLE BOOK.
" SLATE AND BLACK-BOARD EXERCISES.
ADAMS' NEW REVISED ARITHMETIC.
" PRIMARY ARITHMETIC; COLBURN'S MENTAL do.
EMERSON'S FIRST ARITHMETIC.
" SECOND and THIRD do.
RY'S FIRST ARITHMETIC.
" SECOND and THIRD do.
SMITH'S MENTAL ARITHMETIC.
" SECOND do., and THIRD OR NEW do.
DAVIES' TABLE BOOK.
" PRIMARY ARITHMETIC.
" OLD and NEW ARITHMETIC; UNIVERSITY do.
GREENLEAF'S MENTAL "
" COMMON SCHOOL ARITHMETIC.
" NATIONAL "
PERKINS' PRACTICAL ARITHMETIC; HIGHER do
STODDART'S JUVENILE "
" INTELLECTUAL "
" PRACTICAL "
" PHILOSOPHICAL "

Keys to Arithmetics.

KEY TO THOMPSON'S PRACTICAL ARITHMETIC.
" " " HIGHER "
" " ADAMS', EMERSON'S, RY'S, and DAVIES' do.

KEY TO DAVIES' ALGEBRA.
" GREENLEAF'S COMMON SCHOOL ARITHMETIC.
" " NATIONAL "
" " ALGEBRA.
" SMITH'S ARITHMETIC.

Mathematical Books.

DAVIES' ALGEBRA—ELEMENTARY.
" " —BOURDON'S.
" ELEMENTARY GEOMETRY.
" PRACTICAL MATHEMATICS.
" MENSURATION; DAVIES' LEGENDRE'S GEOMETRY.
" ANALYTICAL GEOMETRY; DAVIES' DESCRIPTIVE do.
" SURVEYING AND NAVIGATION.
" SHADES AND SHADOWS; DAVIES' CALCULUS.
SMITH'S ALGEBRA; SMITH'S BIOT'S ANALYTICAL GEOMETRY.
BRIDGE'S ALGEBRA.
LOOMIS' ELEMENTS OF ALGEBRA; LOOMIS' LARGE do.
" GEOMETRY, TRIGONOMETRY, LOGARITHMS.
RY'S FIRST ALGEBRA; RY'S SECOND do.
ROBINSON'S ELEMENTARY ALGEBRA; ROBINSON'S LARGE do
GREENLEAF'S ALGEBRA.
GUMMERE'S SURVEYING; GILLESPIE'S do.
PLAYFAIR'S EUCLID'S GEOMETRY.
DAY'S ELEMENTS OF ALGEBRA; DAY'S LARGE do.

English Grammars.

BROWN'S GRAMMAR; WELD'S do.
WELD'S PARSING BOOK; WELLS' GRAMMAR.
PINNÈO'S PRIMARY GRAMMAR; PINNÈO'S ANALYTICAL do.
BULLION'S ANALYTICAL GRAMMAR; BULLION'S ENGLISH do.
" FIRST LESSONS IN GRAMMAR.
TOWER'S ELEMENTS OF GRAMMAR; KIRKHAM'S do.
SMITH'S GRAMMAR; CLARK'S NEW do.
CLARK'S NEW REVISED GRAMMAR.
GREEN'S FIRST LESSONS IN GRAMMAR.
" INTRODUCTION TO ENGLISH GRAMMAR.
" ELEMENTS OF GRAMMAR; GREEN'S ANALYSIS OF do.
TOWN'S ANALYSIS; McELLIGOT'S YOUNG ANALYSER.
McELLIGOT'S ANALYTICAL MANUAL; BUTLER'S GRAMMAR.

School Geographies.

MITCHELL'S SCHOOL GEOGRAPHY AND ATLAS.
" PRIMARY "
" ANCIENT " "

MITCHELL'S QUARTO GEOGRAPHY; MITCHELL'S PHYSICAL do.
" GEOGRAPHICAL QUESTION BOOK.
" OUTLINE MAPS AND KEY; PELTON'S do.
OLNEY'S SCHOOL GEOGRAPHY AND ATLAS.
" QUARTO GEOGRAPHY; SMITH'S PRIMARY do.
SMITH'S GEOGRAPHY AND AND ATLAS.
" QUARTO GEOGRAPHY; MORSE'S QUARTO do.
PARLEY'S PRIMARY GEOGRAPHY; MONTEITH'S MANUAL OF do.
CORNELL'S PRIMARY GEOGRAPHY; CORNELL'S QUARTO do.
McNALLY'S PRIMARY GEOGRAPHY; COLTON & FITCH'S do.

Dictionaries.

WEBSTER'S QUARTO DICTIONARY; WEBSTER'S ROYAL 8vo. do.
" UNIVERSITY DICTIONARY.
" QUARTO ACADEMIC DICTIONARY; HIGH SCHOOL do.
" SMALL SCHOOL DICTIONARY; POCKET do.
WORCESTER'S 8vo. DICTIONARY; COMPREHENSIVE do.
" PRIMARY DICTIONARY; ACADEMIC do.
COBB'S MINIATURE LEXICON; LADIES' do.; PARLOR do.
DICTIONARY OF POETICAL QUOTATIONS.
WALKER'S PRONOUNCING DICTIONARY; WALKER'S RHYMING do.
MEADOWS' SPANISH AND ENGLISH DICTIONARY.

Astronomy.

GUY'S ASTRONOMY AND KEITH ON THE GLOBES.
MATTISON'S ELEMENTS OF ASTRONOMY.
" HIGH SCHOOL "
BURRITT'S GEOGRAPHY OF THE HEAVENS AND ATLAS.
SMITH'S ILLUSTRATED ASTRONOMY.
OLMSTED'S SCHOOL ASTRONOMY; OLMSTED'S LARGE do.

Anatomy and Physiology for Schools.

CUTTER'S ANATOMY AND PHYSIOLOGY.
" FIRST BOOK IN ANATOMY.
" PRIMARY ANATOMY AND PHYSIOLOGY.
JANE TAYLOR'S PHYSIOLOGY; LAMBERT'S do.; COMSTOCK'S do.

Botany.

WOOD'S FIRST LESSONS IN BOTANY.
" CLASS-BOOK OF "
MRS. LINCOLN'S BOTANY; COMSTOCK'S do.

Works on Bookkeeping.

MAYHEW'S BOOKKEEPING; MAYHEW'S BLANKS to do ; KEY to do.
FULTON & EASTMAN'S BOOKKEEPING.

www.ingramcontent.com/pod-product-compliance
Lightning Source LLC
LaVergne TN
LVHW020936110826
845150LV00004B/881

* 9 7 8 1 4 2 5 5 5 1 7 0 4 *